# NORTON ANTHOLOGY OF
# WESTERN MUSIC

## VOLUME 1: ANCIENT TO BAROQUE

### FIFTH EDITION

# NORTON ANTHOLOGY OF
# WESTERN MUSIC

## VOLUME 1: ANCIENT TO BAROQUE

### FIFTH EDITION

Edited by

## J. Peter Burkholder

and

## Claude V. Palisca

**W. W. NORTON & COMPANY**
**NEW YORK LONDON**

**ISBN 0-393-97990-3 (pbk.)**

W. W. Norton & Company, Inc., 500 Fifth Avenue, New York, N.Y. 10110
    www.wwnorton.com

W. W. Norton & Company Ltd., Castle House, 75/76 Wells Street, London W1T 3QT

5 6 7 8 9 0

# CONTENTS

## Sacred Music in the Era of the Reformation

## Madrigal and Secular Song in the Sixteenth Century

## The Rise of Instrumental Music

# THE SEVENTEENTH CENTURY
## New Styles in the Seventeenth Century

# MAKING CONNECTIONS:
# HOW TO USE THIS ANTHOLOGY

The *Norton Anthology of Western Music* (NAWM) is a companion to *A History of Western Music*, Seventh Edition (HWM), and *Concise History of Western Music*, Third Edition. It is also designed to stand by itself as a collection representing the most significant traditions, trends, genres, national schools, innovations, and historical developments in the history of music in Europe and the Americas.

The editions of the scores are the best available for which permission could be secured, including several new editions especially prepared for NAWM. Where no publication or editor is cited, Claude V. Palisca or I have edited the music from the original source. Each selection is followed by a new, detailed commentary, separate from the discussion of the piece in HWM, that describes the piece's origins, points out its important features and stylistic traits, and addresses issues of performance practice, including any unusual aspects of notation. All foreign-language texts are accompanied by English translations by one or both coeditors, except where another translator is credited. These are literal to a fault, corresponding to the original line by line, often word for word, to facilitate understanding of the ways the composer has set the text.

An anthology of musical scores is greatly enhanced by recordings. Excellent, authoritative recordings of all the items in NAWM are included on the *Norton Recorded Anthology of Western Music*. Many are new to this edition. For music composed prior to the nineteenth century, the performers on the recordings use period instruments and seek to reflect the performance practice of the time, to the extent that we understand it today. The recordings also include performances with period instruments for several works composed during the nineteenth century: symphonies of Beethoven and Berlioz, Clara Schumann's Piano Trio, an oratorio by Mendelssohn, and songs by Bishop and Foster. The ragtime and jazz recordings all feature the original artists. In many periods and genres, musicians were expected to improvise, embellish, or otherwise alter the written music; when these or other discrepancies occur between score and recording, we have provided an explanation in the commentary.

To make listening easier, compact disc numbers and track numbers have been added to the scores—in notched rectangles for the complete 12-CD set and in plain rectangles for the 6-CD Concise set. The boxes are shaded a light gray to make them stand out on the page. The CD number is located in the running head at the top of the page, and the track numbers are placed in the score itself. Tracks are positioned not only at the beginning of each selection or movement but also to mark major sections, themes, and other events in the music, especially those pointed out in the commentaries.

## Why These Pieces?

We have aimed to include outstanding works that represent their makers, genres, and times. But because only a small fraction of the music worthy of attention could be included, it is incumbent on us to explain why we chose the pieces we did. Knowing our thinking will help students and teachers make the best use of this collection.

The title *Norton Anthology of Western Music* (NAWM) needs one important qualifier: this is a *historical* anthology of the Western musical tradition. Rather than serve up great works to be studied in splendid isolation, this anthology seeks to place each piece in a historical context, relating it to the society from which it came and to other music that the composer used as model or inspiration. Studying music in its contexts can illuminate the choices composers made, the values of the society they lived in, and the meanings of the pieces themselves. Just as composers did not create in a musical void, standing aloof from their predecessors and contemporaries, so the historically oriented listener must have access to the primary material in order to establish connections. This anthology invites students and teachers to make such connections.

## Breadth of Repertoire

Making connections depends on having a wide range of examples. The repertoire covered in this edition of NAWM is broader than ever before. Women composers are represented across the centuries—in the twelfth century by Hildegard of Bingen (7) and Beatriz de Dia (9); in the seventeenth by Barbara Strozzi (69) and Elisabeth-Claude Jacquet de la Guerre (78); in the nineteenth by Clara Schumann (123); and in the twentieth by Amy Cheney Beach (134), Bessie Smith (149), Ruth Crawford Seeger (156), Ellen Taaffe Zwilich (169), and Sofia Gubaidulina (171). Music of Spain is covered more fully, and Latin America is now included as well, represented by a medieval cantiga (12), a Renaissance secular villancico (48), works for vihuela (60), a South American Christmas villancico (81), the first opera composed and staged in the New World (80), and a symphonic picture of an Afro-Cuban ritual by Mexico's Silvestre Revueltas (155). The African-American traditions of ragtime, blues, and jazz are included for the first time, with a Joplin rag (136), Bessie Smith's *Back Water Blues* (149), Louis Armstrong's rendition of *West End Blues* (150), Ellington's *Cotton Tail* (152), and Parker and Gillespie's *Anthropology* (159). Also here for the first time are classics of band literature, from Sousa (135) to Husa (167). Coverage of music in the United States and Eastern Europe has been increased, adding pieces by Billings (97), Foster (115), Gottschalk (120), Rachmaninov (139), Gershwin (151), Barber (162), Penderecki (165), Cage (166), Pärt (170), and Sheng (172), who is the first Asian-born composer to be included in any edition of NAWM.

Breadth of repertoire is matched by depth. Several composers are represented by more than one work to permit comparison of early and later styles (for example, Du Fay, Monteverdi, Beethoven, Schubert, Schoenberg, and Stravinsky) and to show distinct approaches by a single composer to diverse genres (for example, Adam de la Halle, Machaut, Josquin, Byrd, Bach, Handel, Haydn, Mozart, and Mendelssohn). Instead of relying solely on excerpts to give a taste of multimovement genres, NAWM includes complete examples of a Gregorian chant Mass,

Baroque keyboard suite, Corelli trio sonata, Vivaldi concerto, Bach cantata, and Haydn symphony, to show how such works are constructed and what types of movement they contain. In the same spirit, complete scenes from operas by Monteverdi, Rameau, Handel, Mozart, Rossini, Weber, and Verdi demonstrate how differently these composers construct a scene.

## Styles and Genres

Perhaps the primary role of a historical anthology is to present examples of the most important styles and genres in music history and to trace their development through time. The generally chronological organization of the book, which follows the order in which these selections are discussed in HWM, highlights changes in both style and genre from ancient Greece (NAWM 1–2), medieval monophony (3–13), and early polyphony (14–23) through the fourteenth century (24–30); the first, middle, and later generations of Renaissance composers (31–36, 37–41, and 42–62); the early, middle, and late Baroque period (63–76, 77–84, and 85–92); the Classic era (93–107); the first and second halves of the nineteenth century (108–126 and 127–135); and the twentieth century before (136–158) and after (159–172) World War II.

Genres, styles, conventions, and forms develop only because composers pick up ideas from each other and replicate or build on them in their own music, a process that can be observed again and again through the pieces in this anthology. The monophonic songs of the troubadours in southern France (8–9), for example, inspired those of the trouvères in the north (10), Minnesinger in Germany (11), and cantiga composers in Spain (12). Later generations of poet-musicians, active in the fourteenth century, wrote polyphonic secular songs and codified standard forms for them, notably the French rondeau (26 and 33), virelai (27), and ballade (34), and the Italian madrigal, caccia, and ballata (28–30). In the Renaissance, new forms and styles of secular song emerged, including the Spanish villancico (48), German Lied (38), Italian frottola and madrigal (49–53), and new types of French chanson (54–55) and songs in English (56–58). A similar path can be traced from the creation of opera in Italy (65–68) through its diffusion to other lands and the many changes of style through the nineteenth (125–131) and twentieth centuries (143 and 161), or in religious music from Gregorian chant (3–5) to the modern style of Pärt (170).

Musicians frequently use an old word to mean new things, so that the very nature of a genre may change. For example, the motet began as a work that added text to existing music (21a), then became a new piece based on chant in the bottom voice (21c), which could be secular, like Adam de la Halle's (22). In the Renaissance, from Dunstable (32) to Lasso (47), the motet was redefined as a polyphonic Latin sacred work with equal voices, and in the seventeenth century it came to include solo works with accompaniment by Grandi (70) and others. Exploring and explaining such changes is a central theme of this anthology and of HWM.

Similar chains of development can be seen in instrumental music. Dance music in the Middle Ages (13) and Renaissance (59) led to stylized dances of many types: independent pieces for keyboard, including those by Byrd (61) and Chopin (117); keyboard dance suites in the Baroque period, such as those by Jacquet de la

Guerre (78) and François Couperin (86), a genre revived in the modern era by Schoenberg (142) and others; and dance movements in other works, including Corelli's trio sonatas (83d) and symphonies from Haydn (104c) to Shostakovich (154). In addition, dance rhythms infect many vocal and instrumental works, from the air in minuet rhythm in Lully's opera *Armide* (77) to the seguidilla from Bizet's *Carmen* (129).

The canzonas of Gabrieli (62) and others established a tradition of extended instrumental works in several sections with contrasting meters, tempos, and moods, leading to the sonatas of Marini (76) and the multimovement sonatas of Corelli (82) and later composers. Out of this tradition emerged the string quartet and other forms of chamber music, from Haydn (103) to Crumb (163). The symphony grew from its Italian beginnings, represented by Sammartini (100), to become the major instrumental genre of the late eighteenth and nineteenth centuries, dominated by Austrian and German composers such as Stamitz (101), Haydn (104), and Beethoven (109). Berlioz's *Symphonie fantastique* (121) and Brahms's Fourth Symphony (132) represent opposite sides of the nineteenth-century division between programmatic and absolute music. The symphony was a continuing presence in the twentieth century, represented here by Webern (144), Stravinsky (146), Shostakovich (154), Still (158), and Zwilich (169).

As suggested by these descriptions, almost every genre has roots in an earlier one. Here is where the evolutionary metaphor so often applied to music history seems most applicable, tracing lines of development both within and between genres. This anthology provides ample material for making these connections. The development of individual genres can be traced by using the Index of Forms and Genres at the back of each volume.

## Techniques

In addition to genres, composers often learn techniques from their contemporaries or predecessors and extend them in new ways. Compositional practices that start in one genre or tradition often cross boundaries over time. To give just one example, imitative counterpoint, developed in the medieval canon (23) and caccia (29), became a structural principle in Renaissance vocal music from the late fifteenth century, illustrated by Josquin's motet *Ave maria . . . virgo serena* (39), through the early seventeenth century, as in Weelkes's madrigal *As Vesta was* (57). The technique was taken over into instrumental music through the canzona (62) and ricercare (75), and the latter developed into the fugue (see the fugues in 84 and 88). Fugal passages occur in many types of work, from oratorios (92c and 124) to the development sections of symphonies (104a and 109), and imitation remains a device learned by every student of Western music.

Forms morph into new forms or combine with others. Binary form, invented for dance music (59a and 78), was used for abstract sonata movements by Domenico Scarlatti (98) and others and developed into sonata form as used in Mozart's piano sonatas (105) and the first movements of symphonies (100, 101, 104a and d, and 109). A small binary form could also be expanded into a longer movement by serving as the theme for a movement in rondo form, as in the finale of Haydn's *Joke* String Quartet (103). The elements of sonata form could in turn be combined with ritornello form in a concerto first movement, as in the concertos by J. C. Bach (102) and Mozart (106), or with rondo form in a sonata-rondo, used for finales by Beethoven (108), Mendelssohn (122), and others.

Styles also cross genres and traditions. Vocal music served as the basis for early instrumental works, like the intabulations and variations of Narváez (60). Moreover, the styles and gestures of vocal music have been imitated by instrumental composers again and again, including recitative and vocal monody in Marini's violin sonata (76), singing styles in piano sonatas by C. P. E. Bach (99) and Mozart (105), and bel canto operatic style in Chopin's nocturnes (118). Musicians cannot afford to know only the literature for their own instrument, for composers are constantly borrowing ideas from other repertoires, and performers need to know how to reflect these allusions to other styles in their performances.

Several selections document the influence of vernacular and traditional music on art music. Medieval English singers improvised polyphony with parallel thirds and sixths, which entered notated music in the thirteenth-century *Sumer is icumen in* (23), fifteenth-century carols (31), and the works of English composer John Dunstable (32) and exercised a profound influence on Continental composers such as Binchois (33) and Du Fay (35). Debussy adapted the texture and melodic idiom of a Javanese gamelan to his own orchestral conception in *Nuages* (138). Stravinsky simulated folk polyphony in *The Rite of Spring* (145). Bartók borrowed elements of Serbo-Croatian song and Bulgarian dance styles in his *Music for Strings, Percussion and Celesta* (147). Still's *Afro-American Symphony* (158) incorporates the twelve-bar blues (149–150), the style of African-American spirituals, and instrumental sounds from jazz. Sheng makes the cellist imitate the sounds and playing styles of Chinese instruments in his *Seven Tunes Heard in China* (172).

Twentieth-century composers have introduced a constant stream of innovations, and this anthology includes a number of pioneering works. Notable are Schoenberg's *Pierrot lunaire* (141), his most famous atonal piece and the first to use *Sprechstimme*; his Piano Suite (142), the first complete twelve-tone work; Webern's Symphony (144), a model of *Klangfarbenmelodie* and pointillism; Stravinsky's *Rite of Spring* (145), whose block construction influenced so many later composers; Babbitt's *Philomel* (164), an early example of combining a live singer with electronic music on tape; Cage's *Music of Changes* (166), one of the first pieces composed using chance operations; Penderecki's *Threnody* (165), which produces novel clusters of sound from a string orchestra; and Adams's *Phrygian Gates* (168), which applies minimalist techniques to create a gradually changing canvas of sound.

### Learning from History

Besides learning from their contemporaries and immediate predecessors, many composers have reached back across the centuries to revive old methods or genres, often producing something remarkably new in the process. Inspired by the ancient Greek idea of suiting music to the rhythm and mood of the words, illustrated here by the *Epitaph of Seikilos* (1), Renaissance composers sought to capture the accents and feelings of the text, evident in motets by Josquin (39) and Lasso (47), in the new genre of the madrigal (50–53), and in the *musique mesurée* of le Jeune (55). Among the tools Renaissance composers borrowed from ancient Greek music and music theory was chromaticism, found in Euripides's *Orestes* (2);

after madrigal composers like Rore (51), Marenzio (52), and Gesualdo (53) used it as an expressive device, it became a common feature in instrumental music as well, such as in Frescobaldi's chromatic ricercare (75), and later composers from Bach (89) to Wagner (128) made it an increasingly central part of the musical language. In a classic example of creating something new by reaching into the distant past, the attempt to revive the principles of ancient Greek tragedy led to the invention of opera and recitative in Peri's *Euridice* (65).

Romantic and modern composers have often sought to revive the spirit of earlier music. Recollections of Baroque music include Beethoven's fugue in his String Quartet in C-sharp minor (110a), Brahms's chaconne in the finale of his Fourth Symphony (132), and Schoenberg's passacaglia in *Nacht* from *Pierrot lunaire* (141a). Webern's Symphony (144) contains elaborate canons modeled on those of the Renaissance, and Hindemith's *Un cygne* (153) resurrects the Renaissance chanson in a modern harmonic language. Messiaen borrowed the isorhythmic techniques of Vitry (24) and Machaut (25) in his *Quartet for the End of Time* (160), and Barber echoed medieval chant, heterophony, and open-fifth harmonies in his picture of a medieval monk (162).

*Reworkings*

In addition to drawing on general styles, genres, and techniques, composers have often reworked particular compositions, a process that can be traced through numerous examples in this anthology. In one notable case, a single chant gave rise to a chain of polyphonic accretions. *Viderunt omnes* (3d) was elaborated by Léonin in an organum for two voices (17), which in turn was refreshed by his successors with new clausulae (18) that substituted for certain passages in Léonin's original. His younger colleague Pérotin wrote a four-voice organum on the same chant (19). Meanwhile, anonymous musicians fitted words to the upper parts of some of the clausulae, creating the new genre of the motet (21a). Later composers borrowed the tenor line of a clausula (21b) or a passage from the original *Viderunt omnes* chant (21c and 22) and added one, two, or three new voices to create ever more elaborate motets.

NAWM contains many other instances in which composers reworked existing music into new pieces, a recurring thread in music history. Anonymous medieval church musicians added monophonic tropes (6) to the chant *Puer natus* (3a) and developed early types of polyphony that add other voices to a chant (14–15). Machaut based the Kyrie of his *La Messe de Nostre Dame* (25) on the chant *Kyrie Cunctipotens Genitor* (3b). Many Renaissance composers wrote masses that rework existing models, including Du Fay's cantus-firmus mass based on his own polyphonic ballade *Se la face ay pale* (36); Ockeghem's mass (37) on Binchois's rondeau *De plus en plus* (33); Josquin's paraphrase mass on the chant hymn *Pange lingua* (40); and Victoria's imitation mass on his own motet *O magnum mysterium* (46). Du Fay elaborated a Gregorian hymn in fauxbourdon style (35), and Luther recast another (42a) as a Reformation chorale (42b), later used by J. S. Bach as the basis for a cantata (90).

Such elaborations of existing material are not confined to religious music. Narváez's *Cancion Milles regres* (60a) is a reworking for vihuela of Josquin's chanson *Mille regretz* (41), and Byrd's *Pavana Lachrymae* (61) recasts Dowland's lute song *Flow my tears* (58) into an idiomatic keyboard piece. Gottschalk's *Souvenir de Porto Rico* (120) uses a melody of Puerto Rican street musicians. Both Berlioz's *Symphonie fantastique* (121) and Crumb's *Black Angels* (163) borrow phrases from the chant *Dies irae*. The Coronation scene from Musorgsky's *Boris Godunov* (130) incorporates a Russian folk song, and Ives's *General William Booth Enters into Heaven* (148) is based on a hymn tune. The theme of the finale of Beach's Piano Quintet (134) is modeled on a theme from Brahms's Piano Quintet. Both Ellington's *Cotton Tail* (152) and Parker and Gillespie's *Anthropology* (159) borrow the harmonic progression from the chorus of Gershwin's song *I Got Rhythm* (151). Copland's *Appalachian Spring* (157) includes variations on a Shaker hymn, Husa's *Music for Prague* (167) derives much of its material from a Czech hymn, and the first movement of Sheng's *Seven Tunes Heard in China* (172) varies the melody of a Chinese song.

## Improvisation

Improvisation has been part of the Western tradition since ancient times. Eleventh-century organum (15) was an improvisatory practice before it was a written one. Singers and instrumentalists from the Renaissance to the early nineteenth century often improvised ornaments and embellishments to decorate the written music, as represented on many of the recordings that accompany this anthology. Lutenists and keyboard players demonstrated their skill through elaborate improvisations, exploring a mode or introducing another work; from these developed the written tradition of the toccata and prelude, represented by examples from Frescobaldi (74), Jacquet de la Guerre (78a), Buxtehude (84), and J. S. Bach (88). Part of the individuality of the keyboard music of C. P. E. Bach (99), Schumann (116), Chopin (118), Liszt (119), Rachmaninov (139), and Scriabin (140) derives from textures or passages that sound improvisatory, however carefully calculated they may be. The invention of sound recording has made possible the preservation of improvisations themselves, which are a fundamental part of the blues and jazz tradition, represented here in the recordings of Jelly Roll Morton (playing Joplin's *Maple Leaf Rag*, 136b), Bessie Smith (149), Louis Armstrong (150b), Ben Webster (soloing in Ellington's *Cotton Tail*, 152), and Charlie Parker (159).

## Reception

Certain pieces won a place in this anthology because contemporary critics or the composers themselves singled them out. A legend developed that when some Catholic leaders sought to ban polyphonic music from church services, Palestrina saved it by composing his *Pope Marcellus Mass* (45). Giovanni Maria Artusi dismembered Monteverdi's *Cruda Amarilli* (63) in his dialogue of 1600, which contains both a critique and a defense of Monteverdi's innovations. Caccini wrote that *Vedrò 'l mio sol* (64) was one of his pioneering attempts to write a new type of solo song. Cesti's *Intorno all'idol mio* (68b) was one of the most frequently cited arias of the mid-seventeenth century. Athanasius Kircher praised the scene of Carissimi's *Jephte* (71) as a triumph of the powers of musical expression. Jean-Jacques Rousseau roundly criticized and Jean le Rond d'Alembert carefully analyzed Lully's monologue in *Armide, Enfin il est en ma puissance* (77b). The first movement of Beethoven's *Eroica Symphony* (109) and Stravinsky's *The Rite of Spring* (145) were both objects of critical uproars after their premieres. Britten's *Peter Grimes* (161) became the first English opera to win international acclaim in over two centuries, and Zwilich's Symphony No. 1 (169) earned her the first Pulitzer Prize awarded to a woman. The reactions to these compositions are exemplars of "reception history," a field that has attracted considerable attention among teachers and historians.

### Relation to Politics

Finally, musical influences are not the only connections that can be made between these pieces. For example, many grew out of a specific political context, and studying the ways those links are reflected in the music can be illuminating. Walther von der Vogelweide's *Palästinalied* (11) is a crusade song, celebrating the Christian warriors from Western Europe who sought to wrest the Holy Land from the Muslims. *Fole acostumance/Dominus* (21b) attacks hypocrisy and deception in the church and in French politics. Lully's operas (77) were part of a political program intended to glorify King Louis XIV of France and centralize his power through the arts. Schütz's *Kleine geistliche Konzerte* (72) were written for reduced forces in response to the Thirty Years' War. Gay's *The Beggar's Opera* (95) spoofed social norms by taking a criminal as its hero. Political commentary is a recurrent theme in twentieth-century music, including Berg's appeal for better treatment of the poor in *Wozzeck* (143), Britten's condemnation of social ostracism in *Peter Grimes* (161), Crumb's reflections on the Vietnam War in *Black Angels* (163), Penderecki's memorial for the first victims of nuclear war (165), and Husa's protest against the Soviet invasion of Czechoslovakia in *Music for Prague 1968* (167).

### Your Turn

All of these and many other potential connections can be made through the works in this anthology. But they remain unrealized until you, the reader, make them real for yourself. We invite you to study each piece for what it shares with others here as well as for its own distinctive qualities. You will encounter much that is unfamiliar, perhaps including pieces you will grow to love and others that may never suit your tastes. At the end, the goal is to understand as much as possible why those who created this music made the choices they did, and how each piece represents a trend, genre, style, and time that played an important role in our long and ever-changing tradition of Western music.

# ACKNOWLEDGMENTS

Any book is a collaborative effort, and teaching materials are especially so. There are many people to thank.

I am indebted first of all to Claude V. Palisca, who devised NAWM as a companion to HWM and compiled its first four editions. Most of the selections and translations are his, and I have incorporated material from his commentaries for those works. I regret that his untimely death kept us from collaborating more closely.

The creative efforts of many others are represented in these pages. W. W. Norton and I appreciate the individuals and publishers cited in the source notes who granted permission to reprint or adapt material under copyright. I am especially grateful to Edward H. Roesner for his edition of Léonin's *Viderunt omnes* and to Rebecca A. Baltzer for her editions of *Factum est salutare/Dominus* and *Fole acostumance/Dominus* and her editorial revisions of Adam de la Halle's *De ma dame vient/Dieus, comment porroie/Omnes*, which were prepared specifically for NAWM. Thomas J. Mathiesen kindly provided phonetic transliterations of the Greek poetry and new engravings of the music for NAWM 1 and 2. Ann Shaffer assisted with the re-editing and typesetting of NAWM 55, 60b, and 72. David Budmen elegantly typeset the other new items that were not reproduced from existing editions. Several experts offered guidance on translations, including Rex Sprouse for Walther von der Vogelweide and Martin Luther, Luis Dávila for the *Cantigas de Santa Maria*, James Franklin for early Latin polyphonic works, and Andrew Dell'Antonio for Latin and Italian selections. I had assistance in writing several of the commentaries, from Patrick Warfield (NAWM 135), Felicia Miyakawa (149–152 and 159), and Roger Hickman (153–154, 163, 165, 168, 170, and 172). Alison Trego helped to assemble scores and researched the backgrounds of dozens of pieces, and Felix O. Cox also offered research support. Thanks to all of them for their assistance.

Members of the Editorial Advisory Board for HWM, especially Jane A. Bernstein, Geoffrey Block, Michael Broyles, Matthew Dirst, Melanie Lowe, Roberta Montemorra Marvin, Kevin N. Moll, Margaret Murata, Larry Starr, and Neal Zaslaw, reviewed the proposed contents and made very helpful suggestions. Russell E. Murray advised on the choice of repertoire and helped to find alternatives. My colleagues at Indiana University offered advice and suggestions, especially David Baker, Halina Goldberg, Jeffrey Magee, and Daniel Melamed. So did former students, notably John Anderies, Felicia Miyakawa, Scott Stewart, and Patrick Warfield. The staff of the Cook Music Library at Indiana University offered every possible assistance. Andrew Dell'Antonio, Claudia Macdonald, Richard Crawford, and Larry Starr reviewed the commentaries, helping me to refine my thinking and writing, clarify important issues, and avoid pitfalls. Edward Swenson also offered helpful suggestions. I appreciate their advice, which has made this a far better book.

Assembling the recordings was an especially complex task, and I am deeply grateful to everyone who contributed. I began with an initial list, matching editions to recordings wherever possible. Russell E. Murray did extensive research to find the high-quality recordings of musical performances that complement the commentary and scores in NAWM. He also worked with Ronnie Thomas from Naxos to ensure that the mastering of each CD was precise. Russell meticulously checked and rechecked each of the disks, and Ronnie carefully mastered the CDs. Justyn Baker, licensing and production manager for Naxos, oversaw the production of the CD sets, and along with Diamond Time, Ltd., negotiated the licensing for each track—a laborious and complicated effort. Luis Lange assisted Justyn in coordinating the licensing and production of the project and obtained all of the source recordings. Their enthusiastic work brought the recording set to fruition, and I greatly appreciate their efforts.

For many works and for the new editions, no satisfactory recordings were available, and Maribeth Anderson Payne energetically located performers and commissioned new recordings. Paul Elliott organized, directed, and sang in several excellent new performances from medieval chant to nineteenth-century parlor songs, collaborating with Concentus, Nigel North, Matthew Leese, Wolodymyr Smishkewych, and Yonit Lea Kosovske. Konrad Strauss and his staff produced the recordings, and Indiana University School of Music generously offered the performing space. New recordings were also contributed by Tonus Peregrinus, under the direction of Antony Pitts; Ellen Hargis with Paul O'Dette; and Mark Rimple, David Douglass, and Mary Springfels of the Newberry Consort. Their wonderful performances have made the set of recordings better and more complete, and I gratefully thank them all.

It has been a pleasure to work with the staff at W. W. Norton. Allison Benter oversaw and coordinated the entire NAWM project, facilitating communication between all of the project's contributors and cheerfully handling every difficulty that came along. She also copyedited the entire manuscript, offered encouragement, and gently nudged me to completion. Kathy Talalay, Michael Ochs, and Courtney Fitch assisted with the copyediting. Courtney also secured permissions and drafted the appendices and indexes. Maribeth Anderson Payne, music editor, has been a constant source of ideas and enthusiasm for NAWM as well as HWM. JoAnn Simony oversaw production, contributed the beautiful design and attractive layout, and found ways to make the schedule work when I fell behind. I cannot thank them all enough for their skill, dedication, care, and counsel.

Thanks finally but most of all to my family, especially Donald and Jean Burkholder, who introduced me to the love of music; Bill, Joanne, and Sylvie Burkholder, whose enthusiasm renewed my own; and P. Douglas McKinney, whose patient support made this book possible. I look forward to sharing the music in this anthology with them, and with all who use and enjoy it.

—*J. Peter Burkholder*
*June 2005*

# RECORDINGS

Recordings accompanying this anthology are available under the titles *Norton Recorded Anthology of Western Music* (12 CDs containing all of the pieces in the two volumes) and *Concise Norton Recorded Anthology of Western Music* (6 CDs containing 92 of the pieces in the two volumes). The corresponding CD numbers are indicated in the scores. Track numbers for both sets of CDs are indicated in the scores as follows:

| 12-CD set |   (tracks indicated in notched boxes):

CD 1: NAWM 1–18
CD 2: NAWM 19–37
CD 3: NAWM 38–57
CD 4: NAWM 58–70
CD 5: NAWM 71–82
CD 6: NAWM 83–92
CD 7: NAWM 93–102 and 104–105
CD 8: NAWM 103 and 106–118
CD 9: NAWM 119–128
CD 10: NAWM 129–140
CD 11: NAWM 141–157
CD 12: NAWM 158–172

| 6-CD set |   (tracks indicated in plain boxes):

CD 1: NAWM 1–46
CD 2: NAWM 47–73 and 77
CD 3: NAWM 74 and 78–103
CD 4: NAWM 104–119
CD 5: NAWM 121–138
CD 6: NAWM 141–172

# PITCH DESIGNATIONS

In this book, a note referred to without regard to its octave register is designated by a capital letter (A). A note in a particular octave is designated in italics, using the following system:

 *C to B*

*c to b*

 *c' to b'*

*c" to b"*

# Epitaph of Seikilos

*Song (epigram)*

FIRST CENTURY C.E.

Copenhagen, National Museum, Inventory No. 14897 (for photograph, see HWM, p. 21, figure 1.10). From Thomas J. Mathiesen, *Apollo's Lyre: Greek Music and Music Theory in Antiquity and the Middle Ages* (Lincoln: University of Nebraska Press, 1999), 149. Reprinted by permission of the University of Nebraska Press. © 1999 by the University of Nebraska Press. Phonetic transliteration by Thomas J. Mathiesen. © 2001 by Thomas J. Mathiesen. Used by permission.

We do not know precisely how the Greek language was pronounced. The phonetic transliteration shown here is based on the phonology of New Testament Greek as described by Friedrich Blass and Albert Debrunner, *A Greek Grammar of the New Testament and Other Early Christian Literature*, rev. and trans. Robert W. Funk (Chicago: University of Chicago Press, 1961). This phonology is almost certainly close to being correct for Seikilos and may not be too far off for the much older Euripides text in NAWM 2. The transliteration should be pronounced as follows:

> i = the sound in "police"
> e = the sound in "red"
> a = the sound in "father"
> o = the sound in "corporal"
> ou = the sound in "moo"
> eu = a diphthong equivalent to e + ou
> th, ph, and ch are lightly aspirated mutes

| Hoson zis phenou | As long as you live, be lighthearted. |
|---|---|
| miden holos su lupou | Let nothing trouble you. |
| pros oligon esti to zin | Life is only too short, |
| to telos ho chronos apeti. | and time takes its toll. |

The Epitaph of Seikilos is a brief song inscribed on a tombstone dating from the first century C.E. (Common Era, equivalent to A.D.). Originally erected in southwestern Turkey, near the modern city of Aydin, the round stone column is now in the National Museum in Copenhagen. The opening lines of the inscription make clear the purpose of the stone:

> I am a tombstone, an icon. Seikilos placed me here as an everlasting sign of deathless remembrance.

The poem that follows is an *epigram,* a short verse that makes a pointed remark, often by wittily juxtaposing contrasting ideas. Here we are encouraged to be cheerful, not in spite of death and the ravages of time but, ironically, because of them. The ethos of the epigram is one of moderation between extremes. The inscription ends with two lines whose meaning is uncertain but which appear to ascribe the poem and perhaps the music to Seikilos.

Above the words of the epigram are letters and other symbols representing pitches in Greek notation. Above these symbols are signs indicating durations. The score included here shows the original notation above the modern transcription with the Greek text and a phonetic transliteration.

The clear rhythmic notation has made this song of particular interest to historians. The notes without rhythmic markings above the alphabetical signs are worth one unit of duration (*protos chronos*), rendered in the transcription as an eighth note. The horizontal dash (—) indicates a *diseme,* worth two units, and the horizontal dash with an upward stroke to the right is a *triseme,* worth three. Note that the duration indicated is that of the syllable, not of the pitch, so that a *diseme* may include two pitches (as in the second line) and the *triseme* one, two, or three (as at the end of each line).

It is possible to transcribe the piece into modern notation using tables given by Alypius in his *Introductio musica,* probably compiled in the late fourth or fifth century C.E. Alypius presented the letter notations for fifteen *tonoi,* each of which places the sequence of intervals in the Greater Perfect System in a specific range (see HWM, p. 18). There are two sets of letters for each tonos—one for vocal pitches and the other for instruments. The *Epitaph of Seikilos* uses the vocal notes of the diatonic Iastian tonos, conventionally transcribed as the two-octave scale from *B* to *b'* with two sharps:

The music reflects the text in several important ways. Most obviously, the four lines of poetry are set to four distinct musical phrases, each the same length (twelve units of time) and each closing with a *triseme* preceded by another long duration. The Greek language had long and short syllables; all the long syllables in the epitaph are set to long durations, so that the music follows the rhythms of the text. Each phrase begins with a rising gesture up to *e'* and then falls to a cadence, paralleling the inflections of speech. The gradual descent through an octave in the final phrase creates a strong sense of closure.

The Iastian tonos is consistent with the moderate ethos of the epigram, balanced between two extremes. In Alypius's arrangement of the fifteen tonoi, the Iastian is number 7, intermediate between the lowest, Hypodorian, and the highest, Hyperlydian. The use of the diatonic genus is also appropriate for an ethos of moderation because it avoids the more extreme emotions associated with the chromatic and enharmonic genera.

The melody is restricted to the central octave from *e* to *e'*. The octave species is the one called Phrygian by Cleonides, with a succession of whole and half steps equivalent to the octave from D to D on the white keys of a piano. The high and low notes receive special emphasis—*e'* as the topmost pitch in all four phrases and *e* as the last note in the piece. The notes *a* and *c♯'* are also prominent as the most frequent notes (each occurs eight times) and the notes used to begin phrases. Today and perhaps also then, the major thirds that begin or end the last three phrases would be perceived as bright, as would the rising fifth at the opening. These bright intervals cast the message of the poem in a somewhat optimistic light.

This melody is interesting also because it conforms closely to Greek theoretical writings on melody. It uses patterns described by theorists such as Cleonides and Aristides Quintilianus: repeating notes, as in the first and fourth phrases; moving up or down the scale, as in the second phrase; and repeating the same interval succession a step lower or higher, as at the end of the third phrase (*c♯'–a*, *b–g*) and the beginning of the fourth (*a–c♯'*, *b–d'*). Subtle melodic resemblances link each phrase to the next. For example, the last four notes of the first phrase are echoed at the beginning of the second; the second and third phrases end with the same three notes and rhythms; and the third and fourth phrases begin with similar contours. Like the poem, the music is more complex and intriguing than it may appear at first hearing.

Although there is no indication of an accompaniment, a singer would likely have accompanied himself or herself on a lyre or other plucked string instrument, perhaps playing the melody in unison (as done on the accompanying recording) or sounding the *a*, *e*, or other prominent notes.

# EURIPIDES (CA. 485–CA. 406 B.C.E.)

*Orestes:* Stasimon chorus

*Greek tragedy*

408 B.C.E.

Vienna, Österreichische Nationalbibliothek, Papyrus G2315 (for photograph, see HWM, p. 21, Figure 1.11). Transcription of fragment from Thomas J. Mathiesen, *Apollo's Lyre: Greek Music and Music Theory in Antiquity and the Middle Ages* (Lincoln: University of Nebraska Press, 1999), 117–18. Reprinted by permission of the University of Nebraska Press. © 1999 by the University of Nebraska Press. For a detailed analysis, see ibid., pp. 117–20. Phonetic transliteration by Thomas J. Mathiesen. © 2001 by Thomas J. Mathiesen. Used by permission.

katolophirome      materos hema sas  
hos' anabakcheui      ho megas holbos ou  
monimos em brotis      ana de lephos hos  
tis akatou thoas      tinaxas demon  
katoldioen      dinon  
ponon      hoos pontou

You wild goddesses who dart across the skies seeking vengeance for murder, we implore you to free Agamemnon's son from his aging fury. We grieve for this boy. Happiness is brief among mortals. Sorrow and anguish sweep down on it like a swift gust of wind on a sloop, and it sinks under the tossing seas.

A small scrap of papyrus dating from the third century B.C.E. contains seven lines of a chorus from *Orestes* by the great Greek playwright Euripides, with musical notation above the words. The tragedy has been dated 408 B.C.E. It seems likely that the music was composed by Euripides himself, who was renowned for his musical settings, but we cannot be certain. This fragment of Greek music is centuries older than the *Epitaph of Seikilos* (NAWM 1) but is presented second here because it poses greater difficulties in reading and reconstructing the music.

Only the center of each line of text and music survives on the papyrus. The missing words can be restored from other copies of the play and are printed in brackets in this transcription. However, this papyrus is the only source for the music, and many of the notes are missing. Any performance of the piece must be a reconstruction, conjecturing what the absent notes might have been. The recordings that accompany this anthology include two very different reconstructions, both based on the assumption that the missing segments of melody probably resembled the notes set to parallel portions of other lines of the text.

In a Greek tragedy, the chorus plays an important role, witnessing and commenting on the events of the drama. This song is a *stasimon,* an ode the chorus sings while standing still in their place in the *orchestra,* a semicircular rim between the stage and the benches of the spectators. In this stasimon, the women of Argos implore the gods to have mercy on Orestes, who murdered his mother Clytemnestra six days before the play begins. He had plotted with his sister Electra to punish their mother for infidelity to their father, Agamemnon. The chorus begs that Orestes be released from the madness that has overwhelmed him since the murder.

The dochmaic rhythm—six syllables in the pattern short-short-short long-short-long—suffuses the poetry and predominates in the music. The dochmaic rhythm was often used in Greek tragedy for passages of intense agitation and grief, so it is perfectly suited to this moment in the play.

Contemporary descriptions of Euripides' music noted that he had a complex, somewhat disjunct melodic style in which the pitch contour and rhythm sometimes departed from the natural contour and rhythm of the text. This characterization fits this melody, which jumps back and forth between a lower and a higher range and includes some rhythmic symbols that modify the textual rhythm.

Plutarch credited Euripides with helping to introduce the chromatic genus into tragedy, and that is also apparent in this melody. The notation indicates a mixture of the diatonic and the chromatic (or possibly the enharmonic) genera. The vocal melody moves in the range *g* to *g'*, combining diatonic tetrachords on *e–f–g–a* and *e'–f' g'–a'* with a chromatic tetrachord on *a–b♭–b♮–d'*. This combination exemplifies both Euripides' fondness for chromaticism and his preference for complexity, which tend to confirm him as the composer. Moreover, the chromaticism combines with the dochmaic rhythm to convey the anguish of the chorus at this moment in the drama.

As noted above, it is possible to read the notation as indicating the enharmonic genus (which uses quartertones) rather than the chromatic. The transcription shown here and one of the two performances on the recordings render the small intervals as chromatic; the other performance renders them as enharmonic (the notes shown here as B♭ are lowered a quartertone, and B is lowered to B♭), producing quite a different effect. The chromatic performance is sung by a unison male chorus. In the enharmonic performance, a female singer (a soloist standing in for the chorus) is accompanied by an aulos (the double-reed instrument of the Greeks) playing in unison with the voice but also holding drones against it. Auloi were used to accompany Greek tragedy, but their precise function is unclear.

Certain musical symbols in this setting are not associated with syllables of text. The transcription and the chromatic performance on the recordings interpret these as notes for instruments, which had their own letter notation. The sign transcribed here as high *g'* may simply indicate a break between lines of text and is omitted in the enharmonic performance. But the *f♯–b* figure in lines 5 and 6 is clearly intended for instruments, read as an interjection between lines in the chromatic performance and as a change of drone in the enharmonic.

# Mass for Christmas Day

*Gregorian chant Mass*

A Gregorian chant Mass includes a variety of elements—some sung, some intoned, and some spoken. Included here are only the portions of the Mass for Christmas Day that are sung by the choir. Some of these, the Proper chants (Introit, Gradual, Alleluia, Offertory, and Communion), have texts and melodies that are unique to this day in the church calendar. The others, the Ordinary chants (Kyrie, Gloria, Credo, Sanctus, Agnus Dei, and Ite, missa est), have texts that are sung in all or most Masses, but each Ordinary text has many musical settings. Beginning in the thirteenth century, Ordinary chants were organized into *cycles* with one musical setting for each text in the Ordinary except the Credo. The edition included here is from the *Liber usualis*, a book of prayers, lessons, and chants for the Roman Catholic services of the Mass and the Office that was first issued in 1952 by the Benedictine monks of Solesmes, France. This cycle is numbered IV in the *Liber usualis*, and the Credo—one of the oldest—is numbered I.

The various elements of the Mass were added at different times, so each has its own history. Neither the chants of the Proper for a given day nor the Ordinary cycle shows any consistency of age or of mode. However, as is true for most feast days, the Proper chants in this Mass are much older than the Ordinary melodies, and the two groups differ somewhat in style. All the Proper chants are derived from psalm-singing, and as a result they tend to include passages of decorated recitation, centering around a single note with embellishing gestures (for example, see the Introit at "et vocabitur nomen ejus," the Gradual at "omnes fines terrae," and the Alleluia at "sanctificatus illuxit"). The Ordinary chants, in contrast, are more like composed melodies, with frequent stepwise motion and little recitation.

Kyrie, Gloria, Sanctus, Agnus Dei, and Ite, missa est from Mass IV, *Liber usualis* (Tournai: Desclée, 1961), 25–28. Credo I from ibid., 64–66. Proper chants from ibid., 408–10. *Gloria Patri* (Lesser Doxology) from ibid., 15–16. Reprinted by permission of St. Bonaventure Publications. English translations for the Proper from *The Saint Andrew Daily Missal,* ed. Dom Gaspar Lefebvre, O.S.B. (St. Paul: E. M Lohmann Co., 1940), 38–40. Translations for the Ordinary adapted from ibid., 519–20, 523–25, 534, and 546. Reprinted by permission.

## INSTRUCTIONS FOR READING SOLESMES CHANT NOTATION

The official Vatican editions of Gregorian chant, prepared by monks at the Benedictine Abbey of Solesmes, use a modernized chant notation based on late medieval forms. The staff has four lines rather than five but follows the familiar principle of alternating lines and spaces for the steps of the scale. A clef designates one line as either middle C (𝄢) or the F below it (𝄢). These are not absolute but relative pitches (although in the accompanying recording, most chants are performed at written pitch). Flat signs are valid only until a new word begins or a vertical division line appears.

The notes are indicated by *neumes,* which may contain one or more notes. The basic noteshape is square (■) rather than round, reflecting the flat quills of medieval copyists. Notes are assumed to have equal durations, with exceptions as specified below. Notes are read from left to right as in standard notation, except when two notes are stacked vertically (▐), in which case the lower note is sung first. Successive notes on the same pitch and syllable are sung as though tied or slightly pulsed. Diamond-shaped notes (♦) are used in descending patterns to save space but have the same duration as square notes. Small notes, called *liquescent neumes* (♪), signify closing the mouth or tongue on a voiced consonant such as "n" or "m" at the end of a syllable. A diagonal stroke of the pen, found in *oblique neumes* (◥), is not a glissando, but rather it indicates two notes—the pitches on which the stroke begins and ends. A wavy line used in some ascending figures, called a *quilisma* (∿), may have signified an ornament; in Solesmes performing style, it is sung normally, but the preceding note is slightly lengthened.

The Solesmes editors added interpretive signs to shape the performance. A dot after a note doubles its value. A horizontal line above or below a note indicates that it is to be lengthened somewhat. Vertical barlines delineate sections (double barline), periods (full barline), phrases (half barline), and smaller units (quarter barline through the top staff line) that are usually marked by pauses of various lengths. In Solesmes performing style, notes are freely grouped in twos and threes (though other approaches are not so rigid); the editors added vertical strokes below some notes to suggest where such groups should begin. The note-like symbol (♩) at the end of each staff is a *custos* (guard), a guide to lead the reader to the first note on the following line.

Performances are also guided by symbols inserted among the words. Most chants are begun by the choir leader, the *cantor,* and an asterisk (✳) shows where the cantor is joined by the rest of the choir. Asterisks are also used to show other changes of performer—for example, between two halves of the choir. The signs *ij* and *iij* (the roman numerals 2 and 3), found in the Kyrie and Alleluia, indicate that the preceding material is to be sung twice or three times.

(a) Introit: *Puer natus est nobis*

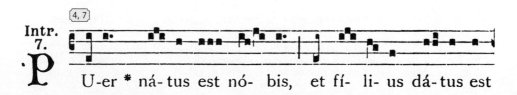

Intr. 7.

(4, 7)

Pu-er ✳ ná- tus est nó- bis, et fí- li- us dá-tus est

nó- bis : cú-jus impé- ri- um super hú- me-rum é-

jus : et vocá- bi-tur nómen é- jus, mágni consí-

li- i Ange- lus. *Ps.* Can-tá-te Dómino cánti-cum nó-

vum : * qui- a mi-rabí- li-a fé- cit. Gló- ri- a Pátri.

E u o u a e.

The Doxology is not written out in chant books, but is performed as follows:

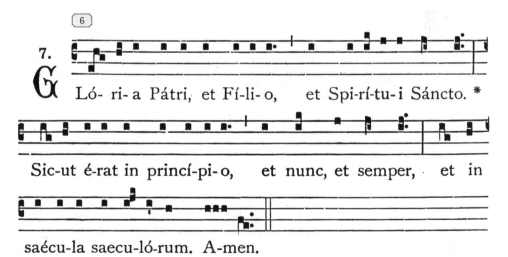

7.

G Ló- ri- a Pátri, et Fí-li- o,     et Spi-rí-tu- i Sáncto. *

Sic-ut é-rat in princí-pi- o,     et nunc, et semper,   et in

saécu-la saecu-ló-rum. A-men.

Puer natus est nobis, et filius datus est
    nobis: cujus imperium super humerum
    ejus: et vocabitur nomen ejus, magni
    consili Angelus.
*Ps.* Cantate Domino canticum novum: quia
    mirabilia fecit.

Gloria Patri, et Filio, et Spiritui Sancto.
    Sicut erat in principio, et nunc, et
    semper, et in saecula saeculorum.
    Amen.

A child is born to us, and a Son is given to
    us; whose government is upon His
    shoulder; and His Name shall be called
    the Angel of great counsel.
*Psalm verse*: Sing ye to the Lord a new
    canticle, because He hath done
    wonderful things.
*Doxology*: Glory be to the Father, and to
    the Son, and to the Holy Spirit. As it
    was in the beginning, is now, and
    ever shall be, world without end. Amen.

The sung portion of the Mass begins with the Introit (from Latin for "entrance"). In the early Middle Ages, the Introit consisted of a psalm preceded and followed by an antiphon (as in NAWM 4a) and was sung during the entrance procession of those conducting the Mass. It later became the practice to sing the psalm after the priest and choir were in place. With no action to accompany the Introit, the text was shortened to the following standard form: the antiphon, one psalm verse, the Lesser Doxology (the formula praising God that is sung after every psalm), and a repetition of the antiphon, producing the form ABB'A.

Two styles of chant appear in this and all other Introits. One style, relatively simple and syllabic, is used to sing the psalm verse (indicated by *Ps.* after a double barline) and the Lesser Doxology. In this recitational manner the melody holds mostly to one pitch, the reciting tone of the mode, with opening rises and cadential falls. Most syllables have one note, and others have two or three. The other style, used for the antiphon, is *neumatic,* with up to seven notes per syllable, and is much more varied in contour.

This Introit is in mode 7, as indicated by the number above the initial letter in this score. Both antiphon and psalm begin with a rising gesture from the mode's final, G, to its reciting tone, D, and end with a descent back to G, creating a melodic arch that is typical of chant. The antiphon often lingers on C, and some of the phrases cadence on A, two important secondary notes in this mode. Individual phrases tend to have an archlike pattern, rising near the beginning, rotating around one or two notes relatively high in the range, then sinking to a cadence.

Although the entrance psalm was originally performed antiphonally, alternating between two halves of the choir, in the later Middle Ages it was sung responsorially, alternating between a soloist and the choir. The cantor sings the opening (up to the asterisk), and the choir completes the antiphon. The psalm verse and Doxology are each begun by soloists (up to the asterisk) and finished by the choir. The Doxology is not written out in full in the chant books because the words were well known to the singers and because it was sung to the same melody as the psalm verse. Instead, music is given for only the first two words (*Gloria Patri*) and the last six syllables, abbreviated to their vowels *E u o u a e* (for *saEcUlOrUm AmEn*). The Doxology is written out here to show how it fits the music. After the Doxology, the antiphon is repeated.

(b) Kyrie

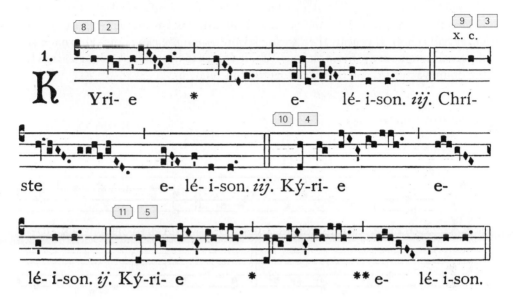

| 8 | 2 | | | | | | 9 | 3 |
|---|---|---|---|---|---|---|---|---|

1.

K Yri- e   *   e- lé- i-son. *iij*. Chrí-

ste   e- lé- i-son. *iij*. Ký-ri- e   e-

lé- i-son. *ij*. Ký-ri- e   *   ** e-   lé- i-son.

| Kyrie eleison. | Lord have mercy. |
|----------------|------------------|
| Christe eleison. | Christ have mercy. |
| Kyrie eleison. | Lord have mercy. |

After the Introit, the choir sings the Kyrie. The Kyrie is the only chant from the Mass whose text is in Greek, showing its origin in the Byzantine Church. Among the musical settings of the Kyrie that may be sung on Christmas Day is this one from the tenth century, known as *Kyrie Cunctipotens Genitor*. (The name comes from an alternative text, known as a *trope*, that can replace the words "Kyrie" and "Christe.") The invocation "Kyrie eleison" is sung three times; then "Christe eleison" is sung three times; then "Kyrie eleison" is sung three times again. Here, a new melody is introduced for each section, and the final statement repeats a phrase, creating an overall form of AAA BBB CCC'.

The chant is classified as being in mode 1. This is very clear in the first "Kyrie eleison," which begins on the reciting tone A, circles around it, then gradually and repeatedly falls to the final D. The "Christe eleison" again starts on A and gradually falls to D. However, the remaining statements of "Kyrie eleison" reverse course, springing up to A, circling around it, and ending on A. The pattern of steps around A (whole step below, whole step and half step above) is the same as the pattern around D, so that medieval theorists recognized A as a *co-final* for mode 1.

Because of their very short text, most Kyries are *melismatic* (with melismas of many notes on several syllables), like this one. A few Kyries, used for Masses that are neither on Sundays nor on feast days, are syllabic to neumatic.

The Kyrie was originally sung in processions and took the form of a *litany*, in which the whole group repeats a short prayer in response to a leader. By the

Middle Ages, Kyries were often performed antiphonally, in alternation between two halves of the choir, as illustrated on the accompanying recording. The cantor begins the first "Kyrie eleison," joined at the asterisk by one half (choir 1); the other half (choir 2) repeats the "Kyrie eleison"; then the two choirs alternate. In the final statement of "Kyrie eleison," choir 1 sings to the asterisk, choir 2 sings to the double asterisk, and both join together on "eleison."

(c) Gloria

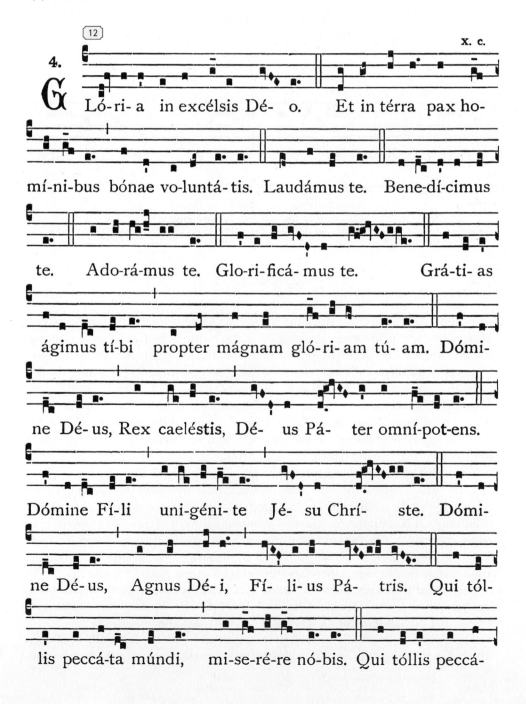

ta múndi,   súscipe depreca-ti-ónem nóstram.   Qui sé-des

ad déxteram Pátris,   mi-se-ré-re nó-bis.   Quó-ni- am tu

só-lus sánctus. Tu só-lus Dóminus. Tu só-lus Altíssimus,

Jé-  su Chrí-    ste.   Cum Sáncto Spí-   ri- tu,   in gló-

ri- a Dé- i Pá- tris.   A-    men.

| | |
|---|---|
| Gloria in excelsis Deo | Glory be to God on high. |
| Et in terra pax hominibus bonae voluntatis. | And on earth peace to men of good will. |
| Laudamus te. Benedicimus te. Adoramus te. Glorificamus te. | We praise thee, we bless thee, we adore thee, we glorify thee. |
| Gratias agimus tibi propter magnam gloriam tuam. | We give thee thanks for thy great glory. |
| Domine Deus, Rex caelestis, | O Lord God, King of heaven, |
| Deus Pater omnipotens. | God the Father Almighty. |
| Domine Fili unigenite Jesu Christe. | O Lord, the only begotten Son, Jesus Christ. |
| Domine Deus, Agnus Dei, Filius Patris. | O Lord God, Lamb of God, Son of the Father. |
| Qui tollis peccata mundi, miserere nobis. | Thou who takest away the sins of the world, have mercy on us. |
| Qui tollis peccata mundi, suscipe deprecationem nostram. | Thou who takest away the sins of the world, receive our prayer. |
| Qui sedes ad dexteram Patris, miserere nobis. | Thou who sittest at the right hand of the Father, have mercy on us. |
| Quoniam tu solus sanctus. | For thou only art holy, |
| Tu solus Dominus. | Thou only art Lord. |
| Tu solus Altissimus, Jesu Christe. | Thou only art most high, O Jesus Christ, |
| Cum Sancto Spiritu, | With the Holy Spirit, |
| In Gloria Dei Patris. Amen. | In the glory of God the Father. Amen. |

The Gloria, or Greater Doxology, is a text that praises God, states the doctrine of the Trinity, and asks for mercy. It is sung only on Sundays and feast days and is omitted in the seasons of Advent (before Christmas) and Lent (before Easter). Thus its presence adds to the festive quality of the Mass for Christmas Day, especially after having been absent during the preceding weeks.

Because the text is long, no Gloria melodies are melismatic; most, including this one, are neumatic, and a few are largely syllabic. This tenth-century melody is in mode 4, closing on E and moving in an octave from a third below to a sixth above. The mode is clear throughout because almost every phrase closes on the final.

There is no standard pattern of repetition for Gloria melodies, but in this Gloria the same melodic ideas recur repeatedly, often varied (see, for example, the many variants of the motive first heard at "bonae voluntatis"). Remarkably, references to the three aspects of the Trinity are all highlighted with the same motive, which occurs nowhere else (the Father at "Deus Pater omnipotens," the Son at "Jesu Christe," and the Holy Spirit at "Sancto Spiritu").

The Gloria and the Credo are unusual among the chants sung by the choir in that they are begun by the priest officiating at the Mass rather than by the cantor. This is a holdover from their original role as texts to be sung by the entire congregation.

After the Gloria, a prayer called the Collect is chanted, and then the Epistle (an extract from one of the letters of the apostle Paul to the Hebrews) is recited. Both are vocalized with very simple formulas.

(d) Gradual: *Viderunt omnes*

mi-nus  sa-lu-

tá-  re sú-  um : ante conspéctum génti- um  re-

ve-lá-  vit * justí-  ti- am sú- am.

Viderunt omnes fines terrae salutare Dei
nostri: jubilate Deo omnis terra.

℣. Notum fecit Dominus
salutare suum: ante conspectum
gentium revelavit justitiam suam.

All the ends of the earth have seen the
salvation of our God; sing joyfully to
God, all the earth.

℣. The Lord hath made known His
salvation; He hath revealed His justice
in the sight of the peoples.

This Gradual exemplifies responsorial psalmody, in which a soloist singing the psalm verse (Psalm 97:2 in the Latin Vulgate, 98:2 in the Protestant Bible) alternates with a choir performing the respond (here taken from verses 3–4 of the same psalm). Unlike the Introit's psalm verse, which followed a recitational formula, this verse is extremely ornate, as was characteristic of chants involving soloists from the choir. The melody is clearly in mode 5, with cadences on the final F at the end of both respond and verse, a range that extends an octave above the final and one step below, many phrases that center on the reciting tone C, and phrase-endings on C and on A (both common in this mode). The note B is often flatted in this mode to avoid the tritone with F. Several flat signs appear in the music; they are valid only until the end of the word.

In performance, the soloist (usually the cantor, sometimes another singer or two singers) sings the opening phrase and is joined by the choir at the asterisk. Then the soloist sings most of the verse, and the choir joins in again at the asterisk. In the Middle Ages, the respond was then repeated by the entire choir (for an ABA form), but in modern practice that repetition is often omitted.

(e) Alleluia: *Dies sanctificatus*

Alleluia. Alleluia.
℣. Dies sanctificatus illuxit
   nobis: venite gentes, et adorate
   Dominum: quia hodie descendit lux
   magna super terram.

Alleluia. Alleluia.
℣. A sanctified day hath shone upon
   us; come ye peoples, and adore the
   Lord; for this day a great light hath
   descended upon the earth.

During most of the year, the Alleluia, another responsorial chant, comes after the Gradual. As in the Gradual, a soloist sings the psalm verse, and the choir responds with "Alleluia" (from the Hebrew *Hallelujah,* meaning "praise Yahweh," or "Jehovah"). The Gradual and Alleluia together form the musical high point of the Gregorian Mass. No ritual actions occur at this point in the service, and the attention of all is focused on the singing of these melodies and texts. The soloist sings the first phrase of "Alleluia" to the asterisk; the choir repeats this (as shown by the repeat mark *ij.*) and continues with the following melisma, the *jubilus.* The soloist sings the verse, joined by the choir for the last words (marked by an asterisk). Finally, the respond is sung again without the repetition, creating an overall ABA'

form. In the Middle Ages, the soloist often sang the "Alleluia," and the choir joined at the melisma, as on the accompanying recording.

The Alleluia for Christmas Day is one of the oldest. Many later Alleluias repeat the entire melody for "Alleluia" on the last word of the verse. Here instead there is a varied repetition of the first phrase of the verse ("Dies sanctificatus illuxit nobis") in the third phrase ("quia hodie descendit lux magna"). The melody is in mode 2, the plagal mode on D, and moves in the normal octave range from A to A. Most phrases end on the final, others on the note below, and several phrases linger on the reciting tone F. Compare this chant to the Kyrie, a mode 1 chant, to see how different are the plagal and authentic modes on the same final of D.

After the Alleluia comes the Gospel, a reading from one of the four New Testament books that relate the life of Jesus. It is chanted by the deacon on a simple recitation formula. A spoken sermon may follow.

(f) Credo

pter nos hómines,   et propter nóstram sa-lú-tem descéndit

de caé-lis.    Et incarná-tus est de Spí-ri-tu Sáncto      ex

Ma-rí- a Vírgi-ne :    Et hómo fáctus est. Cru-ci-fíxus ét-i- am

pro nóbis : sub Pónti- o Pi-lá-to     pássus, et sepúltus est.

Et resurréxit térti- a dí- e,     secúndum Scriptúras.    Et

ascéndit  in caélum : sédet ad déxte-ram Pátris. Et í-te-rum

ventúrus est cum gló-ri- a,     judi-cá-re vívos et mórtu- os :

cú-jus régni non é-rit fí-nis.    Et in Spí-ri-tum Sánctum, Dó-

minum,  et vi-vi-fi-cántem : qui  ex Pátre Fi-li- óque procé-

dit. Qui cum Pátre  et Fí-li- o    simul ado-rá-tur,   et con-

glo-ri-fi-cá-tur : qui locútus est per Prophé-tas.  Et únam sán-

ctam cathó-li-cam   et apostó-li-cam Ecclé-si- am. Confí-

te- or únum baptísma   in remissi- ónem pecca-tó-rum. Et

exspécto resurrecti- ónem mortu-ó-rum. Et ví-tam ventú-

ri saé-cu-li.   A- men.

Credo in unum Deum, Patrem omnipotentem, fac-
torem caeli et terrae, visibilium omnium et
invisibilium.
Et in unum Dominum Jesum Christum Filium Dei
unigenitum. Et ex Patre natum ante omnia saecula. Deum de Deo, lumen de lumine, Deum
verum de Deo vero. Genitum, non factum, con
substantialem Patri: per quem omnia facta sunt.
Qui propter nos homines et propter nostram
salutem descendit de caelis. Et incarnatus est de
Spiritu Sancto ex Maria Virgine: et homo factus
est. Crucifixus etiam pro nobis: sub Pontio
Pilato passus, et sepultus est. Et resurrexit tertia
die, secundum Scripturas. Et ascendit in
caelum: sedet ad dexteram Patris. Et iterum
venturus est cum gloria judicare vivos et mortu
os: cujus regni non erit finis.

Et in Spiritum Sanctum, Dominum, et vivifican-
tem: qui ex Patre, Filioque procedit. Qui cum
Patre, et Filio simul adorator, et conglorificatur:
qui locutus est per Prophetas.
Et unam sanctam catholicam et apostolicam
Ecclesiam.
Confiteor unum baptisma in remissionem pecca-
torum. Et exspecto resurrectionem mortuorum.
Et vitam venturi saeculi. Amen.

I believe in one God, Father Almighty, maker of
heaven and earth, and of all things visible and
invisible.
And in one Lord Jesus Christ, the only-begotten
Son of God. Born of the Father before all ages.
God of God, light of light, true God of true God.
Begotten, not made, being of one substance with
the Father, by whom all things were made. Who
for us humans and for our salvation descended
from heaven. And was made incarnate by the
Holy Spirit of the Virgin Mary, and was made
man. And was crucified for us; under Pontius
Pilate He died, and was buried. And rose again
on the third day, according to the Scriptures.
And ascended into heaven, and sits at the right
hand of the Father. And He shall come again
with glory to judge the living and the dead; of
whose kingdom there shall be no end.
And in the Holy Spirit, Lord and giver of life, who
proceeds from the Father and the Son. Who,
together with the Father and the Son, is wor-
shiped and glorified; who spoke by the prophets.
And one holy, Catholic, and Apostolic
Church.
I acknowledge one baptism for the remission of
sins. And I await the resurrection of the dead.
And the life of the world to come. Amen.

The Credo, or Nicene Creed, is a statement of faith that summarizes the central doctrines of the Catholic Church. This was the last item to be added to the standard form of the Mass (in 1014), and it was the last of the Ordinary chants to be taken away from the congregation and given to the choir. The long association with congregational singing explains why all Credo melodies are syllabic and relatively simple, why there are relatively few Credo melodies, and why Credo melodies are not included in cycles of Ordinary chants. It also explains why the priest begins the chant, singing "Credo in unum Deum" (I believe in one God) before the choir sings the rest of the melody.

Like Gloria melodies, Credo melodies have no standard pattern of repetition, but they do feature a few motives that are repeated and varied to fit the changing accentuations of the text. Note for example the motive on "Patrem omnipotentem," used in various forms more than a dozen times and often preceded by a variant of the figure on "Credo in unum Deum." Although the melody ends on E and therefore is classed as mode 4, almost all the phrases close on G, and B♭ is an unexpectedly common tone (compare the Gloria and Offertory, both in mode 4, in which B♭ never occurs).

The Credo marks the end of the first main division of the Mass, the Liturgy of the Word, which centers on readings and singing more than on ritual actions. It is followed by the Liturgy of the Eucharist, whose focus is the preparation for and giving of communion to the faithful.

(g) Offertory: *Tui sunt caeli*

ti- a    et   judí-       ci-   um praepa-rá-

ti-o    sé-    dis    tú- ae.

Tui sunt caeli, et tua est terra: orbem terrarum, et plenitudinem ejus tu fundasti: justitia et judici‐um praeparatio sedis tuae.

Thine are the heavens, and Thine is the earth: the world and the fullness thereof Thou hast found‐ed; justice and judgment are the preparation of Thy throne.

As the priest begins to prepare the bread and wine for communion, the choir sings the Offertory. Originally, the Offertory was a long responsorial psalm, performed as members of the congregation made donations of bread and wine to the priests, with florid verses sung by a soloist framed by a respond sung by the choir. All that survives today is the respond, whose melismatic character reflects its history as a chant associated with florid solo singing. This Offertory draws its text from a psalm (verse 11 and half of verse 13 from Psalm 88 in the Latin Vulgate, 89 in the Protestant Bible).

The melody is in mode 4, with a final on E and a range from C to C, but it tends to linger on F instead of emphasizing the tenor A. The cantor sings the first words to set the pitch, and the choir joins at the asterisk to complete the chant.

The priest then recites various prayers in a speaking voice for the blessing of the elements and vessels of the Eucharist, the reenactment of Christ's last supper. One prayer that is chanted is the Preface, to a formula that is more melodious than the other simple readings. The Preface serves to introduce the Sanctus.

(h) Sanctus

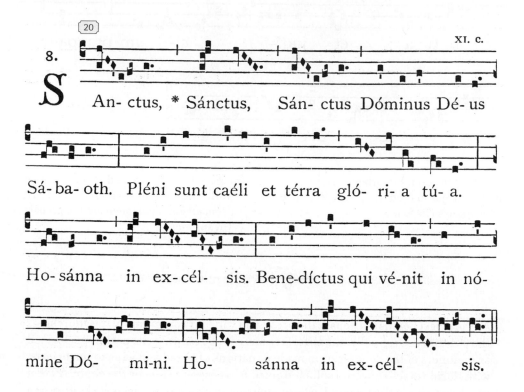

8.

SAn- ctus, * Sánctus,   Sán- ctus Dóminus Dé- us

Sá- ba- oth.  Pléni sunt caéli et térra gló- ri- a tú- a.

Ho- sánna   in ex- cél- sis. Bene-díctus qui vé-nit  in nó-

mine Dó-   mi-ni. Ho-    sánna   in ex-cél-     sis.

| | |
|---|---|
| Sanctus, Sanctus, Sanctus Dominus Deus Sabaoth. Pleni sunt caeli et terra gloria tua. Hosanna in excelsis. | Holy, holy, holy, Lord God of Hosts. The heavens and earth are full of thy glory. Hosanna in the highest. |
| Benedictus qui venit in nomine Domini. Hosanna in excelsis. | Blessed is he who comes in the name of the Lord. Hosanna in the highest. |

The Sanctus begins with the words sung by angels in a vision described in Isaiah 6:3. Sanctus melodies are typically neumatic, as in this eleventh-century setting. The threefold repetitions of "Sanctus" and the twofold "Hosanna" invite musical repetitions. Here, there are both exact repetitions (the third "Sanctus" repeats the first; the second "Hosanna" repeats the previous eleven notes) and varied repetitions (compare the sections from "Pleni" through "excelsis" and from "Benedictus" through the end to each other and to the melody from the second "Sanctus" through "Sabaoth"). The overall form of AA'A" is not uncommon, but the particular sequence of motives (abacd b'cdba' b"cdcdba") is individual and rather lovely in its combination of simplicity with subtly complex variation.

The melody is in mode 8, with a final of G and an octave range from D to D. Frequent cadences on G and phrases that wind above and below it make the mode clear throughout. Compare this chant to the Introit, a mode 7 chant, to see the differences between the authentic and plagal modes on G.

Now the celebrant pronounces the Canon, the prayer consecrating the bread and wine, and the *Pater noster* (the Lord's Prayer, "Our Father").

(i) Agnus Dei

Agnus Dei, qui tollis peccata mundi: miserere nobis.

Agnus Dei, qui tollis peccata mundi: miserere nobis.

Agnus Dei, qui tollis peccata mundi: dona nobis pacem.

Lamb of God, who takest away the sins of the world: have mercy on us.

Lamb of God, who takest away the sins of the world: have mercy on us.

Lamb of God, who takest away the sins of the world: give us peace.

The Agnus Dei, like the Kyrie, was originally a litany, a repeated prayer in which participants respond to a leader. The text consists of a threefold acclamation, "Lamb of God, who takest away the sins of the world," followed by two identical responses, "have mercy on us," and a final response, "give us peace." Despite the two different responses, the three periods of the chant each end with the same music. The beginning of the middle period differs from the other two, creating an overall form of AB CB AB, one of the standard patterns for the Agnus Dei. The opening words "Agnus Dei" in each period are sung by the cantor, with the choir completing the period.

This chant is classed as mode 6, the plagal mode on F. The final is very clear, but the range from E to D could fit either mode 6 or mode 5, the authentic mode on F (compare the Gradual, which is in mode 5, and has a range from low E to high F). Here the tenor may be the deciding factor: there is a strong emphasis on A, the tenor of mode 6, whereas C, the mode 5 tenor, seldom occurs. Each melodic unit describes an undulating arch, and each period rises to a single peak (C in the outer periods, D in the middle one), arrives at a medial cadence on the tenor A, and winds back down to F.

## (j) Communion: *Viderunt omnes*

Viderunt omnes fines terrae salutare Dei nostri.    All the ends of the earth have seen the salvation of our God.

After the faithful and celebrants have partaken of the bread and wine, the choir sings the Communion. This chant was originally a psalm with antiphon, sung antiphonally by the choir during the distribution of the bread and wine. When in the later Middle Ages the chant was moved to follow rather than accompany the giving of communion, it no longer needed to last as long, so the psalm verses were dropped, and only the antiphon remained.

The text of this Communion is the same as that beginning the Gradual. There are no repeated motives in the music, but rather a variety of melodic patterns. The melody is in mode 1, evident in the cadences on the final D, the emphasis on the tenor A, and the range that extends almost an octave above D.

(k) Ite, missa est

1.

- te,

Dé- o

míssa est.

grá-ti- as.

Ite, missa est.

Deo gratias.

Go, the Mass is over.

Thanks to God.

At the end of the Mass, the priest or deacon dismisses the faithful, and the choir replies, "Thanks to God." In the Solesmes Mass cycles, this short text is always sung to the melody of the first "Kyrie eleison." In the accompanying recording, the dismissal is sung by the deacon.

# 4 Chants from Vespers for Christmas Day

*Gregorian chant Office*

(a) First Psalm with Antiphon: Antiphon *Tecum principium* and psalm *Dixit Dominus*

CD 1|24, 27    CD 1|7, 10

TECUM prin-cí- pi- um * in di- e virtú-tis tu- æ, in splendó-ri-bus sanctó-rum, ex ú-te-ro ante lu-cí-fe-rum gé-nu- i te. E u o u a e.

Tecum principium in die virtutis tuae, in splen-
doribus sanctorum, ex utero ante luciferum
genui te.

Thine shall be the dominion in the day of Thy
strength, in the brightness of the Saints, from
the womb before the day star I begot Thee.

25    8

Mediant of 2 accents.                                                    *g*

1. Dí-xit Dóminus Dómino mé-    o ; * Séde a *déxtris* mé-    is.

Antiphon and hymn from *Antiphonale monasticum* (Tournai: Desclée, 1934), 245 and 238 respectively.
Psalm from *Liber usualis* (Tournai: Desclée, 1961), 128, Tone 1g. Reprinted by permission of St.
Bonaventure Publications. English translations from *The Saint Andrew Daily Missal*, ed. Dom Gaspar
Lefebvre, O.S.B. (New York: Benziger Publishing Co., 1956). Reprinted by permission.

1  Díxit Dóminus **Dómino méo**: *
   Séde a *déxtris* **méis**.
2  Donec pónam inimícos **túos**, *
   scabéllum pé*dum tu*ó*rum.
3  Vírgam virtútis túae emíttet
      Dóminus ex **Síon**: *
      domináre in medio inimicó*rum tuó*rum.
4  Técum princípium in díe virtútis túae
      in splendóri**bus** sanctó**rum**: *
      ex útero ante lucíferum *génu*i te.

5  Jurávit Dóminus, et non paenité**bit é**um: *
   Tu es sacérdos in aetérnum
   secúndum órdi*nem Melchi*sedech.
6  Dóminus a **déx**tris **túis**, *
   confrégit in díe írae *súae* **ré**ges.
7  Judicábit in natiónibus, im**pl**ébit ruínas: *

   conquassábit cápita in térra *mul***tór**um.
8  De torrénte in **vía bí**bet: *
   proptérea exal*tábit* **cá**put.
   26  9
9  Glória **Pátri**, et **Fí**lio, *
   et Spirítui **Sáncto**.
10 Sicut érat in princípio, et **núnc**, et **sém**per, *

   et in saécula saecu*lórum*. **Amen.**

The Lord said unto my Lord:
Sit Thou at My right hand.
Until I make Thine enemies
Thy footstool.
The Lord shall send the rod of Thy
   strength out of Sion:
rule Thou in the midst of Thine enemies.
Thine shall be the dominion in the day of
   Thy power amid the brightness of the Saints:
from the womb, before the day star have
I begotten Thee.

The Lord hath sworn, and will not repent:
Thou art a Priest for ever after the order
of Melchisedech.
The Lord at Thy right hand
shall strike through kings in the day of His wrath.
He shall judge among the heathen, He
shall fill the places with dead bodies:
He shall wound the heads over many countries.
He shall drink of the brook in the way:
therefore shall He lift up His head.

Glory be to the Father, and to the Son,
and to the Holy Spirit.
As it was in the beginning, is now, and
   ever shall be,
world without end. Amen.

(b) Hymn: *Christe Redemptor omnium*

Christe Redemptor omnium,
Ex Patre Patris Unice,
Solus ante principium
Natus ineffabiliter

Jesus! Redeemer of the world!
Who, ere the earliest dawn of light,
Was from eternal ages born,
Immense in glory as in might.

Tu lumen, tu splendor Patris,
Tu spes perennis omnium:
Intende, quas fundunt preces.
Tui per orbem famuli.

Immortal Hope of all mankind
In whom the Father's face we see,
Hear Thou the prayers Thy people pour
This day throughout the world to Thee.

Memento, salutis Auctor,
Quod nostri quondam corporis,
Ex illibata Virgine
Nascendo, formam sumpseris.

Remember, O Creator Lord!
That in the Virgin's sacred womb
Thou was conceiv'd and of her flesh
Didst our mortality assume.

Sic praesens testatur dies,
Currens per anni circulum.
Quod solus a sede Patris
Mundi salus adveneris.

This ever-blest recurring day
Its witness bears, that all alone,
From Thy own Father's bosom forth,
To save the world Thou camest down.

Hunc caelum, terra, hunc mare,
Hunc omne, quod in eis est,

O Day! to which the seas and sky,
And earth, and heav'n, glad welcome
      sing;
O Day! which heal'd our misery,
And brought on earth salvation's King.

Auctorem adventus tui
Laudans exultat cantico.

Nos quoque, qui sancto tuo,
Redempti sanguine sumus,
Ob diem natalis tui
Hymnum novum concinimus.

We, too, O Lord, who have been cleans'd
In Thy own fount of Blood divine,
Offer the tribute of sweet song
On this blest natal day of Thine.

Gloria tibi, Domine,
Qui natus es de Virgine,
Cum Patre et Sancto Spiritu
In sempiterna saecula. Amen.

O Jesus! born of Virgin bright,
Immortal glory be to Thee;
Praise to the Father infinite
And Holy Ghost eternally. Amen.

Of the eight daily services that constitute the Office, Vespers is one of the most important. The principal feasts in the Catholic Church have two Vespers services: the first at sunset the evening before and the second at sunset on the feast day itself. Thus, the official name for Vespers on Christmas Day is Second Vespers of the feast of the Nativity of Our Lord (December 25). The excerpts from the Vespers included here exemplify two types of chant that occur in all Office services: the psalm with antiphon and the hymn.

The first full psalm sung in this Office is Psalm 109, *Dixit Dominus* (Psalm 110 in the Protestant Bible). It is preceded and followed by the Antiphon *Tecum principium*, which borrows its text from a verse of the psalm. The antiphon is a simple, mostly syllabic melody in mode 1. Its melodic contour elegantly delineates the phrasing and accentuation of the text while highlighting the most important notes in the mode (the final D, the tenor A, and F) through cadences or repetition. The psalm is sung to a *psalm tone*, a simple melodic formula designed to accommodate verses of any length. There is one psalm tone for each of the eight modes, and the mode of the antiphon determines the mode of the psalm, here mode 1. Each verse of the psalm is sung to the psalm tone, which then is repeated twice more for the Lesser Doxology (here numbered as verses 9–10), a formula of praise to the Trinity.

Psalm verses normally divide into two parts, punctuated by a colon or comma, and psalm tones use melodic motion to reflect this division. The formula for the first half of the verse has three components: an *intonation*, a rising figure used only in the first verse of the psalm (here the notes F–G–A); recitation on the *reciting tone*, the tenor of the mode; and the *mediant*, a cadence to close the first half. As shown here, in mode 1 the mediant rises from the tenor A to B♭ on the next-to-last accented syllable, returns to A, falls to G on the last accented syllable, and returns again to A. (The open noteheads show what note to sing when there are two unaccented syllables after an accent, rather than one.) The last two accented syllables are shown in boldface here and in modern chant books as a guide for the singers. When the first half of the psalm verse is especially lengthy, a *flex* (inflection), a melodic fall of a step or third, serves as a resting point.

The second half of the verse begins with more recitation on the tenor and then concludes with a final cadence called a *termination*. Each psalm tone has a variety of terminations designed to provide a smooth flow back to the antiphon, and by convention the form of termination is indicated after the antiphon over the letters "E u o u a e," which stand for the syllables "saEcUlOrUm AmEn," at the end of the Doxology. In this case, the termination closes on G with a G–A figure on the last accented syllable, shown in boldface, preceded by G and F for the previous two syllables, shown in italics. (Because the piece is not over until the antiphon repeats, the psalm tone itself does not have to close on the final of the mode.)

Office psalms were sung antiphonally, alternating verses or half verses between two halves of the choir. On the accompanying recording, the cantor begins the antiphon to set the pitch, and the full choir joins in at the asterisk. Then the cantor sings the first half of the first psalm verse, half the choir completes it, and the two halves of the choir alternate verses until both join together in the reprise of the antiphon.

The hymn *Christe Redemptor omnium* hails the arrival of the Savior on this day of his birth. Hymns as a genre are strophic—that is, the number of lines, the syllable count, and the structure of all the stanzas are the same. This hymn has seven stanzas of four lines each, each line containing eight syllables. There is no regular pattern of accents, and rhymes occur only occasionally. The English translation included here is a rhyming, metrical version that can be sung to the chant, rather than a literal rendering. The setting of this hymn is simple, with no more than two notes per syllable. It may have been performed rhythmically rather than with the free durations of prose texts and psalms.

# ASCRIBED TO WIPO OF BURGUNDY (CA. 995–CA. 1050)

## *Victimae paschali laudes*

*Sequence*

FIRST HALF OF THE ELEVENTH CENTURY

1 Victimae paschali laudes immolent Christiani.

To the Paschal Victim let Christians offer songs of praise.

2 Agnus redemit oves: Christus innocens Patri reconciliavit peccatores.

The Lamb has redeemed the sheep; sinless Christ has reconciled sinners to the Father.

3 Mors et vita duelo conflixere mirando: dux vitae mortuus, regnat vivus.

Death and life have engaged in miraculous combat; the leader of life is slain, yet living he reigns.

*Liber usualis*, 780. "Chant: Sequence For The Solemn Mass of Easter Day," from Richard Hoppin, ed., *Anthology of Medieval Music* (New York: Norton, 1978), 15. © 1978. Used by permission of W. W. Norton & Company, Inc.

4  Dic nobis Maria, quid vidisti in via? Sepulcrum Christi viventis, et gloriam vidi resurgentis:

Tell us, Mary, what you saw on the way? I saw the sepulchre of the living Christ and the glory of His rising;

5  Angelicos testes, sudarium, et vestes. Surexit Christus spes mea: praecedet suos in Galilaeam.

The angelic witnesses, the shroud and vesture. Christ my hope is risen; He will go before His own into Galilee.

6  [Credendum est magis soli Mariae veraci quam Judaeorum turbae fallaci.]

The truthful Mary alone is more to be believed than the deceitful crowd of Jews.

7  Scimus Christum surrexisse a mortuis vere: tu nobis, victor Rex, miserere. Amen. Alleluia.

We know that Christ has truly risen from the dead. Thou conqueror and king, have mercy on us. Amen. Alleluia.

—(?) WIPO OF BURGUNDY

—TRANS. RICHARD HOPPIN

Among the many sequences that were sung in the Middle Ages, *Victimae paschali laudes* is one of only five that are retained in the liturgy and standard modern chant books. When the Council of Trent (1545–63) eliminated most sequences, this one was kept because it was widely used and associated with Easter, the most important feast day of the Christian calendar. It was sung as part of the liturgy at Mass and was also incorporated into sacred dramas performed at Easter. The text describes Jesus' resurrection and the redemption that Christians believe He brings to humankind.

In one medieval manuscript, this sequence is ascribed to Wipo (ca 995–ca. 1050), chaplain to Holy Roman Emperor Henry III. He may have written the text, or both text and music, but it is also possible that the piece was written by someone else and attributed to Wipo simply because he was an eminent clergyman.

Sequences of the ninth through the eleventh centuries typically follow the form A BB CC . . . N, comprising an opening sentence with its own musical phrase, a series of paired sentences (each with the same number of syllables and set to the same music), and a final unpaired sentence. In its original form, *Victimae paschali laudes* lacked the final unpaired sentence, but in modern chant books, verse 6 (marked here by brackets) is omitted, bringing this sequence into line with the usual pattern. There was a more urgent reason than mere conformity for making this change: that verse, with its reference to "the deceitful crowd of Jews," evokes the ancient calumny that Jews were responsible for the death of Jesus, part of an anti-Jewish tradition that modern church leaders have apologized for and have sought to uproot.

As is common in early sequences, the number of syllables increases through the first three verses and then recedes to the mean. Verses 4–7 each have internal rhymes, reflecting the predilection of Frankish writers for rhyming and scanning texts in newly composed chants. The melody likewise features musical rhymes that lend it coherence: verses 2–3 and 6–7 begin with the same phrase, and all verses and most internal phrases close with a stepwise descent to D, usually G–F–E–D.

**6**

# Tropes on *Puer natus*: *Quem queritis in presepe* and Melisma

*Texted trope (liturgical drama) and untexted trope*

LATE TENTH CENTURY

CD 1|30

Trope to the Antiphon

Quem que- ri- tis in pre- se- pe pas-

[Shepherds]

-to- res di- ci- te Sal- va- to- rem

xris- tum do- mi- num in- fan- tem pan- nis in-

-vo- lu- tum se- cun- dum ser- mo- nem an-

[Midwives]

-ge- li- cum Ad- est hic par- vu- lus cum

Ma- ri- a ma- tre su- a de qua du- dum va-

-ti- ci- nan- do i- sa- i- as di- xe- rat pro- phe- ta

Ec- ce vir- go con- ci- pi- et et pa-

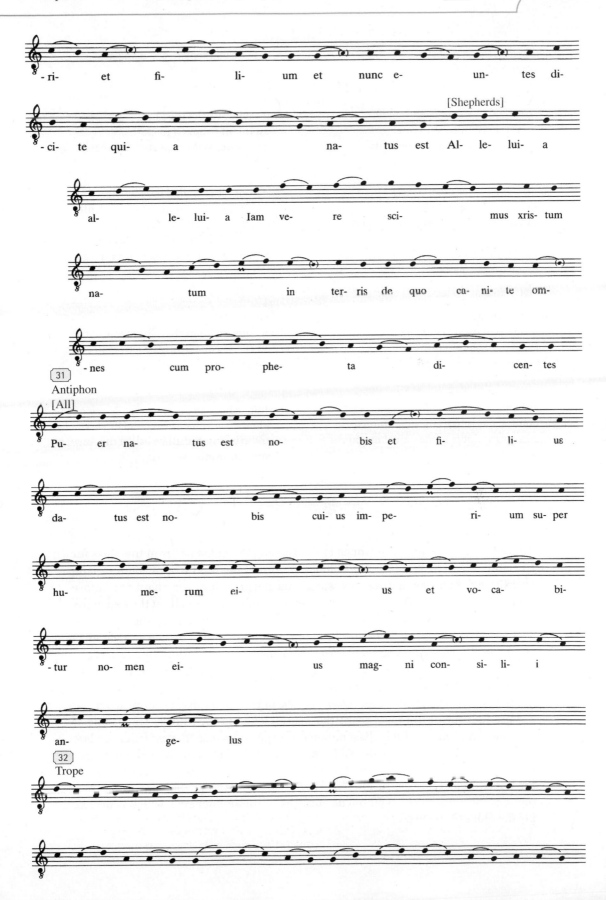

[MIDWIVES]

Quem queritis in presepe,
    pastores, dicite?

Whom do you seek in the manger,
    shepherds, tell us?


[SHEPHERDS]

Salvatorem, Christum Dominum,
    infantem pannis involutum,
    secundum sermonem angelicum.

Our savior, Christ the Lord,
    an infant wrapped in cloths,
    according to the report of the angels.


[MIDWIVES]

Adest hic parvulus cum Maria,
    matre sua, de qua dudum
    vaticinando Isaias dixerat propheta:
    Ecce virgo concipiet et
    pariet filium; et nunc euntes
    dicite quia natus est.

The infant is attended here by Mary,
    his mother, about whom a little while
    ago the prophet Isaiah foretold:
    behold a virgin will conceive and
    give birth to a son; and now as you go
    tell that he is born.


[SHEPHERDS]

Alleluia, alleluia!
Iam vere scimus Christum natum
    in terris, de quo canite omnes
    cum propheta dicentes:

Alleluia, alleluia!
Now truly we know that Christ was born
    on earth, concerning which let all sing
    with the prophet, saying:


[ALL]

Puer natus est nobis, et filius datus est
    nobis: cujus imperium super humerum
    ejus: et vocabitur nomen ejus, magni
    consilii angelus.

A child is born to us, and a Son is given to us;
    whose government is upon His shoulder;
    and His Name shall be called the Angel of
    great counsel.

This selection includes two tropes to the Introit *Puer natus est* from the Mass for
Christmas Day (NAWM 3a). These illustrate two of the ways tropes could expand
an existing chant: by adding new words and music before the chant (or before
each phrase or section) and by adding untexted melismas, usually at the end of the
chant or of a section. Both kinds of trope add length, emphasizing the chant and
increasing its grandeur. The third kind of trope, adding text to an existing melisma, is not shown here. The texted trope also adds an explanation, or gloss, clari-
fying how the text of the original chant, which is often taken from a psalm, relates
to the particular feast being celebrated.

In this case, the texted trope, *Quem queritis in presepe*, is also a liturgical drama,
a short dialogue or dramatic scene that was attached to the liturgy. This is one of
the oldest and most widely disseminated liturgical dramas, dating from the late
tenth century. The version shown here, which differs in some melodic passages
from the earliest sources, is contained in an eleventh-century manuscript from
St. Yrieix, near Limoges in France. There is a very similar dialogue for Easter,
*Quem queritis in sepulchro* (Whom do you seek in the sepulcher?), which is probably the older of the two.

In the Christmas dialogue, the midwives caring for the Christ child ask the shepherds whom they seek in the manger. The shepherds answer that they are looking for an infant in swaddling clothes, Christ the Savior, as the angels foretold. The midwives explain that the child was born to Mary, a virgin. The shepherds rejoice in the knowledge that they have confirmed the birth of Christ, and they then introduce the singing of the Introit. The words of the trope set the stage for the Introit and indeed for the entire Mass.

The melody is in mode 7, the mode of the Introit, with a strong emphasis on the final G and tenor D. There are a number of notable melodic recurrences that help to create the sense of a dialogue. When the shepherds first respond, they begin by repeating the midwives' melody. The same opening motive begins the second half of the midwives' reply (at "Ecce virgo concipiet"). The shepherds' final acclamation echos the first part of the midwives' reply, at least in its general outline of beginning on D, rising to high G, and falling back to D. In addition to these similarities at the beginnings of phrases, there are musical rhymes at cadences. The first three phrases all end with the same cadence, G–A–G–F–G. Then the last words of the shepherds' first statement, "sermonem angelicum," introduce a new ending formula that returns three more times: at the middle and end of the midwives' next response ("Isaias dixerat propheta" and "quia natus est") and at the end of the entire dialogue ("propheta dicentes"). These varied repetitions of one another's melodic material convey the sense of a conversation between the midwives and shepherds, and lend continuity and unity to the entire composition.

One late-tenth-century manuscript includes instructions for when and where the dialogue is to be performed: "On the day of the nativity of the Lord, at the station of St. Peter [a place along the side of the church], they begin the trope before the office is said [i.e., before the Mass begins with the Introit]." Exactly how and by whom it is to be performed is not specified, and even the identities of the characters in the dialogue have to be inferred from context. Perhaps the boys of the choir played the role of the midwives and the men the role of the shepherds, as in the recording accompanying this anthology. The recording continues with all voices singing the antiphon and added melisma, but the psalm verse and doxology are omitted. The performance differs in some small details from the transcription printed here.

# HILDEGARD OF BINGEN (1098–1179)

*Ordo virtutum*: Chorus, *In principio omnes*

*Sacred music drama*

CA. 1151

VIRTUES

| In principio omnes creature viruerunt, | In the beginning all creatures flourished, |
|---|---|
| in medio flores floruerunt; | they bloomed in the middle of flowers; |
| postea viriditas descendit. | after that greenness declined. |
| Et istud vir proeliator vidit et dixit: | The warrior [Christ] saw this and said: |
| Hoc scio, sed aureus numerus nondum est plenus. | "This I know, but the golden number is not yet complete. |
| Tu ergo, paternum speculum aspice: in corpore meo fatigationem sustineo, parvuli etiam mei deficiunt. | You, therefore, look upon the Father's reflection: in my body I endure fatigue, even my children weaken. |
| Nunc memor esto, quod plenitudo quae in primo facta est arescere non debuit, et tunc in te habuisti quod oculus tuus numquam cederet usque dum corpus meum videres plenum gemmarum. | Now be mindful, for the fullness that was made at the beginning did not need to wither, and at that time you believed that you would not turn away your eye until you could see my body covered with gems. |
| Nam me fatigat quod omnia membra mea in irrisionem vadunt. | It wearies me that all my followers fall into mockery. |

Pater, vide, vulnera mea tibi ostendo.

Ergo nunc, omnes homines, genua vestra ad
    Patrem vestrum flectite, ut vobis manum suam
    porrigat.

Father, behold, I show you my wounds."

Now, therefore, all humankind, bend your
    knees before your Father, that he may offer
    his hand to you.

Hildegard, founder and abbess of the convent in Rupertsberg, Germany, was famous for her prophetic powers and revelations. Her morality play with music, *Ordo virtutum* (The Virtues, ca. 1151), is unusual for its time because, unlike the liturgical dramas such as *Quem queritis in presepe* (NAWM 6), it is not a supplement to the Mass of a certain feast. Rather, it is an independent Latin play, an edifying entertainment for Hildegard's select community of noblewomen. The characters, singing in plainchant, include the Patriarchs and Prophets, sixteen female Virtues (including Humility, Love, Obedience, Faith, Hope, Chastity, Innocence, and Mercy), a Happy Soul, an Unhappy Soul, and a Penitent Soul. The Devil, bereft of divine harmony, can only shout and bellow; it is the only part that is spoken rather than sung.

The play begins with a chorus of Patriarchs and Prophets who express their wonder at the sight of the richly robed Virtues. Souls in a procession beg the Virtues for divine insight, alternating solos with choral responses. But the Devil tempts the Souls, and one Unhappy Soul succumbs and follows him, only to return later, bedraggled, hurt, and repentant. The Devil tries to reclaim her, but the Virtues, led by Humility, protect her and capture and bind the Devil. Though victorious, the Virtues lament the spoiling of the green, blossoming paradise and invoke the militant Christ, who urges them to aspire to the blessed conditions of the time of creation.

The final chorus, which serves as an epilogue, consists of four rhymed lines followed by a prose speech by Christ and ends with a short prayer. The melody is in mode 3, keeping mostly to the range of that mode, *d* to *e'*. It rises to *g'* at "oculus tuus" (your eye) and "ad Patrem" (to the Father), perhaps to emphasize those words, and elsewhere three times touches low *c*. This expanded range of a twelfth is typical of late Frankish chant. Periods and other strong endings in the text are marked by cadences on the final E. The tenor of this mode, C, plays no part in the structure; rather, the fifth degree, B, is the most frequent resting point.

The rhyme of the opening two lines is paralleled by an identical cadence formula in the music. The next two rhymed lines do not use the same closing pattern because the second serves as an introduction to Christ's speech. Frequently, phrases begin with the rising fifth *e–b'*, which opens the chorus and recurs seven times, sometimes leading to similar melodic contours. A few other melodic figures appear more than once, but for the most part, the melody unfolds in a constantly varied stream. The chorus ends with a melismatic flourish on the final word.

# BERNART DE VENTADORN (?CA. 1130–CA. 1200)

## Can vei la lauzeta mover

*Canso (troubadour song)*

CA. 1170–80

Can vei la lauzeta mover
de joi sas alsas contral rai,
que s'oblid' e · s laissa chazer
per la doussor c'al cor li vai,
ai! tan grans enveya m'en ve
de cui qu'eu veya jauzion,
meravilhas ai, car desse
lo cor de dezirer no · m fon.

Ai, las! tan cuidava saber
d'amor, e tan petit en sai,
car eu d'amar no · m posc tener
celeis don ja pro non aurai.
Tout m'a mo cor, e tout m'a me,
e se mezeis e tot lo mon;
e can se · m tolc, no · m laisset re
mas dezirer e cor volon.

Anc non agui de me poder
ni no fui meus de l'or' en sai

When I see the lark beating
its wings joyfully against the sun's rays,
which then swoons and swoops down
because of the joy in its heart,
oh! I feel such jealousy
for all those who have the joy of love,
that I am astonished
that my heart does not immediately melt with desire!

Alas! I thought I knew so much
of love, and I know so little;
for I cannot help loving a lady
from whom I shall never obtain any favor.
She has taken away my heart and myself,
and herself and the whole world;
and when she left me, I had nothing left
but desire and a yearning heart.

I have no power over myself,
and have not had possession of myself

Music adapted from and text and translation taken from Hendrik van der Werf, *The Chansons of the Troubadours and Trouvères* (Utrecht, 1972), 91–95, where versions of the melody appearing in five different sources are given, showing surprising consistency among readings. The dot splitting two letters of a word, as in e · s, indicates a contraction.

que · m laisset en sos olhs vezer
en un miralh que mout me plai.
Mirahls, pus me mirei en te,
m'an mort li sospir depreon,
c'aissi · m perdei com perdet se
lo bels Narcisus en la fon.

De las domnas me dezesper;
ja mais en lor no · m fiarai;
c'aissi com las solh chaptener,
enaissi las͜c deschaptenrai.
Pois vei c'una pro no m'en te
vas leis que · m destrui e · m confon,
totas las dopt' e las mescre,
car be sai c'atretals se son.

D'aisso's fa be femna parer
ma domna, par qu'e · lh o retrai,
car no vol so c'om deu voler,
e so c'om li devada, fai.
Chazutz sui en mala merce,
et ai be faih co · l fols en pon;
e no sai per que m'esdeve,
mas car trop puyei contra mon.

Merces es perduda, per ver,
et eu non o saubi anc mai,
car cilh qui plus en degr'aver
no · n a ges, et on la querrai?
A! can mal sembla, qui la ve,
qued aquest chaitiu deziron

que ja ses leis non aura be,
laisse morir, que no l'aon!

Pus ab midons no · m pot valer
precs ni merces ni · l dreihz qu'eu ai,
ni a leis no ven a plazer
qu'eu l'am, ja mais no · lh o dirai.
Aissi · m part de leis e · m recre;
mort m'a, e per mort h respon,
e van m'en, pus ilh no · m rete,
chaitius, en issilh, no sai on.

since the time when she allowed me to look into her eyes,
in a mirror which I like very much.
Mirror, since I was reflected in you,
deep sighs have killed me,
for I caused my own ruin, just as
fair Narcissus caused his by looking in the fountain.

I despair of ladies;
I shall not trust them ever again;
just as I used to defend them,
now I shall condemn them.
Since I see that *one* of them does not help me
against her who is ruining and destroying me
I fear them all and have no faith in them,
for I know they are all the same.

My lady shows herself to be [merely] a woman
(and that is why I reproach her)
in that she does not want what one should want,
and she does what is forbidden her.
I have fallen out of favor,
and have acted like the fool on the bridge;
and I do not know why this has happened to me,
unless it was because I tried to climb too high.

Mercy is gone, that is sure,
and I never received any of it,
for she who should have the most mercy
has none, and where else should I seek it?
Oh! how difficult it is for a person who sees her
to imagine that she would allow to die this poor
     yearning wretch,
and would not help the man
who can have no help but her!

Since pleas and mercy and my rights
cannot help me to win my lady,
and since it does not please her
that I love her, I shall speak to her about it no more.
So I am leaving her and her service;
she has killed me, and I reply with death,
and I am going sadly away, since she will not accept
my service, into exile, I do not know where.

| Tristans, ges no · m auretz de me, | Tristan, you will hear no more of me, |
| qu'eu m'en vau, chaitius, no sai on. | for I am going sadly away, I do not know where, |
| De chantar me gic e · m recre, | I am going to stop singing, |
| e de joi d'amor m'escon. | and I flee from love and joy. |

One of the best-preserved songs by the troubadour Bernart de Ventadorn is a lover's complaint, the main subject of the entire troubadour repertory. The poem is in Occitan, a language then spoken in what is now southern France. This is a *canso,* a strophic song about love. More specifically, it is about *fine amour,* or courtly love, an idealized love through which the lover is refined by his discreet and respectful adulation of an unattainable woman.

The song is strophic, each stanza but the last having eight lines rhymed ababcdcd, and each line has eight syllables. The music to which all the stanzas are sung has a new phrase for each line of poetry except the seventh, which repeats the music for the fourth line.

There are several versions of the melody, notated in different sources with slight variants between them. These variants suggest that the melody was conveyed through oral tradition for some time before being written down. To illustrate this variation, the accompanying recording presents a slightly different version from the one printed here.

In both versions, the melody is in the first mode. The first two phrases establish the mode, beginning on the final D, rising to the tenor A, circling around it, and cadencing on A. The rest of the melody rises and falls through graceful arches in mostly stepwise motion, twice touching high D. The version shown here sustains momentum by avoiding a cadence on the final until the very end, as the internal phrases close on the more active tones of G, F, and E. The version on the recording cadences on D after the fourth line, making the fourth and seventh phrases slightly different. The third phrase (at "Que s'oblid'") and eighth phrase (at "Lo cor de dezirer") both have figures that are written like noteheads with tails; these are sung as two pitches, the main note and the note a step down (if the tail goes down) or up (if the tail goes up).

Whether the troubadour songs were sung in a particular rhythm is a much-debated question, because the notation does not indicate rhythm but the poetry is metrical. The accompanying performance treats the rhythm freely but moves more quickly when there is more than one note on a syllable, keeping the syllables, rather than the notes themselves, roughly even in duration. Another approach is to give stressed syllables a value twice as long as unstressed syllables. The accompanying recording features the voice without accompaniment, which is most likely how such songs were performed. Alternatively, the singer might have been joined by an instrument playing the melody, playing a drone, or improvising an accompaniment.

This canso has seven eight-line stanzas and a closing four-line stanza sung to the second half of the melody, emphasizing the melodic closure. Because of time constraints, only the first two stanzas are included on the accompanying recording, but the entire poem should be read to fully understand its meaning. Each stanza introduces a new twist, and the poet's situation gradually becomes clearer with each one.

# Comtessa de Dia (fl. late twelfth to early thirteenth century)

## A chantar

*Canso (troubadour song)*

SECOND HALF OF TWELFTH CENTURY

| | |
|---|---|
| A chantar m'er de so qu'ieu non volria, | To sing I must of that which I would rather not, |
| tant me rancur de lui cui sui amia, | so bitter I am towards him who is my love: |
| car ieu l'am mais que nuilla ren que sia; | for I love him more than anyone; |
| vas lui no · m val merces ni cortesia, | my kindness and courtesy make no impression on him, |
| | |
| ni ma beltatz ni mos pretz ni mos sens, | nor my beauty, my virtue, or my intelligence; |
| c'atressi · m sui enganad' e trahia | so I am deceived and betrayed, |
| com degr' esser, s'ieu fos desavinens. | as I should be if I were unattractive. |

Melody transcribed by Hendrik van der Werf, *The Extant Troubadour Melodies* (Rochester: Author, 1984), 13. Gerald A. Bond, text editor. Text and translation used by permission of Hyperion Records Ltd., London, England.

D'aisso · m conort car anc non fi faillenssa,

amics, vas vox per nulla captenenssa,
anz vos am mais non fetz Seguis Valenssa;

e platz me mout quez eu d'amar vox
    venssa,
lo mieus amics, car etz lo plus valens;
mi faltz orguoill en ditz et en parvenssa,

e si etz francs vas totas autras gens.


Be · m meravill com vostre cors s'orguoilla,

amics, vas me, per qu'ai razon qu'ieu · m
    duoilla;
non es ges dreitz c'autr' amors vos mi
    touilla
per nuilla ren que · us diga ni acuoilla;
e membre vos cals fo · l comenssamens
de nostr' amor! ja Domnedieus non vuoilla
qu'en ma colpa sia · l departimens.

Proesa grans qu'el vostre cors s'aizina
e lo rics pretz qu'avetz m'en ataïna,
c'una non sai, loindana ne vezina,
si vol amar, vas vos non si'aclina;

mas vos, amics, etz ben tant conoissens
que ben devetz conoisser la plus fina:
e membre vos de nostres covinens.

Valer mi deu mos pretz e mos paratges,

e ma beltatz e plus mos fis coratges,

per qu'ieu vos mand lai on es vostr'
    estatges
esta chansson que me sia messatges;
ieu vuoill saber, lo mieus bels amics gens,
per que vos m'etz tant fers ni tant
    salvatges;
non sai si s'es orguoills o mal talens.

Mas aitan plus vuoill li digas, messatges,

qu'en trop d'orguoill ant grant dan maintas
    gens.

One thing consoles me: that I have never
    wronged you,
my love, by my behavior towards you;
indeed I love you more than Sequin loved
    Valensa;
and I am glad that my love is greater than
    yours,
my love, since you are the more worthy;
you are haughty towards me in your words
    and your
demeanor, yet you are friendly to
    everybody else.

I am amazed how disdainful you have
    grown,
my love, towards me, which gives me good
    reason to grieve;
it is not right that another love should take
    you away from me,
whatever she may say to attract you;
and remember how our love began!
God forbid
that I should be to blame for our parting.

The great prowess which you have
and your fine reputation worry me,
for I know no woman, near or far,
who would not turn to you, if she were
    inclined to love;
but you, my love, are discerning enough
to know who loves you most truly;
and remember the agreement we made.

My reputation and my noble birth should
    sway you,
and my beauty, and above all my faithful
    heart;
therefore I send to you where you dwell

this song to be my messenger;
I want to know, my noble love,
why you are so haughty and disdainful
    towards me;
I do not know whether it is pride or malice.

But most of all I want you to tell him,
    messenger,
that excess of pride has been the downfall
    of many.

According to a *vida* (life), or biographical tale, from about a century after she lived, "Beatrix, comtessa de Dia [Countess of Dia], was a beautiful and good woman, the wife of Guillaume de Poitiers. And she was in love with Rambaud d'Orange and made about him many good and beautiful songs." It is not known which parts of this account are legendary and which parts are true. She has tentatively been identified with "Beatrix comitissa," named in a document of 1212 as the daughter of Count Isoard II of Dia.

Like NAWM 8, *A chantar* is a canso in the Occitan language. However, in this song the tables are turned, and it is the woman in love who writes of the pride and disdain of her male lover. It has been suggested that the poetry of the female troubadours (called *trobairitz*) is more realistic and less artificial than that of their male peers, as if the women were speaking from real life experience rather than of an idealized love circumscribed by conventions. *A chantar* is the only song by a trobairitz for which the music is known to have survived.

The canso consists of five seven-line stanzas with the rhyme scheme aaaabab, followed by a final couplet that is sung to the same music as the last two lines of the preceding stanzas. While the a rhymes vary from stanza to stanza, the b rhymes are the same throughout the poem ("-ens"), linking the stanzas together. The melody used with each stanza repeats phrases in the pattern ab ab cdb, creating an overall form of AAB:

| Sections | A | | A | | B | | |
|---|---|---|---|---|---|---|---|
| Musical phrases | a | b | a | b | c | d | b |
| Rhyme scheme | a | a | a | a | b | a | b |

The A and B sections have a musical rhyme because both end with the same musical phrase. AAB form, with or without a musical rhyme, is found in several troubadour songs and many songs of the trouvères and Minnesinger.

On the accompanying recording, the singer is unaccompanied and sings in relatively free rhythm, moving more quickly when there are two or three notes on a syllable to maintain roughly equal durations among the syllables. As in NAWM 8, the round noteheads with tails indicate two pitches, the main note and the note a step down (if the tail goes down) or up (if the tail goes up).

# ADAM DE LA HALLE (CA. 1240–?1288)

### *Jeu de Robin et de Marion*: Rondeau, *Robins m'aime*

### *Musical play*

CA. 1284

CD 1|38

*Chorus:*
Ro - bins  m'ai - me,  Ro - bins  m'a,  Ro - bins  m'a  de - man - dé - e,

Si  m'a - ra.  *Solo:*  Ro - bins  m'a - ca - ta  co - te - le  D'es - car - la - te

bonne et  be - le,  Sous - ka - nie et  chain - tu - rele A - leu - ri - va!

*Chorus:*
Ro - bins  m'ai - me,  Ro - bins  m'a,  Ro - bins  m'a  de - man - dé - e,  Si  m'a - ra.

| | |
|---|---|
| Robins m'aime, | Robin loves me, |
| Robins m'a, | Robin has me, |
| Robins m'a demandée | Robin asked me |
| Si m'ara. | if he can have me. |
| Robins m'acata cotele | Robin bought me a skirt |
| D'escarlate bonne et belle | of scarlet, good and pretty, |
| Souskanie et chainturele. | a bodice and belt. |
| Aleuriva! | Hurray! |
| Robins m'aime, | Robin loves me, |
| Robins m'a, | Robin has me, |
| Robins m'a demandée | Robin asked me |
| Si m'ara. | if he can have me. |

From Friedrich Gennrich, *Troubadours, Trouvères, Minne- und Meistergesang* (Cologne, 1951), 38.

46

Adam de la Halle, one of the last and most famous of the trouvères, was born in Arras and studied in Paris. In 1283 he traveled to Italy with his patron Robert II, count of Artois, and there he entered the service of Robert's uncle, Charles of Anjou. In Naples, Adam composed and staged for his two patrons the musical play *Le jeu de Robin et de Marion* (The Play of Robin and Marion, ca. 1284). Like many other secular dramas of its time, it is a spoken play that features music. However, it includes far more music than its contemporaries, and a few of the songs have polyphonic settings. Indeed, Adam is one of very few medieval composers who is known to have composed both monophonic and polyphonic works. It has been suggested that Adam may have borrowed some of the songs in the play, but the range of styles from popular to elevated is characteristic of his music. The plot and poetry of the play draw on the genre of lyric poem known as a *pastourelle*, a dialogue between a shepherdess and a knight who courts her.

Typical of the tuneful songs in the play is *Robins m'aime*, sung by Marion at the opening. It is a monophonic rondeau in the form ABaabAB, using separate letters for each musical phrase, capitals for the refrain, and lower case when the same music appears with new words. This pattern is slightly different from the standard form of the fourteenth-century rondeau (see NAWM 26). We can be reasonably certain about the rhythm because the tune also appears as a line in a polyphonic motet whose notation shows the exact durations.

The music is written as a single melodic line, but its dancelike rhythm seems to invite instrumental accompaniment. In the recording that accompanies this anthology, instruments first play the melody and then accompany the singer. Medieval musicians freely adapted secular vocal music for instruments in any combination they desired, and this performance embodies that spirit.

# WALTHER VON DER VOGELWEIDE (?CA. 1170–?CA. 1230)

## Palästinalied (Nū alrēst lebe ich mir werde)

*Minnelied*
?CA. 1228

CD 1|39

Nū al - rēst lebe ich mir wer - de,
daz rei - ne lant und ouch die er - de,

sīt mīn sün - dic ou - ge siht
den man sō vil ē - ren giht.

mirst ge-schehen des ich ie bat, ich bin ko - men

an die stat, dā got men-nisch - lī - chen trat.

| | |
|---|---|
| Nū alrēst lebe ich mir werde, | Now for the first time I live worthily, |
| sīt mīn sündic ouge siht | since my sinful eye sees |
| Daz reine lant und ouch die erde, | the Holy Land and also the earth |
| den man sō vil ēren giht. | to which one so much honor assigns. |
| Mirst geschehen des ich ie bat, | To me has happened what I have always prayed for, |
| ich bin komen an die stat, | I have come to the city |
| dā got mennischlīchen trat. | where God walked as a human being. |
| | |
| Schoeniu lant rīch unde hēre, | Of the beautiful lands, rich and glorious, |
| swaz ich der noch hān gesehen, | that I so far have seen, |
| sō bist duz ir aller ēre: | you are the most deserving of honor: |
| waz ist wunders hie geschehen! | what a miracle happened here! |
| Daz ein magt ein kint gebar, | That a maiden bore a child, |
| hēre über aller engel schar, | Lord over all the multitude of angels, |
| was daz niht ein wunder gar? | was that not absolutely a miracle? |

From Hugo Moser and Joseph Müller-Blattau, *Deutsche Lieder des Mittelalters: Von Walther von der Vogelweide bis zum Lochamer Liederbuch* (Stuttgart: Ernst Klett, 1968), 39–40.

| Hie liez er sich reine toufen, | Here He in purity was baptized, |
|---|---|
| daz der mensche reine sī; | so that each person could be pure; |
| dō liez er sich hie verkoufen, | then he let himself be sold, |
| daz wir eigen wurden frī. | so that we who are in bondage would be set free. |
| Anders waeren wir verlorn; | Otherwise, we would be lost; |
| wol dir, sper, kriuz unde dorn! | hail to you, spear, cross, and thorn! |
| Wē dir, heiden, daz ist dir zorn! | Woe to you, heathens, this enrages you! |
| | |
| Kristen, juden unde heiden | Christians, Jews, and heathens |
| jehent daz diz ir erbe sī. | all claim that this [land] is their inheritance. |
| Got sol uns ze reht bescheiden | May God decide justly for us |
| durch die sīne namen drī. | for the sake of His three names. |
| Al diu welt diu strītet her: | All the world is fighting here; |
| wir sin an der rehten ger: | we are desirous of the right; |
| reht ist daz er uns gewer. | it is just for Him to defend us. |

Walther von der Vogelweide was perhaps the most famous of the Minnesinger. Little is known of his life other than what he wrote in his songs, although a payment record confirms that he was a traveling singer. Most of his songs are love poems, but perhaps his best known work is the *Palästinalied* (Palestine Song), in the relatively new genre of the crusade song. Such songs described the experiences of those who undertook the Crusades and sought to inspire others to follow their example. Walther may have composed this song around 1228–29, when Holy Roman Emperor Frederick II negotiated a treaty that gave Christians control of Jerusalem, which was formerly under Egyptian rule. Although the text describes seeing the Holy Land, it is not known whether Walther actually traveled there.

The poem is in Middle High German and has seven stanzas, four of which are included here. Each stanza is sung to the same melody and has the same rhyme scheme: ab ab ccc. That pattern is reflected in the melody's form, AAB, with the the two couplets each set to the same melody (A) and the final three lines set to a new melody (B) that shares the same last phrase. The musical form parallels that of *A chantar* (NAWM 9), though the rhyme scheme differs:

| Sections | A | | A | | B | | |
|---|---|---|---|---|---|---|---|
| Musical phrases | a | b | a | b | c | d | b |
| Rhyme scheme | a | b | a | b | c | c | c |

Since the nineteenth century, scholars of German poetry have called this AAB structure *bar form*. The A section is known as the *Stollen*, the B section as the *Abgesang*.

In Walther's notation of this song, the pitches are clear, but the rhythm is not specified. The transcription printed here and the performance on the accompanying recording differ in some details, but both assume that each syllable receives the same duration except for the last syllable in each section, which is twice as long.

The song was originally notated as a monophonic line without accompaniment, but scenes depicted in contemporary artwork often include instrumentalists playing along with singers. On the recording, the vocal line is joined by a *rebec* (a bowed string instrument) and a lute, playing sometimes in unison with the voice, sometimes in heterophony, and sometimes in improvised polyphony. The instruments also play before and between stanzas.

# Cantiga 159, *Non sofre Santa Maria*, from *Cantigas de Santa Maria*

*Cantiga (song)*

CA. 1270–90

Music from Alfonso X El Sabio, *Cantigas de Santa María: Nueva transcripción integral de su música según la métrica latina*, ed. Roberto Pla (Madrid: Música Didáctica, 2001), 290. Text from Afonso X, O Sábio, *Cantigas de Santa Maria*, ed. Walter Mettmann (Edicións Xerais de Galicia, 1981), 541–42.

Non sofre Santa Maria
de seeren perdidosos
os que as sas romarias
son de fazer desejosos.

E dest' oyd' un miragre
de que vos quero falar,
que mostrou Santa Maria,
per com' eu oy contar,
aūuns romeus que foron
a Rocamador orar
como mui bõos crischãos,
simplement' e omildosos.

Non sofre Santa Maria . . .

E pois entraron no burgo,
foron pousada fillar
e mandaron conprar carne
e pan pera seu jantar
e vynno; e entre tanto
foron aa Virgen rogar
que a seu Fillo rogasse
dos seus rogos piadosos

Non sofre Santa Maria . . .

E mandaran nove postas
meter, asse Deus m' anpar,
na ola, ca tantos eran;
mais poi-las foron tirar,
acharon end' hūa menos,
que a serventa furtar-
lles fora, e foron todos
poren ja quanto queixosos.

Non sofre Santa Maria . . .

E buscaron pela casa
pola poderen achar,
chamando Santa Maria
que lla quiesse mostrar;
e oyron en un' arca
a posta feridas dar,
e d' ir alá mui correndo
non vos foron vagarosos.

Non sofre Santa Maria . . .

Holy Mary does not allow
losses to befall
those who desire
to undertake Her pilgrimages.

In this regard, listen to a miracle
that I want to tell to you,
that Holy Mary performed,
as I heard it recounted,
for some pilgrims who went
to Rocamador to pray,
like many good Christians,
simply and humbly.

Holy Mary does not allow . . .

After they entered the town,
they went to an inn,
and ordered and paid for meat
and bread for their supper,
and wine; and in the meantime
they went to pray to the Virgin
that she pray to Her Son for them
with Her merciful prayers.

Holy Mary does not allow . . .

And they ordered nine chops of meat,
as God is my witness, to be put
into the pot, for that's how many they were;
but when they pulled them out,
they found one fewer,
for a servant girl had robbed
them, and they were all
complaining a lot about it.

Holy Mary does not allow . . .

And they searched throughout the house
trying to find it,
calling to Holy Mary
that she reveal it to them;
and they heard in a trunk
the chop hitting the side,
and they went running over to it quickly,
they were not loitering.

Holy Mary does not allow . . .

| | |
|---|---|
| E fezeron log' a arca | And they had the trunk |
| abrir e dentro catar | opened and looked inside, |
| foron, e viron sa posta | and they saw their chop |
| dacá e dalá saltar; | jumping back and forth; |
| e sayron aa rua | and they ran into the streets |
| muitas das gentes chamar, | and called to many people, |
| que viron aquel miragre, | who saw that miracle, |
| que foi dos maravillosos | which was one of the most marvelous |
| | |
| Non sofre Santa Maria . . . | Holy Mary does not allow . . . |
| | |
| Que a Virgen groriosa | That the glorious Virgin |
| fezess' en aqual logar. | had performed in that place. |
| Des i fillaron a posta | So they took the chop |
| e fórona pendorar | and hung it |
| per hũa corda de seda | on a silken cord |
| ant' o seu santo altar, | in front of Her holy altar, |
| loando Santa Maria, | praising Holy Mary, |
| que faz miragres fremosos. | who performs beautiful miracles. |
| | |
| Non sofre Santa Maria . . . | Holy Mary does not allow . . . |

The *Cantigas de Santa Maria* is a collection of over 400 songs (*cantigas*) in honor of the Virgin Mary, preserved in four handsomely illustrated manuscripts. King Alfonso el Sabio (the Wise) of Castile and Léon, a kingdom in northwestern Spain, supervised its preparation around 1270–90 and may have written some of the poems and melodies. Although religious, such songs were sung not in church services but for entertainment, at a time when religious sentiments were a part of everyday life.

A brief explanatory note, which is not sung, is at the beginning of each cantiga. The sung parts that follow include several verses, each preceded and followed by the refrain that states the moral of the song. Every tenth cantiga in the collection is a song of praise for Mary. The others describe miracles that Mary performed to protect the faithful from harm, to heal the sick or wounded, and to rescue those in peril. One of the most down-to-earth is this song, whose introductory note says that it relates "How Holy Mary caused to be discovered a chop of meat that was stolen from some pilgrims in the city of Rocamador."

The melody is simple and bouncy with a constantly repeating figure transcribed here as a quarter note and two eighth notes. The music for the refrain also appears in the second half of each verse, with different words. Indicating repetitions of music by letter and of text through capitalization, the overall form can be diagrammed A ba A ba A … ba A. Within both a and b sections, a short musical phrase repeats four times with varying endings, so that the entire song is spun out of only two brief ideas. The range is very narrow—only a sixth.

Based on contemporary accounts, the refrain was typically sung by a chorus and the verses by a soloist, as on the accompanying recording. In that performance, the fourth and fifth verses are spoken rather than sung in order to emphasize the climax of the story, when the miracle occurs. The modal final is G, but the prominent Fs in the refrain suggest that the Bs should be performed as B♭s. On the recording, the performers sing B♭s rather than Bs in the a sections but not the contrasting b section; this produces an effect similar to that of shifting back and forth between Dorian and Mixolydian modes on G.

Like most medieval songs outside the liturgy, these cantigas could either be sung unaccompanied or with instruments. The recording offers one possibility for accompaniment: *nakers* (a small drum of the Middle Ages) beating a lively pattern and a *rebec* (a bowed string instrument) varying between phrases of the melody, a drone, and improvised counterpoint, joined on the refrains by a pipe and *oud* (lute).

## La quarte estampie royal, from *Le manuscrit du roi*

*Estampie*

LATE THIRTEENTH CENTURY

From Timothy McGee, *Medieval Instrumental Dances* (Bloomington: Indiana University Press, 1989), 64.
Reprinted by permission.

**13** FROM *LE MANUSCRIT DU ROI* *La quarte estampie royal*

Instrumentalists who played music for dancing during the Middle Ages usually played from memory or improvised, so very few dance melodies were written down. However, a thirteenth-century song manuscript known as *Le manuscrit du roi* (The Manuscript of the King), now in the French national library in Paris (Bibliothèque Nationale fonds français 844), includes eight dance tunes identified as "royal estampies." The manuscript was probably commissioned around 1250–70 by Guillaume of Villehardouin, prince of Moria. The inclusion of these dance tunes suggests that they were highly esteemed, but what connection they may have had to the royal court is unclear.

The *estampie* is a dance in a fast triple meter that features a series of phrases, each played twice but with a different ending each time. The first time, the cadence is referred to as *open* (*ouvert*) because it ends on a note a step or two above the modal final and thus sounds incomplete; the second time, the phrase cadences on the final and is therefore referred to as *closed* (*clos*). In the transcription included here, the two cadences are shown as first and second endings with a repeat mark at the end of the first ending. The same open and closed endings were meant to be played with each successive phrase, so in the medieval manuscripts it was not necessary to write them out after the first few notes. The material shown here between vertical brackets was supplied by the editor, but any medieval performer would have known to play it.

The final of this estampie is F, and the mode initially seems to be mode 6, with a range extending a fourth below the final and a melodic emphasis on A, the tenor of that mode. Later, the melody ranges an octave above the final, reminding us that late medieval melodies often do not fit neatly into one of the standard church modes.

On the accompanying recording, this estampie is played on a medieval fiddle, which sometimes adds brief drones on its open strings to enrich the tune. It is accompanied by a *bendir*, a frame drum from Morocco played with the fingers and hand.

# Organa from *Musica enchiriadis*

*Parallel organum and mixed parallel and oblique organum*

CA. 850–900

(a) *Tu patris sempiternus es filius*, in parallel organum at the fifth below

Principal Voice
Organal Voice

Tu  pa - tris  sem - pi - ter - nus  es  fi - li - us.

Tu patris sempiternus es filius.          You of the father are the everlasting son.

(b) *Sit gloria domini*, in parallel organum at the fifth below, with octave doublings

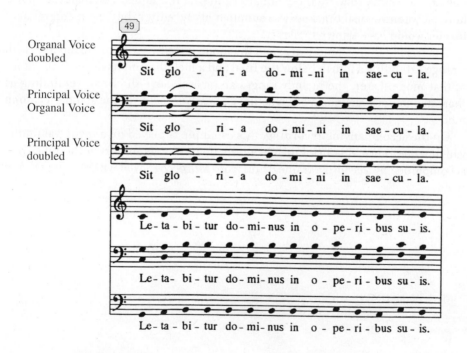

Organal Voice
doubled

Sit  glo - ri - a  do - mi - ni  in  sae - cu - la.

Principal Voice
Organal Voice

Sit  glo - ri - a  do - mi - ni  in  sae - cu - la.

Principal Voice
doubled

Sit  glo - ri - a  do - mi - ni  in  sae - cu - la.

Le - ta - bi - tur  do - mi - nus in  o - pe - ri - bus su - is.

Le - ta - bi - tur  do - mi - nus in  o - pe - ri - bus su - is.

Le - ta - bi - tur  do - mi - nus in  o - pe - ri - bus su - is.

Sit gloria domini in saecula.          May the glory of the Lord be forever;
Laetabitur dominus in operibus suis.          the Lord will rejoice in his works.

From *Musica enchiriadis and Scolica enchiriadis,* trans. with intro. and notes by Raymond Erickson, ed. Claude V. Palisca (New Haven: Yale University Press, 1995), 19, 24, and 27–28. Reprinted by permission.

(c) *Rex caeli domine*, in mixed parallel and oblique organum

Principal Voice
Organal Voice

Rex  cae - li   do - mi - ne   ma - ris   un - di - so - ni.

Ty - tan - is   ni - ti - di   qual - li - di - que   so - li.

Te  hu - mi - les  fa - mu - li   mo - du - lis  ve - ne - ran - do  pi - is.

Se  iu - be - as   fla - gi - tant va - ri - is   li - be - ra - re   ma - lis.

Rex caeli domine maris undisoni,
Tytanis nitidi squalidique soli.

King of Heaven, Lord of the roaring sea,
of the shining Titan (Sun) and the squalid earth,

Te humiles famuli modulis venerando piis,

Your humble servants, worshipping you with
pious melodies,

Se iubeas flagitant variis liberare malis.

Beseech you, as you command, to free them
from diverse ills.

*Musica enchiriadis* (Music Handbook, ca. 850–900) was one of the most widely read music treatises in the Middle Ages. It is a practical manual that includes instruction in the theory and practice of church music. One of the topics covered in the treatise is how to perform diaphony ("singing together"), or organum, which is music sung extemporaneously rather than from notation. The three selections shown here are examples from the treatise. They should be thought of not as compositions but as models for how such polyphony was expected to be sung. In every case, one of the voices—called the principal voice—was taken from a chant. The other voice—the organal voice—was derived from the principal voice according to a set of simple rules that were described in the treatise for singers to apply during performance. This made it unnecessary to write out the added part.

*Tu patris sempiternus es filius* is an example of parallel organum at the fifth below, which was probably an ancient practice even before *Musica enchiriadis* described it. The principal voice, singing the chant, is joined by the organal voice a perfect fifth below, producing a more resonant sound than unison singing.

*Sit gloria domini* illustrates the possibilities of doubling one or both voices at the octave to enrich the sonority further. Here the principal voice is doubled an octave lower and the organal voice an octave higher, but other combinations are also allowed by the treatise. Such doubling might have occured naturally in choirs that included both men and boys, whose voices lie in different ranges.

Organum at the fourth below was more complex because of the way the writer of *Musica enchiriadis* described notes and scales. He laid out the system of notes as a series of disjunct tetrachords: *G–A–B♭–c, d–e–f–g, a–b–c'–d', e'–f♯'–g'–a'*, and so on. This scale system is ideal for parallel fifths because it lacks diminished fifths. (Try playing the tetrachords on the keyboard to confirm this.) However, this system does contain augmented fourths, such as *B♭–e* and *f–b*, which must be avoided in organum at the fourth. In the example included here, the presence of B♭ in the lower octave and B♮ in the upper octave is indicated in the transcriptions of the first and third selections; in *Sit gloria domini*, the low B is natural because it must duplicate the principal voice at a perfect octave.

The writer indicated that in order to prevent the organal voice from sounding a tritone below the principal voice, it must not move below *c* during a segment of chant that includes *e* or below *g* when the chant includes *b*. The organal voice must remain stationary until it can move in parallel perfect fourths without creating a tritone. The sequence *Rex caeli domine* is an example of how this system works in practice, producing organum that sometimes features parallel motion and at other times resembles a melody over a drone, called oblique motion. Seconds or thirds, still considered dissonances, are permitted while the organal voice is not moving. At the end of a phrase, if the organal voice would form a second or third with the principal voice, it moves instead to join the chant on a unison.

All three styles of organum illustrated here could be sung by a group with little or no rehearsal, since the rules for deriving the organal voice from the principal voice are clear and relatively simple. However, the system demonstrated by the *Rex caeli domini* example foreshadowed new possibilities. Although mixed parallel and oblique organum was still a method for singing polyphony extemporaneously rather than composing pieces, the system can be seen in retrospect as the first step toward a polyphony of truly independent voices.

# *Alleluia Justus ut palma*, from *Ad organum faciendum*

*Alleluia in free organum*

CA. 1100

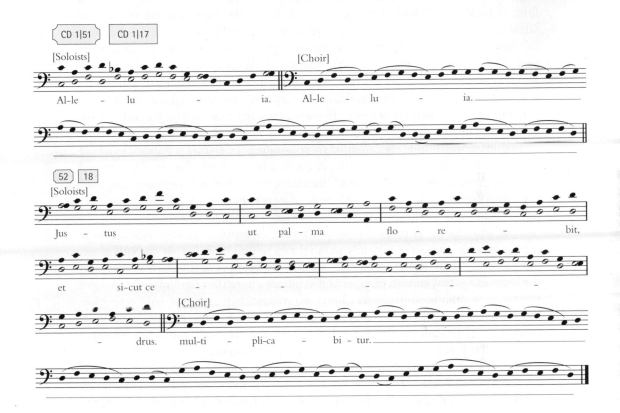

Alleluia.
Justus ut palma florebit,
et sicut cedrus multiplicabitur.

Alleluia.
The righteous shall flourish like a palm tree
and shall multiply like a cedar.

*Ad organum faciendum* (On Making Organum) describes how to sing or compose organum. This anonymous treatise dates from around 1100 and survives in three manuscripts, the earliest and most complete of which is housed at the Ambrosian Library in Milan. The writer presented this organum, based on the plainchant *Alleluia Justus ut palma*, as an example. In accordance with the practice at the time, the only portions of the chant that were set in polyphony were those traditionally performed by soloists: the opening intonation of "Alleluia," and most of the verse. The rest of the respond and the final word of the verse were sung by the choir and were not treated polyphonically. Only the polyphonic portions appear in the treatise, but the chant is included here to show how such a piece would actually have been performed.

In this transcription, the principal voice (singing the chant) is notated in whole notes and the organal (added) voice is notated in black noteheads. The organal voice sings one note for each note of the chant, except for one melisma sung with the last chant note on "-lu-" of "Alleluia." The organal voice is above the principal voice for most of this organum, but the voices sometimes cross.

This example illustrates the style of free organum, or note-against-note organum, which features not only parallel and oblique motion, as in NAWM 14, but also similar and contrary motion. Contrary motion is particularly common at the beginnings and ends of phrases and at points where the chant melody changes direction. Similar motion occurs when both voices move in the same direction but the interval between them changes. Most phrases use some parallel motion in fourths or fifths, but parallel octaves and unisons are largely avoided. Oblique motion occurs only when the chant melody repeats a note.

The great majority of the time, the two voices form a perfect consonance—unison, octave, fifth, or fourth. Phrases begin on an octave, unison, or fifth, and end on an octave or unison, the most restful consonances. At the ends of several phrases, the cadence is strengthened by motion from a third to a unison or from a sixth to an octave. The cadences sound smoother because both voices move by step. They also sound more emphatic because the third and sixth were considered dissonances, and placing them just before the purest consonance of a unison or octave produced a strong sense of resolution.

This setting of *Alleluia Justus ut palma* can be thought of as a composition, but it also served as a model for how to improvise free organum in performance. By demonstrating how a new, independent voice could be added to an existing melody, such music laid the foundation for the later development of polyphony.

## Jubilemus, exultemus

*Versus in Aquitanian polyphony*

EARLY TWELFTH CENTURY

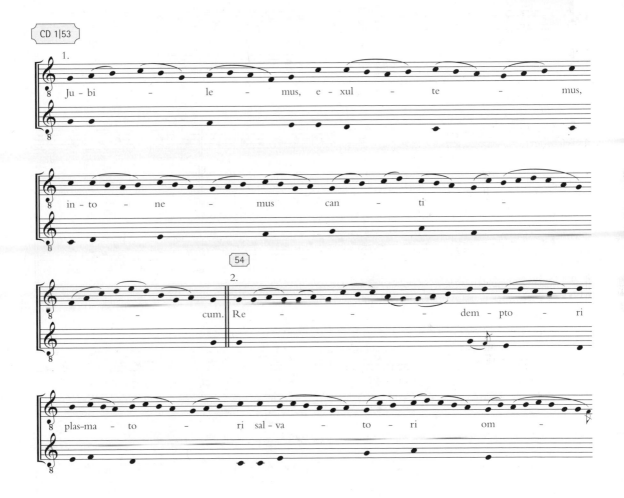

Paris, Bibliothèque Nationale, fonds latin 1139, fol. 41. For two different metrical transcriptions, see *Saint-Martial Polyphony*, ed. Bryan Gillingham (Henryville, Ottawa, and Binningen: Institute of Mediaeval Music, 1994), 7–9, and *The Polyphony of Saint Martial und Santiago de Compostela*, ed. Théodore Karp (Berkeley: University of California Press, 1992), vol. 2, pp. 178–81. A facsimile of the page is in Carl Parrish, *The Notation of Medieval Music* (New York: Norton, 1957), Plate XXI, and a facsimile of the entire manuscript is published in *Paris, Bibliothèque nationale, fonds latin 1139 d'après les manuscrits conservés à la Bibliothèque nationale de Paris*, ed. Bryan Gillingham (Ottawa: Institute of Mediaeval Music, 1987).

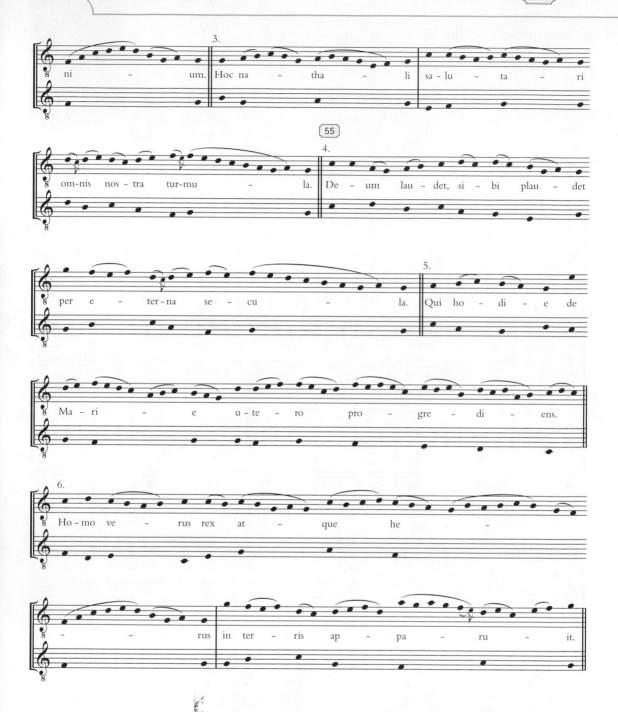

ni - um. Hoc na - tha - li sa - lu - ta - ri

om-nis nos - tra tur-mu - la. De - um lau - det, si - bi plau - det

per e - ter-na se - cu - la. Qui ho - di - e de

Ma - ri - e u - te - ro pro - gre - di - ens.

Ho - mo ve - rus rex at - que he -

- rus in ter - ris ap - pa - ru - it.

| | |
|---|---|
| Jubilemus exultemus, intonemus canticum | Let us rejoice, exult, and sing a song |
| Redemptori plasmatori, salvatori omnium. | to the redeemer, creator, savior of all. |
| Hoc nathali salutari omnis nostra turmula | For this blessed birth, let our whole congregation |
| Deum laudet sibi plaudet per eterna secula. | praise God and eternally applaud. |
| Qui hodie de Marie utero progrediens | He who today issued from Mary's womb |
| Homo verus rex atque herus in terris apparuit. | a true man, appeared on earth as a king and lord. |
| Tam beatum ergo natum cum ingenti gaudio | In such a blessed birth, then, with boundless delight, |
| | |
| Conlaudantes, exultantes benedicamus Domino. | praising and exulting together, let us bless the Lord. |

This two-part setting of a rhymed metrical text is from a manuscript that was copied in the early twelfth century in or near Limoges, a city in the duchy of Aquitaine, now southwest France. The manuscript contains historical chronicles of Limoges along with tropes, versus, musical dramas, and Office services from the surrounding area. The music is written in the Aquitanian notation of that region. Now in the French national library in Paris, the manuscript was for centuries in the Abbey of St. Martial in Limoges. Because of these associations, the style represented by this piece is called Aquitanian polyphony or St. Martial polyphony.

The text is a *versus*, a rhythmic, rhymed poem in Latin. The internal rhymes (such as "Jubilemus," "exultemus," and "intonemus" in the first line) make the poetry especially lively and interesting. Since the poem ends with the phrase "Benedicamus Domino" (Let us bless the Lord), it can be considered a trope on *Benedicamus Domino*. This liturgical formula was used in Office services and in the Mass when *Ite, missa est* was not sung, suggesting that the versus may have been sung as part of the liturgy. However, the music seems not to be borrowed from an existing chant melody.

The anonymous composer set anywhere from one to seventeen notes in the upper part to each note in the lower part, called the tenor. Theorists at the time distinguished between two polyphonic styles or textures, both exemplified here. Extended passages with only one to three notes in the upper part for each tenor note, as at "Deum laudet, sibi plaudet" and "Tam beatum ergo natum," are in *discant* style. Passages in which the upper part is relatively melismatic compared to the tenor, as in the first two verses, are called *organum*. The latter is today known as *florid organum* to distinguish it from other styles of organum.

Because there are often two or more notes in the upper part for each tenor note, the sonorities between the voices are much more varied and include many more dissonances than the sonorities in note-against-note organum (compare NAWM 15). However, as in the earlier style, the ends of phrases are marked with unisons or octaves, usually approached in contrary motion, which created a strong sense of closure.

The scribe notated the florid upper voice above the slower tenor part in score format, but the text underlay and alignment of the notes are not consistently clear. Although the poetry has consistent iambic meter, which might suggest a regular alternation of short and long notes in the tenor, the number of notes in the upper voice makes this unlikely. For this reason, most performers treat the rhythm freely, as in chant.

# LÉONIN (FL. CA. 1150S–CA. 1201)

## Viderunt omnes

*Organum duplum*

SECOND HALF OF THE TWELFTH CENTURY

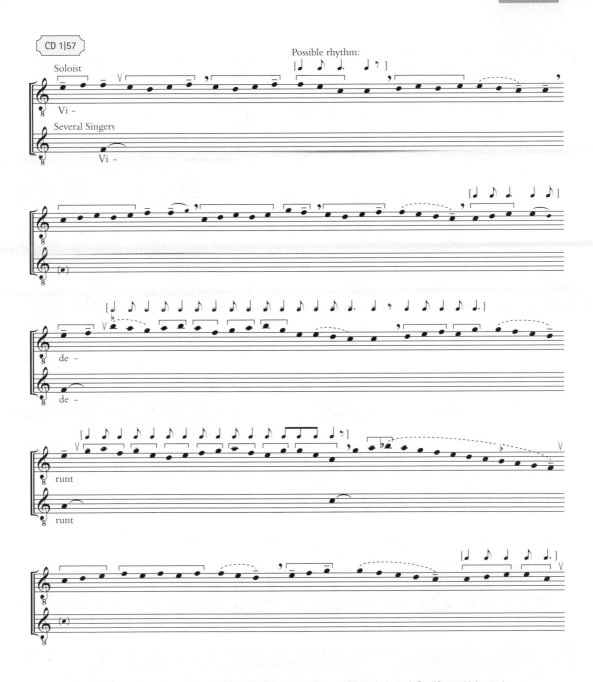

Edited by Edward H. Roesner from Wolfenbüttel, Herzog August Bibliothek, cod. Guelf. 628 Helmstad. (W1), fol. 25r–25v. Chant from Paris, Bibliothèque nationale, fonds lat. 1112, 20r. © Copyright 2005 Edward H. Roesner. Used by permission.

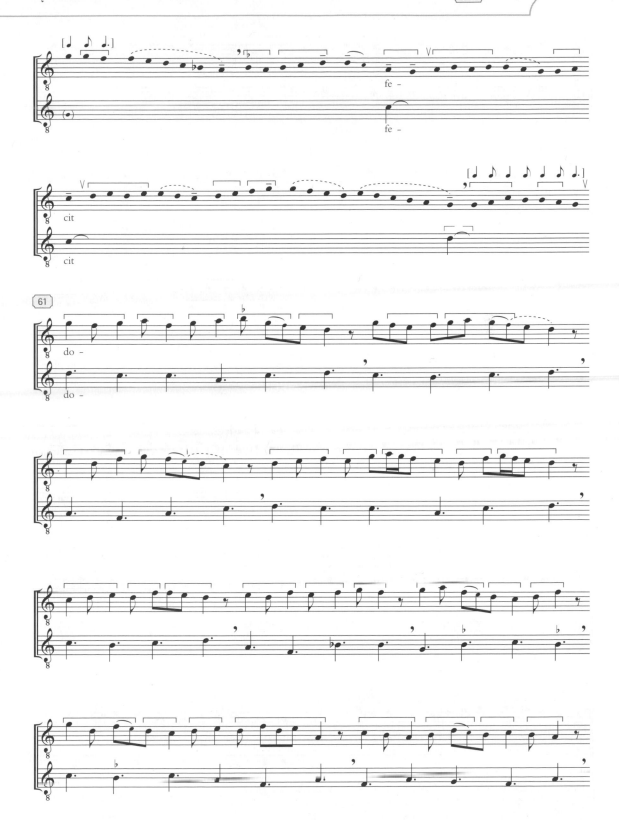

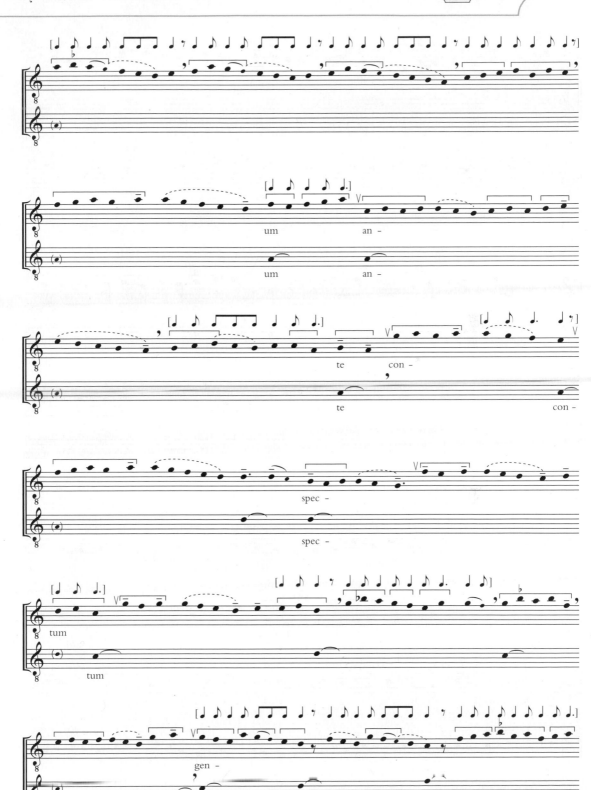

| | |
|---|---|
| Viderunt omnes fines terrae salutare Dei nostri: jubilate Deo omnis terra. | All the ends of the earth have seen the salvation of our God; sing joyfully to God, all the earth. |
| ℣. Notum fecit Dominus salutare suum: ante conspectum gentium revelavit justitiam suam. | ℣. The Lord hath made known His salvation; He hath revealed His justice in the sight of the peoples. |

One of the most glorious accomplishments of the Middle Ages is the body of polyphony composed during the twelfth and thirteenth centuries by musicians associated with the Cathedral of Notre Dame in Paris for the services there and in other churches. Although it is not entirely clear whether he composed all of the music himself, Léonin is credited with compiling a *Magnus liber organi* (Great Book of Polyphony) that contained two-voice settings of the solo portions of the responsorial chants for major feasts. The original *Magnus liber* does not survive, but the repertory is preserved in several thirteenth-century manuscripts that include additions and substitutions by later composers.

This setting of the Gradual *Viderunt omnes* from the Mass for Christmas Day (see NAWM 3d) is found in the oldest of these manuscripts. Now housed in Wolfenbüttel, Germany, this source was prepared for a priory (a religious house) in St. Andrews, Scotland, during the first half of the thirteenth century and was probably copied there or in England. We cannot be certain that it represents Léonin's original version of this piece, but it probably resembles the original verion as closely as any in existence.

Performances of this piece must have seemed magnificent to listeners during the Middle Ages. As the first responsorial chant in the Mass for Christmas Day, it would probably have been the first polyphony to be heard during that service at Notre Dame, and it would have had a powerful effect. It is grand both in sound and in size, lasting about three times as long as the original chant.

As was typical during this period, only the solo portions are in polyphony, with the choral portions remaining in plainchant. The alternation between polyphony and monophony magnifies the contrast between solo and choral performance that was already present in the original chant. Here, the first two words of the respond and all but the last two words of the verse are set polyphonically. The notes of the chant appear in relatively long values in the lower voice, sung by a small choir of about five voices, and above the chant is a much more florid upper line sung by a soloist. The lower voice came to be called the *tenor* (from Latin *tenere*, "to hold") because it holds the chant, and the upper voice is called the *duplum* (Latin for "second"). Only the polyphonic portions appear in the manuscripts because the choir would have performed from a separate book of plainchant. The version of the chant included here is taken from a manuscript used in Paris during the Middle Ages and differs in a few details from the version in modern chant editions (compare NAWM 3d).

Besides the contrast between chant and polyphony, Léonin employed two contrasting styles of polyphony: florid organum and discant (compare NAWM 16). The opening passage is in organum. The four notes of "Viderunt" are stretched out into unmeasured sustained notes of indefinite duration to form the tenor. Against this, the soloist sings melismatic phrases, always singing the same syllable as the tenor. The melismas are broken at irregular intervals by cadences and pauses that were marked by vertical strokes in the original notation and are rendered here as wedges or breath marks. The fluid melody—nonperiodic and loosely segmented—strongly suggests that this is a written version of a style developed through improvisatory practice.

At the word "omnes," there is a brief passage in discant style. In this section, the tenor moves more quickly, the duplum has one to three notes for each note of the tenor, and both parts sing in a strictly measured rhythm with repeating patterns known as rhythmic modes. The rhythm of the tenor is in mode 5, a series of equal long notes transcribed as dotted quarters, and the duplum is in mode 1, alternating long and short notes transcribed as quarter and eighth notes respectively. In some cases the quarter note is split into smaller notes, demonstrating a practice known as *fractio modi* (division of the mode).

The treatment of text in the original chant largely determined where Léonin used organum or discant style. Organum, with long sustained notes in the tenor, was appropriate for portions of the original chant that were syllabic or neumatic. Where the original chant was highly melismatic, it was necessary for the tenor to move along more quickly in discant style so that the whole piece would not be unduly lengthened. Thus, in this setting of *Viderunt omnes*, there are four passages in discant: at the beginning of "omnes"; on "dominus" (the longest); at "suum" (the briefest); and on "revelavit." All of these end with a cadence in organum style, and in between them are sections of organum. Such self-contained sections, setting one or more words on syllables from the chant and ending with a cadence, are known as *clausulae* (sing. *clausula*, Latin for a clause or phrase in a sentence). Clausulae may be in organum or discant style; most of Léonin's discant clausulae close with a flourish in organum style to make a strong cadence.

In both organum and discant, the onset of a new tenor note is normally accompanied by a perfect consonance (unison, octave, fifth, or fourth) between the parts. At the close of extended phrases, Léonin sometimes wrote a seventh moving to an octave (as at "-de-" of "Viderunt") or a second moving to a unison (as at "-nes" of "omnes") in what resembles a modern appoggiatura. The discant sections are articulated by rests that break up the melodies into easily understood phrases.

Horizontal brackets above the music show the original notegroups, or *ligatures*. These brackets are included in modern editions because the Notre Dame composers used ligatures to notate the rhythmic modes. At "dominus," the pattern of three notes in a ligature followed by several ligatures with two notes indicates that the rhythm is in mode 1. This edition uses dotted slurs to transcribe notegroups with diamond-shaped noteheads (used for descending figures) and adds a flat above the note B when singers would probably have sung B♭ to avoid the tritone with F or to provide a smoother contour.

   It is not certain whether the upper part in the sections in organum style should be sung in modal rhythm or more freely. In most passages, the notation does not show the pattern of ligatures for any of the rhythmic modes, which suggests that Léonin intended a free performance like the one on the accompanying recording. But in some passages, such as the first phrase on "-runt" of "Viderunt," there is a regular pattern of ligatures that suggests mode 1, as shown by the notes above the staff. Both rhythmic and free renditions can be heard on modern recordings of Léonin's organum. Some scholars have suggested that the twelfth-century original was free, but that later generations preferred to hear the upper line in modal rhythm.

## 18

# Clausulae on *Dominus*, from *Viderunt omnes*

*Substitute clausulae*

LATE TWELFTH OR EARLY THIRTEENTH CENTURY

(a) *Dominus*, clausula No. 26

From *Le Magnus Liber Organi de Notre-Dame de Paris*, vol. 5, *Les Clausules à deux voix du manuscrit de Florence, Biblioteca Medicea-Laurenziana, Pluteus 29.1, Fascicule V*, ed. Rebecca A. Baltzer (Monaco: Éditions de l'Oiseau-Lyre, 1995), 17 and 20.

(b) *Dominus*, clausula No. 29

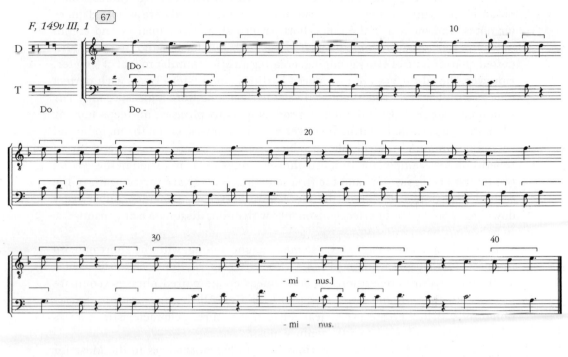

Composers after Léonin frequently wrote new discant clausulae to replace passages on the same segment of chant that were used in Léonin's organum. A manuscript of Notre Dame polyphony that was probably copied in Paris during the 1240s and is now in Florence, Italy, contains dozens of such *substitute clausulae*, including ten that set the phrase of chant from *Viderunt omnes* on the word "Dominus." Any of these could have been used at the Mass for Christmas Day in place of the parallel passage in Léonin's setting of *Viderunt omnes* (NAWM 17). The collection of clausulae in this manuscript is ordered according to the day in the church year when the clausula might be sung. The two included here are numbers 26 and 29 in the collection.

In both of these clausulae, the chant is in the tenor with a repeating rhythmic pattern, and the duplum adds a free counterpoint above it. The recurring rhythmic figures in the tenor give these clausulae greater shape and coherence than Léonin's clausula on this same segment of chant. Such rhythmic patterning is a common feature of clausula and motet tenors throughout the thirteenth century. In both of the clausulae included here, the pattern breaks near the end to signal the final cadence.

Clausula No. 26 uses rhythmic mode 5 in the tenor and alternates between modes 5 and 1 in the duplum. Mode 5 is a series of perfect longs (notes whose duration spans three *tempora*, the basic unit of time), notated here as dotted quarter notes, and mode 1 is the long-short pattern shown as a quarter and eighth note. The repeating rhythmic pattern in the tenor emphasizes the first and third dotted quarter note of every grouping, creating an effect similar to that of $\frac{6}{8}$ meter. However, the editor has not introduced barlines, and instead treats each perfect long as a unit, numbering them as if each perfect long were a measure of $\frac{3}{8}$. The duplum either rests with the tenor, producing short phrases, or keeps moving when the tenor rests, resulting in longer melodic phrases. Often the melodic and rhythmic contours in the duplum produce a sense of paired phrasing and varied repetition; for example, the first two phrases (longs 1–8) are varied in the second two phrases (longs 9–16), and the first four (longs 1–16) are varied again in the second four (longs 17–32). If the piece were barred in $\frac{6}{8}$ meter, almost every downbeat would have a perfect consonance with either dissonance or consonance in between.

Both voices in clausula No. 29 use mode 2 (short-long, with the short note on the beat), which gives this clausula a very different rhythmic character. Once again, the rhythmic repetitions in both voices create paired phrases (compare longs 1–8 with 9–16 and longs 17–24 with 25–32). All these repetitions, variations, and pairings create a very clear sense of structure, a characteristic that was greatly important for thirteenth-century music.

In the context of a complete performance of *Viderunt omnes* in the Mass for Christmas Day, any clausulae used for *Dominus* would have been performed by the same forces as in Léonin's setting (NAWM 17): about five voices on the tenor, and a soloist on the duplum. However, such clausulae found a new life as motets when words were added to the duplum. On the accompanying recordings these clausulae are sung by two soloists to facilitate comparison to the motets in NAWM 21.

# PÉROTIN (FL. LATE TWELFTH AND EARLY THIRTEENTH CENTURIES)

## Viderunt omnes

*Organum quadruplum*

LATE TWELFTH OR EARLY THIRTEENTH CENTURY

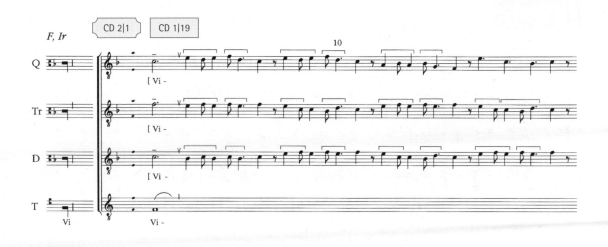

From *Le Magnus Liber Organi de Notre-Dame de Paris*, vol. 1, *Les Quadrupla et Tripla de Paris*, ed. Edward H. Roesner (Monaco: Éditions de l'Oiseau-Lyre, 1993), 1–14.

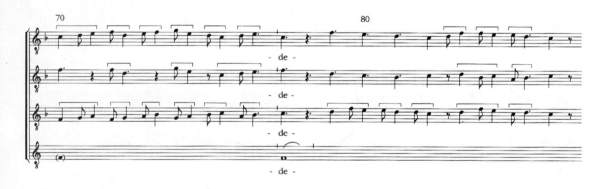

- runt

- runt

- runt

- runt

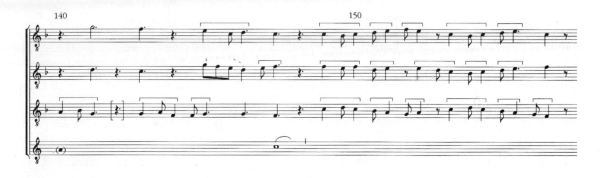

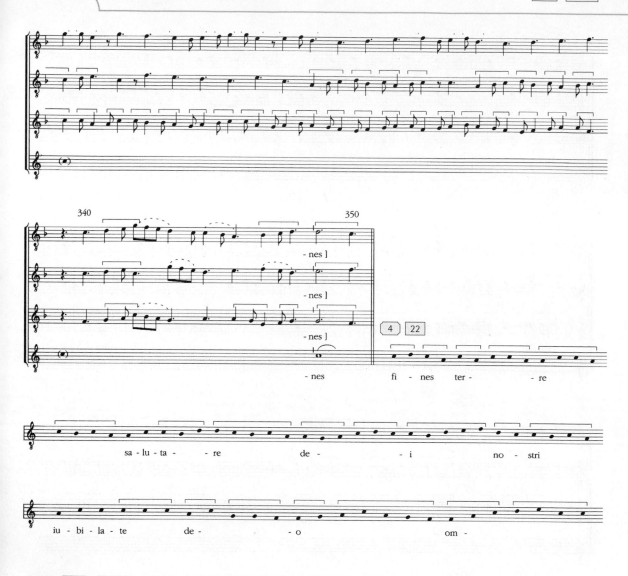

- nes ]

- nes ]

- nes ]

4   22

- nes        fi  -  nes  ter  -     -  re

sa - lu - ta -     - re        de -        - i        no - stri

iu - bi - la - te        de -        - o                om -

- nis                    ter -     - ra.

Viderunt omnes fines terrae salutare Dei nostri: jubilate Deo omnis terra.
℣. Notum fecit Dominus salutare suum: ante conspectum gentium revelavit justitiam suam.

All the ends of the earth have seen the salvation of our God; sing joyfully to God, all the earth.
℣. The Lord hath made known His salvation; He hath revealed His justice in the sight of the peoples.

Among several pieces ascribed to Pérotin is this setting of the Gradual *Viderunt omnes* from the Mass for Christmas Day (see NAWM 3d), the same chant Léonin elaborated in NAWM 17. The two settings had the same purpose, function, and intended audience. They also have the same general structure: only the solo portions of the original chant are set in polyphony; the choral portions remain in plainchant; and the polyphonic portions alternate between organum (with sustained notes in the tenor) and discant (in which the tenor moves more rapidly, in steady rhythm). However, Léonin composed for only two voice parts—tenor and duplum—and Pérotin composed for four voice parts, adding a *triplum* (the third voice from the bottom) and *quadruplum* (the fourth) to produce a much richer sound.

In Léonin's organum sections, the rhythm was probably unmeasured, but in Pérotin's setting, all the upper parts use the rhythmic modes throughout. This reflects his generation's preference for modal rhythm and also solves the practical problem of coordinating the parts.

As in Léonin's setting, the longest discant clausula is on "dominus" (where the longest melisma is in the original chant), and shorter passages in discant appear at the beginning of "omnes," on "suum," and on "revelavit." Reflecting the preference of later generations for discant wherever possible, Pérotin included two additional discant passages, on "-ta-" of "salutare" and on "gentium." In the discant sections, the upper voices often rest with the tenor, but sometimes one or more voices sing through the tenor rests to maintain forward motion.

In order to sustain the interest of listeners during the very lengthy sections in organum style, Pérotin used various kinds of repetition to achieve a balance of unity and variety. Several phrases are repeated in one, two, or all three upper voices, exactly or with slight variations (see the quadruplum at the beginning of the piece and all three voices at longs 243–98 of the respond). Some figures are also repeated at a new pitch levels (see the duplum at longs 20–27 of the respond and all three voices in the verse at longs 154–72). As demonstrated several times near the beginning of this piece, Pérotin frequently employed a device called *voice exchange*, when two voices trade figures, as the duplum and triplum do at longs 8–19. Often the use of voice exchange or varied repetition results in pairs of phrases that exhibit antecedent-consequent relationships. Johannes de Garlandia, who wrote a treatise on rhythm in Notre Dame polyphony, remarked that complementary phrases of this kind occurred particularly in a style of organum called *copula*, which he said was intermediate between discant and organum.

Pérotin also used harmony to create interest and forward momentum. Phrases generally end with perfect consonances among all four voices, but many phrases (including the first several) begin with one or more dissonances (seconds, thirds, sixths, or sevenths) against the tenor, setting up an expectation of resolution. Especially emphatic arrivals, such as those at the end of the respond and the verse, are marked with what we today would call appoggiaturas.

At the beginning of the respond and again at the beginning of the verse, the editor of this edition has transcribed the clefs and first notes of the original notation and has indicated the range of each voice. The ranges overlap, and all three upper voices cross below the tenor at several points, although the triplum and quadruplum tend to lie a little higher than the duplum and tenor. Directions for performing such music at Notre Dame Cathedral indicate that the upper parts were each performed by one singer, with about five singers on the tenor to ensure a seamless performance.

*Ave virgo virginum*

*Conductus*

LATE TWELFTH OR EARLY THIRTEENTH CENTURY

Florence, Biblioteca Medicea-Laurenziana, MS Pluteus 29.1 (F), fol. 240r–240v.

95

| | |
|---|---|
| Ave virgo virginum | Hail, virgin of virgins, |
| Verbi carnis cella, | shrine of the word made flesh, |
| In salutem hominum | who for man's salvation |
| Stillans lac et mella. | drips milk and honey. |
| Peperisti dominum, | You bore the Lord; |
| Moysi ficella, | you were a rush-basket for Moses; |
| O radio | O, from your rays |
| Sol exit, et luminum | the sun goes forth, and the star |
| Fontem parit stella. | brings forth a fountain of light. |
| | |
| Ave, plena gratia, | Hail, full of grace, |
| Caput Zabulonis | chief of Zebulun, |
| Contrivisti spolia | the spoils of robbers |
| Reparans predonis. | you restore. |
| Celi rorans pluvia | Like rain, falling from heaven |
| Vellus Gedeonis, | on the fleece of Gideon, |
| O filio | with your son |
| Tu nos reconcilia, | reunite us, |
| Mater Salomonis. | O mother of Solomon! |
| | |
| Virgo tu mosayce | You, Virgin, |
| Rubus visionis, | bramble-bush of the Mosaic vision, |
| De te fluxit sylice | from you flowed the fountain |
| Fons redemptionis. | through the rock of redemption. |
| Quos redemit calice | Those Christ has redeemed through the chalice |
| Christus passionis, | of his passion, |
| O gaudio | O, may he clothe them with the joy |
| Induat glorifice | of his glorious |
| Resurrectionis. | resurrection. |

This thirteenth-century conductus is preserved in one of the three main manuscripts of Notre Dame polyphony, suggesting that it may have been composed for use at the Cathedral of Notre Dame in Paris. Conductus were rhymed, metrical, strophic Latin poems on sacred or serious topics, set either monophonically or in polyphony. Like much of the Latin poetry written during the later Middle Ages, this poem is addressed to the Virgin Mary, praising her and seeking her assistance. This polyphonic setting was probably used in special devotions and processions.

The three strophes are each sung to the same music. (The third strophe is omitted from the accompanying recording.) In each strophe, the first two couplets have identical music in all parts. This creates an AAB form, which was more common in secular song than in sacred music during this era. Each line has seven or six syllables and occupies two measures of $\frac{6}{8}$ in the transcription, except for the seventh line of each stanza, which has only four syllables and fills just one measure. In the original manuscript, the short melodic phrases are clearly set off by strokes, and the poetry uses trochaic meter (alternating accented and unaccented syllables), suggesting transcription in rhythmic mode 1 as shown here. The regular alternation of quarter and eighth notes in that mode is enlivened by *fractio modi* (division of the mode), in which a note is divided into two or more smaller notes (shown here by eighth and/or sixteenth notes beamed together).

In the original manuscripts, conductus are notated in score format, with notes to be sung simultaneously presented in vertical alignment. The text is written only under the lowest notated voice, the tenor, but all three voices sing the words at the same time. The three voices overlap in range, with the tenor extending from *e* to *f'*, the duplum (second voice from the bottom) from *e* to *d'*, and the triplum (third voice up) from *b♭* to *g'*.

As in discant, the sonority at the beginning of each rhythmic unit (here, each dotted quarter) is usually consonant, most often an open octave, fifth, or fifth plus octave, but dissonances occur freely in between. However, conductus differ from discant clausulae in that the tenor line is newly composed rather than borrowed from chant.

# Motets on Tenor *Dominus*

*Motets*

THIRTEENTH CENTURY

(a) *Factum est salutare/Dominus*

[*actor in MS.]

Edited by Rebecca A. Baltzer from Florence, Biblioteca Medicea-Laurenziana, Plut. 29, fol. 408v.
Translation adapted from Susan A. Kidwell, "The Integration of Music and Text in the Early Latin Liturgical
Motet" (Ph.D. dissertation, University of Texas at Austin, 1993). Used by permission.

[* MS has A.]

### DUPLUM

| | |
|---|---|
| Factum est | Salvation |
| salutare | was made known |
| conspectu | in the sight |
| notum gentium. | of the people. |
| A rege | By King |
| mundus Cesare | Caesar, the world |
| describitur. | is defined. |
| Factor omnium | The maker of all, |
| rex nascitur | the King, is born |
| salvare | to save |
| quod periit. | that which has perished. |
| Ergo Lazare | Therefore, Lazarus, |
| post triduum | after three days, |
| iam compare. | now appear. |
| Tardare | To delay |
| nimis fatuum | the exceedingly foolish |
| sanare | or to heal |
| quartum mortuum | a man dead for four days |
| numquam voluit | was never desired |
| Dominus. | by the Lord. |

### TENOR

| | |
|---|---|
| Dominus | Lord |

—TRANS. SUSAN A. KIDWELL

(b) *Fole acostumance/Dominus*

Edited by Rebecca A. Baltzer from Munich, Bayerische Staatsbibliothek, Mus. ms. 4775, Complex A, fol. 1v–2r. Translation by Rebecca A. Baltzer. Used by permission.

DUPLUM

| | |
|---|---|
| Fole acostumance | Foolish custom |
| me fait que je chant, | makes me sing, |
| car nus mes n'avance | for I can advance |
| par asotillance | neither by accomplishment |
| ne par chant. | nor by song. |
| Mes en remembrance | But for remembrance's sake |
| ai fet cest novel deschant, | I have composed this new motet [discant], |
| que duel et pesance | since the valiant |
| doivent avoir molt grant | ought to have much more |
| li vaillant; | grief and worry; |
| quant envie | because Envy |
| et vilanie | and Villainy |
| vet de jor en jor montant, | increase from day to day, |
| cortoisie | Courtesy |
| avec s'amie | with her friend |
| largesce s'en vet fuiant. | Largesse flees from them. |
| Papelardie, | Religious Hypocrisy [pope-flattering]— |
| que Dex la maudie! | may God curse it! |

| | |
|---|---|
| Que que nus en die, | Whatever anyone may say, |
| vait mes avant; | it continues to advance; |
| n'est nus en vie, | there is no one alive |
| por qu'il en mesdie, | who in return for slandering it |
| que l'en ne l'en voist blasmant. | is not blamed for doing so. |
| Chascuns le vet redotant, | Everyone lives in fear, |
| n'il n'est mie | and this is not |
| grant folie, | at all foolish, |
| car li plus riche et li plus poissant | for the richest and most powerful |
| vont mes tel vie menant; | lead this kind of life; |
| valor ne sens ne clergie | neither reputation nor wisdom nor knowledge— |
| ne vont mes nule riens prisant; | no one values anything anymore; |
| tot ont mes truant. | these wretches have everything. |
| Morte est France | Dead is France |
| par tel decevance | because of such deception |
| et par tel faus semblant. | and because of such false seeming. |
| Tant est mes plaine de tel viltance, | She is so full of such evil |
| que trestoz li monz s'en vait gabant; | that the whole world mocks her; |
| c'est grant duels et grant mescheance, | it is a great sorrow and great misfortune |
| quant tel guile dure mes tant, | that such guile endures so long, |
| qu'ipocrisie | that Hypocrisy |
| sor tote rien vivant | makes every living thing |
| va compaignie | abandon companionship |
| et grant despense eschivant. | and great generosity. |
| Trop sont chiche, anguoisseus et tenant, | They are very stingy, anguished, and greedy, |
| signorie | lordship |
| ne baillie | and power |
| ne vent refusant, | they do not refuse, |
| mes de lor bien ne se sent nus. | but no one gets any of their goods [favors]. |

TENOR

| | |
|---|---|
| Dominus | Lord |

—TRANS. REBECCA A. BALTZER

(c) *Super te/Sed fulsit/Primus tenor/Dominus*

From *English Music of the Thirteenth and Early Fourteenth Centuries,* ed. Ernest H. Sanders, Polyphonic
Music of the Fourteenth Century 14 (Monaco: Éditions de l'Oiseau-Lyre, 1979), 170. Translation adapted
from ibid., 239.

| Super te Ierusalem | Over thee, Jerusalem, |
|---|---|
| de matre virgine | from the virgin mother |
| ortus est in Bethlehem | has arisen in Bethlehem |
| deus in homine | God in man; |
| ut gygas substancie | like a giant of twin substance |
| processit gemine | he has come forth |
| virginis ex utero | from the virgin's womb |
| sine gravamine | without effort; |
| non fuit feconditas | this pregnancy did not occur |
| hec viri semine. | through human seed. |

DUPLUM

| Sed fulsit virginitas | Rather, her virginity received its splendor |
|---|---|
| de sancto flamine | from the Holy Spirit; |
| ergo pie virginis | therefore, pious virgin's |
| flos pie domine | flower, pious Lord, |
| da medelam criminis | bring us the remedy for our crime |
| matris pro nomine | for the name of Thy mother, |

| ne nos preda demonis | lest we fall prey to the devil |
| simus pro crimine | for our crime, |
| quos preciosi sanguinis | we who the flood of Thy precious blood |
| emisti flumine. | has ransomed. |

TENOR

| Dominus | Lord |

These pieces illustrate three stages in the development of the motet. All three are based on the same chant melody, the melisma on *Dominus* from the Gradual *Viderunt omnes* (NAWM 3d), which we have seen set in discant style by Léonin (in NAWM 17), two anonymous composers (NAWM 18), and Pérotin (in NAWM 19). As is customary, each motet is identified by a title made up of the first words of each voice from highest to lowest.

Typical of the earliest motets, *Factum est salutare/Dominus* is a direct adaptation of a discant clausula. It was created by adding words to the upper voice of the clausula on *Dominus* in NAWM 18a, which appears earlier in the same manuscript of Notre Dame polyphony (now in Florence). Since the music was already written, the poet had to accommodate his text to the number of notes in each phrase of the duplum, which resulted in varying line lengths and accentuations. When set with text, the duplum may also be termed the *motetus*.

As is true of many early motets, the text for the duplum is a trope on the words of the chant from which the tenor is taken, in this case the verse of *Viderunt omnes*:

| Notum fecit Dominus salutare suum: | The Lord hath made known His |
|    ante conspectum gentium revelavit |    salvation; He hath revealed His justice in |
|    justitiam suam. |    the sight of the people. |

It was customary for tropes and early motets to borrow words or sounds from the original chant text. This practice is demonstrated in this motet and indicated by the underlined words in the poetry: "Dominus" at the end of the motet, and "notum," "salutare," "conspectu(m)," and "gentium" near the beginning. The endings "-um" and "-are" are repeated as rhymes throughout the motet, and another word-ending from the original chant, "-it," is also used as a rhyme.

Besides borrowing sounds, the words of the motetus reflect on the meaning of the chant text and of the holiday it celebrates, the nativity of Jesus. The first four lines summarize the chant's verse, from Psalm 97:2 (98:2), and the rest refer to incidents in the life of Jesus. The contrast between the power of Jesus as king of salvation and the power of earthly kings like Caesar was drawn both by Jesus himself ("render unto Caesar the things that are Caesar's, and to God the things that are God's," in Mark 12:17) and in the story of his crucifixion (John 19:12–15). Raising Lazarus from the dead was a sign of Jesus' power as savior. The multiple allusions to the Bible create a sermon in miniature, drawing together ideas that the listener might not have thought to relate.

This first motet is like a gloss upon a gloss, a text (a gloss in words) added to what already was a musical elaboration (a gloss in music) of the original chant. Because of its sacred text, it could have been performed in place of the original clausula, as part of the Gradual at the Mass for Christmas Day, although we cannot be certain that it was. Since the motet is complete in itself, it could also have been sung in devotions or as entertainment for an audience of churchmen or courtiers who were well enough educated to follow the web of allusions.

A motet called *Error popularis/Dominus* appears just a few pages after *Factum est* in the same manuscript. It borrows the tenor from *Factum est*, states it twice, and adds a new, more quickly moving melody in the duplum with a secular Latin text. Such a piece, with words unrelated to the original chant or Christmas Mass, could have been performed as entertainment or in devotions, but not in the service. *Error popularis* was later reworked by another poet, who substituted a French text for the Latin one to produce the second motet included here, *Fole acostumance/Dominus*, which appears in three later manuscripts (the Munich source, used for this edition, also includes *Factum est*). Such a chain of transformations illustrates the way that polyphony was viewed in the thirteenth century: as common property, material that could be used, altered, and adapted to new uses.

The tenor of *Fole acostumance* is identical to that of *Factum est* except that the section on "Do-" appears twice (the repetition begins at measure 41, marked with roman numeral II). Phrases in the duplum are longer than in *Factum est*, often overlapping the tenor rests, and the use of only three rhymes throughout the motet lends the poetry clarity and coherence. The poem is a blistering attack on envy, villainy, hypocrisy, deception, and greed, and was apparently inspired by conflict with or within the church. The only connection to the original chant text is through sound: the last line of the poem begins with "m" and ends with "nus," coordinated with the "-mi-" and "-nus" of "Dominus" in the tenor.

As we have seen, the first stage of motet composition consisted of adding text to an existing discant clausula, and subsequent developments included writing a new duplum to an existing tenor or writing a new text for an existing motet. In all of these cases, the composer reworked what was already a polyphonic piece. A different approach was to use a fragment of a chant to create a new tenor and add one or more voices above it, producing a motet that is not directly related to a discant clausula. This procedure quickly became the most common approach.

An example of such a motet is *Super te/Sed fulsit/Primus tenor/Dominus*, which uses the first half of the *Dominus* melisma (minus its first two notes) stated twice (measures 1–18 and 19–36, paralleling measures 3–21 of *Factum est*). The rhythmic pattern differs from the previous motets, and occasionally notes are omitted, repeated, or inserted. This motet exists in two variants: the four-voice version shown here, from a manuscript in Worcester, England, and a three-voice version in a French manuscript. The latter lacks the "Primus Tenor" (first tenor) part, which thickens the texture and adds a third to the final sonority—traits of English music in the late Middle Ages. The English version is probably the older.

The poetry in this motet was apparently written before the music, as shown by the regular line lengths and rhyme scheme. A single Latin poem was used for the upper two voices, the first half for the triplum, and the second for the duplum. The subject, the birth of Jesus to the Virgin Mary, is appropriate to the Christmas season, but the motet was more likely sung in private devotions than as part of the Gradual at Mass.

With occasional exceptions, the upper voices do not rest at the same time as each other or at the same time as the tenor on *Dominus*. As a result, the music moves continuously. This is typical of motets with three or four voices and strongly differentiates these later motets from those of the early thirteenth century such as *Factum est*. As became standard during the century, almost every measure in this transcription begins with a sonority of perfect consonances, usually fifth plus octave, but both consonance and dissonance occur freely in between.

In the manuscript of *Super te,* the Primus Tenor has no words, and the second tenor has only the word *Dominus* at the beginning, without designations for where the syllables are to be sung. Some scholars and performers have interpreted the lack of text underlay in motet tenors to mean that these lines should be performed by instruments. Current thinking is that all parts were sung by solo voices, and that is how all three motets are performed on the accompanying recordings.

# ADAM DE LA HALLE (CA. 1240–?1288)

## De ma dame vient/Dieus, comment porroie/Omnes

Motet

CA. 1260s–1280s

Adapted by Rebecca A. Baltzer from *The Montpellier Codex*, ed. Hans Tischler, vol. 3 (Madison: A-R Editions, 1978), 112–15. Translation adapted from the one by Susan Stakel and Joel C. Relihan in ibid., vol. 4, pp. 92–93.

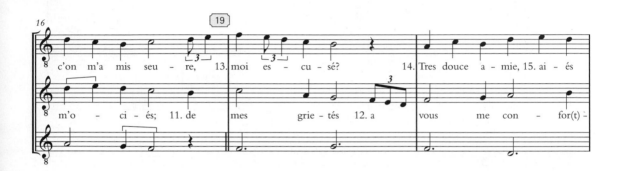

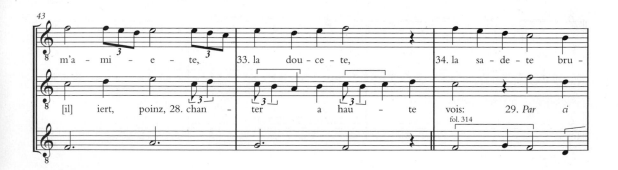

### TRIPLUM

| | |
|---|---|
| *De ma dame vient* | From my lady comes |
| li gries maus, que je trai, | the grievous pain which I bear |
| don't je morrai, | and of which I will die, |
| s'esperance ne me retient, | if hope does not keep me alive, |
| et la grant joie que j'ai. | along with the great joy that I have. |
| Car j'aperçoi bien et sai, | For I see well and know |
| c'o[n] m'a grevé et mellé, | that others have hurt my chances and caused misunderstandings, |
| | |
| si qu'ele m'a tout ausi qu'entroublié, | and she has as good as forgotten me, |
| qui en soloie estre audeseure. | who used to be uppermost in her mind. |
| Dieus, quant verrai l'eure, | God, when will I see the hour |
| qu'aie a li parlé | when I shall have talked with her |
| et, de ce c'on m'a mis seure, | and, of that for which they have blamed me, |
| moi escusé? | be excused? |
| Tres douce amie, | Sweet friend, |
| aiés de moi pitié, | have pity on me, |
| por Dieu merci! | for God's sake, mercy! |
| Onques n'ama, qui por si peu haï, | Never has anyone loved, and then for so little been hated, |
| | |
| ne deservi ne l'ai mie; | nor have I deserved it; |
| ains est par envie, | rather it is out of envy |
| k'on en a mesdit, | that they have slandered me, |
| et en leur despit | and to spite them, |
| maintenant irai | now I will go |
| et pour aus crever ferai | and, to make them burst with anger, |
| melleur samblant, que je ne devroie. | will pretend to be happier than I should. |
| *Fui toi, gaite, fai moi voie,* | Get away, watchman, make way for me, |
| *par ci p[a]ssent gens de joie;* | for here pass joyful people; |
| tart m'est, que j'i soie, | it is past time that I be there— |
| encore m'i avés vous nuisi. | again have you done me harm. |
| Si serai je mieus de li, | I will get along better with her |
| c'onques ne fui, se seulete | than ever before, if alone |
| enqui en un destour | searching in a byway |
| truis m'amiete, | I find my beloved, |
| la doucete, | the sweet one, |
| la sadete brunete, | the charming, dark-haired one, |
| savourosete, | the luscious one, |
| cui Dieus doinst boin jour. | to whom God grant a fine day. |

### MOTETUS

| | |
|---|---|
| Dieus, coument porroie | God, how can I |
| trouver voie | find a way |
| d'aler a celi, | to go to him |
| qui amiete je sui? | whose lover I am? |
| Çainturele, va i en lieu de mi, | Little belt, go there instead of me, |
| quar tu fus sieve ausi, | for you were his too; |
| si m'en conquera mieus. | in that way I'll accomplish more. |
| Mes coument serai sanz ti, Dieus? | But how will I get along without you? God! |

| | |
|---|---|
| Ceinturele, mar vous vi! | Little belt, a curse on you! |
| Au desceindre m'ociés; | In unbuckling, you kill me; |
| de mes grietés | from my sorrows |
| a vous me confor(t)toie, | I took comfort |
| quant je vous sentoie, aymi, | when I smelled on you, alas, |
| a la savour de mon ami. | the scent of my lover. |
| Ne pour quant d'autres en ai | Nevertheless, from others I have |
| a claus d'argent et de soie | articles of silver and of silk |
| pour mon user. | for my use. |
| Moi, lasse, comment porroie | Alas! how can I |
| sans celi durer, | endure without the one |
| qui me tient en joie? | who is the source of my joy? |
| Ceinturele, celi proie, | Little belt, beg him |
| qui la m'envoia; | who sent it to me; |
| puisque je ne puis aler la, | since I cannot go there, |
| qu'il en viengne ennuit ci, | let him come to me here at night, |
| droit au jour failli, | as soon as the day fades, |
| pour faire tout ses bo[i]ns. | to fulfill all his needs. |
| Et il m'orra, quant [il] iert, poinz, | He will hear me at the right time, |
| chanter a haute vois: | singing out loud: |
| *Par ci va la mignotise,* | There goes frolic, |
| *par ci ou je vois.* | there where I go. |

TENOR

Omnes                     All

—TRANS. SUSAN STAKEL AND JOEL C. RELIHAN

Adam de la Halle's *De ma dame vient/Dieus, comment porroie/Omnes* is one of the few thirteenth-century motets whose composer we know. Since it combines the court tradition of trouvère song with the newer form of the motet, it is possible that Adam composed it for his patrons Robert II, count of Artois, or Charles of Anjou.

Adam borrowed from a variety of sources to create this piece. The tenor uses the melisma on "omnes" from the Gradual *Viderunt omnes* (see NAWM 3d), transposed down a fifth. Adam gives the melody a distinctive rhythmic profile and states it four times (measures 1–16, with the end of each statement marked by a double bar). He then repeats the same process twice, giving the melody two new rhythmic patterns that are each repeated four times (see measures 17–32 and 33–48). The motetus (or duplum) begins with the refrain from Adam's own monophonic rondeau *Diex, comment porroie*, transposed, and closes with another borrowed refrain (shown here in italics). The triplum also quotes several lines of poetry from other songs (shown in italics). This complex web of references to other music and poetry must have added to the intellectual appeal of this piece, and demonstrates motet composers' continued interest in alluding to more than one source (see NAWM 21a).

The piece uses the new notation known as Franconian, after Franco of Cologne, which indicates a precise rhythm for each note. The more exact notation allowed the composer greater freedom from the rhythmic modes than was possible in earlier motets, such as those in NAWM 21. Here the tenor is still in modal rhythm, alternating modes 1 (as in measures 2–4) and 5 (as in measures 17–19), and mode 1 patterns often underlie the upper voices as well. (In this edition, perfect longs are transcribed as dotted half notes rather than dotted quarter notes, as in NAWM 17–21, so mode 1 alternates half and quarter notes.) But many smaller durations are used in the motetus and especially in the triplum, so that they move much faster than the tenor. Each voice has its own rhythmic character, with the triplum moving most rapidly, and they seldom move in rhythmic unison for an entire measure. Almost never does either upper voice have the same rhythm for two successive measures, giving the music a constant variety.

These rhythmic differences between the parts are characteristic of Franconian motets. In this case, they also add to the piece's meaning. The poem in the triplum is in the voice of a man who describes his pain at being separated from his lady; the motetus is in the voice of the lady, who is searching for a way to send word to tell him that he should come to her. It is hard for modern listeners to imagine how thirteenth-century audiences could hear motets with two texts, the most common type of motet in France, and understand both texts at once. But in this work, the use of two separate texts creates a special poignancy as the two lovers express their anguish at being apart, yearn to be together, and voice their feelings simultaneously, unable to hear each other.

*Sumer is icumen in*

*Rota*

CA. 1250

*English Music of the Thirteenth and Early Fourteenth Centuries,* ed. Ernest H. Sanders, Polyphonic Music of the Fourteenth Century 14 (Monaco: Éditions de l'Oiseau-Lyre, 1979), 5–7. Translations from ibid., 210.

| | |
|---|---|
| Sumer is icumen in, | Summer is come, |
| Lhude sing cuccu! | sing loud, cuckoo! |
| Groweþ sed and bloweþ med | The seed grows and the meadow blooms, |
| and springþ the wde nu. | and now the wood turns green. |
| Sing cuccu! | Sing, cuckoo! |
| | |
| Awe bleteþ after lomb, | Ewe bleats after lamb, |
| lhouþ after calve cu. | cow lows after calf, |
| Bulluc sterteþ, | bullock leaps, |
| bucke verteþ, | buck [he-goat?] farts, |
| murie sing cuccu! | sing merrily, cuckoo! |
| Cuccu, cuccu, | Cuckoo, cuckoo! |
| wel singes þu cuccu, | You sing well, cuckoo. |
| ne swik þu naver nu! | Don't ever stop now! |

| | |
|---|---|
| LATIN TEXT: | |
| Perspice Christicola, | Observe, worshipper of Christ, |
| que dignacio; | what gracious condescension! |
| celicus agricola | The heavenly husband, |
| pro vitis vicio, | because of the vine's imperfection, |
| filio, | not sparing his son, |
| non parcens exposuit | exposed him |
| mortis exicio. | to death's destruction. |
| Qui captivos | The prisoners, |
| Semivivos | who are half-dead |
| a supplicio | on account of the death sentence, |
| Vite donat | he restores to life, |
| et secum coronat | and crowns them at his side |
| in celi solio. | on heaven's throne. |

—Trans. Ernest H. Sanders

One of the treasures of medieval polyphony is *Sumer is icumen in,* also known as the Summer Canon, the only known piece of six-part polyphony before the fifteenth century. It was composed around 1250, probably in Reading, England, where the manuscript in which it is preserved was copied and housed in an abbey. The main text, in English, is a celebration of spring; the Latin text (not sung on the recording) was probably added to make this clearly recreational piece suitable for the manuscript of Latin polyphony in which it appears. Despite the English text, the counterpoint is too complex to imagine that this could be folk or popular music, or indeed anything other than entertainment music intended to be performed by those learned in church polyphony.

This piece combines two forms that were common in England at the time: the *rota* and the *rondellus*. The bottom two voices, marked "Pes" (foot), create a small rondellus, a form in which voices begin together and then exchange parts:

| Pes 1 | a | b |
|-------|---|---|
| Pes 2 | b | a |

Together, they form a harmonic foundation, which they repeat throughout the piece. Above them, two, three, or four voices join in a rota, a round or perpetual canon at the unison. Each voice sings the same music, but enters at a different time: the first together with the Pes and the others at two-measure intervals.

Once all the voices have entered, the harmonies alternate between F–A–C–F sonorities on each downbeat and G–B♭–D or similar sonorities on the second half of each measure. The emphasis on imperfect consonances and on full triads is typical of English music of the thirteenth and fourteenth centuries. Other common traits of English music include melodies that modern listeners hear as in the major mode (it was not described as a mode until the sixteenth century, when it was called Ionian); alternation between chords on the first and second degrees of the scale; short, periodic phrases of two or four measures; and preference for rhythmic modes 1 and 5.

On the accompanying recording, the performers demonstrate three different possibilities for performance: over the repeating Pes, one voice sings the entire vocal line, then two voices sing it in canon, then four voices. Since no ending for the piece is indicated, all singers could stop together or, as in the recording, each could stop in turn upon reaching the end of the melody, leaving the Pes singers to sing the final cadence.

# PHILIPPE DE VITRY (1291–1361)

*In arboris/Tuba sacre fidei/Virgo sum*

*Motet*

CA. 1320

24

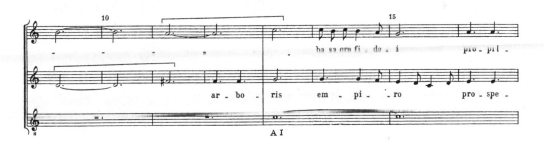

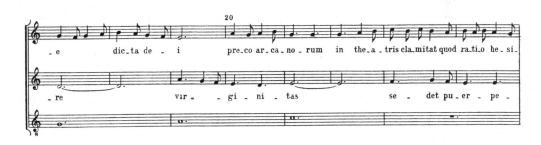

From Philippe de Vitry, *Complete Works*, ed. Leo Schrade, with new introduction and notes by Edward H. Roesner (Monaco: Éditions de l'Oiseau-Lyre, 1984), 32–34.

### DUPLUM (MOTETUS)

| | |
|---|---|
| In arboris empiro prospere | At the top of the tree auspiciously |
| virginitas sedet puerpere | sits virginity expecting child, |
| mediatrix fides in medio, | with faith, the midwife, in the middle, |
| cum stipite cecata ratio | along with the trunk, blind reason, |
| insecuta septem sororibus, | followed by seven sisters |
| sophismata sua foventibus; | fostering its sophisms. |
| hec ut scandat dum magis nititur | Reason strives to climb higher |
| debilitas ramorum frangitur. | until the fragile branches break. |
| Petat ergo fidei dexteram | Therefore let her seek the right hand of faith |
| vel eternum nitetur perperam. | or tread the wrong path forever. |

### TRIPLUM

| | |
|---|---|
| Tuba sacre fidei, | The trumpet of holy faith |
| proprie dicta Dei. | is rightly called God's word. |
| Preco arcanorum | The teller of secrets |
| in theatris clamitat | proclaims in the theaters |
| quod ratio hesitat, | what reason, |
| basis peccatorum, | the basis of sinners, |
| fatendum simpliciter | hesitates to say simply |
| credendumque firmiter | and believe firmly |
| morive necesse: | or one must die. |
| Deum unum in tribus | That God is one in three |
| personis equalibus | equal persons, |
| et tres unum esse; | and the three are one; |
| virginem non semine | that the virgin by no seed |
| viri set spiramine | of man but by the breath |
| verbi concepisse; | of the word conceived; |
| ipsam semper virginem | that she, always a virgin, |
| Deum atque hominem | to God and man |
| mundo peperisse; | in the world gave birth. |
| sed transnaturalia | But since such |
| ista cum sint omnia | supernatural things |
| credentibus vita | are life to those who believe, |
| neces negligentibus, | death to those who ignore, |
| nature quod gressibus | let what by natural steps |
| ratio potita | reason has acquired |
| in premissis dubium | from premises beget |
| gignat et augurium; | doubts and prophesies. |
| igitur vitetur | Therefore reason is shunned |
| et fides per quam via | and faith, by means of which |
| apud archana dia | secret divine truths |
| clarior habetur, | become clearer, |
| semper imitetur. | should always be obeyed. |

### TENOR

| | |
|---|---|
| Virgo sum. | I am a virgin. |

*In arboris/Tuba sacre fidei/Virgo sum* is one of the motets attributed to Philippe de Vitry in the *Ars nova* treatise that preserves his teachings. He probably wrote the motet around 1320.

The texts of the motetus and triplum are closely related: they are both about the Virgin Mary and express the need to follow faith rather than reason. These texts also both refer to the subject of the plainchant tenor, *Virgo sum* (I am a virgin). Such interconnections and references between the texts were part of the appeal that motets had for their primary audience, educated clerics, courtiers, and nobles. Despite its religious theme, this motet was probably not performed in church but as entertainment and in devotions at court or clerical gatherings.

Vitry usually observed the accents of the poetic lines in his setting, but not the rhythm of speech. The contours and segmentation of the melodies follow the lines of poetry, but neither the rhymes nor the meanings of the lines are reflected in the shape of the melodies.

The principal innovation that characterized the music of Vitry and his contemporaries and led to the label *ars nova* (new art) was the invention of notation that allowed note values to be divided into either two or three equal parts. This new notation allowed a far greater variety of rhythmic patterns than were available in earlier systems of notation. In Franconian notation, which had been used in the late thirteenth century, the basic time unit (*tempus*, equivalent to a breve) always appeared in a group of three called a *perfection*, making triple time the universal meter. Moreover, the breve itself was divided into three equal semibreves; if there were only two, the second was twice as long as the first, maintaining the triple division. In contrast, Ars Nova notation allowed for duple or triple division at several different levels, known as *mode* (division of the long), *time* (division of the breve), and *prolation* (division of the semibreve). Triple divisions were called perfect, duple divisions imperfect (or, for prolation, major and minor respectively).

At the opening of this motet, the long (transcribed as a dotted whole note, as at measure 17) is divided into two breves (dotted half notes), making the mode imperfect. This duple division is highlighted in the transcription through the use of barlines. In the upper voices, each measure is a breve, and in the tenor (the lowest voice), each measure is a long, extending over two measures in the other parts. The breve, in turn, is divided into two semibreves (dotted quarter notes, as at measure 2), making the time also imperfect. Only the prolation, the division of semibreves into minims, is triple (major prolation, represented in the transcription by three eighth notes, as at measure 14).

The form of the piece is created by repetitions in the tenor. The tenor melody consists of two statements (called *colores*) of the same phrase of chant (in measures 13–84 and 85–118). In the second color, the note values are diminished by half; here the melody moves mostly in breves (dotted half notes) rather than in longs (dotted whole notes). Each statement of the chant is divided into three segments, or *taleae* (cuttings). The first three taleae (measures 13–36, 37–60, and 61–84) have identical rhythmic patterns in the tenor. The last three taleae (measures

85–96, 97–108, and 109–118) have the same rhythm as the first three taleae, with the note values reduced by half. (In the final talea, the rests at the end are omitted to allow a conclusive ending with all three voices sounding.) This kind of organization, called *isorhythm* ("equal rhythm"), evolved from the shorter repeating patterns in the tenors of thirteenth-century motets, such as NAWM 21 and 22.

Near the end of each talea, three types of intensification occur. In the original notation, after the first four notes of the tenor, the next three notes were written in red ink, which indicated that the division of the long (dotted whole note) into breves temporarily changed from duple to triple (see measures 25–30 and the parallel point in each later talea). The scribe indicated this change with a direction written at the beginning of the tenor part: "Black notes are imperfect [duple division] and red notes are perfect [triple division]." This change of ink color, called "coloration," is indicated in the transcription by open brackets under the tenor. (The brackets over each staff indicate ligatures in the original notation, as in NAWM 17–23.)

In all six taleae, the rhythms of the upper parts as well as the tenor during this "colored" section are isorhythmic—one pattern governing the first color, another the second. Moreover, all these "colored" sections use a technique called *hocket* (from the French *hoquet*, meaning "hiccup"), in which the upper voices alternate singing and resting to project a single although choppy melodic line. A long note follows each of the "colored" sections, and succeeding this is a proliferation of short notes in both upper parts until a new talea begins, marked by long notes in all parts. Even if a listener does not notice the rhythmic repetition in the tenor, the presence of these other features at the same point in each talea gives the music a shape that can easily be heard if one knows to listen for it. Moreover, when the tenor doubles its pace in the last three taleae, the other parts also become somewhat more active, creating a satisfying rhythmic intensity toward the end of the piece.

Apart from the hockets, the three voices are mostly independent of each other. On the longer notes, with only a few exceptions, the parts meet on octaves, fifths, fourths, thirds, and sixths, with the perfect consonances marking the points of greatest stability. For the very end of the motet, Vitry used the strongest cadence available in Ars Nova style; known as a double leading-tone cadence, it consists of a major third and major sixth expanding out to a perfect fifth and octave, with both upper voices rising a half step and the lowest voice descending a step. The use of accidentals as indicated here was called *musica ficta* (feigned music) because it involved notes outside the standard gamut. The manuscript includes several accidentals, such as the C♯ in measure 117; other notes would likely have been altered chromatically by the singers in order to avoid tritones, smooth the melody, or provide more satisfactory cadences, and these are suggested by the editor with accidentals above the staff.

Vitry's motets were probably performed by one singer on each part, as on the present recording. Some modern performers use an instrument for the tenor, reasoning that the long notes and lack of text underlay make the line better suited for instrumental performance.

# GUILLAUME DE MACHAUT (CA. 1300–1377)

*La Messe de Nostre Dame*: Kyrie

*Mass (Mass Ordinary cycle)*

CA. 1364

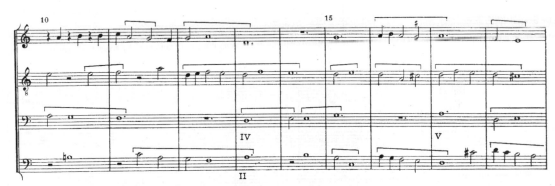

*The Works of Guillaume de Machaut,* ed. Leo Schrade, vol. 2, Polyphonic Music of the Fourteenth Century 3 (Monaco: Éditions de l'Oiseau-Lyre, 1956), 37–40.

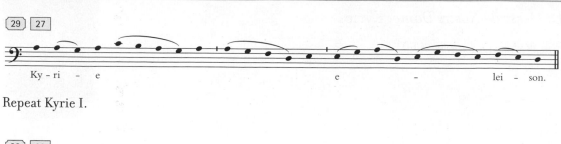

Ky – ri – e        e – lei – son.

Repeat Kyrie I.

Chri – ste        e – lei – son.

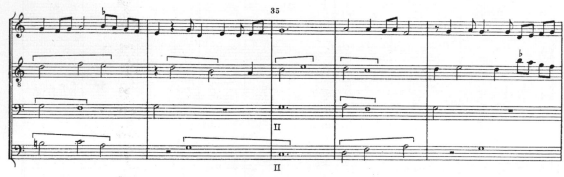

Repeat chant Christe.

Kyrie eleison.          Lord have mercy.
Christe eleison.        Christ have mercy.
Kyrie eleison.          Lord have mercy.

Guillaume de Machaut probably wrote *La Messe de Nostre Dame* (Mass of Our Lady) in the 1360s for performance at a Mass for the Virgin Mary that was celebrated each Saturday in a chapel of the Cathedral at Reims. When his brother Jean died in 1372, the observance became a memorial Mass for Jean, thanks to an endowment the brothers had given the church. An oration for Guillaume's soul was added after his death in 1377. Because of the endowment, this mass continued to be performed in their honor weekly for several decades.

Machaut used two styles in the mass. The Kyrie, Sanctus, Agnus Dei, and Ite, missa est are isorhythmic, based on chants for those texts, while the Gloria and Credo are generally syllabic and homophonic (except for isorhythmic Amens) and are not based on chant.

The Kyrie is typical of the isorhythmic movements. The tenor melody is taken from the plainchant *Kyrie Cunctipotens Genitor*, which we saw in NAWM 3b (although Machaut used a slightly different version of the chant). The chant has four segments of melody—Kyrie eleison, Christe eleison, a new setting of Kyrie eleison, and a longer variant of the latter—and all four are set by Machaut. The last Kyrie (measure 67) begins like the second Kyrie (measure 50), emphasizing the similarity between the original chants.

In the first Kyrie (measures 1–27), the twenty-eight notes of the chant are divided into seven statements of a four-note talea in the tenor (see measures 1–4 for the first statement). In addition, the contratenor is mostly isorhythmic with a talea of twelve measures (compare measures 1–12 with 13–24), and the upper voices are partially isorhythmic over the same span (see especially measures 9–12 and 21–24). The beginning of each talea is marked with a roman numeral in the score. In the Christe (measures 28–49) and second Kyrie (measures 50–66), both tenor and contratenor are exactly isorhythmic, with taleae of seven measures in the Christe and eight measures in Kyrie II, and the upper parts are again partly isorhythmic (for example, see measures 30–32, 37–39, and 44–47 of the Christe in all voices). The last, extended Kyrie (measures 67–95) has the longest talea in the tenor, fourteen measures, with the contratenor repeating a seven-measure pattern and the upper parts cycling with the tenor (compare measures 70–74 with 84–88 and 78–79 with 92–93). The rhythmic repetitions in other voices make the taleae in the tenor easier to hear, as do the recurring measures where all four voices sustain a long tone.

Characteristics of this Kyrie that are common in the rest of Machaut's music include the syncopations at the level of the quarter note (semibreve, in the original notation) and eighth note (minim) and the occasional use of hocket, as in measures 30–31 and 34 of the Christe.

The tenor and contratenor together provide the harmonic foundation for the more quickly moving upper voices. The harmony reflects the mode of the chant, mode 1 on D. Each section begins and ends on $d$–$a$–$d'$–$a'$, a very stable sonority of perfect consonances. Most final cadences and some internal cadences use the double-leading-tone cadence with octave doubling in the upper part, producing parallel octaves and fifths. In between, a sense of forward motion is achieved through frequent sonorities with thirds or sixths, which required resolution to perfect consonance, and Machaut returns frequently enough to sonorities on D to keep the mode clear.

Chant Kyries were often performed in antiphony, with alternation between two halves of the choir (see NAWM 3b). A similar practice was often used for polyphonic settings, with alternation between soloists singing the polyphony and the choir singing the original chant, as on the accompanying recordings. Such a performance proceeds as follows:

| Kyrie: | Polyphony (Kyrie I) | CD 2|28 | CD 1|26 |
|---|---|---|---|
| | Chant | CD 2|29 | CD 1|27 |
| | Polyphony (Kyrie I) | | |
| Christe: | Chant | CD 2|30 | CD 1|28 |
| | Polyphony (Christe) | CD 2|31 | CD 1|29 |
| | Chant | | |
| Kyrie: | Polyphony (Kyrie II) | CD 2|32 | CD 1|30 |
| | Chant | CD 2|33 | CD 1|31 |
| | Polyphony (Kyrie III) | CD 2|34 | CD 1|32 |

Alternatively, the polyphonic settings could be repeated to produce the threefold statements of "Kyrie eleison" and "Christe eleison."

# GUILLAUME DE MACHAUT (CA. 1300–1377)

*Rose, liz, printemps, verdure*

*Rondeau*

MID-FOURTEENTH CENTURY

From Guillaume de Machaut, *Oeuvres complètes*, vol. 5, ed. Leo Schrade (Monaco: Éditions de l'Oiseau-Lyre, 1977), 11–12.

| | | | |
|---|---|---|---|
| A | 1 | Rose, liz, printemps, verdure, | Rose, lily, spring, greenery, |
| | 2 | Fleur, baume et tres douce odour, | flower, balm, and the sweetest fragrance, |
| B | 3 | Belle, passes en doucour, | beautiful lady, you surpass in sweetness. |
| a | 4 | Et tous les biens de Nature, | And all the gifts of nature |
| | 5 | Avez dont je vous aour. | you possess, for which I adore you. |
| A | 6 | Rose, liz, printemps, verdure, | Rose, lily, spring, greenery, |
| | 7 | Fleur, baume et tres douce odour. | flower, balm, and the sweetest fragrance. |
| a | 8 | Et quant toute creature | And, since beyond any creature's |
| | 9 | Seurmonte vostre valour, | your virtue excels, |
| b | 10 | Bien puis dire et par honour: | I can honestly say: |
| A | 11 | Rose, liz, printemps, verdure, | Rose, lily, spring, greenery, |
| | 12 | Fleur, baume et tres douce odour, | flower, balm, and very sweet fragrance, |
| B | 13 | Belle, passes en doucour. | beautiful lady, you surpass in sweetness. |

Rondeaux were love songs in the centuries-old tradition of the trouvères. They were probably performed most often as entertainment at court, where a cultivated audience would have appreciated the wordplay of their texts and the intricacies of their music. *Rose, liz* is preserved with Machaut's other polyphonic chansons in manuscripts prepared under his own supervision. The earliest manuscript (from ca. 1350) lacks the triplum, or top voice, suggesting that Machaut added it later. Indeed, Machaut composed most of his polyphonic chansons for three voices rather than four; here, the triplum is essentially decorative rather than integral to the structure of the work.

The rondeau is a form in which the full refrain, heard at the beginning and the end, contains all of the music in the piece. In *Rose, liz* the first part of the refrain (A in the diagram below) has two lines and the second part (B) has one. The first couplet (a), of two lines, is set to the music of the first part of the refrain and is followed by a reprise of that first part of the refrain. The second couplet (ab), of three lines, uses the music of the entire refrain, and the whole refrain returns at the end. Each time the refrain returns, in part or in whole, it has new layers of meaning added by the intervening lines.

The musical form for the thirteen-line song is ABaAabAB (capital letters indicate that both the music and the text of the refrain are sung):

| Lines of poetry: | 1 | 2 | 3 | 4 | 5 | 6(=1) | 7(=2) | 8 | 9 | 10 | 11(=1) | 12(=2) | 13(=3) |
|---|---|---|---|---|---|---|---|---|---|---|---|---|---|
| Rhyme: | a | b | b | a | b | a | | b | | a | b | b | a | | b | | b |
| Sections of music: | A | | B | a | | A | | | a | | b | A | | | B |

The first section of the refrain ends without finality on the note D, and the second section closes on C, the song's tonal center. The two sections are linked by similar final rhymes (on *-our*) and by a kind of musical rhyme (compare measures 20–25 and 32–37). The harmonic relationship between the sections—in which the last tenor note of the final cadence is a step lower than that of main internal cadence—is common in Medieval music, and the overall structure reflects the harmonic motion of the typical cadence, in which the tenor descends a step to the final.

Like most of Machaut's polyphonic songs, *Rose liz* is constructed around a two-voice framework in which the tenor serves as a slower-moving support to the cantus, which is the only voice provided with a text (although all of the voices may have been sung). The contratenor reinforces or complements the tenor in the same range, and the triplum shares the upper octave and exchanges motives with the cantus. A diatonic figure of a stepwise descending fourth dominates the tenor part and at one point is taken up by the triplum (see tenor, measures 1–2, and triplum, measures 15–16). Thirds and sixths sweeten the harmony, but the ends of poetic lines are marked by cadences on open fifth and octave sonorities.

As in the *Messe de Nostre Dame*, Machaut alternated segments of music with different rhythmic profiles. Some measures sustain a chord without motion (for instance, measures 2 and 10); some move only in quarter notes (as do measure 8–9); but in most measures, at least one voice moves on most or all of the eighth notes. To create this activity, Machaut often reused the same rhythmic figures; those in measures 4, 5, 6, and 7 of the cantus recur several times throughout the song.

Characteristic of French fourteenth-century secular music are the long melismas at the beginning of lines and sometimes also in the middle. These melismas, occupying as much as four measures, do not fall on important words, nor even necessarily on accented syllables, but they serve a formal and decorative function.

Machaut's polyphonic chansons were probably performed by singers, one on each part. The untexted lines might have been sung on neutral syllables, or all voices might have sung the text together, as on the accompanying recording. Some modern performances use instruments for the untexted lines, usually with a different timbre on each line to keep the parts clear.

# JOHANNES CICONIA (CA. 1370–1412)

*Sus une fontayne*

*Virelai*

CA. 1400

27

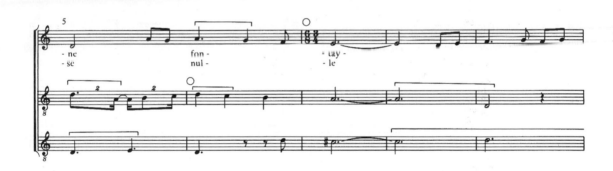

\* *Ob* : prefatory stave
  *MOe* : mensuration signs

From *The Works of Johannes Ciconia*, ed. Margaret Bent and Anne Hallmark, Polyphonic Music of the Fourteenth Century 24 (Monaco: Éditions de l'Oiseau-Lyre, 1985), 170–74.

| A | 1 | Sus une fontayne en remirant | By a fountain, while gazing around, |
|---|---|---|---|
| | | Oÿ chanter si douchement | I heard [someone] singing so sweetly |
| | | Que mon cuer, corps et | That my heart, body, and thoughts |
| | | pensement, | |
| | | Remanent pris en atendant | Were held in waiting |

| b | 2 | D'avoir merchi de ma dolour | To have mercy for my pain |
|---|---|---|---|
| | | Qui me trepount au cuer forment | Which resounds in my heart so strongly |
| b | 3 | Seul de vëoir ce noble flour, | Only to see this noble flower, |
| | | Qui tant cantoit suavement. | who was singing so sweetly. |
| a | 4 | Que chois' null' say en recivant | Knowing nothing of my chances, I feel |
| | | Pavour, tremour et angosment | Fear, trembling, and anguish, |
| | | Que fere duis certaynement | Which I can certainly endure, |
| | | Tant sui de ly vëoir desirant. | So much do I desire to see her. |

| A | 5 | Sus une fontayne en remirant | By a fountain, while gazing around, |
|---|---|---|---|
| | | Oÿ chanter si douchement | I heard [someone] singing so sweetly |
| | | Que mon cuer, corps et | That my heart, body, and thoughts |
| | | pensement, | |
| | | Remanent pris en atendant. | Were held in waiting. |

Ciconia's *Sus une fontayne* is representative of the Ars Subtilior but of only one facet of its composer, who wrote in a wide variety of styles and genres. He was born around 1370 in or near Liège, in Flanders, and trained there as a choirboy but spent most of his career in Italy. He began working in Rome during the 1390s, then spent time in Pavia at the court of Gian Galeazzo Visconti around 1398–1401, and finally moved to Padua. It was likely in Pavia, a center for the Ars Subtilior in Italy, that Ciconia wrote this virelai, because the fountain in its first line was a symbol for the Visconti family. Ciconia paid homage to an older composer who also spent time in Pavia, Philippus de Caserta, by quoting words and music from the openings of three of his ballades: *En remirant* (measures 11–18), *En atendant* (measures 56–59), and *De ma dolour* (measures 74–80). These quotations are woven so smoothly into the texture that only listeners who know the earlier works would notice them. Like the rhythmic and notational complexity of this music, the quotations were probably intended for the appreciation of Ciconia's patron and the elite at the Pavia court.

   The Ars Subtilior style is marked by a complexity of rhythm and notation that was unmatched until the twentieth century and is illustrated in *Sus une fontayne*. As in all fourteenth-century French polyphonic chansons, the cantus (top voice) carries the main melody, the tenor supports and forms cadences with the cantus, and the contratenor fills in between and around the other two voices. However, in this song the three voices often move in different meters. At the beginning, for example, each voice has a different mensuration sign, indicating a unique meter.

Beats are subdivided in different ways (often duple against triple), the meter in one voice may be displaced to produce extended syncopations (as at measures 12–16 of the cantus), and mensuration changes frequently, sometimes for one note (see measure 11 of the contratenor). The result is a rhythmic surface of astonishing variety.

Ciconia lent the piece coherence through the form, harmony, cadences, and rhythm. The form is a virelai, an AbbaA form in which A is the refrain (measures 1–55, to the text marked 1 and 5); b is a contrasting musical phrase sung twice to different words (measures 56–95, to the couplets marked 2 and 3), and a is the last part of the stanza, with new words to the music of the refrain (the text marked 4). (In the performance on the accompanying recording, the a section is omitted, resulting in an AbbA form.) As is true of many virelais, the b sections feature different endings, the first harmonically open (on E) and the second closed (on D, a step lower). But the end of the A section (on a unison G) sounds most final of all. Melismas and phrases are even longer than in Machaut's chansons, creating an expanded form with increased rhythmic and stylistic possibilities. Cadences (as at measure 5) and sustained sonorities (as at measure 7) provide guideposts for both performers and listeners. Each successive phrase has a distinctive rhythmic profile, which also helps to give the piece shape. The rhythmic and metric complexity demands skilled performers, but it also generates momentum and sustains tension between points of rest, helping to create long-breathed phrases and a large-scale form. With all the conflicting meters and rhythms, it is remarkable how euphonious the music sounds.

Some modern performances of this piece use solo voices for all three parts, while others use instruments for the tenor and contratenor. Although the former is perhaps more likely how chansons were performed in the fourteenth century, using instruments of contrasting timbres can highlight the independence of each line and the remarkable rhythmic complexity of the piece.

# JACOPO DA BOLOGNA (FL. 1340–?1386)

## Fenice fù

Madrigal

CA. 1360

28

From Nino Pirrotta, ed. *Music of Fourteenth-Century Italy*, vol. 4, *Jacobus de Bononia, Vicentius de Arimino*, *Corpus mensurabilis musicae* 8 (Amsterdam: American Institute of Musicology, 1963), 6. © Hänssler Verlag, D-71087 Holzgerlingen. Used by permission of A-R Editions.

Fenice fù e vissi pura e morbida,
Et or son trasmutat' in una tortora
Che volo con amor per le belle ortora

A phoenix was I who lived pure and tender,
and now I am transformed into a turtledove
that flies with love through the beautiful orchards.

STANZA 2

Arbor[e] secho [mai] n'aqua torbida.
No' me deleta may per questo dubito.
Va ne l'astate l'inverno viene subito.

Neither dry trees nor muddy waters
ever delight me, because of this doubt:
summer is fleeting, winter quickly follows.

RITORNELLO

Tal vissi e tal me vivo e posso scrivere
C'ha donna non è più chè honesta vivere.

So I lived and so I live and can write,
which, for a woman, is no more than to live honestly.

Not much is known of Jacopo da Bologna's life, but he served the ruling family of Milan, the Visconti, during the 1340s and 1350s, interrupted by a period at the court of Verona in about 1349–52. *Fenice fù*, which was probably one of his last compositions, appears in two northern Italian manuscripts that were copied around 1410, the Codex Reina from northeast Italy and the Squarcialupi Codex from Florence.

The poem, whose meaning is elusive, has the form typical of the fourteenth-century madrigal: two stanzas of three lines followed by a two-line ritornello. The music for the stanza is heard twice and the ritornello once. The two voices have the same text and were both meant to be sung. Unlike the practice in the the treble-dominated style of Machaut (NAWM 26), the voices are relatively equal, except during extended florid runs in the upper part on the last accented syllable of each line. In two places (measures 7–9 and 24–25) the voices are in imitation, one immediately echoing the other, and in two short passages (measures 9 and 16) they engage in hocketlike alternation. The strongest cadences, including those at the end of each section, converge on a unison, which differs from the usual French cadence formed by widening to an octave.

The rhythm in this madrigal is typical of the early Italian Trecento style. Both voices exhibit elaborate divisions of the beat that may have derived from a tradition of improvisation. The notation of the stanzas calls for imperfect division of the breve (transcribed as a half note) into two semibreves (quarter notes). In the Italian system, these can be further subdivided in various ways (producing eighth and even sixteenth notes in the transcription), allowing florid scales and runs. In the ritornello, the breve is perfect (transcribed as a dotted half note) and may be divided into three imperfect semibreves (three quarter notes) or two perfect semibreves (two dotted quarter notes), which can in turn be subdivided. The flexible Italian notation was perfectly suited for music in this style.

# GHERARDELLO DA FIRENZE (CA. 1320–CA. 1362)

*Tosto che l'alba*

*Caccia*

MID-FOURTEENTH CENTURY

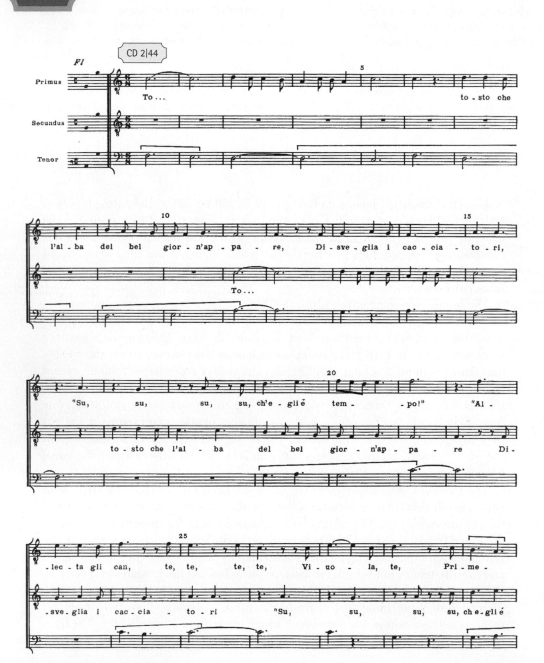

From *Italian Secular Music*, ed. W. Thomas Marrocco, Polyphonic Music of the Fourteenth Century 7 (Monaco: Éditions de l'Oiseau-Lyre, 1971), 109–12.

| | |
|---|---|
| Tosto che l'alba del bel giorn' appare, | As soon as the dawn of the fine day appears, |
| Disveglia i cacciatori, | it wakes up the hunters. |
| "Su, su, su, ch'egli è tempo!" | "Up, up, up, for it's time!" |
| "Allecta gli can, te, te, Viuola, te, Primera, te!" | "Call the dogs, you, Viuola, you, Primera, you!" |
| Su alto al monte con buon cani a mano | Up high on the hill with good dogs at hand |
| E gli bracchet' al piano. | and the hounds on the level ground. |
| Et nella piaggia ordine ciascuno. | And on the slope everyone in his place. |
| I' veggio sentire uno d'i nostri miglior bracchi. | I see one of our best hounds sniffing. |
| "Sta avisato!" | "Be forewarned!" |
| "Bussate d'ogni lato." | "Beat [the bushes] on every side." |
| "Ciascun le macchie che Quaglina suona!" | "Everyone, the bushes where Quaglina is barking!" |
| "Aio, aio, a te la cerbia vene." | "Ai-yo, ai-yo, the deer is coming toward you." |
| Carbon l'a prese ed in boccha la tene. | Carbon has caught her and is holding her in his mouth. |

RITORNELLO

| | |
|---|---|
| Del monte que' che v'era su gridava, | From the hilltop someone shouts, |
| "All'altra, all'altra," e suo corno sonava. | "Get the other one!," and sounds his horn. |

Gherardello was a priest and prior in Florence, Italy. He was best known in his own time for liturgical works, but few survive. His secular music includes ten madrigals, five monophonic ballatas, and this caccia, presumably composed and sung for the amusement of the educated elite in Florence.

The caccia is a fourteenth-century Italian genre that combines virtuosity—for both the composer and performer—with humor. The two upper parts form a canon at the unison, the second voice singing exactly the same melody and text as the first voice but entering several measures later. They are accompanied by a freely composed, untexted tenor in relatively long notes. The three voices cadence together in measure 94, followed by a short concluding ritornello with another canon in the top voices and freely composed tenor.

The word "caccia" means "hunt," referring to the second voice chasing after the first, but many such works are about hunting, as is true here. The poem does not tell a story so much as evoke a series of scenes, like a hunting tapestry turned into song. The rhyme scheme is irregular, but most of the lines are either seven or eleven syllables long, as was typical of Italian poetry for the next several centuries. (In counting syllables, successive vowels are usually elided, even from one word to the next; for example, the last line of the poem is counted as eleven syllables because of such elisions.) Through the canonic imitation, the composer combined the voices to create humorous juxtapositions, as when "up, up!" from the third line of text in the second voice alternates with "you, Viuola, you" from the fourth line (at measures 26–28). The shouts of "Aio!" and the imitation of hunting horn calls at "suo corno sonava" (sounds his horn) in the ritornello add realistic and humorous touches.

In the ritornello, the staff for the tenor has a key signature with one flat, while the upper voices have none. This notational convention, sometimes called *partial signature*, was apparently adopted as a matter of convenience: the tenor line might consistently include flatted B's (for example, to form a perfect fifth below F in one of the upper parts) while an upper part might include both B-flats and B-naturals. This made it useful to have a signature with one flat in the tenor but none in the upper part. We will see this notation in other late-fourteenth- and fifteenth-century works, including NAWM 30.

# FRANCESCO LANDINI (CA. 1325–1397)

## *Non avrà ma' pietà*

*Ballata*

LAST QUARTER OF THE FOURTEENTH CENTURY

From *The Works of Francesco Landini*, ed. Leo Schrade, Polyphonic Music of the Fourteenth Century 4 (Monaco: Éditions de l'Oiseau-Lyre, 1958), 144–45. © Hänssler Verlag, D-71087 Holzgerlingen. Used by permission.

| A | 1 | Non avrà ma' pietà questa mia donna, | She will never have mercy, this lady of mine, |
|---|---|---|---|
|   |   | Se tu non faj, amore, | if you do not see to it, Love, |
|   |   | Ch'ella sie certa del mio grande ardore. | that she is certain of my great ardor. |
| b | 2 | S'ella sapesse quanta pena i' porto | If she knew how much pain I bear— |
|   |   | Per onestà celata nella mente | for honesty's sake concealed in my mind— |
| b | 3 | Sol per la sua bellecça, che conforto | only for her beauty, other than which |
|   |   | D'altro non prende l'anima dolente, | nothing gives comfort to a grieving soul, |
| a | 4 | Forse da lej sarebbono in me spente | perhaps by her would be extinguished in me |
|   |   | Le fiamme che la pare | the flames which seem to arouse in |
|   |   | Di giorno in giorno acrescono 'l dolore. | me from day to day more pain. |
| A | 1 | Non avrà ma' pietà questa mia donna, | She will never have mercy, this lady of mine, |
|   |   | Se tu non faj, amore, | if you do not see to it, Love, |
|   |   | Ch'ella sie certa del mio grande ardore. | that she is certain of my great ardor. |

—B. D'Alessio Donati

During the thirteenth and early fourteenth centuries, ballate (sing. *ballata*, from *ballare*, to dance) were associated with dancing, but the polyphonic ballate of the late fourteenth century were stylized works for elite audiences, meant to be sung and listened to for their own sakes. Landini was the leading ballata composer, with about 140 to his credit. His *Non avrà ma' pietà* was well known, with copies in the Squarcialupi Codex and several other northern Italian manuscripts, and is typical of the form and of Landini's style.

A three-line refrain called the *ripresa* (A, measures 1–29) is sung both before and after a seven-line stanza. The first two pairs of lines in the stanza, which were called *piedi*, have their own musical phrase (b, measures 30–57), and the last three lines, the *volta*, use the same music as the refrain (a). The first of the two piedi has an open (*verto*) ending on A, the second a closed (*chiuso*) ending on G, the same step-down relationship from internal to final cadence that we saw in NAWM 26 and 27. The form resembles that of a virelai (see NAWM 27).

Like Machaut's chansons, Landini's ballate are built around a two-voice framework comprising the cantus and the tenor. These two voices form cadences to mark the end of each line of poetry (as at measures 11, 17, and 29) and also occasionally within lines. At most of these cadences the upper voice decorates its rising stepwise motion by first descending a step and then skipping up a third, sometimes called an "under-third cadence" (or "Landini cadence"), though it is common in French as well as Italian music). The contratenor fills out the counterpoint and adds rhythmic interest. As in the music of Vitry, Machaut, and Ciconia (see NAWM 24–27)—but not Landini's Italian predecessors—most of the cadences are double-leading-tone cadences, either notated or created through the *musica ficta* expected from the performers.

Like Machaut, Landini used frequent syncopation, varied rhythms, and many sonorities containing thirds and sixths, which gave this ballata its sweetness and charm. Elements that differentiate Landini's style from Machaut's include melismas on the first and penultimate syllables of each line, with clear, almost syllabic text-setting elsewhere; less angular contratenors; and smoother, more stepwise and rhythmically regular melodies in both cantus and tenor.

As in French chansons, the tenor and contratenor are untexted. Modern performers often play those lines on instruments, but it is more likely that all three parts were sung, as on the accompanying recording.

# 31   *Alleluia: A newë work*

*Carol*

FIRST HALF OF THE FIFTEENTH CENTURY

From Oxford, Bodleian Library, MS Arch. Selden b. 26, ff. 21v–22. Edition from *Mediaeval Carols*, ed. John Stevens, Musica Britannica 4 (London: Stainer and Bell, 1952), 22–23. © 1952, 1958 by The Musica Britannica Trust. Reproduction by permission of Stainer & Bell, Ltd. English words modernized in spelling but not in form; modern equivalents given in brackets.

Alleluia, alleluia, alleluia.

1. A newë [new] work is come on hond [hand],
Through might and grace of Goddës sond
 [God's messenger],
To save the lost of every lond [land],
 Alleluia, alleluia,
For now is free that erst [once] was bond [in
 bondage];
We mow [may] well sing alleluia.

2. By Gabriel begun it was:
Right as the sun shone through the glass
Jesu Christ conceivëd was,
 Alleluia, alleluia,
Of Mary mother, full of grace;
Now sing we here alleluia.

3. Now is fulfilled the prophecy
Of David and of Jeremy [Jeremiah],
And also of Isaie [Isaiah],
 Alleluia, alleluia,
Sing we therefore both loud and high:
Alleluia, alleluia.

4. Simeon on his armës right
Clippëd Jesu full of might
And said unto that barne [child] so bright,
 Alleluia, alleluia;
I see my Savïour in sight;
And sung therewith alleluia.

5. Then he said, withoutë lece [without untruth]:
Lord, thou seeth thy servant in peace,
For now I have that I ever chece [choose],
 Alleluia, alleluia.
All ourë joyës [our joys] to increase
There saintës singeth alleluia.

6. Alleluia, this sweetë song,
Out of a greenë branch it sprong [sprang].
God send us the life that lasteth long!
 Alleluia, alleluia.
Now joy and bliss be them among
That thus can sing alleluia.

This anonymous carol survives only in a manuscript containing thirty-two carols that was copied about 1450 and is now at Oxford University. Like all fifteenth-century English carols, this one consists of a number of stanzas, each sung to the same music in alternation with a *burden,* or refrain. The text mixes the Latin "Alleluia" with an English poem about the incarnation of Jesus, a frequent theme of carols.

As in several other carols, there are two burdens, one for two voices and the other, a variation of the first, for three voices. Both are sung at the outset, and either both or just the second are repeated after each verse. In the first burden, the two parts move mostly in parallel thirds or sixths, sometimes crossing, and close on an octave or unison at the end of each phrase. In the second burden, the three voices move mostly in parallel $^6_3$ sonorities: the middle voice presents a variant of the top melody from the first burden, the upper voice parallels it a fourth above (with some decoration), and the bottom voice moves mostly a third below the middle voice, and thus a sixth below the top voice. At cadences and some other points, the voices move out from parallel thirds and sixths to fifths and octaves (see measures 15–16 and 17–19 for examples). These streams of $^6_3$ sonorities are typical of English polyphony, which featured longer successions of parallel thirds and sixths unmediated by perfect consonances than did Continental polyphony before the 1420s. The predominance of thirds and sixths, minimal presence of dissonance, regular phrasing, and primarily homorhythmic textures exemplified by this carol gave English music its distinctive "sweet" sound and exercised a profound influence on Continental composers.

Streams of imperfect consonances also appear in the music for the stanzas, marked *verse.* In most carols, the stanzas are set in free two-part counterpoint. This carol is unusual in its alternation among monophonic, three-part, and two-part textures. The first two lines of each stanza are each sung first in unison, and then in three-part, mostly parallel polyphony. The three-part sections strongly resemble the improvised tradition of English *faburden,* in which a chant melody appears in the middle voice, paralleled a fourth above and a third below, with a fifth below to mark the beginnings and ends of phrases. (Compare the related practice of *fauxbourdon* in NAWM 35, which differs somewhat in procedure but sounds very similar and was probably derived from faburden.) The rest of the stanza alternates unison, two-part, and three-part writing, with a brief recollection of the burden at the word "alleluia."

In the manuscript, the text is printed beneath the lowest part, but all parts are to sing the text together. Although the editor has marked the three-part sections "chorus," such carols were probably sung by one singer on each part, as in most polyphony of the time. The recording accompanying this anthology includes only one verse, followed by the second burden.

# JOHN DUNSTABLE (CA. 1390–1453)

## Quam pulchra es

*Motet or cantilena*

FIRST HALF OF THE FIFTEENTH CENTURY

| | |
|---|---|
| Quam pulchra es et quam decora, | How beautiful you are, and how graceful, |
| carissima in deliciis. | dearest one, my delight. |
| Statura tua assimilata est palme, | Your stature is like a palm tree, |
| et ubera tua botris. | and your breasts like clusters of grapes. |
| Caput tuum ut Carmelus, | Your head is like Carmel; |
| collum tuum sicut turris eburnea. | your neck is like an ivory tower. |
| Veni, dilecte mi, | Come, my beloved, |
| egrediamur in agrum, | let us go out into the fields, |
| et videamus si flores fructus parturierunt | and let us see if the grape blossoms have borne fruit |
| si floruerunt mala Punica. | and the pomegranates are in bloom. |
| Ibi dabo tibi ubera mea. | There I will give you my breasts. |
| Alleluia. | Alleluia. |

—ADAPTED FROM THE SONG OF SOLOMON 7:4–12

Dunstable wrote numerous three-part settings of liturgical or biblical texts. Most of them are based on chant melodies, but this antiphon on a biblical text is freely composed. It was written before 1430 and appears in a manuscript from about that time.

Unlike earlier motets, there is no strong difference in character between the tenor (the lowest voice) and the other voices. All are similar in style and importance, and most often they move and declaim the text together. The musical texture of the piece—largely homophonic with short melismas at the ends of both main sections (measures 26–29 and 55–58)—resembles that of a conductus or its English relative, the cantilena.

Unfettered by a cantus firmus or an isorhythmic scheme, Dunstable freely determined the form of the music, guided only by the text. He divided the piece into two sections, roughly equal in length. The first, measures 1–30, comprises abbreviated versions of verses 6, 7, 5, and 4 of Chapter 7 from The Song of Solomon; the second, beginning at "Veni," draws on verses 11–12, with an added "alleluia." The strongest cadences delineate the ends of Bible verses (measures 9, 18, 22, 29, 38, and 54), and others mark internal phrases.

In addition to the musical form being determined by the text, many musical phrases are molded to the rhythm of the words—for example, in the declamation of "statura tua assimilata est," "mala Punica," and "ibi dabo tibi." Although most of the text-setting is syllabic, many cadences feature brief melismas. The final word in both sections is set off by a cadence, particularly extensive melismas, and livelier rhythm.

The frequent use of melodic thirds and the occasional outlining of a triad (as in the middle voice in measures 9–11 or the top voice in measures 43, 46, and 55–56) give Dunstable's melodies a character rather different from fourteenth-century melodies by Machaut or Landini. The counterpoint is also quite different. Almost every vertical sonority is consonant, and thirds and sixths are prominent, both typical traits of English music at the time. Some passages feature the parallel $^6_3$ sonorities common in English polyphony, especially at cadences (as in measures 12–15 and 52–54), but most phrases offer much greater variety of sonority. Variety is also evident in the rhythm: despite the relative rhythmic simplicity, no two successive measures have the same rhythmic pattern.

The piece projects a strong tonal center of C, which is the opening note, the most frequent cadential note, and the root of the final open-fifth-octave sonority. It is not "in C major," but in a mode on C, later named Ionian by Glareanus. The cadences to C are not tonic-dominant cadences, but typical modal cadences of the time: D–F–B to C–G–C, as in measures 8–9, sometimes decorated with the under-third cadence, as at the end. Other cadences are on D, F, and G, all important notes in the Ionian mode.

All of these traits—relative equality of voices, free structure based on the text, sensitivity to text declamation, pervasive consonance, variety in sonority and rhythm, and strong tonal center—became characteristic of music in the fifteenth and sixteenth centuries.

Like other polyphony of the time, this was probably performed by one singer per part, unaccompanied, as on the recording accompanying this anthology. Note the change of tempo at the words "et videamus," increasing the pace by the proportion of three new beats in the time of two former ones.

# Binchois (Gilles de Bins) (ca. 1400–1460)

*De plus en plus*

*Rondeau*

CA. 1425

From *Die Chansons von Gilles Binchois*, ed. Wolfgang Rehm, Musikalische Denkmäler 2 (Mainz: B. Schott's Söhne, 1957). Reproduced by permission of European American Music Distributors.

| A | 1 | De plus en plus se renouvelle | More and more renews again, |
|---|---|---|---|
|  | 2 | Ma doulce dame gente et belle, | my sweet lady, noble and fair, |
|  | 3 | Ma voulonté de vous veir. | my wish to see you. |
| B | 4 | Ce me fait le tres grant désir | It gives me the very great desire |
|  | 5 | Que j'ai de vous oir nouvelle. | I have to hear news of you. |
| a | 6 | Ne cuidiés pas que je recelle, | Do not heed that I hold back, |
|  | 7 | Comme a tous jours vous este celle | for always you are the one |
|  | 8 | Que je veul de tout obeir. | whom I want to follow in every way. |
| A | 9 | De plus en plus se renouvelle | More and more renews again, |
|  | 10 | Ma doulce dame gente et belle, | my sweet lady, noble and fair, |
|  | 11 | Ma voulonté de vous veir. | my wish to see you. |
| a | 12 | Hélas, se vous m'estiés cruelle | Alas, if you were cruel to me, |
|  | 13 | J'auvoie au cuer angoisse telle | I would have such anguish in my heart |
|  | 14 | Que je voudroye bien mourir, | that I would want to die. |
| b | 15 | Mais ce seroit sans déservir, | But this would do you no wrong, |
|  | 16 | En soustenant vostre querelle. | while supporting your cause. |
| A | 17 | De plus en plus se renouvelle | More and more renews again, |
|  | 18 | Ma doulce dame gente et belle, | my sweet lady, noble and fair, |
|  | 19 | Ma voulonté de vous veir. | my wish to see you. |
| B | 20 | Ce me fait le tres grant désir | It gives me the very great desire |
|  | 21 | Que j'ai de vous oir nouvelle. | I have to hear news of you. |

Binchois composed *De plus en plus* around 1425. At the time, he was probably in the service of William Pole, earl of Suffolk, one of the English noblemen assisting in the occupation of northern France. The upbeat opening, the relatively full harmony, the many harmonic thirds and sixths, and the great number of melodic thirds and triadic figures probably reflect the influence of English music. The appearance of this piece in a manuscript copied in Italy around 1430 demonstrates that Binchois's music was widely disseminated, even though he spent most of his career in and around the Burgundian court.

The text is a love poem in the tradition of courtly love, or *fine amour*. The poetic form is a rondeau, like Machaut's *Rose, liz* (NAWM 26), but the first part of the refrain (A) consists of three lines and the second part (B) of two (rather than two lines and one line respectively, as in the Machaut). The rhyme scheme is different as well. The refrain contains all of the music, which is also set to the words of the couplets (a and b). The full refrain text with its music is heard only at the beginning and the end.

The quickly moving cantus (the topmost melody) indulges in runs, dotted figures, and syncopations. The slower-moving tenor (the middle voice) provides a foundation, harmonizing the cantus mostly in thirds and sixths, and resolving to octaves at cadences. The contratenor (the bottom voice in the score, though its melody crosses both above and below that of the tenor) enlivens the rhythm and fills in the harmony, often supplying the third note in a triad.

In this chanson, Binchois used imperfect tempus and major prolation, tran-scribed as two dotted quarters per measure (compare NAWM 24). Each measure is usually subdivided into two groups of three eighth notes, but often, particular-ly in the tenor, three quarter notes appear instead, producing a hemiola effect.

The music fits the shape and structure of the poem. The cantus declaims the text in a mostly syllabic setting with melismas at cadences. Each line of poetry occupies four measures of music, producing a proportion of 3:2 between the two musical sections. A cadence marks the end of each poetic line, with the tenor-cantus pair moving from a sixth to an octave or from a third to a unison. The cadential motion to the octave from the sixth (changed to major when necessary by *musica ficta*) is usually decorated in the cantus with the third below the last note of the cadence. In most of the cadences, syncopation causes a dissonance in the upper voice before the penultimate note, a type of dissonance later called a *suspension*.

Binchois treated the end of the A section (measure 12) differently from the other cadences. After tenor and cantus cadence on G (measure 11), the tenor and contratenor close on D with F♯ in the cantus. The major third leaves us in sus-pense, intensified by a rest, as we anticipate the second section of the music. The end of the B section is more conventional, with a descending series of third-sixth sonorities that resolve to a fifth and an octave. Here, the only surprise is the cadential note D; earlier cadences had suggested C or G as the likely final.

Such polyphonic chansons were probably sung by three unaccompanied voic-es, as in the recording that accompanies this anthology. Alternatively, the two lower lines could be played by instruments.

# GUILLAUME DU FAY (CA. 1397–1474)

*Resvellies vous*

*Ballade*

1423

From Guillaume Dufay, *Opera omnia*, ed. Heinrich Besseler, vol. 6 (American Institute of Musicology, 1964), 25–26. © Hänssler Verlag, D-71087 Holzgerlingen. Used by permission of A-R Editions.

grant hon - neur et no - ble sei - gnou - ri - e;

Ce vous con - vient ung chas - cum fai - re fe - ste, Pour bien grig -

nier la bel - le com-pagny - e; Char - le gen - til,

Char - le gen - til,

Char - le gen - til,

C

c'on dit de Ma - le-tes -

-te.

| | |
|---|---|
| Resvellies vous et faites chiere lye | Awake and be merry, |
| Tout amoureux qui gentilesse ames | all lovers who love gentleness; |
| Esbates vous, fuyes merancolye, | frolic and flee melancholy. |
| De bien servir point ne soyes hodés | Tire not of serving yourself well, |
| Car au jour d'ui sera li espousés, | for today will be the nuptials, |
| Par grant honneur et noble seignourie; | with great honor and noble lordship, |
| Ce vous convient ung chascum faire feste, | and it behooves you, everyone, to celebrate |
| Pour bien grignier la belle compagnye; | and join the happy company. |
| Charle gentil, c'on dit de Maleteste. | Noble Charles, who is named Malatesta. |
| | |
| Il a dame belle et bonne choysie, | He has chosen a lady, fair and good, |
| Dont il sera grandement honnourés; | by whom he will be greatly honored, |
| Car elle vient de tres noble lignie | for she comes from a very noble lineage |
| Et de barons qui sont mult renommés. | of barons who are much renowned. |
| Son propre nom est Victoire clamés; | Her name is Victoria, |
| De la colonne vient sa progenie. | and she descends from the Colonnas. |
| C'est bien rayson qu'a vascule requeste | Thus it is right that his appeal be heard |
| De cette dame mainne bonne vie. | to live honestly with this lady. |
| Charle gentil, c'on dit de Maleteste. | Noble Charles, who is named Malatesta. |

"Awake and be merry," this ballade tells lovers. Guillaume Du Fay composed it in 1423 for the marriage of Carlo Malatesta and Vittoria Colonna, niece of Pope Martin V. At the time, Du Fay was serving the Malatestas, the ruling family of Rimini and Pesaro. The acclamation "noble Charles," addressed to the bridegroom, is set in long notes with fermatas, which illustrates a traditional French technique for emphasizing a person's name. Following that statement, the family name Malatesta is set to a spree of rapid triplets in the cantus. Perhaps the bouncy triplet rhythm at the line "Pour bien grignier la belle compagnye" (and join the happy company) is also a reflection of the text.

The standard aab musical form of the ballade repeats for each stanza. The last line of each stanza is a refrain (measures 50–67). The florid treatment at the end of each line of the poem follows the refined ballade tradition. In the a section and refrain, Du Fay employed imperfect tempus with major prolation, equivalent to $\frac{6}{8}$ (the breve, here transcribed as a dotted half-note, is divided into two parts, each containing three minims or eighth notes). In the b section, he used perfect tempus with minor prolation, equivalent to $\frac{3}{4}$ (the breve is divided in three semibreves, each containing two minims). Hemiolas and syncopations abound throughout. Both the a section and the refrain end with the same closing passage, creating a musical rhyme. An unusual feature of this chanson is the imitation between the cantus (top voice) and the tenor at measures 7–10, briefly involving the contratenor as well at measures 15–19 and 60–64.

*Resvellies vous* combines elements of three main traditions of the fourteenth century: from the French Ars Nova, the ballade form and syncopations; from the Ars Subtilior, the rapid, complex rhythmic passages; from the Italian Trecento, the smooth vocal melodies, the syllabic declamation of some passages, and the change of meter; and from all three traditions, the cantus-tenor framework and the elaborate melismas at the ends of lines of poetry. These are signs of Du Fay's characteristic blending of traits from diverse styles.

The melismatic passages in the cantus, with their rapid runs and triplet figures, may seem more suited to instrumental than vocal performance, yet they can be performed convincingly by a trained singer. The lower parts are mostly untexted and could have been sung or played on instruments. However, in the original sources, all three parts have text at the words "Charle gentil" (noble Charles) in the refrain, making it clear that Du Fay intended for all three performers to sing the name of the patron for whose wedding the piece was written. The accompanying recording presents only the first verse of the ballade, with instruments on the lower parts and on several of the melismas in the cantus.

# GUILLAUME DU FAY (CA. 1397–1474)

*Conditor alme siderum*

*Hymn in fauxbourdon style*

CA. 1430

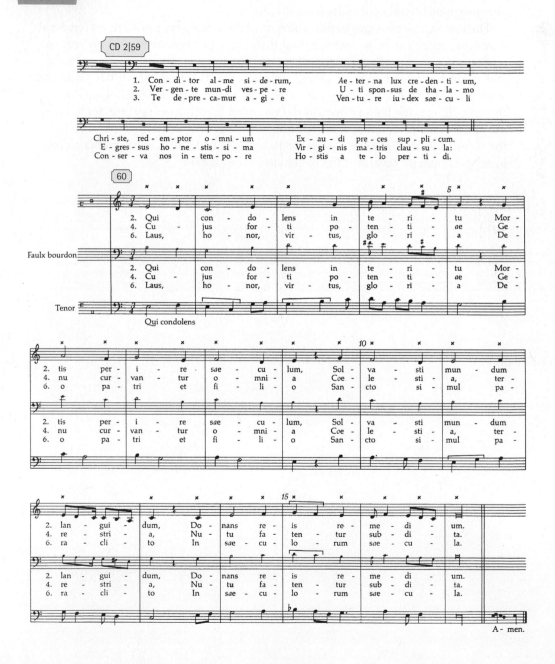

From Guillaume Dufay, *Opera omnia*, ed. Heinrich Besseler, vol. 5 (American Institute of Musicology, 1966), 39. © Hänssler Verlag, D-71087 Holzgerlingen. Used by permission of A-R Editions.

Conditor alme siderum,
Aeterna lux credentium,
Christe redemptor omnium
Exaudi preces supplicum.

Bountiful creator of the stars,
eternal light of believers,
Christ, redeemer of all,
hear the prayers of the supplicants.

Qui condolens interitu
Mortis perire saeculum,
Solvasti mundum languidum,
Donans reis remedium:

You who suffer the ruin
of death, the perishing of the race,
who saved the sick world,
bringing the healing balm.

Vergente mundi vespere
Uti sponsus de thalamo,
Egressus honestissima
Virginis matris clausula.

As the world turns toward evening,
the bridegroom from his chamber
issues forth from the most chaste
cloister of the Virgin mother.

Cujus forti potentiae
Genu curvantur omnia
Coelestia, terrestria,
Nutu fatentur subdita.

You, before whose mighty power
all bend their knees,
celestial, terrestrial,
confessing subjection to his command.

Te deprecamur agie
Venture judex saeculi
Conserva nos in tempore
Hostis a telo perfidi.

We entreat you, holy
judge of the days to come,
save us in time
from the weapons of the perfidious.

Laus, honor, virtus, gloria
Deo patri, et filio,
Sancto simul paraclito
in saeculorum saecula.

Praise, honor, virtue, glory
to God the Father, and Son,
and also to the Holy Protector,
time everlasting.

During the late Middle Ages and Renaissance, it was a frequent custom for a chorus and soloists to sing alternate stanzas when performing a plainchant hymn. The chorus always sang the monophonic chant, but the soloists might have sung polyphony, either improvised or composed. Du Fay and other composers wrote numerous polyphonic settings for the even-numbered stanzas of hymns, which were meant to be performed by soloists, but the odd-numbered stanzas continued to be sung by the choir to monophonic chants.

This hymn setting is in the style of fauxbourdon, a notational practice that apparently derived from the improvised English tradition of faburden (see discussion for NAWM 31). Du Fay placed the chant, slightly decorated, in the cantus (the x's mark the notes of the chant). He wrote a tenor part that began an octave lower and then moved mostly in sixths against the chant, expanding to an octave at cadences. A third voice, not written down (but often indicated in the music by the word "faulxbourdon"), could be sung at the interval of a perfect fourth below the cantus, producing a succession of $\frac{6}{3}$ sonorities, except where the bottom voice moved out to an octave. In this edition, that voice is transcribed in small notes. As long as the outer voices form a harmonic sixth or octave, the middle voice is consonant with both, but there are some passing dissonances where the outer voices contract to a fifth (as on the last eighth note of measures 2, 3, and 4). Fauxbourdon's emphasis on consonant sonorities, especially thirds and sixths, became characteristic of Renaissance music, even though its strict parallelism eventually came to sound archaic.

Although we do not know whether Gregorian chant hymns were sung in a particular rhythm (listen to the recording of NAWM 4b), by the fifteenth century musicians often regularized the performance of hymns into a succession of longs and breves (respectively, noteheads with and without stems). In Du Fay's setting, this is reflected by the alternation of half and quarter notes in triple meter. In a full performance of this hymn, the chant would be sung for each odd-numbered verse and the polyphony for each even-numbered verse. The accompanying recording includes just the first two verses, to give an example of each.

# Guillaume Du Fay (CA. 1397–1474)

*Se la face ay pale*       *Missa Se la face ay pale*: Gloria

*Ballade*       *Cantus-firmus mass*

1430s       CA. 1450s

(a) *Se la face ay pale*

From Guillaume Dufay, *Opera omnia,* ed. Heinrich Besseler, vol. 6 (American Institute of Musicology, 1964), 36. © Hänssler Verlag, D-71087 Holzgerlingen. Used by permission of A-R Editions.

| | |
|---|---|
| Se la face ay pale, | If my face is pale, |
| La cause est amer, | the cause is love, |
| C'est la principale, | that is the principal reason, |
| Et tant m'est amer | and for me it is so bitter |
| Amer, qu'en la mer | to love, that in the sea |
| Me voudroye voir; | I would like to throw myself; |
| Or, scet bien de voir | then, seeing this, she would know well, |
| La belle a qui suis | the fair lady to whom I belong, |
| Que nul bien avoir | that to have any happiness |
|    Sans elle ne puis. |    without her I am not able. |
| | |
| Se ay pesante malle | If I have a heavy load |
| De dueil a porter, | of grief to bear, |
| Ceste amour est male | [it is because] this love is difficult |
| Pour moy de porter; | for me to endure; |
| Car soy deporter | because to enjoy oneself |
| Ne veult devouloir, | she does not want to allow, |
| Fors qu'a son vouloir | so that her own will |
| Obeisse, et puis | one must obey, and since |
| Qu'elle a tel pooir, | she has such power, |
|    Sans elle ne puis. |    without her I am not able. |
| | |
| C'est la plus reale | She is the most regal woman |
| Qu'on puist regarder, | that one could ever see. |
| De s'amour leiale | From loyal love for her |
| Ne me puis guarder, | I cannot keep myself. |
| Fol sui de agarder | Foolish am I for looking at her |
| Ne faire devoir | and for not wanting |
| D'amours recevoir | to receive love |
| Fors d'elle, je cuij; | from anyone but her, I think; |
| Se ne veil douloir, | if I want not to be sad, |
|    Sans elle ne puis. |    without her I am not able. |

(b) *Missa Se la face ay pale*: Gloria

From Guillaume Dufay, *Opera omnia,* ed. Heinrich Besseler, vol. 3 (American Institute of Musicology, 1964), 4–13. © Hänssler Verlag, D-71087 Holzgerlingen. Used by permission of A-R Editions.

64   47

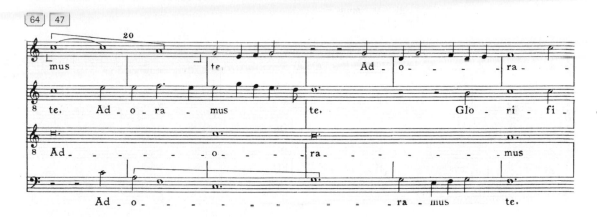

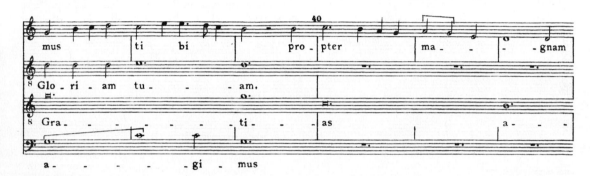

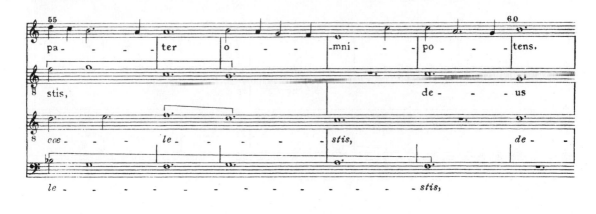

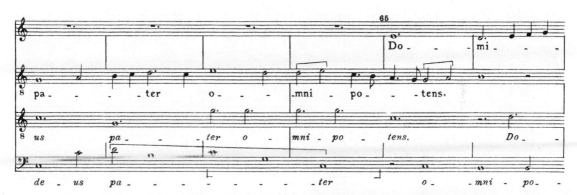

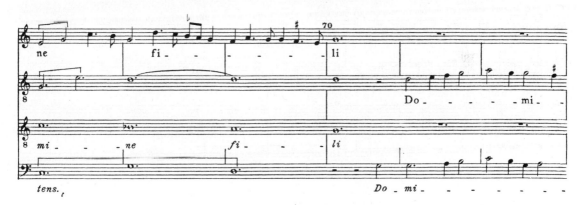

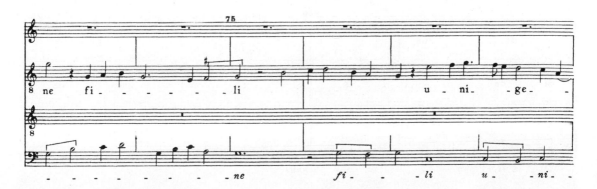

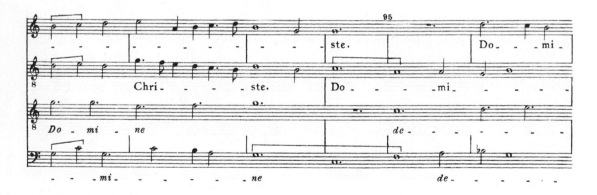

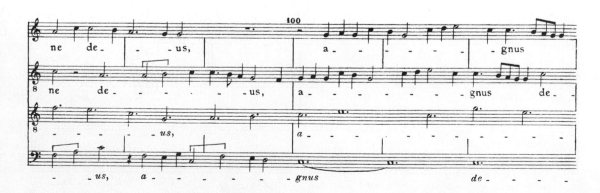

67  50

68  51

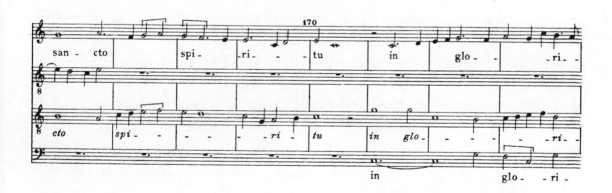

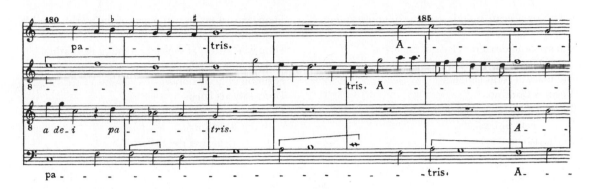

69   52

Gloria in excelsis Deo
Et in terra pax hominibus bonae voluntatis.
Laudamus te. Benedicimus te. Adoramus te.
    Glorificamus te.
Gratias agimus tibi propter magnam gloriam tuam.
Domine Deus, Rex caelestis,
Deus Pater omnipotens.
Domine Fili unigenite Jesu Christe.
Domine Deus, Agnus Dei, Filius Patris,
Qui tollis peccata mundi, miserere nobis.

Glory be to God on high.
And on earth peace to men of good will.
We praise thee, we bless thee, we adore thee, we
    glorify thee.
We give thee thanks for thy great glory.
O Lord God, King of heaven,
God the Father Almighty.
O Lord, the only begotten Son, Jesus Christ.
O Lord God, Lamb of God, Son of the Father.
Thou who takest away the sins of the world, have
    mercy on us.

| | |
|---|---|
| Qui tollis peccata mundi, suscipe deprecationem nostram. | Thou who takest away the sins of the world, receive our prayer. |
| Qui sedes ad dexteram Patris, miserere nobis. | Thou who sittest at the right hand of the Father, have mercy on us. |
| Quoniam tu solus sanctus. | For thou only art holy, |
| Tu solus Dominus. | Thou only art Lord. |
| Tu solus Altissimus, Jesu Christe. | Thou only art most high, O Jesus Christ, |
| Cum Sancto Spiritu, | With the Holy Spirit, |
| In Gloria Dei Patris. Amen. | In the glory of God the Father. Amen. |

Du Fay composed *Se la face ay pale* during the 1430s while he was serving as master of the chapel at the court of the duke of Savoy. He may have written it for the duchess, Anne de Lusignan. In comparison with his earlier ballade *Resvellies vous* (NAWM 34), this one shows many changes in Du Fay's style, including his blending of national characteristics. Instead of following the fixed form of the fourteenth-century ballade (aab), he composed the music freely to suit each line of text. Only the use of three stanzas, the closing refrain line, and the final melisma are retained from the ballade tradition. Other French characteristics include frequent syncopation and an angular contratenor line with many large leaps. English influence is demonstrated in the pervasive consonance with only a few ornamental dissonances, the prevalence of thirds and sixths, the relatively short and well-articulated phrases, the relative equality between cantus and tenor melodies, and the triadic figures that suffuse the final melisma. Both English and Italian traits are evident in the smooth, mostly stepwise melodies and in the primarily syllabic treatment of the text.

In the 1450s, Du Fay was back at the court of Savoy after several years in Cambrai. He may have written *Missa Se la face ay pale* for a special occasion at court during that time, for he used the tenor of his earlier ballade as a cantus firmus, perhaps to honor his patrons.

The structure of the mass is carefully designed. Du Fay applied mensural proportions to multiply the durations of the ballade tenor by varying amounts. As a result, the cantus firmus is heard at different speeds in various movements and sections. In the Kyrie, Sanctus, and Agnus Dei, the duration of each note of the ballade tenor is doubled. In the Gloria and in the Credo, the cantus firmus is heard in the tenor three times, first at triple the normal durations, then at double the durations, and finally at its original pace.

Because of the way the editor has transcribed the original notation, these proportions may be easier to hear than to see, but they can be easily understood in terms of beats rather than note values. In the entire ballade and in the Gloria at measures 119–58, the beat is transcribed as a quarter note; elsewhere in the Gloria, the beat is rendered as a half note. Thus in the first section of the Gloria (measures 1–118), each beat of the original ballade tenor is now three beats long, corresponding to a full measure of triple time in the other voices. In the second section, at "Qui tollis" (measures 119–58), each beat of the original chanson tenor is now two beats long, corresponding to a measure of duple time in the other voices. Finally, in the third section, at "Cum sancto spiritu" (measures 159–98), the tenor moves at its original pace, and the beats and measures in all four voices correspond equally.

The form of this Gloria, delineated by the calculated restatement of the tune, is further marked by the inclusion of a duet preceding each entrance of the cantus firmus. Additionally, a briefer duet divides the cantus firmus into two halves in each section. Each of the Gloria's three sections has the same internal proportions, which are also of interest. They are easiest to see in the last section: six measures of duet without the tenor, eighteen measures with the tenor, three measures of rest in the tenor, and twelve final measures of tenor (stopping the count where the tenor reaches its last note). These proportions of 6:18:3:12, or 2:6:1:4, feature numbers whose ratios form those of the perfect fifth (3:2) and octave (2:1), the same ratios represented in the proportional scheme of the whole movement (3:2:1). Moreover, the ratio of the first segment of duet and tenor melody (measures 159–82) to the second (measures 183–97)—2+6 to 1+4, or 8 to 5—approximates the Golden Section, a ratio beloved of mathematicians, architects, and composers, especially Du Fay. This intricate numerical structure shows the enduring influence of the links between music and number that were promulgated by theorists from Pythagoras through Boethius and beyond.

More evident to the listener than these proportions is the way that the source ballade gradually emerges from obscurity to recognizability. Although the tenor melody is present from the outset, it only becomes easy to recognize during the final statement, when it is included with its original durations. Then, at the end, the tenor is joined by other borrowings from the original ballade. At measures 192–96 of the Gloria, Du Fay borrowed material from all three voices of the final melisma of the ballade (measures 25–29), sometimes exactly and otherwise in paraphrase. Such borrowings from multiple voices of the model occur frequently in masses whose cantus firmus is drawn from a polyphonic work.

Each voice of the mass is a distinct layer with its own melodic and rhythmic logic and function. The tenor provides the scaffolding, around which everything else is coordinated. The bassus, the lowest voice, joins with the tenor to provide the harmonic foundation, often providing the lowest note at cadences. The top two voices, the superius and the contratenor altus, are the most active, moving in smooth, mostly stepwise lines varied with skips and leaps, and occasionally echoing each other (see measures 1–4 and 14–15 for brief examples). The rhythmic diversity the top voices provide, each measure different from the last, is typical of Du Fay and was part of the variety that was prized by commentators at the time. Despite the diverse roles the voices play, they are more equal than in earlier music, with sixth-to-octave cadences forming between superius and altus (such as measures 12–13), altus and bassus (measures 27–28), tenor and bassus (measures 33–34), and superius and bassus (measures 36–37), as well as the usual cadences between superius and tenor.

Besides the use of the ballade tenor throughout the mass, another feature that links each movement is the use of a *head-motive*, a musical idea that appears at the beginning of every movement, thereby establishing a relationship between the sections. Each movement of the mass begins in the superius with a variant of the motive that in the Gloria is set to the words "Et in terra pax." The motive is also alluded to within movements, as in the Gloria at measures 40, 88, 119, 165, and 184. The movements of the mass are also linked because all are in the same mode. Although the ballade is clearly centered on C and many of the internal cadences in the mass movement also close on C, Du Fay centered the mass on F. With the tune in the tenor, he was able to close the first and final sections of the Gloria on F in bassus and superius (measures 118 and 198), but the middle section on C (measure 158).

Consonance and dissonance are carefully controlled. The strongest dissonances are suspensions, all properly resolved (for example, at measures 33, 36, 72, and 81), while other dissonances, mainly between beats, pass quickly. Du Fay obviously worked to include as many thirds and sixths as possible, which produced many triads (to use modern terminology) on the strong beats.

According to long-standing liturgical tradition, the opening words of the Gloria, "Gloria in excelcis Deo" (Glory be to God on high), are always sung by the priest. For this reason, Renaissance composers never included these words in their settings of the Gloria. In all likelihood, Du Fay's mass would have been sung by four soloists, though in modern times it is often performed by choirs. The long tones of the tenor in isorhythmic movements such as this one have prompted many modern performers to use instruments on the tenor and sometimes on the bassus as well, either instead of or doubling the singers. However, the historical evidence for this practice is uncertain.

# Jean de Ockeghem (ca. 1420–1497)

## Missa De plus en plus: Agnus Dei

*Cantus-firmus mass*

SECOND HALF OF THE FIFTEENTH CENTURY

37

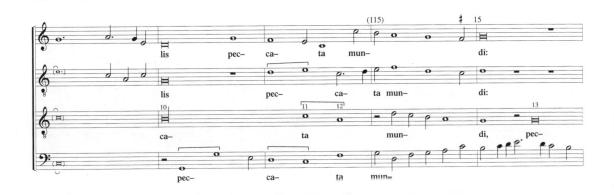

From Johannes Ockeghem, *Masses and Mass Sections*, vol. 2, *Masses Based on Secular Settings*, ed. Jaap van Benthem (Utrecht: Koninklijke Vereniging voor Nederlandse Muziekgeschiedenis, 1994–2000), 31–35. Used by permission of the Royal Society for Music History of the Netherlands.

Go to Agnus 2

Return
to Agnus 1
and 2nd
ending

Agnus Dei, qui tollis peccata mundi: miserere
    nobis.
Agnus Dei, qui tollis peccata mundi: miserere
    nobis.
Agnus Dei, qui tollis peccata mundi: dona nobis
    pacem.

Lamb of God, who takest away the sins of the world:
    have mercy on us.
Lamb of God, who takest away the sins of the world:
    have mercy on us.
Lamb of God, who takest away the sins of the world:
    give us peace.

It is not known when or for what occasion Jean de Ockeghem wrote *Missa De plus
en plus.* He may have chosen Binchois's chanson *De plus en plus* (NAWM 33) as a

model in order to pay tribute to the older composer, with whom he may have studied and upon whose death he wrote the lament *Mort tu as navré.*

Ockeghem used the tenor of Binchois's chanson as a cantus firmus in the tenor of his mass. Yet he freely changed the rhythm and at times interpolated decorative passages between the notes of the original tenor. To facilitate comparison of these works, the editor of this edition added numbers above the tenor line to indicate the notes drawn from Binchois's model according to their position in the original chanson tenor (repeated notes in the latter are omitted in the numbering). The chanson tenor is presented twice in full with some further repetition—first in Agnus Dei 1 (notes 1–28) and Agnus Dei 2 (notes 29–52, plus notes 1–8 again), then again in the reprise of Agnus Dei 1 with a new closing passage marked here as a second ending (notes 1–17, 1–52, and 1–8). In this closing passage (measures 120–37), there are very few interpolated notes, making the chanson tenor melody more apparent than in other sections of the work. However, the rhythmic differences from the original render the borrowing less easy to hear than the direct quotation of both melody and rhythm at the end of Du Fay's *Missa Se la face ay pale* (NAWM 36b).

Several cadences in the mass fall at the ends of the chanson's phrases, as on notes 8, 17, and 34 (measures 7, 18, and 56 of the mass, corresponding to cadences in measures 4, 8, and 14 of the chanson). However, Ockeghem manipulated the cantus firmus so that the final cadences for each section strongly project the modal center of G. According to theorists of the time, the mode of a polyphonic piece was defined by the modes of the tenor and cantus. Here, the cantus and tenor parts both close on G and move in the range from a fifth below G to a fifth or sixth above it, establishing the mode of the piece as mode 8, with a final of G and a tenor of C. At the end of the first Agnus Dei (measures 29–30), the tenor and cantus close on C, the modal tenor. To achieve this, Ockeghem ended the section on note 28 (C) from the chanson tenor—the first note of the B section of Binchois's rondeau—rather than note 27 (D), the cadence note of Binchois's A section. Since the last note of the chanson tenor (note 52) is D rather than G, Ockeghem repeated the first eight notes of the chanson tenor at the end of the second and third statements of Agnus Dei (measures 87–101 and 134–37) in order to close on G. Through these manipulations, as well as the rhythmic transformations and interpolated notes, Ockeghem completely reworked Binchois's melody to create his own unique work.

Ockeghem achieved a full harmonic sound by including three different consonant pitches in the simultaneous sonorities (forming what we call triads), except in the last chords of important cadences, where he included only perfect consonances. Where the tenor or the lowest voice descends at a cadence, one or more voices syncopate to cause a suspension. With few exceptions, the only other dissonances are brief passing tones. This gives the music an overwhelmingly euphonious sound.

As is typical of Ockeghem's music, the phrases are long and many of the cadences are blurred by motion in other voices, producing a sense of sustained, ongoing movement. Cadences on G between cantus and tenor at measures 7 and 15 are both obscured by the bassus, which maintains the momentum. Because the frequent pauses and clear phrasing in Du Fay's music seem to reflect Italian and English influences, Ockeghem's more continuous flow and fondness for syncopation may reflect a concentrated French style that Ockeghem gained during his almost half century at the French royal court.

Some editorial indications in this edition are worth noting. At the beginning of the score, the editor included the original clefs for each part and the overall range for each voice within this movement. The altus and bassus (marked "contratenor" and "contratenor 2" respectively) have particularly wide ranges, as is customary in Ockeghem's music. In order to preserve Ockeghem's original notation, the editor did not reduce the note values; the O mensuration sign translates as $\frac{3}{1}$ meter, so the whole note gets the beat. Also, since neither barlines nor ties were used in Ockeghem's notation, the editor included barlines only where they do not interfere with the note values; where a tie would be necessary in modern notation, as from measure 9 to measure 10 in three of the parts, the original note value is preserved and a dotted barline is inserted for reference. Suggested alterations according to *musica ficta* are indicated above the staff, though some could be questioned. In measures 7–8, the tenor and cantus form a cadence, calling for the F in the cantus to be raised a half step according to the rules of *musica ficta*; but would a singer really sing an F♯ against C♮ in two other parts?

# HENRICUS ISAAC (CA. 1450–1517)

*Innsbruck, ich muss dich lassen*

*Lied*

CA. 1500

G. Forster, *Ein Ausszug guter alter und neuer teutscher Liedlein* (Nürnberg, 1539). Music and translation copyright © 1961 by Noah Greenberg and Paul Maynard. Copyright renewed. First appeared in *An English Songbook* published by Doubleday, 181–84. Reprinted by permission of Curtis Brown, Ltd.

| | |
|---|---|
| Innsbruck, ich muss dich lassen, | Innsbruck, I must leave you; |
| ich fahr dahin mein Strassen, | I am going on my way |
| in fremde Land dahin. | into a foreign land. |
| Mein Freud ist mir genommen, | My joy is taken from me, |
| die ich nit weiss bekommen, | I know not how to regain it, |
| wo ich im Elend bin. | while in such misery. |
| | |
| Gross Leid muss ich jetzt tragen, | I must now endure great pain |
| das ich allein tu klagen | which I confide only |
| dem liebsten Buhlen mein. | to my dearest love. |
| Ach Lieb, nun lass mich Armen | O beloved, find pity |
| im Herzen dein erbarmen, | in your heart for me, |
| dass ich muss dannen sein. | that I must part from you. |
| | |
| Mein Trost ob allen Weiben, | My comfort above all other women, |
| dein tu ich ewig bleiben, | I shall always be yours, |
| stet treu, der Ehren fromm. | forever faithful in honor true. |
| Nun muss dich Gott bewahren, | May the good Lord protect you |
| in aller Tugend sparen, | and keep you in your virtue |
| bis dass ich wiederkomm. | for me, till I return. |

—TRANS. NOAH GREENBERG
AND PAUL MAYNARD

Henricus Isaac wrote two settings of this melody and text, probably while he was in the service of Holy Roman Emperor Maximilian I between about 1497 and 1512. Innsbruck was the emperor's favorite city and one of his official residences. This setting may have been composed for the departure of the emperor and his court from Innsbruck in either February 1500 or December 1501.

During the very late fifteenth and early sixteenth centuries, the polyphonic *Lied* was usually either an arrangement of a folk or popular song or a setting of a newly composed melody. In either case, Lieder were intended for use at court or in elite circles. By this period, the preferred texture for secular music was four parts rather than three, as had been standard during the fifteenth century (see NAWM 33, 34, and 36a). In four-voice Lieder, the tune may be in the tenor or the cantus, and the setting may use cantus-firmus style, imitation, or homophony. It is not known whether Isaac used an existing song for this Lied or if he devised the tune and poetry himself, though the latter perhaps is more likely. The melody is in the cantus, and the other voices mostly harmonize with it in simple homophony, modeled on the style of Italian songs that Isaac had encountered while living in Florence. Such homophonic, strophic settings in four parts became typical for many kinds of vernacular songs in the sixteenth century. Isaac's other setting of the same melody is in a very different style, more typical of the German Lied at this time, with the tune in canon in the tenor and altus.

Each line of the poem is set to its own musical phrase and separated from the next line by a rest. Phrases usually end with suspensions leading to cadences on the mode's final, F, or tenor, C, and a cadence on G marks the midpoint of each stanza. That the piece is modal rather than tonal is apparent from the cadences, which move out from a sixth to an octave, and also from the occasional triads on E♭, a whole step below the final, which would rarely occur in a piece in F major.

The editor included the original clefs and note values at the beginning of the piece, revealing that the middle voices are in essentially the same range and that the note values have been reduced by half to make the notation look more familiar to modern singers. There are three verses of poetry, all sung to the same music. On the accompanying recording, only the top line is sung, and the others are played by instruments. Later in the sixteenth century, this melody was adapted to sacred words and became widely known as the chorale *O Welt, ich muss dich lassen* (O world, I now must leave thee).

# JOSQUIN DES PREZ (CA. 1450–1521)

*Ave Maria . . . virgo serena*

**39**

*Motet*

CA. 1484–85

Edited by Alejandro Enrique Planchart. Used by permission. Reprinted from Allan W. Atlas, *Anthology of Renaissance Music* (New York: W. W. Norton, 1998), 159–65.

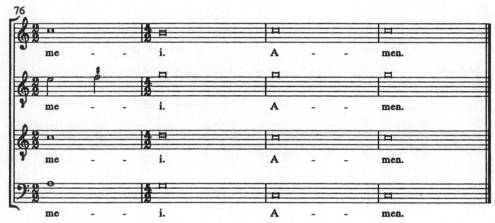

| Ave Maria, gratia plena, | Hail Mary, full of grace, |
| Dominus tecum, Virgo serena. | the Lord is with you, serene Virgin. |
| | |
| Ave, cujus conceptio | Hail to her whose conception, |
| Solemni plena gaudio, | full of solemn jubilation, |
| Caelestia, terrestria | fills heaven and earth |
| Nova replet laetitia. | with new joy. |
| | |
| Ave, cuius nativitas | Hail to her whose birth |
| Nostra fuit solemnitas: | was our solemn feast, |
| Ut lucifer, lux oriens, | like the morning star, the light of day, |
| Verum solem praeveniens. | anticipating the true sun [Christ]. |
| | |
| Ave, pia humilitas, | Hail, pious humility, |
| Sine viro fecunditas, | fruitful without a man, |
| Cuius annuntiatio | whose annunciation |
| Nostra fuit salvatio. | was our salvation. |

| | |
|---|---|
| Ave, vera virginitas, | Hail, true virginity, |
| Immaculata castitas, | immaculate chastity, |
| Cuius purificatio | whose purification |
| Nostra fuit purgatio. | purged our sins. |
| | |
| Ave, praeclara omnibus | Hail, most excellent in all |
| Angelicis virtutibus, | angelic virtues, |
| Cuius fuit assumptio | whose assumption was |
| Nostra glorificatio. | our glorification. |
| | |
| O Mater Dei, | O Mother of God, |
| Memento mei. | remember me. |
| Amen. | Amen. |

*Ave Maria . . . virgo serena* was perhaps Josquin's most popular motet, as demonstrated by its inclusion in numerous manuscripts and its placement as the first work in Ottaviano Petrucci's first published collection of motets in 1502. Its cumbersome title is necessary to distinguish it from another motet Josquin wrote that also begins "Ave Maria." *Ave Maria . . . virgo serena* was copied into a manuscript in about 1485, making it the earliest datable piece by Josquin. Its text and structure suit the liturgical and musical practices of Milan, where Josquin was employed by a member of the city's ruling Sforza family from about 1484 to 1489, so it seems likely that he wrote it around 1484–85.

The text, in praise of the Virgin Mary, begins with two lines from a medieval sequence, continues with five metered and rhymed stanzas, and ends with a two-line prayer. The form of the poem determined the form of the music, reflecting Josquin's interest in clear delineation of the text. For each couplet or strophe, Josquin composed a unique musical treatment. Each section ends with a cadence on C, the tonal center, demonstrating Josquin's concern for pitch organization. Glareanus, in his *Dodekachordon*, classified the mode of this motet as Hypoionian (mode 12) because of its final on C and ranges of at least a fifth above and fourth below the final in the tenor and the superius, which were the two voices that Renaissance theorists considered to define the mode in a polyphonic work.

Josquin's setting of the words shows both variety and expressivity. The opening couplet is composed as a series of points of imitation (measures 1–15). Each phrase of text is given a musical subject that is taken up by each voice in turn, working from highest to lowest in what may be a musical representation of angels hailing Mary. Before the last voice finishes its phrase, a different voice begins the next phrase with a new subject, preserving the musical continuity and perhaps suggesting the unremitting praises of the heavenly host. At "virgo serena" (serene Virgin), the final phrase of the first couplet (measures 12–15), all the voices sing together for the first time, and the rhythmic activity accelerates to the eighth-note level, emphasizing the conclusion of the first section. This increase in activity, often called a "drive to the cadence," is a technique Josquin probably learned from Ockeghem.

When the first strophe begins, the texture changes from imitation to homophony. The first line, hailing Mary's conception, is presented twice, in parallel sixths and then in parallel $^6_3$ sonorities that are reminiscent of fauxbourdon (measures 16–20). By the time that Josquin composed this piece, fauxbourdon was archaic, and the use of an older style gave listeners the sense of a sacred and dignified mood. The second line, "full of solemn jubilation," suggests both fullness and solemnity because all four voices are in homophony for the first time in the motet (measures 20–22). In the remainder of the strophe, Josquin staggered rhythms between the parts to represent the multitude of heavenly and earthly voices (measures 22–27). The end of the strophe is marked with the most emphatic cadence so far in the piece.

Josquin varied the texture constantly through the rest of the piece, alternating duets with three- and four-part writing, and points of imitation with homophony. The meter shifts to triple time at two different points (measures 47 and 68), providing contrast. A particularly expressive moment comes at the end when the music slows and the singers declaim in rhythmic unison and simple harmonies, "O mother of God, remember me. Amen" (measures 73–79). It is as if the composer—on his own behalf, and also for his singers, his patron, and the congregation—set aside his artistry to speak directly and modestly to the Virgin Mary, pleading for his soul.

This motet is often sung by choirs today, but in Josquin's time it was probably performed by only a few singers, perhaps as few as one per part. It is a rewarding piece to sing; each part is equally interesting and important, the texture changes continually, and the melodies unfold smoothly and logically, yet with constant rhythmic and melodic interest.

# JOSQUIN DES PREZ (CA. 1450–1521)

*Missa Pange lingua*: Kyrie and part of Credo

*Paraphrase mass*

CA. 1515–20

(a) Kyrie

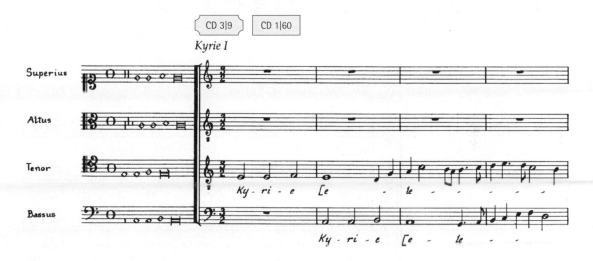

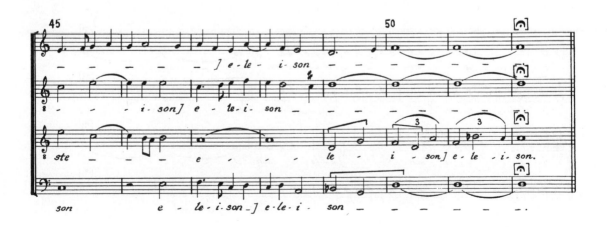

Kyrie eleison.        Lord have mercy.
Christe eleison.      Christ have mercy.
Kyrie eleison.        Lord have mercy.

(b) Credo, excerpt: *Et incarnatus est* and *Crucifixus*

dex-te-ram Pa-tris.   Et i-te-rum ven-tu-rus est   cum glo-ri-a,   ju-di-ca-

Et i-te-rum ven-tu-rus est   cum glo-ri-a,   ju-di-ca-

se-det ad dex-te-ram Pa-tris.   Et i-ter-rum ven-tu-rus est cum glo-ri-a, ju-di-ca-

dex-te-ram Pa-tris.   Et i-te-rum ven-tu-rus est   cum glo-ri-a,   ju-di-ca-

re   vi-vos et   mor-tu-os   cu-jus re-gni   non

re vi-vos et   mor-tu-os   cu-jus re   -   gni   non

re   vi-vos et mor-tu-os   cu-jus re-gni   non

re vi-vos et mor-tu-   os   cu-jus re   -   gni non   -

e - rit fi - nis.

e - rit fi - nis.

e - rit fi - nis.

e - rit fi - nis.

| | |
|---|---|
| Et incarnatus est de Spiritu Sancto ex Maria Virgine: et homo factus est. Crucifixus etiam pro nobis: sub Pontio Pilato passus, et sepultus est. Et resurrexit tertia die, secundum Scripturas. Et ascendit in caelum: sedet ad dexteram Patris. Et iterum venturus est cum gloria judicare vivos et mortuos: cujus regni non erit finis. | And was made incarnate by the Holy Spirit of the Virgin Mary, and was made man. And was crucified for us; under Pontius Pilate He died, and was buried. And rose again on the third day, according to the Scriptures. And ascended into heaven, and sits at the right hand of the Father. And He shall come again with glory to judge the quick and the dead; of whose kingdom there shall be no end. |

Since Ottaviano Petrucci did not print *Missa Pange lingua* in any of his collections of Josquin des Prez's masses (published in 1502, 1505, and 1514), it is likely that it was one of the last that Josquin composed. It first appeared in the anthology *Missae tredecim* (Thirteen Masses) in 1539, eighteen years after Josquin's death.

The mass is based on the melody of the hymn *Pange lingua gloriosi* (text by St. Thomas Aquinas), assigned to second Vespers on the feast of Corpus Christi (*Liber usualis*, p. 957). The six strophes of the hymn are sung to the melody given below with the first strophe.

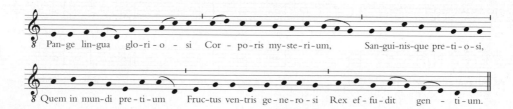

| | |
|---|---|
| Pange lingua gloriosi | Sing, tongue, of the glorious |
| Corporis mysterium, | body's mystery |
| Sanguinisque pretiosi, | and of the precious blood, |
| Quem in mundi pretium | ransom of the world, that |
| Fructus ventris generosi | the fruit of the generous womb, |
| Rex effudit gentium. | the king of all peoples, poured forth. |

Josquin based all the movements of the mass—though not all its subdivisions—on the hymn melody. Rather than placing the chant in a single voice as a cantus firmus line, he paraphrased it in all the voices. Josquin adapted the six phrases of the hymn melody as subjects for polyphonic imitation, making imitation the primary structural device rather than the layering of voices around a cantus firmus. A mass based on this procedure—paraphrasing a melody in all voices and treating motives derived from it in points of imitation—is called a *paraphrase mass*.

The Kyrie follows the hymn faithfully. The movement has three sections (Kyrie I, Christe, and Kyrie II), and in each section Josquin paraphrased two of the hymn's six phrases. The last notes of the second, fourth, and sixth phrases of the hymn determine the modal degrees on which each section of the Kyrie closes—respectively G, D, and E.

The tenor takes the lead at the outset, following the contour of the hymn's first phrase exactly, then adding effusive decoration before cadencing on the last note of the hymn's first phrase, C (see measures 1–5). The bassus imitates the same figure a fifth lower but diverges more from the original hymn. The superius and altus repeat the tenor and bassus phrases an octave higher (measures 5–9); such alternation of paired voices is typical of Josquin's music. The second phrase of the hymn is then paraphrased in a three-voice point of imitation. The first several notes of the hymn phrase (C–D–C–C–B–A) are reworked to create a motive in the bassus (C–C–D–C–A–B–A in measures 9–11) that is imitated exactly by tenor and superius at one–measure intervals. But the rest of the hymn phrase (C–B–A–G) is more loosely paraphrased, as all three voices indulge in repeated descending figures, each decorated in a different way, with energy sustained by faster rising scale figures (measures 12–16). This heightened activity is typical of Josquin's "drive to the cadence."

The third and fourth phrases of the hymn are paraphrased in the Christe, again with imitation in paired voices. To achieve maximum variety, Josquin varied the combinations of voices, the order of entrances, and the intervals of imitation. Also typical of Josquin's music is the way that each motive begins as a clear statement of the original hymn phrase in long notes and then becomes progressively more active and more distant from the source.

In the final Kyrie, the fifth and sixth phrases of the hymn are treated a bit more freely. For example, the fifth phrase is missing its opening note, and the sixth phrase is paraphrased differently in each voice. Searching for the hymn's contour in all four voices in measures 60–70 provides a striking lesson in Josquin's inventiveness in reworking given material. Several motives are repeated either in sequence or at pitch in a most striking manner.

Excerpts from the *Credo* demonstrate Josquin's attention to text expression. The solemn proclamation at "Et incarnatus est" (And he was made incarnate by the Holy Spirit out of the Virgin Mary, and was made man) is declaimed in block chords, with the top voice paraphrasing the first line of the hymn. Such homophonic passages often appear in sixteenth-century works, alone or in alternation with points of imitation. For the word "Crucifixus" (crucified), Josquin took advantage of the plaintive semitone motion in the hymn's opening. The following passage, mostly on new material, features alternating imitative and homophonic phrases. Some motives suggest word-painting, including the burst of activity at "Et resurrexit" (and was resurrected) and the rising line at "Et ascendit in caelum" (and ascended into Heaven).

As we have seen in some other scores, the editor has included the original notation at the beginning of each section. The composer specified the text underlay in the excerpt from the *Credo*, and the music perfectly suits the rhythm and accentuation of the words. In the *Kyrie*, the original music contained only the word "Kyrie" or "Christe" at the beginning of each part and "eleison" at the end; the editor has added text repetition (the text shown in brackets) to fit the musical rhythm. With these additions, one can consider each section to be a three-fold statement of the text (for instance, the three statements of "Kyrie eleison" begin at measures 1, 5, and 9 of Kyrie I). In a performance at a Mass, the *Kyrie* as written here could be performed once and be sufficient for the liturgy, which requires each sentence to be said three times. Otherwise, each section would be sung three times or alternated with chant, as in NAWM 25.

# JOSQUIN DES PREZ (?) (CA. 1450–1521)

*Mille regretz*

*Chanson*

CA. 1520

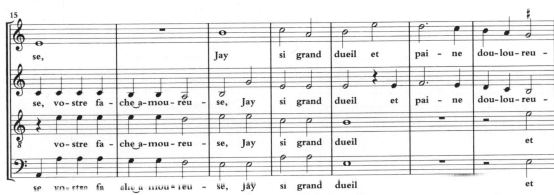

Reprinted by permission of the publisher from *Chanson and Madrigal, 1480–1530: Studies in Comparison and Contrast, A Conference at Isham Memorial Library, September 13–14, 1961*, edited by James Haar, 143–46, Cambridge, Mass.: Harvard University Press. Copyright © 1964 by the President and Fellows of Harvard College.

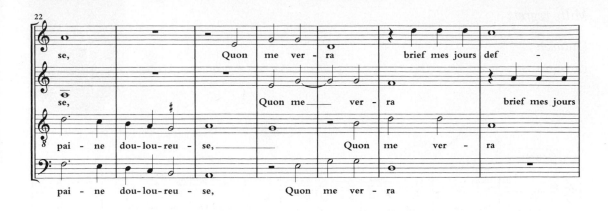

| | |
|---|---|
| Mille regretz de vous habandonner | A thousand regrets at deserting you |
| Et d'eslonger vostre fache amoureuse, | and leaving behind your loving face. |
| Jay si grand dueil et paine douloureuse, | I feel so much sadness and such painful distress, |
| Qu'on me verra brief mes jours definer. | that it seems to me my days will soon dwindle away. |

*Mille regretz* is simpler and more homophonic than most of Josquin's chansons and in some ways is more characteristic of music by the next generation of composers. For these reasons, and because a large number of works that were once attributed to Josquin are now known to be by other composers, several scholars have questioned its attribution to Josquin. Yet it is credited to him from its first appearance in any source, only a decade after his death. If it is by Josquin, it is one of his last chansons, and it demonstrates his interest in keeping up with the most modern styles.

There is evidence to suggest that Josquin composed it for Holy Roman Emperor Charles V and presented it to him in person in 1520, when the emperor was in Brussels, near where Josquin was living in Condé sur l'Escaut. After Josquin's death, it became one of his most popular chansons, especially in Spain, where Charles spent most of his time. It was known in Spain as "La cancion del Emperador" (The Song of the Emperor), confirming the link to Charles and perhaps to Josquin. It was later reworked in a mass by Cristóbal de Morales and arranged for vihuela (a guitar-shaped lute) by Luis de Narváez (see NAWM 60a).

Chansons by Binchois (NAWM 33), Du Fay (NAWM 36a), Ockeghem, and other composers who were active before the 1470s are treble-dominated—the cantus is the most important voice, the tenor accompanies the cantus in two-part counterpoint, and the other voices are added around the cantus-tenor framework. In this chanson and others by composers from Josquin's generation, all the voices are essential. The cadences are not all formed between cantus (the top voice) and tenor (the third voice down) but may occur between any two voices.

As is typical of music by Josquin and his contemporaries, each phrase of text is given a distinctive musical phrase that fits the rhythm and meaning of the words. The texture also changes from phrase to phrase, alternating between homophony and imitation, and between various combinations of two, three, or all four voices. The sadness of the song is conveyed especially by the many descending lines, as at "regretz," "paine doulourouse" (painful distress), and "brief mes jours definer" (my days will soon dwindle away).

The piece is in mode 3 (Phrygian), as demonstrated by the frequent cadences on E (including the final cadence) and the ranges of cantus and tenor from low C or D to high E. The only cadence note other than E is A, an important note in the mode (and the tenor of its plagal relative, mode 4). Several of the cadences, including the final sonority, include thirds, as was becoming more common during this period. In the fifteenth century, pieces and sections typically closed on perfect consonances, such as an octave or a fifth and octave.

All the parts were meant to be sung, as evident in the appropriate text-setting and in the various textures—such as alternating pairs of voices and imitation between the parts—that suggest complete equality between the parts. Most likely, the song was intended for one singer on each part, as was standard in the sixteenth century.

# MARTIN LUTHER (1483–1546)

*Nun komm, der Heiden Heiland* and *Ein' feste Burg*

*Chorales*

1524 AND 1529

## (a) Attributed to St. Ambrose: Hymn, *Veni redemptor gentium*

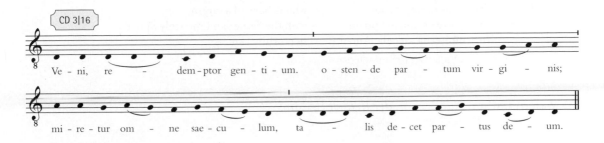

| Veni, redemptor gentium, | Come, Savior of nations, |
|---|---|
| ostende partum Virginis; | display the offspring of the Virgin. |
| miretur omne saeculum: | Let all ages marvel |
| talis decet partus deum. | that God granted such a birth. |

| Non ex virili semine, | Not from man's seed, |
|---|---|
| sed mystico spiramine | but by the Holy Spirit's power |
| Verbum Dei factum est caro | the Word of God is made flesh |
| fructusque ventris floruit. | and blooms as the fruit of the womb. |

| Alvus tumescit Virginis, | The womb of the Virgin swells, |
|---|---|
| claustrum pudoris permanet, | yet the fortress of her purity is not breached, |
| vexilla virtutum micant, | the sparkling banners of virtue |
| versatur in templo Deus. | turn it into a temple of God. |

| Procedat e thalamo suo, | He comes forth from his chamber, |
|---|---|
| pudoris aula regia, | the royal hall of purity, |
| geminae gigas substantiae | a giant of twofold substance in one, |
| alacris ut currat viam. | eager to run his course. |

| Egressus eius a Patre, | He comes to us from the Father, |
|---|---|
| regressus eius ad Patrem; | and he returns to the Father; |
| excursus usque ad infernos | he goes down to Hell |
| recursus ad sedem Dei. | and returns to the seat of God. |

From Einsiedeln, Benediktinerkloster, Musikbibliothek, MS 366 (twelfth century), after *Hymnen: Die mittelalterlichen Hymnenmelodien des Abendlandes*, ed. Bruno Stäblein, Monumenta mododica medii aevi 1 (Kassel: Bärenreiter, 1956), 273–74.

| | |
|---|---|
| Aequalis aeterno Patri, | Equal to the eternal Father, |
| carnis tropaeo cingere, | victory clothed in our flesh, |
| infirma nostri corporis | the weaknesses of our bodies |
| virtute firmans perpeti. | your virtues shall forever strengthen. |
| | |
| Praesepe iam fulget tuum | Now your crib gleams, |
| lumenque nox spirat novum, | the night gives forth a new light, |
| quod nulla nox interpolet | because darkness cannot enter in, |
| fideque iugi luceat. | faith perpetually shines. |
| | |
| Gloria tibi, Domine, | Praise be to you, Lord, |
| Qui natus es de virgine, | who is born of a virgin, |
| Cum Patre et sancto Spiritu, | with the Father and the Holy Spirit, |
| in sempiterna saecula. Amen. | in eternity. Amen. |

—ATTRIBUTED TO ST. AMBROSE

(b) Martin Luther, *Nun komm, der Heiden Heiland*

Nun komm der Hei – den Hei – land, Der Jung – frau – en Kind er – kannt, Dass sich wun – der al – le Welt. Gott solch' Ge – burt ihm be – stellt.

| | |
|---|---|
| 1. Nun komm, der Heiden Heiland, | Now come, Savior of the heathens, |
| Der Jungfrauen Kind erkannt, | child, known to be born of the Virgin. |
| Dass sich wunder alle Welt, | Let all the world marvel |
| Gott solch' Geburt ihm bestellt. | that God such a birth for him ordained. |
| | |
| 2. Nicht von Manns Blut noch von Fleisch, | Not from man's blood nor from flesh, |
| Allein von dem Heil'gen Geist | but alone from the Holy Spirit |
| Ist Gott's Wort worden ein Mensch | has God's Word become a human being, |
| Und blühet ein Frucht Weib'sfleisch. | and blooms fruit of a woman's flesh. |
| | |
| 3. Der Jungfrau Leib schwanger ward, | The Virgin became pregnant, |
| Doch blieb Keuschheit rein bewahrt, | But her virginity was kept pure, |
| Leucht herfür manch' Tugend schon, | There shines forth many a virtue indeed, |
| Gott da war in seinem Thron. | There God was on his throne. |

From *Eyn Enchiridiom oder Handbuchlein . . . geystlicher gesenge und Psalmen* (Erfurt, 1524). Spellings modernized.

4.  Er ging aus der Kammer sein,
    Dem kön'glichen Saal so rein,
    Gott von Art und Mensch ein Held
    Sein Weg er zu laufen eilt.

He went out of his chamber,
the royal hall so pure,
God by nature and as man a hero,
he hurries to run his course.

5.  Sein Lauf kam vom Vater her
    Und kehrt' wieder zum Vater,
    Fuhr hinunter zu der Höll',
    Und wieder zu Gottes Stuhl.

His path came to us from the Father,
and returned to the Father;
went down to Hell,
and back to God's throne.

6.  Der du bist dem Vater gleich,
    Führ hinaus den Sieg im Fleisch,
    Dass dein ewig Gott's Gewalt
    In uns das krank' Fleisch enthalt.

You, who are equal to the Father,
bring forth the victory in the flesh,
that your eternal God's power
our sickly flesh preserves.

7.  Dein Krippen glänzt hell und klar,
    Die Nacht gibt ein neu Licht dar.
    Dunkel muss nicht kommen drein,
    Der Glaub' bleibt immer im Schein.

Your crib shines bright and clear,
the night gives forth a new light.
Darkness must not come into it,
Faith stays always in the light.

8.  Lob sei Gott dem Vater ton;
    Lob sei Gott seim ein'gen Sohn,
    Lob sei Gott dem Heiligen Geist
    Immer und in Ewigkeit.

Praise be to God the Father,
Praise be to God his only Son,
Praise be to God the Holy Spirit
Forever and in eternity.

—MARTIN LUTHER

## (c) Martin Luther, *Ein' feste Burg*

Transcribed from Joseph Klug, *Geistliche Lieder auffs new gebessert* (Wittenberg, 1533).

1. Ein' feste Burg is unser Gott,
   ein gute Wehr und Waffen.
   Er hilft uns frei aus aller Not,
   die uns jetzt hat betroffen.
   Der alt böse Feind,
   mit Ernst ers jetzt meint;
   groß Macht und viel List
   sein grausam Rüstung ist,
   auf Erd ist nicht seins Gleichen.

   A sturdy fortress is our God,
   a good defense and weapon.
   He helps us free from all afflictions
   that have now befallen us.
   The old, evil enemy
   now means to deal with us seriously;
   great power and much cunning
   are his cruel armaments;
   on Earth is not his equal.

2. Mit unsrer Macht ist nichts getan,
   wir sind gar bald verloren;
   es streit' für uns der rechte Mann,
   den Gott hat selbst erkoren.
   Fragst du, wer der ist?
   Er heißt Jesus Christ,
   der Herr Zebaoth,
   und ist kein andrer Gott,
   das Feld muß er behalten.

   With our own strength is nothing done,
   very soon we are entirely lost;
   but fighting for us is the righteous man,
   whom God himself has chosen.
   Do you ask, who he is?
   His name is Jesus Christ,
   the Lord Sabaoth,
   and there is no other God;
   he must hold the battlefield.

3. Und wenn die Welt voll Teufel wär
   und wollt uns gar verschlingen,
   so fürchten wir uns nicht so sehr,
   es soll uns doch gelingen.
   Der Fürst dieser Welt,
   wie saur er sich stellt,
   tut er uns doch nichts;
   das macht, er ist gericht'.
   Ein Wörtlein kann ihn fällen.

   And if the world were full of devils
   who wanted to devour us entirely,
   we would not fear so much,
   we will succeed nevertheless.
   The prince of this world,
   no matter how angry he appears,
   he will nevertheless do nothing to us;
   that means, he is already judged.
   A little word can bring him down.

4. Das Wort sie sollen lassen stahn
   und kein' Dank dazu haben;
   er ist bei uns wohl auf dem Plan
   mit seinem Geist und Gaben.
   Nehmen sie den Leib,
   Gut, Ehr, Kind und Weib,
   laß fahren dahin,
   sie haben's kein' Gewinn,
   das Reich muß uns doch bleiben.

   The Word they shall leave standing
   and receive no thanks for this;
   he is certainly with us on the battlefield
   with his spirit and talents.
   They may take your life,
   goods, honor, child, and wife,
   let all this occur,
   yet from it they have no profit;
   The Kingdom still remains for us.

—MARTIN LUTHER

(d) Johann Walter (1496–1570), *Ein' feste Burg*, setting for four voices

From Johann Walter, *Sämtliche Werke*, ed. Otto Schröder, vol. 1, *Geistliches Gesangbüchlein* (Wittenberg 1551), part 1, *Deutscher Gesänge* (Kassel: Bärenreiter, 1953), 26–27. Used by permission.

1 WB    2 BZ  (Darin mit dem Text der 1. und 3. Strophe; diese beiden auch in LC und Ba.)    3 GC

In the early years of the Lutheran church, Martin Luther regarded music as a crucial tool for propagating the new faith. Especially important were the congregational hymns in the vernacular that became known as *chorales* (from the German word for "chant"), which gave the people in the pews a role in the music of church services and also could be sung at home as part of private devotions. Luther and his colleagues often used or adapted existing German devotional songs as chorales or created chorales by writing new religious words for well-known secular songs, as in the retexting of *Innsbruck, ich muss dich lassen* (see NAWM 38) for the chorale *O Welt, ich muss dich lassen* (O world, I now must leave thee). The examples presented here demonstrate two other main sources for chorales: adaptations of Gregorian chants and new melodies in contemporary style.

The text of the hymn *Veni redemptor gentium* was attributed to St. Ambrose of Milan (ca. 340–397), but it was most likely not actually written by him. The earliest known form of the melody, shown here, is found in a twelfth-century hymnal from Einsiedeln, Germany. It was used as an Office hymn during Advent season before Christmas. Luther adapted the text as a chorale for Advent by translating the eight verses into rhyming metric poetry in German, changing the number of syllables per line from eight (common in Latin hymns) to seven. In addition to transposing the melody up a fourth, he indicated specific rhythms and changed several of the notes so that each phrase has a single highest note and so that the last phrase is the same as the first. These changes converted a chant in free rhythm into a melody in the style of Luther's time, which the congregation would probably have found more appealing and easier to sing. Luther made his adaptation in 1523 or 1524, and in the latter year the chorale was published in one of the first collections of chorales to be printed. J. S. Bach later used this chorale as the basis for two cantatas (see NAWM 90).

The most famous of all chorales is *Ein' feste Burg*, whose text and music are credited to Luther. It was first printed in a 1529 chorale collection, but no copies of that volume survive. The edition shown here is transcribed from the oldest extant publication, from 1533. The words, based on Psalm 46, are a stirring statement of faith in God's power to protect believers, and they must have been a great comfort during the bitter and often bloody battles over religious doctrine in Europe during the sixteenth century. The melody reinforces this image of strength with the repeated opening notes, frequent returns to the opening high note, and several descending scale figures that lead to the mode's final (F) or tenor (C). The mode is Ionian, mode 11 in Glareanus's set of twelve modes, transposed a fourth higher to F; Luther associated the Ionian mode with hymns of faith. The rhythm demonstrates Luther's careful attention to the proper setting of text, with long notes for the stressed syllables and shorter notes for most unstressed ones. Since the eighteenth century, Luther's forceful, almost jaunty rhythm has usually been smoothed out into mostly even note values.

The tune of *Ein' feste Burg* may draw some elements from a melody by Luther's younger contemporary, the Meistersinger Hans Sachs (1494–1576). It follows bar form—AAB—as was customary in the songs of the Minnesinger (see NAWM 11) and Meistersinger. As in many of the Meistersinger's songs, the A and B sections end with the same musical phrase.

Beginning soon after the first chorales were composed, Lutheran composers created four-part settings of chorales for performance by the choir during services—separately or alternating verses with the congregation singing in unison—or for singing in schools, in private devotions, or as recreation. The leader in this practice was Johann Walter, whose first collection of four- and five-voice chorale settings, the *Geystliches Gesangk Buchleyn* (Little Book of Spiritual Songs), was published in 1524. In later editions, Walter added several settings of *Ein' feste Burg*, including the one printed here. He followed the tradition of the German Lied in placing the tune in the tenor, essentially unchanged, and surrounding it with free counterpoint in the other voices. Phrase endings in the tenor are often overlapped by one or more voices, maintaining the forward momentum until the end of each section. The cadence at the end of the first section (measures 8–9) includes a triad on the lowered seventh degree (E♭) just before the final three chords. This was a very common cadential formula throughout the sixteenth century.

On the accompanying recordings, *Veni redemptor gentium* is sung by a chant choir, as it would have been in Catholic services, and *Nun komm, der Heiden Heiland* is sung in unaccompanied unison by a mixed congregation of men and women, as was the practice in Lutheran services during Luther's lifetime. Only the first verse of the chant hymn and verses 1, 3, 4, 7, and 8 of the chorale are included on the recordings, but both texts are printed here in their entirety in order to show how Luther adapted the Latin original. The recordings also include two verses of *Ein' feste Burg* in congregational unison and one verse in Walter's polyphonic setting. The edition of Walter's setting includes alternate text underlay for some passages, printed in smaller letters.

# LOYS BOURGEOIS (CA. 1510–CA. 1561)

## Psalm 134 (*Or sus, serviteurs du Seigneur*)

*Metrical psalm*

CA. 1551

(a) Psalm 134, *Or sus, serviteurs du Seigneur*

1. Or sus, serviteurs du Seigneur,
   Vous qui de nuict en son honneur
   Dedans sa maison le servez,
   Louez-le, et son nom eslevez.

   Arise, you servants of the Lord,
   you who by night in his honor
   serve him in his house,
   praise him, and lift up his name.

2. Levez les mains au plus sainct lieu
   De ce tressainct temple de Dieu,
   Et le los qu'il a merité
   Soit par vos bouches recité.

   Lift up your hands to the holiest place
   of this most holy temple of God,
   and may the praise that He deserves
   be recited by your mouths.

3. Dieu qui a fait et entretient
   Et terre et ciel par son pouvoir,
   Du mont Sion, où il se tient,
   Ses biens te face appercevoir.

   May God who made and maintains
   the earth and heavens by his power,
   from Mount Zion, where he resides,
   let you experience his blessings.

   —CLÉMENT MAROT AND
   THÉODORE DE BÈZE

From Clément Marot and Théodore de Bèze, *Les psaumes en vers français avec leurs mélodies* (Geneva, 1562), 447.

(b) William Kethe (d. CA. 1608): Psalm 100, *All people that on earth do dwell* (CA. 1559)

1.  All people that on earth do dwell,
    Sing to the Lord with chereful voyce:
    Him serve with feare, his praise forthe tell:
    Come ye before him, and reioyce.

2.  The Lord, ye knowe, is god in dede:
    Without our aide, he did vs make:
    We are his folke: he doeth vs fede,
    And for his shepe he doeth vs take.

3.  Oh, entre then his gates with praise:
    Approche with ioye his courtes vnto:
    Praise, laude, and bleses his Name always:
    For it is semely so to do.

4.  For why? the Lord our God is good:
    His mercie is for euer sure:
    His trueth at all times firmely stoode,
    And shal from age to age indure.

<br>

1.  All people that on earth do dwell,
    Sing to the Lord with cheerful voice:
    Him serve with fear, his praise forth tell:
    Come ye before him, and rejoice.

2.  The Lord, ye know, is God indeed:
    Without our aide, he did us make:
    We are his folk: he doth us feed,
    And for his sheep he doth us take.

3.  Oh, enter then his gates with praise:
    Approach with joy his courts unto:
    Praise, laud, and bless his Name always·
    For it is seemly so to do.

4.  For why? the Lord our God is good:
    His mercy is forever sure:
    His truth at all times firmly stood,
    And shall from age to age endure.

—WILLIAM KETHE

Music and text from Robin A. Leaver, *"Goostly psalmes and spirituall songs": English and Dutch Metrical Psalms from Coverdale to Utenhove 1535–1566* (Oxford: Clarendon Press, 1991), 237. Reprinted by permission of Oxford University Press.

In Calvinist churches such as the Reformed Church and Presbyterian Church, congregational singing in the vernacular was as important as in the Lutheran Church. The spiritual leader of the Reformed movement, Jean Calvin (1509–1564), believed that humans could not give God anything better than God had given humans, and so he insisted that only texts from the Bible, especially psalms, should be sung in church. Since psalms had verses of varying lengths and thus were difficult for congregations to sing together, Calvinist poets prepared rhymed, metric, strophic translations of psalms in the vernacular, which were called *metrical psalms*. These were set to simple, syllabic tunes—most newly composed, some adapted from chants or other melodies—and published in collections called *psalters*.

The most famous metrical psalm tune is the one included here, composed (or perhaps adapted) by Loys Bourgeois for the version of Psalm 134 by Clément Marot and Théodore de Bèze. The melody first appeared in the Genevan Psalter, *Trente Quatre Pseaumes de David* (Thirty-Four Psalms of David), published in 1551. The popularity of this melody may owe something to its almost perfect shape. It matches the four-line poetic stanzas with four brief phrases of eight notes each. The first three phrases share the same rhythm and move almost entirely by step, with one skip or leap before the last three notes. The last phrase slightly alters the rhythm and introduces more skips, creating a sense of finality by breaking the pattern set in the preceding phrases. The four phrases end with near-rhymes: three stepwise half notes that rise in the first and third phrases and descend in the second and fourth. Each phrase has a single high note, the highest of which is C in the last phrase. In perfect symmetry, the high point of the phrase gradually shifts from the last note of the first phrase (A) to the third note from the end of the second phrase (B♭), the third note from the beginning of the third phrase (A), and the first note of the final phrase. The successive phrase-endings on A, G, F, and F create a gradual descent that balances the ascent from F to A in the first phrase. Additionally, each individual phrase includes a unique balance of ascending and descending elements. It takes longer to describe this melody than is required to sing it, but that a simple melody can feature such richness of detail may explain why it is so memorable and enduring.

Metrical psalm singing was adopted by English Protestants living in exile on the Continent during the reign of Mary I (r. 1553–58), who had restored Catholicism in England. When Elizabeth I succeeded Mary and revived the Church of England, she allowed psalm singing, and it soon became a regular part of church services as well as devotions at home. In English-language psalters, including the English Psalter of 1561, William Kethe's metrical translation of Psalm 100 was associated with Bourgeois's tune, which eventually became known as "Old Hundredth." It has been the most frequently printed tune in English-language psalters and hymnals for over four hundred years. Over the years, several rhythmic variants have been introduced, including a version in which all the notes are the same length.

On the recordings, both the French and the English psalms are sung by a mixed congregation of men and women without accompaniment, as was the sixteenth-century practice. Two verses of each are included.

# WILLIAM BYRD (CA. 1540–1623)

*Sing joyfully unto God*

*Full anthem*

1580s–1590s

From *The Byrd Edition,* gen. ed. Philip Brett, vol. 2, *The English Anthems,* ed. Craig Monson (London: Stainer & Bell, 1983), 82–90. ©1983 Stainer & Bell Ltd. Reproduced by permission. The pitch has been transposed up a minor third from C to E♭ to conform with how, according to the editor, the original scheme of clefs was read.

William Byrd composed *Sing joyfully unto God*, a setting of the first four verses of Psalm 81, sometime during the 1580s or early 1590s. It was one of his most popular anthems, appearing in many manuscripts from the time, and had a long career, being printed in anthologies of English church music in 1641 and again in the eighteenth century. It is a full anthem, the English equivalent of the choral motet, as opposed to a verse anthem, which is scored for soloists with instrumental accompaniment, often alternating with the choir. Anthems were performed in Church of England services and used for home devotions. The composition of such sacred music with text in the vernacular rather than in Latin was a defining contribution of the Reformation.

Several distinctive traits distinguish Byrd's style from those of other composers, such as Josquin (NAWM 39–40), Palestrina (NAWM 45), Victoria (NAWM 46), or Lasso (NAWM 47). In the music of Byrd, cadences are more frequent, imitation is freer and almost constant, homophony is rare, and the voice lines are often more angular and energetic.

This anthem is in the Ionian mode, number 11 in Glareanus's scheme of twelve modes, with a final of C (transposed here to E♭, as explained below) and a range in soprano 1 and tenor of about an octave above the final. Byrd made both the mode and the structure of phrases clear through the many cadences, most on the final or tenor of the mode (as transposed here, E♭ and B♭ respectively). The typical cadence includes bass motion of a fifth down or fourth up (as in measures 4–5 and 9–10). This type of cadence became increasingly common over the course of the sixteenth century and is the ancestor of the modern dominant-to-tonic cadence. However, during the sixteenth century, most such cadences still included a suspension, which was a remnant of the older sixth-to-octave cadence.

In the first point of imitation (measures 1–10), involving only four of the six parts, the subject is treated freely; the rising fifth of the first entrance is answered with a second, fourth, and octave. Vigorous leaps bring to life texts such as "Sing loud" (measure 10) or "Take the song" (measure 26). Melodies consisting mostly of skips and leaps, such as soprano 2, tenor, and bass in measures 10–12, are not unusual. This style contrasts strongly with the largely stepwise motion in music by Josquin or Palestrina. Leaps are especially common in the bass, even two successive leaps in the same direction (see measures 14–15), as the bass sounds the root of each successive triad (to use modern terminology).

Homophonic texture is infrequent in this piece; more often, two or more voices move together in rhythmic unison, as at "Blow the trumpet in the new moon" (measures 30–38), where the fanfare-like figures evoke the text. Byrd paid close attention to the rhythm of the words as well as their meaning. Unstressed syllables most often fall on weak beats, while stressed syllables appear on the main beats (whole notes in the transcription) or are accented by syncopation.

This anthem was originally notated a minor third lower, with no key signature; the first note of each part, in its original clef, is shown at the beginning. The particular combination of clefs has been interpreted by some modern scholars as a notational convention that implies a transposition up a minor third, as shown here and as sung on the accompanying recording. Such a convention would have been useful at a time when singers rarely encountered key signatures other than a single flat (see NAWM 38, 42, 43, and 46 for examples of the latter). Yet not all modern authorities agree on this interpretation. Some sources for the piece include an organ accompaniment, as shown here, but it is probably not by Byrd. The piece was probably composed for unaccompanied voices, as it is performed on the recording.

# GIOVANNI PIERLUIGI DA PALESTRINA

(1525/6–1594)

*Pope Marcellus Mass*: Credo and Agnus Dei I

*Mass*

CA. 1560

## (a) Credo

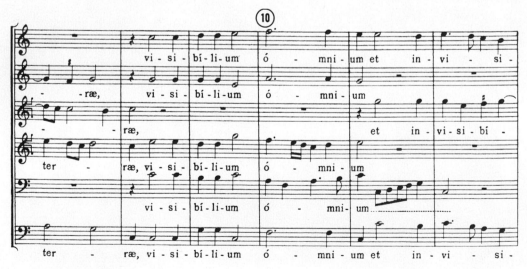

First published in Palestrina, *Missarum Liber secundus* (Second Book of Masses, Rome, 1567). From *Opere complete di Giovanni Pierluigi da Palestrina,* ed. Raffaele Casimiri, vol. 4 (Rome: Edizione Fratelli-Scalera, 1939): 177–87 and 194–96. Reprinted by permission of the Fondazione Istituto Italiano per la Storia della Musica, Rome.

242

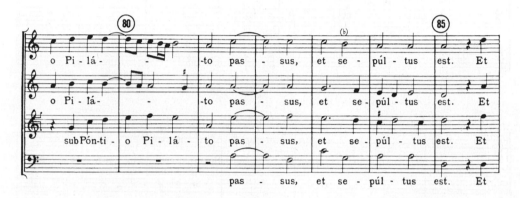

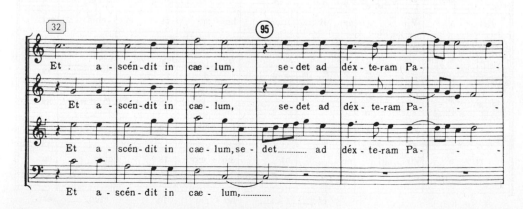

Credo in unum Deum, Patrem omnipotentem, fac-
torem caeli et terrae, visibilium omnium et
invisibilium.

Et in unum Dominum Jesum Christum Filium Dei
unigenitum. Et ex Patre natum ante omnia saecula. Deum de Deo, lumen de lumine, Deum
verum de Deo vero. Genitum, non factum, consubstantialem Patri: per quem omnia facta sunt.
Qui propter nos homines et propter nostram
salutem descendit de caelis. Et incarnatus est de
Spiritu Sancto ex Maria Virgine: et homo factus
est. Crucifixus etiam pro nobis: sub Pontio
Pilato passus, et sepultus est. Et resurrexit tertia
die, secundum Scripturas. Et ascendit in
caelum: sedet ad dexteram Patris. Et iterum
venturus est cum gloria judicare vivos et
mortuos: cujus regni non erit finis.

Et in Spiritum Sanctum, Dominum, et vivifican-
tem: qui ex Patre, Filioque procedit. Qui cum
Patre, et Filio simul adorator, et conglorificatur:
qui locutus est per Prophetas.

Et unam sanctam catholicam et apostolicam
Ecclesiam.

Confiteor unum baptisma in remissionem pecca-
torum. Et exspecto resurrectionem mortuorum.
Et vitam venturi saeculi. Amen.

I believe in one God, Father Almighty, maker of
heaven and earth, and of all things visible and
invisible.

And in one Lord Jesus Christ, the only-begotten
Son of God. Born of the Father before all ages.
God of God, light of light, true God of true God.
Begotten, not made, being of one substance with
the Father, by whom all things were made. Who
for us humans and for our salvation descended
from heaven. And was made incarnate by the
Holy Spirit of the Virgin Mary, and was made
man. And was crucified for us; under Pontius
Pilate He died, and was buried. And rose again
on the third day, according to the Scriptures.
And ascended into heaven, and sits at the right
hand of the Father. And He shall come again
with glory to judge the living and the dead; of
whose kingdom there shall be no end.

And in the Holy Spirit, Lord and giver of life, who
proceeds from the Father and the Son. Who,
together with the Father and the Son, is wor-
shiped and glorified; who spoke by the prophets.

And one holy, Catholic, and Apostolic Church.

I acknowledge one baptism for the remission of
sins. And I await the resurrection of the dead.
And the life of the world to come. Amen.

(b) Agnus Dei I

| Agnus Dei, qui tollis peccata mundi: miserere nobis. | Lamb of God, who takest away the sins of the world: have mercy on us. |

The relation of this mass to Pope Marcellus II, who reigned for only twenty days in 1555, is uncertain. It became Palestrina's most famous mass thanks to a legend that he composed it in order to demonstrate to the Council of Trent (1545–63) that it was possible to write a polyphonic mass that was reverent in spirit and did not obscure the words, thus saving polyphonic music from condemnation by the church. The legend is probably untrue, but it was widely believed in part because the text of the mass is set so clearly. Unlike the other masses we have seen (NAWM 25, 36b, 37, and 40), and unlike most of Palestrina's masses, this one is not based on an existing piece of music.

The Credo is a particularly challenging section of the mass to compose because of the importance and length of the text. In this setting, Palestrina abandoned imitation for the sake of clear diction and brevity. The voices pronounce a given phrase, not in the staggered manner of imitative polyphony, but simultaneously in the same rhythm, etching the text in the hearer's consciousness. Palestrina avoided monotony by dividing the six-voice choir into smaller groups and combining the different voices in constantly varying ways. He reserved the full six-voice ensemble for climactic or particularly significant phrases, such as "per quem omnia facta sunt" (by whom all things were made); this is the first instance when all six voices sing together, and it creates a musical image for the word "all." The six voices also sing together on the phrase "Et incarnatus est" (And was made incarnate), a point Palestrina emphasized because it is one of the central mysteries of the Christian faith. Other portions of the text are sung by three, four, or five voices at a time. Because there is little of the usual imitation or repetition, some voices do not sing some phrases of the text. Where clarity of the text is not an issue, as in the closing passage on "Amen" (measures 186–97), Palestrina returns to his more customary imitative style.

The section beginning at measure 13 illustrates Palestrina's flexible approach to musical textures. One group of four voices sings "Et in unum Dominum" (And in one Lord), and another group of four voices answers by repeating those words and completing the thought ("Jesum Christum"). Then "Filium Dei unigenitum" (only-begotten Son of God) is sung by three voices, symbolizing the three-in-one essence of the Trinity. The texture here is like that of fauxbourdon (see NAWM 35), which by Palestrina's time was considered old-fashioned or even crude. Yet Palestrina applied the sound of fauxbourdon to great effect here and elsewhere in the Credo; harmonies of sixths and thirds provide relief from the almost constant fifth-third combinations, and the texture also suggests the sacred by evoking the aura of a distant but still remembered past.

Throughout this section of the Credo, each phrase closes on a sixth-to-octave cadence. Palestrina preserved forward motion by postponing a full cadence until measure 27 and by beginning the next phrase immediately after each cadence with a syncopated sonority that enters on the next half beat (the next quarter note, in this transcription). He also used syncopation to stress accented syllables, such as the first syllables of "Dominum" and "Jesum." These syncopations contribute to a constantly varying rhythmic surface in which no two successive measures have the same rhythm.

As was common in setting the Credo, Palestrina divided the text into smaller sections. He set the portion beginning at "Crucifixus" for only four voices (measure 74), then returned to six voices at "Et in Spiritum Sanctum" (measure 116). He often illustrated the text through musical imagery. Some of the imagery is obvious, such as when the voices descend together at "descendit de caelis" (descended from Heaven) in measures 53–58, and when the upper voices ascend at "Et ascendit in caelum" (And ascended into Heaven) in measures 92–94. Other imagery is more subtle, such as when four voices sing "consubstantialem" (of one substance) in measures 40–42; this is a variant of the previous phrase and thus "of one substance" with it.

Palestrina used a similar approach for the Gloria of this mass, which also has a long and theologically crucial text. But the movements with shorter texts would be too brief if set in the same way, so there Palestrina turned to imitation and development of motives to create movements of sufficient weight and splendor, aware that the familiar text would be heard and understood as it was reinforced by repetition in all voices.

In Agnus Dei I, the opening subject is sung nine times, each statement differing somewhat from the others, in a point of imitation that lasts fifteen measures. "Qui tollis peccata mundi" (who takes away the sins of the world) is also treated imitatively, but the subject is even more varied from one voice to another, and whole phrases repeat in different voices with alterations in the counterpoint (compare measures 15–19 to measures 19–23), producing an intense development of the musical material. Each voice sings accented syllables on different beats, spinning out its line at its own pace, though at times two voices move together in parallel tenths (see measures 15–18, cantus and bassus I). The final phrase, "miserere nobis" (have mercy on us), receives similar treatment.

Palestrina's melodies typically move by step, and any skips or leaps are usually followed by stepwise motion in the opposite direction to fill in the gap. The counterpoint is mainly consonant. According to strict rules, only certain dissonances are allowed, all preceded and followed by consonances. These include passing tones, neighbor tones, suspensions, and cambiatas (figures in which a voice skips a third down from a dissonance to a consonance and then moves up a step to the expected tone of resolution, as in the cantus at measures 6–7 of the Agnus Dei). Final sonorities of each section and of major subsections most often include thirds—not merely the open fifths and octaves typical in earlier music.

In the original publications of the *Pope Marcellus Mass*, repetitions of text were not indicated even when they were clearly intended by the composer. In the edition included here, the repetitions have been supplied in italics by the editor, as in the cantus and tenor II in measures 16–18 of the Credo. As printed, the music is almost wholly diatonic, but singers likely added alterations through *musica ficta*, as indicated by the editor above the staff. Of the three required statements of "Agnus Dei" (see NAWM 3i), only the first is included here. For the second, singers either would have repeated the first or would have sung plainchant. Palestrina scored the last statement for seven voices (Agnus Dei II, omitted in this anthology).

# TOMÁS LUIS DE VICTORIA (1548–1611)

*O magnum mysterium*

*Missa O magnum mysterium*:
Kyrie

**46**

*Motet*

CA. 1570

*Imitation mass*

CA. 1580s

(a) *O magnum mysterium*

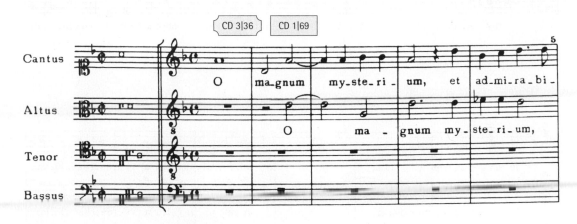

First published in Victoria, *Motectae* (Venice, 1572). From Tomás Luis de Victoria, *Opera omnia*, vol. 2, *Motetes I–XXI*, ed. Felipe Pedrell, rev. ed. Higinio Anglès, Monumentos de la música española 26 (Barcelona: Instituto español de musicología, 1965–68), 7–9. Reprinted by permission of Consejo Superior de Investigationes Científicas (C.S.I.C.).

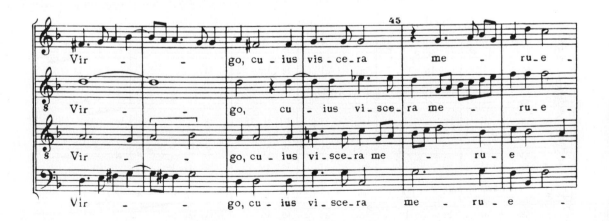

O magnum mysterium, et admirabile
sacramentum, ut animalia
viderent Dominum natum,
iacentem in praesepio.
O beata Virgo,
cuius viscera meruerunt portare
Dominum Iesum Christum. Alleluia.

O great mystery and awesome
sacrament, that the animals
should see the Lord, newly born,
lying in the manger.
O blessed Virgin,
whose womb was worthy of bearing
the Lord Jesus Christ. Alleluia.

(b) *Missa O magnum mysterium*: Kyrie

First published in Victoria, *Missae . . . liber secundus* (Rome, 1592). From *Thomae Ludovici Victoria Abulensis Opera omnia,* ed. Felipe Pedrell, vol. 2 (Leipzig: Breitkopf & Härtel, 1902–13), 6–9. Reproduced by permission of Consejo Superior de Investigaciones Científicas (C.S.I.C.).

Kyrie eleison.        Lord have mercy.
Christe eleison.      Christ have mercy.
Kyrie eleison.        Lord have mercy.

*O magnum mysterium* is Victoria's most widely known piece and is a favorite of modern choirs. He likely composed it during his early years in Rome, where he went to study at age seventeen, and it was published in his first book of motets in 1572. Written for the Feast of the Circumcision on January 1, the motet conveys the mystery, awe, reverence, and joy of the Christmas season through the use of expressive motives, affecting harmonies, and contrasting textures. About twenty years after composing the motet, Victoria used it as the basis for an *imitation mass*, a mass in which each movement is based on the same polyphonic work and all voices of that work are adapted in the mass, but none is used as a cantus firmus. The motet (NAWM 46a) exemplifies Victoria's style, and the first movement of the mass (NAWM46b) illustrates how an imitation mass differs from a cantus-firmus mass (see NAWM 36b and 37) or paraphrase mass (see NAWM 40).

Like Josquin (see NAWM 39–41), Victoria was fond of paired imitation. That is evident at the beginning of the motet, where the cantus and altus are paired and are echoed several measures later by the tenor and bassus. Victoria used some expressive license in composing the subject. Palestrina almost always would follow a leap with stepwise motion in the opposite direction, but Victoria sometimes continued with another leap or with stepwise motion in the same direction. In this motet, the large leaps of a fifth, both down and up, capture the sense of "magnum" (big, large, or great), and the combination of these fifths with the rising and falling semitone on "mysterium" suggests a sense of mystery.

Victoria turned to homophony in measures 16–26 and changed the number of voices every two or three measures to create maximum variety of texture. (In this score, measure numbers are at the upper right of the measure, rather than at the beginning of the measure.) The poignant false relation (F♮ in one voice followed immediately by F♯ in another) in measures 20–21 exemplifies an aspect of Victoria's expressive vocabulary that would not appear in the music of Palestrina. Elsewhere similar fluctuations occur between E and E♭, C and C♯, and B♭ and B♮, lending the music color and fluidity. Imitation, again with paired voices, resumes for the final clause of the first sentence, "iacentem in praesepio" (lying in the manger, in measures 27–39). After a brief silence, all four voices exclaim in awe, "O beata Virgo" (O blessed Virgin), and the outer voices weave a florid garland around the sustained inner voices. The final "Alleluia" is first set homophonically in a dancelike triple meter, then imitatively in duple.

The mode is transposed mode 2 (Hypodorian), with a final on G, one flat in the key signature, and a range in both cantus and tenor of about a fifth above and a fourth below the final. As would be expected in this mode, most strong cadences are on G, with others on D (measures 9, 25) and B♭ (measure 48), the fifth and third of the mode. At both of the main cadences—at the end of the first sentence (measure 39) and at the end of the piece—B♮ is included in the final sonority, creating a full major triad (as we would describe it); such a substitution of a major third (later sometimes called a "Picardy third") for the modally prescribed minor third became common for final cadences in music composed during the seventeenth and eighteenth centuries.

The first section of the motet has two main points of imitation—at the opening and at "iacentum in praesepio"—and these are both adapted by Victoria in the Kyrie movement of his *Missa O magnum mysterium*. The first Kyrie parallels measures 1–16 of the motet, featuring paired imitation between cantus and altus followed by an almost exact repetition in tenor and bassus. Yet the motives are considerably reworked so that the mass actually features two related subjects (one in cantus and tenor, the other in altus and bassus) fashioned from the motet's single subject. The entire polyphonic texture of the motet is reproduced in all voices, yet each voice is altered in subtle and interesting ways, showing what more can be done with the existing material. The Christe is based on a freely invented subject, as is frequently the case in imitation masses, but it retains the device of paired entrances. The second Kyrie is based on the point of imitation at "iacentum in praesepio" in the motet, especially on measures 30–39, again reworking the entrances and the counterpoint.

In discussing imitation masses, there is potential for confusion in terminology. In the term "imitation mass," the word "imitation" refers to the relationship between the mass and the polyphonic work it imitates, which is referred to as its *model*. But "imitation" is also used to describe the relation between voices, as one voice imitates a melody that another has just presented, and this sort of imitation is a characteristic that imitation masses typically share with paraphrase masses. Indeed, just by looking at or hearing this Kyrie and the Kyrie from Josquin's *Missa Pange lingua* (NAWM 40), one may not be able to tell which is the imitation mass and which the paraphrase mass. This is because they differ in how they relate to the source of musical material (respectively, a polyphonic work and a monophonic melody), but not in style or texture (both use imitative counterpoint). To avoid this potential confusion, some music historians use the terms *model mass* or *parody mass* instead of *imitation mass*.

As was becoming common in the later sixteenth century, most of the chromatic alterations, even at cadences, were marked by the composer rather than left to be determined by the singers, as had previously been the frequent practice. In comparing the motet and mass, note that the two editors have chosen different ratios of reduction for the original notation; as a result, the primary beat is transcribed as a quarter note in the motet but as a half note in the mass. (The opening of the original notation is shown at the beginning of the motet.) Both pieces are sung on the accompanying recordings by male choirs with boys on the upper parts, as was customary because of the proscription against women singing in church.

# ORLANDO DI LASSO (1532–1594)

*Tristis est anima mea*

*Motet*

CA. 1565

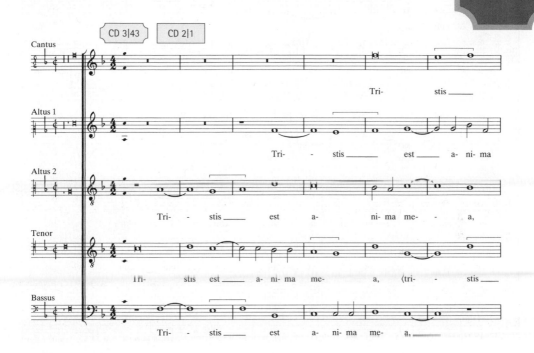

First published in Lasso, *Modullorum secundum volumen* (Paris, 1565). From Orlando di Lasso, *The Complete Motets*, vol. 4, *Motets for Six Voices from Primus liber concentuum sacrorum (Paris, 1564); Motets for Four to Ten Voices from Modullorum secundum volumen (Paris, 1565)*, ed. Peter Bergquist, Recent Researches in the Music of the Renaissance 105 (Madison, Wisc.: A-R Editions, 1966), 89–92. Used by permission.

| Tristis est anima mea usque ad mortem: | Sad is my soul, even unto death; |
|---|---|
| sustinete hic et vigilate mecum: | abide here and watch with me. |
| nunc videbitis turbam, quae | Soon you will see the crowd that |
| circumdabit me: vos fugam capietis, | will encircle me; you will take flight, |
| et ego vadam immolari pro vobis. | and I shall go to be sacrificed for you. |

*Tristis est anima mea* was published first in 1565 and again in the *Magnus opus musicum*, a collection of Lasso's motets that was issued posthumously in 1604 by his sons. It is a setting of a Responsory text for Maundy Thursday, the day before Good Friday, which commemorates Jesus' crucifixion. The text is drawn from the words Jesus said to his disciples the night before he was crucified (Matthew 26:38, Mark 14:34). Lasso was famous in his own time for his forceful and imaginative projection of his texts, and this motet features numerous examples.

The bassus introduces a motive of a descending semitone, F–E, on "Tristis" (sad). At first harmonized consonantly, the motive is treated as a suspension when it is repeated in other voices (measures 3–7). Lasso's use of semitones to express sadness and dissonant suspensions to achieve emotional tension rather than to prepare a cadence were techniques that were common in midcentury madrigals (see NAWM 50–53) but were still unusual in sacred music.

The second phrase of text is split into two units because of their different connotations. At measure 15, "sustinete" is interpreted in the sense not only of "abide" but also of "sustain"; the notes are sustained and then rise relatively slowly through sweet harmonies created by parallel tenths between altus I and bassus and alternating fifths and sixths between tenor and bassus. The contrasting faster motion at "vigilate mecum" (stay alert with me) suggests wakefulness (Jesus reproached his disciples several times for falling asleep on their watch). Lasso avoided a proper cadence on C at the end of this section (measure 27) to open the way for the declamatory proclamation "nunc videbitis" (soon you will see), repeated with increasing fervor at a higher pitch and with fuller sound.

The following section features even more vivid musical imagery. Starting in measure 35, the phrase "circumdabit me" (will encircle me) is illustrated by a figure, imitated in all the parts, that circles around its opening note. Here the semitones C–B–C and D–E♭–D and the range of a diminished fourth between B♮ and E♭ evoke through small intervals the press of the crowd around Jesus and also suggest a mournful feeling. Such use of chromatic alterations for text expression and depiction contrasts strongly with the almost wholly diatonic music of Palestrina. The phrase "Vos fugam capietis" (you will take flight) is portrayed musically by a point of imitation, called *fuga* (flight) in Italian; moreover, there are eleven entrances of the subject, symbolizing the eleven disciples who ran away when the twelfth, Judas, joined the angry crowd that beat and captured Jesus. Once again there is no cadence, and instead Lasso leads directly to the words "et ego vadam immolari pro vobis" (and I shall go to be sacrificed for you), set mostly homophonically in all the voices. Such alternation between imitation and homophony is typical of sixteenth-century polyphony, and here Lasso used it to project the text most forcefully.

In the last measures of the motet, the composer returned to imitation—both direct and in inversion—of a quickly moving scalar figure over a pedal point that seems to suggest the original meaning of *immolare*: to sprinkle grains of wheat (*mola*) over the sacrificial victim. This surge of activity leads to the only real full cadence in the work, marking the only period in the Latin text.

Thus, all the aspects of the musical setting were stimulated by the words: the rhythm, accentuation, and melodic contour of each motive; harmonic effects and cadences; changes of texture; devices such as suspensions and imitation; and, of course, clever illustration of the meanings and images in the text.

The editor has added text repetitions that are enclosed in triangular brackets. These were left out of the original source, but the music's rhythm and accentuation make clear what words the composer intended to be repeated, and the proper place-ment is easy to surmise. Lasso marked almost all the intended accidentals, leaving only the obvious leading tones at cadences to be supplied by the performers.

# JUAN DEL ENCINA (1468–1529)

## *Oy comamos y bebamos*

*Villancico*

LATE FIFTEENTH CENTURY

From *La obra musical de Juan del Encina*, ed. Manuel Morais (Salamanca: Centro de Cultura Tradicional, 1997), 199–200. Departamento de Cultura, Diputacion de Salamanca. Used by permission.

Oy comamos y bebamos
y cantemos y holguemos,
*que mañana ayunaremos.*

Today let's eat and drink
and sing and have a good time,
*for tomorrow we will fast.*

Por onrra de sant Antruejo
parémonos oy bien anchos,
enbutamos estos panchos,
rrecalquemos el pellejo,
que costumbr'es de conçejo
que todos oy nos hartemos,
*que mañana ayunaremos.*

To honor Saint Carnival
today let's end up very fat,
let's stuff our bellies,
let's stretch our skin,
for it's a custom of the council
that today we all gorge ourselves,
*for tomorrow we will fast.*

Honrremos a tan buen santo
porque en hambre nos acorra;
comamos a calca porra,
que mañana ay gran quebranto.
Comamos, bebamos tanto,
hasta que nos rrebentemos,
*que mañana ayunaremos.*

Let's honor this good saint
so that in hunger he may assuage us;
let's eat at top speed,
for tomorrow there will be great affliction.
Let's eat, let's drink so much,
until we burst,
*for tomorrow we will fast.*

Beve, Bras; más tú, Beneyto;
beva Pidruelo y Llorente.
Beve tú primeramente,
quitarnos has deste preito.
En bever bien me deleyto.
Daca, daca, beveremos,
*que mañana ayunaremos.*

Drink Bras; and you more, Beneyto;
drink Pidruelo and Llorente.
You drink first;
let's give up arguing about it.
Drinking delights me.
Give here, let's all drink,
*for tomorrow we will fast.*

Tomemos oy gasajado,
que mañana biene la muerte;
bevamos, comamos huerte;
vámonos para el ganado,
no perderemos bocado,
que comiendo nos iremos,
*que mañana ayunaremos.*

Let's take pleasure today,
for tomorrow comes death;
let's drink, let's eat heartily;
[then] let's return to our herd,
let's not lose a mouthful,
for eating we will go,
*for tomorrow we will fast.*

Encina was the first major Spanish playwright and a leading exponent of the villancico during the late fifteenth century, when he was in the service of the duke of Alba. Like many of his compositions, this villancico was included in the Cancionero Musical de Palacio, a manuscript anthology compiled in the 1490s for the court of Isabella and Ferdinand.

The villancico was devised and cultivated at court and among the aristocracy as a Spanish alternative to the French chanson. Despite their aristocratic origins, villancicos are in a quasi-popular style and often have texts that evoke the life of Spanish peasants. From troubadour songs about shepherd girls to the eighteenth-century French queen Marie Antoinette dressing up as a shepherdess, aristocrats amused themselves with representations of life in the lower classes, and the villancico is part of that tradition. *Oy comamos y bebamos* pretends to be a shepherd's song for Fat Tuesday, the day before the fasting and renunciation of Lent begin on Ash Wednesday. The text is humorous yet reassuring to its intended audience: it suggests that peasants are content with their place in the social order as long as they can eat and drink their fill. The music is also designed to sound rustic, with a primarily homophonic texture, simple harmonies (mostly what we would call root-position triads), and dancelike rhythms that use hemiola effects to shift between $\frac{6}{8}$ and $\frac{3}{4}$ meters.

Villancicos vary in form, but all include a refrain, called an *estribillo*, and one or more stanzas, called *coplas*. Here the refrain has three lines, and the stanzas have seven. Musically, the stanzas begin with a section called *mudanza* ("change") that includes two statements of a musical unit, each set to two lines of poetry. In many villancicos, the mudanza presents new material, but here it uses the last two-thirds of the refrain. The last three lines of each stanza, called the *vuelta* ("return" or "repetition"), repeat the music of the refrain. As in most villancicos, only the last line of the refrain text is repeated at the end of each stanza. When the mudanza includes only new material, the resulting form is aB ccaB ccaB, and so forth (using letters for musical repetitions and capitalization to show textual repetition). However, in this villancico, the three brief phrases of the refrain repeat throughout, in the pattern abC bcbcabC bcbcabC, and so forth. The essential aspect of the villancico form is the two-fold repetition of a segment of music at the beginning of each stanza, followed by the repetition of the music of the refrain, culminating in a textual refrain.

As in most fifteenth-century villancicos, the text appears only in the upper voice, which carries the main melody. The other parts may have been sung or may be performed on instruments, as they are in the recording accompanying this anthology. On that recording, the singer and players both add decorative embellishments to later stanzas, following the typical performing practice of the time.

# MARCO CARA (CA. 1465–1525)

*Io non compro più speranza*

*Frottola*

CA. 1500

Note values halved. Notes in the lute part with dots under them are played with an upward stroke. Bars through the lute staves are original. Those between the voice part and lute accompaniment are added by the present editors to show the implied metrical organization. This version was published by Franciscus Bossinensis in his *Tenori e contrabassi intabulati col sopran in canto figurato per cantar e somar col lauto, libro primo* (Venice, 1509); the original version in four parts was published by Ottaviano Petrucci in Frottole I (Venice, 1504). This edition from *Le Frottole per canto e liuto intabulate da Franciscus Bossinensis,* ed. Benvenuto Disertori (Milan: Ricordi, 1964), 390–91. Copyright by CASA RICORDI-BMG RICORDI S.p.A., Milan. Reprinted by permission.

| Io non compro più speranza | I'll buy no more hope, |
|---|---|
| Ché gli è falsa mercancia. | which is fake goods. |
| A dar sol attendo via | I can't wait to give away |
| Quella poca che m'avanza. | the little that I have left, |
| Io non compro più speranza | I'll buy no more hope, |
| Ché gli è falsa mercancia. | which is fake goods. |
| | |
| Cara un tempo la comprai, | Once I bought it at a high price; |
| Hor la vendo a bon mercato | now I sell it cheap; |
| E consiglio ben che mai | and I would advise that never |
| Non ne compri un sventurato | should the wretched buy it; |
| Ma più presto nel suo stato | rather let them in their condition |
| Se ne resti con costanza. | remain in constancy. |
| Io non ... | I'll buy ... |
| | |
| El sperare è come el sogno | To hope is like a dream |
| Che per più riesce in nulla, | that mostly results in nothing, |
| El sperar è proprio il bisogno | and hoping is truly the need |
| De chi al vento si trastulla, | of him who plays with the wind. |
| El sperare sovente anulla | Hoping often annihilates |
| Chi continua la sua danza. | the one who continues its dance. |
| Io non ... | I'll buy ... |

Marco Cara spent most of his career at the ducal court in Mantua in northern Italy, working for the Gonzaga family from 1494 to 1525. *Io non compro più speranza*, one of many frottole that Cara composed for performance at the Mantuan court, was published in Ottaviano Petrucci's first book of frottole (Venice, 1504) in its original four-part version with the top part to be sung and the rest to be either sung or played by instruments. It was subsequently arranged for voice and lute and published in the form transcribed here by Franciscus Bossinensis in 1509.

The text wittily suggests that it is better to be without hope than to suffer disappointment when the person one loves does not return the affection. Although suffering in love is still a theme in songs of this time, as in the old tradition of *fine amour* or courtly love, this poet does not laud faithfulness but rather takes a more cynical—and amusing—position. Additionally, his sixteenth-century merchant "shoptalk" implies a courtly mocking of the rising merchant class.

The lute tablature (a notation that indicates where the player should put his or her fingers and which strings to pluck) has a barline every four beats, as preserved in this transcription. But the music actually moves in a dance rhythm of six beats per measure, as marked by the barlines inserted between the voice and the lute parts. These six beats are organized sometimes as three groups of two and at other times as two groups of three, producing the hemiola effect so characteristic of frottole, canzonettas, and other popular song types during the sixteenth and early seventeenth centuries. A similar rhythmic effect is found in Encina's villancico in NAWM 48. Like villancicos, frottole were written for aristocratic entertainment but in a mock-popular style, evident in their simple melodies and harmonization primarily with what are now called root-position triads.

Although the term "frottola" is applied to musical settings of various types of popular poetry, this song manifests the poetic and musical form of the frottola proper, also called *barzelletta*. The poem consists of a four-line *ripresa*, whose first two lines are immediately repeated and then return as a refrain, and a six-line *stanza*, consisting of two two-line *piedi* ("feet") and a two-line *volta* ("return" or "repetition"). These terms derive from those asociated with the earlier ballata (see NAWM 30). The music is coordinated with this poetic structure through the scheme shown below.

This structure resembles that of the villancico (see NAWM 48), whose stanzas likewise begin with two pairs of two lines each, followed by a repetition of the music of the refrain that culminates in a repetition of both music and text.

| Music mm. | Poetic lines | Rhyme | Poetic form |
|---|---|---|---|
| | **Ripresa** | | |
| 1–3 | Io non compro più speranza | a | Ripresa |
| 4–6 | Ché gli è falsa mercancia. | b | |
| 7–9 | A dar sol attendo via | b | |
| 10–12 | Quella poca che m'avanza. | a | |
| 13–15 | Io non compro più speranza | a | Refrain |
| 16–27 | Ché gli è falsa mercancia. | b | |
| | **Stanza 1** | | |
| 1–3 | Cara un tempo la comprai | c | Piede |
| 4–6 | Hor la vendo a bon mercato | d | |
| 1–3 | E consiglio ben che mai | c | Piede |
| 4–6 | Non ne compri un sventurato | d | |
| 7–9 | Ma più presto nel suo stato | d | Volta |
| 10–12 | Se ne resti con costanza. | a | |
| 13–15 | Io non compro più speranza | a | Refrain |
| 16–27 | Ché gli è falsa mercancia. | b | |

# JACQUES ARCADELT (CA. 1507–1568)

## Il bianco e dolce cigno

*Madrigal*

CA. 1538

Note values halved. Published in *Il primo libro di Madrigali d'Archadelt a quatro con nuova gionta impressi* (Venice, 1539); first edition lost but probably from 1538. This edition from Arcadelt, *Opera omnia,* ed. Albert Seay, vol. 2, *Madrigali: Libro primo,* Corpus mensurabilis musicae 31 (American Institute of Musicology, 1970), 38–40. © Hänssler Verlag, D-71087 Holzgerlingen. Used by permission of A-R Editions.

| | |
|---|---|
| Il bianco e dolce cigno | The white and sweet swan |
| Cantando more. Et io | dies singing. And I, |
| Piangendo giung' al fin del viver mio. | weeping, come to the end of my life. |
| Stran' e diversa sorte, | Strange and different fate, |
| Ch'ei more sconsolato, | that it dies disconsolate, |
| Et io moro beato. | and I die happy— |
| Morte che nel morire, | a death that in dying |
| M'empie di gioia tutt'e di desire. | fills me fully with joy and desire. |
| Se nel morir' altro dolor non sento, | If when I die no other pain I feel, |
| Di mille mort' il dì sarei contento. | with a thousand deaths a day I would be content. |

—ALFONSO D'AVALOS

Jacob Arcadelt's first book of madrigals was enormously popular. First printed in 1538, it went through 58 editions, the last of which was printed in 1654, over a century after its first appearance. Among its contents was the most famous of the early madrigals, *Il bianco e dolce cigno*, composed in the mid-1530s while Arcadelt was in Florence and reprinted in many anthologies.

Unlike a frottola, the poem used in a madrigal is not strophic and has no refrain or other repetition. This poem freely alternates lines of seven and eleven syllables with a free rhyme scheme (abb cdd ee ff). (Note that in Italian, vowels often elide; for example, the "-co" at the end of "bianco" and the "e" that follows are elided and treated as one syllable.) The poetic imagery is based on the traditional beliefs that swans sing only when they die and that sexual climax resembles a "little death" (a euphemism often used by Renaissance poets). Ironies abound: at the moment of death, the swan sings and yet is disconsolate, while the poet—experiencing a different kind of death—weeps but is filled with joy and desire, wishing as many such deaths as possible. The sentiment is at once surprising, amusing, and erotic.

Arcadelt's setting is primarily homophonic and has clearly marked rhythms, as in a frottola (see NAWM 49). But the first three lines do not follow the structure of the poem, as was customary in a frottola. The first cadence (measure 5) occurs in the middle of the second line of poetry, completing the thought and the sentence. The end of that line runs into the third, following the second sentence as it continues through the line ending (an effect called *enjambment*). Thus, Arcadelt preserved the syntax and meaning of the text and also underscored the word "more" (dies) with a dissonant suspension. At "Et io piangendo" (And I weeping), he illustrated the sharp contrast between the swan's song and the lover's tears with an excursion to an E♭ triad. The juxtaposition of major triads a whole step apart, causing a tritone relation between A and E♭ (measure 6), becomes a metaphor for death; this same relation exists between the triads on B♭ and C at "morire" (to die) in measure 26 and at "morir" in measure 31. Although the work is through-composed, without the repetitive form of a frottola or villancico, Arcadelt did occasionally introduce repetitions of both words and music, often with subtle variations (measures 10–15 repeat measures 5–10 with voices exchanging material, and later measures 38–42 repeat measures 34–38).

Arcadelt departed from the prevailing homophony at "stran' e diversa sorte" (strange and different fate) to suggest a musical image of difference. Then, at "mille mort' il di" (a thousand deaths a day), twelve single or paired entries sing a lilting motive. The multiple imitative entries evoke the idea of a high number, and the contentment conveyed by the motive and its rising and falling contour remind us of the metaphorical meaning of "death."

Madrigals were customarily performed with one voice on each part at upper-class gatherings that could include mixed groups of men and women. Sometimes instruments replaced one or more of the voice parts. In general, madrigals were intended for the pleasure of the performers themselves, rather than for an audience. Since each singer read only his or her line out of a partbook, one enjoyable aspect of sight-singing was the surprise of hearing how the parts fit together. Here, for example, the images created by changing between homophony and polyphony would only be recognized in performance.

# Cipriano de Rore (1516–1565)

*Da le belle contrade d'oriente*

*Madrigal*

CA. 1560–65

From Cipriano de Rore, *Opera omnia,* ed. Bernhard Meier, Corpus mensurabilis musicae 14 (American Institute of Musicology, 1969), 96–99. © Hänssler Verlag, D-71087 Holzgerlingen. Used by permission of A-R Editions.

Da le belle contrade d'oriente
Chiar' e lieta s'ergea Ciprigna, ed io
Fruiva in braccio al divin idol mio
Quel piacer che non cape' humana mente,
Quando senti dopp'un sospir ardente:
"Speranza del mio cor, dolce desio,
T'en vai, haimè! Sola mi lasci! Adio!
Che sarà qui di me scur' e dolente?
Ahi crud' amor! Ben son dubbios' e
　　corte
Le tue dolcezze, poi ch'anchor ti godi,
Che l'estremo piacer finisc' in pianto."
Ne potendo dir più cinseme forte
Iterando gl'ampless' in tanti nodi,
Che giamai ne fer più l'edro o l'acanto.

From the fair regions of the East,
clear and bright rose Venus, and I
enjoyed in the arms of my divine idol
the pleasure that no human mind can understand,
when I heard after a burning sigh:
"Hope of my heart, sweet desire,
you go, alas! Alone you leave me! Farewell!
What will become of me, gloomy and sad?
O cruel love! Much too tentative and
　　brief are
your sweet caresses. Besides, you even take delight
in seeing this extreme pleasure end in tears."
Unable to say more, she held me tight,
repeating her embraces in many coils,
more than ever heather or acanthus made.

—ANONYMOUS

Cipriano de Rore probably composed *Da le belle contrade d'oriente* near the end of his life, since it was published posthumously, in his last collection of madrigals. The text is both erotic and moving: pleasant lovemaking is followed by the woman's complaint that her lover is about to leave her, leading to embraces that suggest both her passion and her desire to keep her lover close to her.

The poem is a sonnet, a form with fourteen eleven-syllable lines divided between an octave (the first eight lines) and sestet (the last six lines). Following the model set by the poet Francesco Petrarca (or Petrarch, 1304–1374), the anonymous poet further divided the octave into two quatrains and the sestet into two tercets, with an overall rhyme scheme of abba abba cde cde. (This differs from the Shakespearean sonnet, which has ten-syllable lines in the rhyme scheme abab cdcd efef gg.) Typically, the octave sets up a situation, and the sestet provides a twist or culmination.

In his setting, Rore marked the division between octave and sestet with the longest rest in the piece for all voices (measure 41), and he clearly delineated the divisions between quatrains and tercets with cadences at measures 21 and 56. He also observed the rhythm of the words very closely, placing longer notes on accented syllables, as in the first phrase. At times this produces syncopation, as it does in measures 13–15 and 49–51. As is typical of madrigals, Rore's setting is through-composed but occasionally repeats a phrase with some variation, especially at the end (compare measures 69–73 to measures 76–80).

This work represents the second generation of the madrigal, when five and six parts were common. The fifth voice is labeled *quintus* (Latin for "fifth"). Rore varied the texture from one voice to five, with diverse combinations of two, three, and four voices in between. Such changes of texture help to indicate the shift between the poet's narration and the woman's speech. The opening narration closes with a passage for the four lowest voices (measures 21–25). Then as the woman begins to speak, the top voice reenters and carries the leading melody throughout her entire speech (measures 25–56) while the others accompany. When she ceases to speak, the top voice briefly drops out and the lower voices resume the narration (measures 56–57).

Words and feelings are conveyed through striking musical devices. The ascent of the planet Venus is depicted with ascending scales that rise as much as a twelfth in the bassus. The woman's first phrase, "Speranza del mio cor" (Hope of my heart), brightly rises in the top line supported by major triads, suggesting hopefulness. At "Te'n vai, haimè" (You go, alas!), melodic half steps and minor thirds convey sadness, heightened by frequent rests that evoke sighs or sobs. At "sola mi lasci" (alone you leave me), the uppermost voice sings alone, with a rising chromatic line; such chromaticism, inspired by the use of chromatic intervals in ancient Greek music (see NAWM 2), was understood as a sign for grief. Later in the piece, Rore indulged in graphic musical images sometimes called *madrigalisms*. Closely consecutive entrances of the motive on "cinseme forte" (hold me tight) depict the meaning of the words, and in the last two lines multiple repetitions and fast runs represent the coils of embraces that resemble the climbing vines of heather or acanthus.

The harmony also reflects the poetry. The modal center is clearly F, and the piece is in mode 6 (Hypolydian), with both tenor and cantus moving primarily in the range from low C to high D. But during the woman's emotional speech, the harmony goes far afield, touching triads as distant as E major on the sharp side (measures 36–37) and D♭ major in the flat direction (measure 48) and including stark juxtapositions such as A major with C minor (measures 40–41). Half a century later, Claudio Monteverdi credited Rore with starting a "second practice" in which the melody and harmony were ruled by the text and were freed from the restrictions of strict modal counterpoint; he must have had compositions such as this in mind.

In the edition included here, the barlines are indicated between staves but not within each staff in order to preserve the feel of the original notation, which had no barlines. The value of some notes extends beyond the next barline, such as the dotted quarter note at the end of the first measure.

# Luca Marenzio (1553–1599)

*Solo e pensoso*

*Madrigal*

1590s

**52**

First published in Luca Marenzio, *Il nono libro de madrigali a 5 voci* (Venice: Gardano, 1599). This edition from *Music and Patronage in Sixteenth-Century Mantua,* ed. Iain Fenlon, vol. 2 (Cambridge: Cambridge University Press, 1982), 99–105. Reprinted with the permission of Cambridge University Press.

52 LUCA MARENZIO *Solo e pensoso*

Solo e pensoso i più deserti campi
Vo misurando a passi tardi e lenti;
E gl'occhi porto, per fuggire, intenti,
Dove vestigio uman l'arena stampi.
Altro scherno non trovo che mi scampi
Dal manifesto accorger de le genti;
Perchè negli atti d'allegrezza spenti
Di fuor si legge com'io dentro avampi:
Si ch'io mi credo homai che monti e
    piagge
E fiumi e selve sappian di che tempre
Sia la mia vita, ch'è celata altrui.
Ma pur sì aspre vie nè sì selvagge
Cercar non sò, ch'Amor non venga sempre
Ragionando con meco, et io con lui.

—FRANCESCO PETRARCA (PETRARCH)

Alone and pensive, the deserted fields
I measure with steps deliberate and slow;
and my eyes I hold in readiness to flee
from a place marked by human footsteps.
No other defense I find that can save me
from the peering eyes of people;
because when laughter and cheer are spent,
from outside can be read my inner flame.
So I have come to believe that mountains and
    beaches
and rivers and woods know of what fibers
is made my life, hidden from others.
Yet paths neither so rough nor wild
can I find where Cupid does not seek me always
to debate with me, and I with him.

This madrigal, published in Marenzio's ninth book of madrigals in the year of his death, is one of his most celebrated. A setting of a sonnet by Petrarch, it is a masterpiece of sensitive musical imagery, harmonic refinement, and deft counterpoint. The chromatic scale in the topmost voice, rising deliberately one half-step per measure from $g'$ to $a''$ and then descending to $d''$, represents the poet's measured steps as he wanders pensively in the deserted fields. This chromatic scale is not only effective as tone painting, it also represents a new musical resource, because composers prior to Marenzio's generation had never extended chromatic motion for more than a few semitones in one direction. The descending arpeggios in the lower voices paint a forbidding, desolate landscape.

The jagged melodic subject imitated by all the voices in measures 25–33 depicts the poet's darting eyes as he looks for a hiding place—he fears that his eyes will reveal his inner fire. He feels safe among the mountains, beaches, rivers, and woods that already know him. These surroundings are depicted musically: the mountains by a series of leaps (measures 88–92) and the flowing rivers by eighth-note runs spanning a seventh passed from voice to voice (measures 93–100). When the poet complains that he cannot find terrain rough enough to discourage Cupid from following him, the voices stumble over each other in syncopations, suspensions, and cross-relations (measures 111–21). A subject that gallops head-long down an octave in dotted notes represents Cupid in hot pursuit, while two of the voices repeat the phrase "cercar non sò" (I cannot find).

Despite the chromaticism, *Solo e pensoso* is clearly in the mode of G, specifically mode 7 (Mixolydian), as indicated by the range of the cantus and tenor. G is the most common cadential note, followed by the modal tenor D. The end of the sonnet's octave (the first eight lines) is marked by a strong cadence on D and a pause that delineate the two sections of the poetic form (octave and sestet) through harmonic means.

In comparing *Solo e pensoso* with the madrigals of Arcadelt and Rore (see NAWM 50–51), we see the vocal lines becoming more complex and harder to sing with each generation. Although earlier madrigals were intended almost solely for convivial singing, for the entertainment of the singers themselves, late-sixteenth-century madrigals such as Marenzio's were often conceived for professional groups of singers, who played an increasingly important role at courts in northern Italy.

# CARLO GESUALDO (CA. 1561–1613)

## "Io parto" e non più dissi

*Madrigal*

CA. 1600

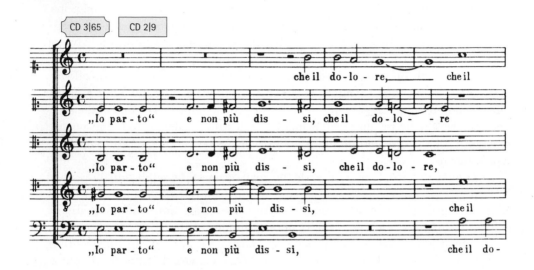

First published in Carlo Gesualdo, *Madrigali a cinque voci libro sesto* (Gesualdo, 1611). This edition from Gesualdo, *Sämtliche Madrigale für fünf Stimmen*, ed. Wilhelm Weismann, vol. 6, *Sechstes Buch* (Hamburg: Ugrino Verlag, 1957), 29–32. © 1957 by Ugrino Verlag, Hamburg. Assigned to VEB Deutscher Verlag für Musik, Leipzig. Reprinted by permission of Bärenreiter Music Corporation.

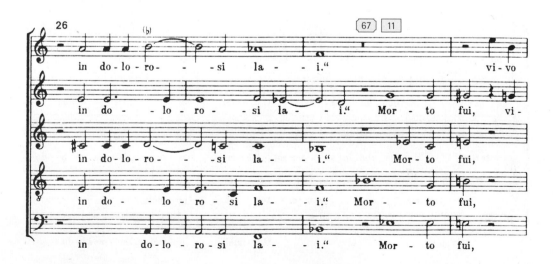

"Io parto" e non più dissi che il dolore
Privò di vita il core.
Allor proruppe in pianto e disse Clori
Con interrotti omèi:
"Dunque ai dolori io resto. Ah, non fia
    mai
Ch'io non languisca in dolorosi lai."
Morto fui, vivo son che i spirti spenti

tornaro in vita a sì pietosi accenti.

"I depart." I said no more, for grief
robbed my heart of life.
Then Clori broke out in tears and said,
with interrupted cries of "Alas":
"Hence in pain I remain. Ah, may I
    never
cease to pine away in sad laments."
Dead I was, now I am alive, for my
    spent spirits
return to life at the sound of such
    pitiable accents.

Although this madrigal was first published in 1611, it may have been composed in the late 1590s. It exemplifies Carlo Gesualdo's use of contrasts between chromatic and diatonic, dissonant and consonant, homophonic and imitative, and slowly and quickly moving passages to heighten the emotions and dramatic impact of the poem.

The text is full of strong images and changes in tone that made it well suited for Gesualdo's musical style. The poem hinges on surprise: it begins with a grief-stricken scene of two lovers parting and then turns erotic as the speaker implies that the couple has just made love (when he refers to his "spent spirits") and that the woman's distress arouses him again ("Dead I was, now I am alive"). The sudden change to present tense in the last sentence suggests that something more may ensue before he departs.

Each segment of text receives individual treatment. The first line is set to three distinct musical ideas: simple, matter-of-fact recitation for "Io parto" (I depart), set off with a rest to suggest the quotation marks; a chromatic rise to a half cadence for the speaker's comment that he said no more, implying unspoken pain; and an expression of grief through a descending line and a suspension on "dolore" (grief). The last figure is immediately intensified by a repetition a semitone higher with the descending whole steps altered to half steps (measure 6) and an ending on a very distant harmony (F♯ rather than C, as in measure 5). Similarly, the second line is split into two musical ideas: simple recitation on "Privò" and then descending imitative entries that represent a heart breaking. Chromaticism marks words associated with sadness, such as "pianto" (tears, measures 13–15) and "ai dolori io resto" (I remain in pain, measures 20–23), and the interrupted cries of "alas" are depicted with short rests that break into each part like breaths between sobs (measures 17–19). When Clori begins to speak (measure 20), the three upper parts declaim against the bass in the same way that the three lower parts did for the opening words of her male lover.

The music of the penultimate line (measures 28–37) contains three separate images: of death, through a chromatic succession of sustained chords; of renewed life, through a diatonic motive in rapid motion, close imitation, and syncopation; and of exhaustion—or the expending of spirits—through a rapid descending scale figure. In the last line, Gesualdo indulged in a pun by setting the word "accenti" (accents) with ornamental runs of the kind that when improvised were called *accenti*.

Despite his fragmentation of the poetic text through this great variety of musical figures and textures, Gesualdo achieved continuity by avoiding conventional cadences and thus linking each phrase to the next. Although often chromatic, the madrigal is clearly in mode 3 (Phrygian), as demonstrated by the first and final sonorities and by the ranges of the cantus and tenor (second part from the bottom). Gesualdo emphasized the main steps of the mode at beginnings and endings of lines and at pauses—E, the final (measures 1, 4, 7, 15, 23, 29, and 43–44); C, the tenor (measures 5 and 12); A, the tenor of the related plagal mode (measures 17, 21, 26, and 37); and G (measures 11, 40, and 42) and B (measures 3, 25, and 40), the other strong notes in the mode.

# CLAUDIN DE SERMISY (CA. 1490–1562)

*Tant que vivray*

*Chanson*

CA. 1527

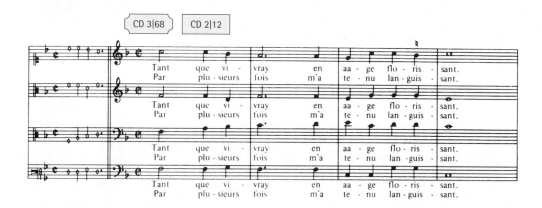

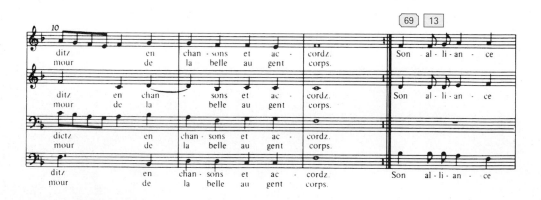

From Claudin de Sermisy, *Collected Works,* vol. 1, *Chansons,* ed. Gaston Allaire and Isabelle Cazeaux (American Institute of Musicology, 1974), pp. 99–100. © Hänssler Verlag, D-71087 Holzgerlingen. Used by permission of A-R Editions, Inc.

| | |
|---|---|
| Tant que vivray en aage florissant, | As long as I am able-bodied, |
| Je serviray d'amours le roy puissant | I shall serve the potent king of love |
| En fais en ditz en chansons et accordz. | through deeds, words, songs, and harmonies. |
| Par plusieurs fois m'a tenu languissant, | Many times he made me languish, |
| Mais apres deul m'a faict rejoyssant | but after mourning, he let me rejoice, |
| Car j'ay l'amour de la belle au gent | because I have the love of the fair lady |
| corps. | with the lovely body. |
| Son alliance | Her alliance |
| C'est ma fiance, | is my betrothal. |
| Son cueur est mien, | Her heart is mine, |
| Le mien est sien, | mine is hers. |
| Fy de tristesse, | Shun sorrow. |
| Vive lyesse, | Live in merriment, |
| Puisqu'en amour a tant de bien. | because there is so much good in love. |

70 14

| | |
|---|---|
| Quand je la veulx servir et honorer, | When I want to serve and honor her, |
| Quand par escriptz veulx son nom decorer, | when I want to adorn her name with words, |
| Quand je la veoy et visite souvent, | when I see and visit her often, |
| Ses envieux n'en font que murmurer; | those jealous of her do nothing but whisper; |
| Mais nostre amour n'en scauroit moins durer; | but our love would not last any less, |
| Autant ou plus en emporte le vent. | however far the wind carries the rumors. |
| Maulgré envie, | Despite jealousy, |
| Toute ma vie, | all my life, |
| Je l'aymeray | I will love her |
| Et chanteray; | and sing of her; |
| C'est la premiere, | She is the first, |
| C'est la derniere | she is the last |
| Que j'ay servie et serviray. | that I have served and will serve. |

—CLÉMENT MAROT

Claudin de Sermisy probably wrote *Tant que vivray* for the French royal court, where he spent most of his career. Parisian publisher Pierre Attaingnant included it in a collection of chansons that was printed in early 1528. It became one of the most popular chansons of its era and was reprinted many times during the following century.

*Tant que vivray* represents a new type of chanson cultivated in France beginning in the 1520s and characterized by repetitive form, lighthearted words, lively rhythms, and syllabic and homophonic textures. The text of this chanson has two strophes, each sung to the same music, and the parallel structure and rhyme schemes of lines 1–3 and 4–6 of each stanza are highlighted through musical repetition, creating an AAB form for each strophe. Sectional repetitions like these are found in other light forms of the period, such as the frottola and canzonetta, but not in the madrigal. The poem expresses the happy feelings of a contented lover; the many short lines and quick rhymes in the second half of each stanza seem especially to suggest the bubbling up of joy.

The setting is syllabic and mostly homophonic. Even the apparent imitation between altus and tenor in measures 13–18 is simply the result of repeating short phrases in three-part homophony with the middle part alternating between the two inner voices. The principal tune is in the cantus, but the other parts are also tuneful and rewarding to sing, as is appropriate in a piece intended for amateurs to sing for their own enjoyment. The harmony consists mostly of what we would call root-position triads and strongly defines the pitch center of F. At some cadences, as the voices declaim the text together, a traditional suspension becomes an accented dissonance (for example, the $c''$ in measure 3).

Because the same music is used for more than one set of words, it is evident that the composer did not set out to illustrate specific words or phrases in the text, but the general spirit of the setting captures the good cheer and optimism of the poem. The rhythms are lively and well suited to the words. The ends of the long lines of text are set to relatively long notes, and short lines end with repeated notes, thereby emphasizing the form of the poetry. The long-short-short rhythm that opens the piece became a characteristic feature of chansons; the same rhythm in diminution begins the B section, which moves along more rapidly than the first section, as suits its more active text.

Chansons such as this were usually sung by one voice per part. Alternatively, some or all parts could be played by instruments, or a performer could sing the top part while playing the bass line and notes from the other parts on the lute. The adaptability of such chansons is attested by a large number of arrangements for various forces. In the performance on the accompanying recording, a lute accompanies the singers, and some of the singers add embellishments during the second verse.

# CLAUDE LE JEUNE (CA. 1528–1600)

## Revecy venir du printans

*Chanson*

LATE SIXTEENTH CENTURY

Published in *Le Printemps* (Paris: Ballard, 1603). This edition adapted from that of Henry Expert in *Les maîtres musiciens de la Renaissance française*, 12 (Paris: Alphonse Leduc, 1900), 11–27.

Le Ca-nard s'e-gay-e plon-jant, Et se la-ve coint de-dans l'eau:
Et la grû' qui four-che son vol Re-tra-ver-se l'air et s'en va.

**[73] Rechant à 5**

Re-ve-cy ve-nir du Prin-tans L'a-mou-reuz' et bel-le sai-zon.

**[2] Chant à 3**

Le So-leil é-clai-re lui-zant D'u-ne plus sé-rei-ne clair-té:

Du nu-a - ge l'om-bre s'en - fuit, Qui se ioû' et court et noir-cît Et fo-retz et champs et cou taus.

Le la-beur hu-main re-ver-dît, Et la prê' dé-cou-vre ses fleurs.

**75**
**Rechant à 5**

Re-ve-cy ve-nir du Prin - tans L'a-mou-reuz' et bel - le sai - zon.

[3]  **Chant à 4**

De Ve-nus le filz Cu-pi — don   L'u-ni-vers se-mant de ses trais,

De sa flam-me va ré-chau — fér, A-ni-maus, qui vo-let en l'air,

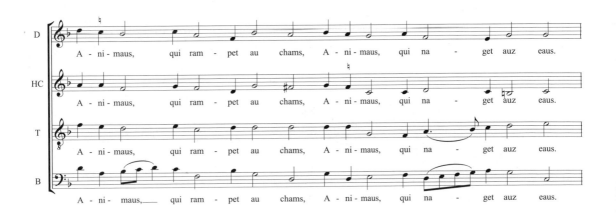

A-ni-maus, qui ram-pet au chams, A-ni-maus, qui na — get auz eaus.

Ce qui mes - me-ment ne__ sent pas, A-mou-reux se fond de plai - zir.

Ce qui__ mes - me-ment ne sent pas, A-mou-reux se__ fond de plai - zir.

Ce qui mes - me-ment ne sent pas, A-mou-reux se fond__ de plai - zir.

Ce qui mes - me-ment ne sent pas, A-mou-reux se fond de plai - zir.

**77**

**Ce reste est à 5**

Re - ve - cy ve - nir du Prin - tans L'a-mou - reuz' et bel - le sai - zon.

Re - ve - cy ve - nir du Prin - tans L'a-mou - reuz' et bel - le sai - zon.

Re - ve - cy ve - nir du Prin - tans L'a-mou - reuz' et bel - le sai - zon.

Re - ve - cy ve - nir du__ Prin - tans L'a-mou - reuz' et__ bel - le sai - zon.

Re - ve - cy ve - nir du Prin - tans L'a-mou - reuz' et bel - le sai - zon.

[4] **78**

Ri - on aus - si nous: et cher - chon Les é-bas et ieus du Prin - tans:

Ri - on aus - si nous: et cher - chon Les é-bas et__ ieus du Prin - tans:

Ri - on aus - si__ nous: et cher - chon Les_ é-bas__ et ieus__ du Prin - tans:

Ri - on aus - si nous:__ et cher - chon Les é-bas__ et ieus__ du Prin - tans:

Ri - on aus - si nous: et cher - chon Les é-bas et ieus du Prin - tans:

Revecy venir du Printans
L'amoureuz' et belle saizon.

Le courant des eaus recherchant
Le canal d'été s'éclaircît:
Et la mer calme de ces flots
Amolit le triste courrous:
Le Canard s'egaye plonjant,
Et se lave coint dedans l'eau;
Et la grû' qui fourche son vol
Retraverse l'air et s'en va.

Revecy venir du Printans
L'amoureuz' et belle saizon.

Here again comes the Spring,
the amorous and fair season.

The currents of water that seek
the canal in summer become clearer;
and the calm sea the waves'
sad anger soothes.
The duck, elated, dives
and washes itself quietly in the water.
And the crane that branches off in flight
recrosses the air and flies away.

Here again comes the Spring,
the amorous and fair season.

| | |
|---|---|
| Le Soleil éclaire luizant | The sun shines brightly |
| D'une plus séreine clairté: | with a calmer light. |
| Du nuage l'ombre s'enfuit, | The shadow of the cloud vanishes |
| Qui se ioû' et court et noircît. | from him who sports and runs and darkens. |
| Et foretz et champs et coutaus | Forests and fields and slopes |
| Le labeur humain reverdît, | human labor makes green again, |
| Et la prê' découvre ses fleurs. | and the prairie unveils its flowers. |
| | |
| Revecy venir du Printans | Here again comes the Spring, |
| L'amoureuz' et belle saizon. | the amorous and fair season. |
| | |
| De Venus le filz Cupidon | Cupid, the son of Venus, |
| L'univers semant de ses trais, | seeding the universe with his arrows, |
| De sa flamme va réchaufér, | with his flame he will rekindle |
| Animaus, qui volet en l'air, | animals that fly in the air, |
| Animaus, qui rampet au chams, | animals that crawl in the fields, |
| Animaus, qui naget auz eaus. | animals that swim in the seas. |
| Ce qui mesmement ne sent pas, | Even those that feel not, |
| Amoureux se fond de plaizir. | in love they melt in pleasure. |
| | |
| Revecy venir du Printans | Here again comes the Spring, |
| L'amoureuz' et belle saizon. | the amorous and fair season. |
| | |
| Rion aussi nous: et cherchon | Let us, too, laugh, and let us seek |
| Les ébas et ieus du Printans: | the sports and games of Spring: |
| Toute chose rit de plaizir: | everything smiles with pleasure; |
| Sélebron la gaye saizon, | let us celebrate the merry season. |
| | |
| Revecy venir du Printans | Here again comes the Spring, |
| L'amoureuz' et belle saizon. | the amorous and fair season. |

Claude Le Jeune composed *Revecy venir du printans* sometime during the late 1500s, and it was published after his death. It exemplifies *musique mesurée* (measured music), which reflected a new approach to poetry and music that was practiced in elite circles in late-sixteenth-century France.

The poets of the Académie de Poésie et de Musique (Academy of Poetry and Music), founded in 1570 under the patronage of King Charles IX, sought to unite poetry and music as in ancient times. They wrote strophic French verses in ancient classical meters, which they called *vers mesurés à l'antique* (measured verses in ancient style), substituting the ancient Greek and Latin quantities of long and short syllables for the modern stress accents. Since the French language lacked any consistent distinction between long and short vowels, the theorists of *vers mesuré* created a system in which syllables were assigned long and short values. Composers such as Le Jeune set these verses accordingly, with long notes for the long vowels and notes half as long for the short vowels, producing *musique mesurée*. Through this fusion of poetry and music, the poets and composers associated with the Académie sought to revive the ethical effects of ancient Greek music and thereby improve society. Such goals reflect the ideals of Renaissance humanism, although neither a revival of Greek *ethos* nor social improvement seems to have been the result. Instead, the varying patterns of long and short notes in *musique mesurée* were adopted in later French styles of setting texts, including the *air de cour* (court air) and French opera in the seventeenth century (see NAWM 77b).

In this chanson, the following pattern of long (L) and short (S) syllables is used almost throughout: SS LS LS L L. This results in rhythmic groupings of quarter notes in the pattern 2 3 3 2 2. Although identical to a popular hemiola rhythm used by Cara in his frottole (see NAWM 49) and later by Monteverdi in his canzonettas (see NAWM 66a), the rhythm here derives from a different source, namely an attempt to emulate ancient Greek poetic meter. Melismas, most of no more than four notes, relieve the uniformity of rhythm and add lightness and charm to the individual parts.

The refrain, or *rechant*, is for five voices, and the strophes, or *chants*, are successively for two, three, four, and five voices. The five voice parts are labeled with French rather than Latin terms: *Dessus* for superius, *Taille* for tenor, *Haute-Contre* for contratenor altus, *Basse-Contre* for contratenor bassus, and *Cinquiesme* for quintus (both mean "fifth"). These terms continued in use for French vocal and instrumental music from the Renaissance through the eighteenth century. In the performance on the accompanying recording, some of the vocal lines are doubled by instruments, as was a frequent practice of the time.

# THOMAS MORLEY (1557/8–1602)

## *My bonny lass she smileth*

*Ballett*

CA. 1595

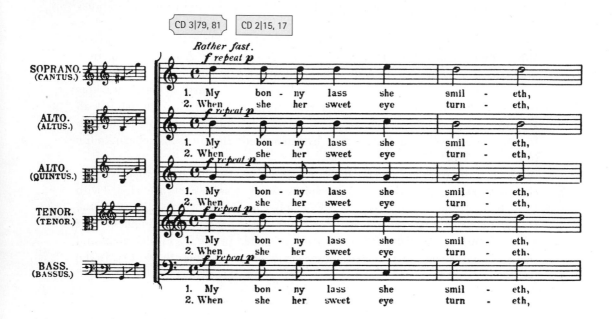

From Thomas Morley, *First Book of Ballets to Five Voices* (London, 1595; reprinted 1600), ed. Edmund Horace Fellowes, The English Madrigal School 4 (London: Stainer and Bell, 1913), 23–25. Dynamic markings added by the editor.

The *ballett* was the English form of the Italian *balletto*, a light, homophonic, strophic song for three or more singers, distinguished by dancelike rhythms and "fa-la-la" refrains. Thomas Morley composed *My bonny lass she smileth* in the early 1590s and published it in his *First Book of Balletts to Five Voices* in 1595. He based it on *Questa dolce sirena* by Giacomo Gastoldi (ca. 1544–1609), the leading Italian composer of balletti.

The poem is light and witty. There are two strophes, marked 1 and 2 in the score. In the first half of each strophe, the poet speaks about the beloved in the third person. In the second half, he addresses her directly to make a surprising request: smile less and look at me less directly, or I will quite burn up with passion. The lighthearted mood and sly wit are nicely matched by the musical setting.

The ballett is in two repeated sections, creating the form AABB. The entire ballett, including repeats, is sung to the words of the first strophe and then repeated for the second strophe, so that every line of text is sung twice. Each section has two parts: two lines of verse set homophonically with the main melody in the top voice accompanied by root-position triads in the other voices, followed by a more contrapuntal setting for the "fa-la-la" refrain, which includes some imitation and rhythmic disjunction between the voices. Although the second "fa-la" passage changes to triple meter, the two sections have the same proportions, heavily weighted toward the nonsense syllables; in both sections, the verse fills four measures and the refrain fills nine.

The lack of a key signature and the presence of several F naturals remind us that the ballet is in mode 7 (Mixolydian) rather than in G major.

Music like this was principally designed for the performers themselves. Several elements make this piece especially satisfying to sing, including the spritely rhythms, changing textures, and attractive melodies in every voice part. Such pieces were probably sung with one voice on each part but could also have been performed with one or more part played by a viol. Today balletts are often treated as choral music, usually for small choirs of two to five on a part, and editors often supply dynamic markings (as here) and piano reductions to facilitate rehearsal.

# Thomas Weelkes (CA. 1573–1623)

*As Vesta was*

*Madrigal*

CA. 1601

From *Madrigals: The Triumphs of Oriana*, ed. Edmund Horace Fellowes, The English Madrigal School 32 (London: Stainer and Bell, 1923), 175–88. Dynamic markings added by the editor.

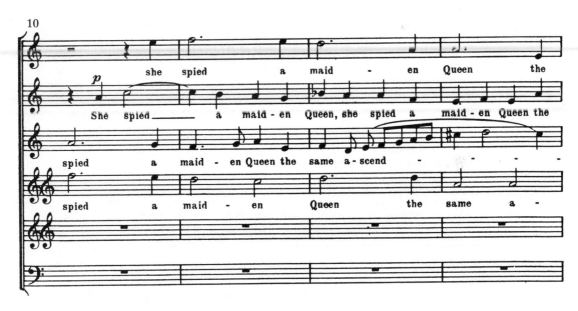

57 THOMAS WEELKES *As Vesta was*

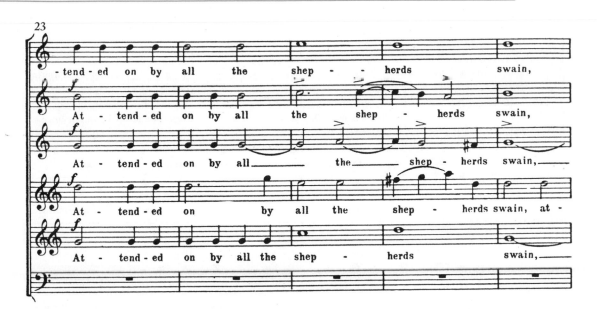

84  20

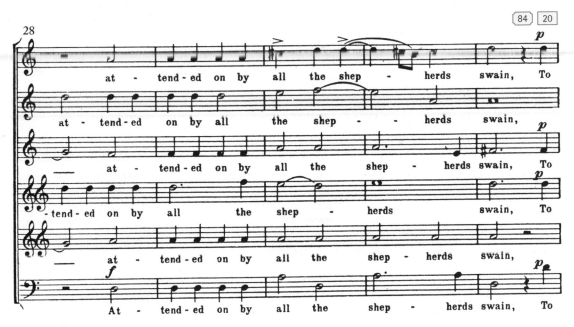

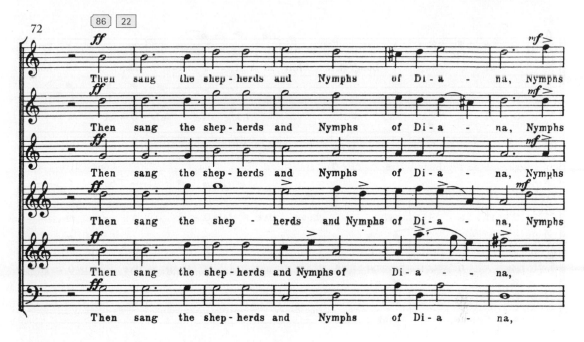

This madrigal was Thomas Weelkes's contribution to *The Triumphs of Oriana*, a collection of twenty-five madrigals by twenty-three different composers in honor of England's Queen Elizabeth, published by Thomas Morley in 1601. All of the madrigals in the collection end with the words "Long live fair Oriana," a poetic name for Elizabeth. Weelkes wrote his own poem in five rhymed couplets to praise the queen. In it, he refers to Elizabeth, who never married, as the "maiden Queen" (measures 11–12) and surrounds her with adoring attendant shepherds (the gentlemen of her court). He also links her to Vesta, Jupiter's unmarried sister, who was the Roman goddess of fire, hearth, and home, and invokes Diana, Greek goddess of virginity and the hunt, whose nymphs abandon her to join the shepherds in singing praises to Elizabeth.

Weelkes wrote this poem using words and images that could be readily depicted in music, making this madrigal a textbook example of word-painting. "Vesta" and the "maiden queen," as females, are described only by the upper four voices of the ensemble (measures 1–22). "Latmos hill" is suggested by a four-note climbing figure, followed by falling scalar figures for "descending" (measures 4–9) and a rising scale for "ascending" (measures 12–22). The lower voices join in at "Attended on by all the shepherds swain" (measures 23–32), representing the male shepherds with deeper voices and "all" with the first appearance of all six voices at once. The crowd of Diana's nymphs running down the hill is depicted with descending scales in imitative polyphony and alternating groups of paired voices (measures 36–46). The phrases "two by two," "three by three," and "together" are set respectively for two pairs of voices, two groups of three, and all six voices together (measures 47–51). Likewise, when Diana is left "all alone," the words are sung by a single mournful soprano (measures 56–57). The nymphs and shepherds mingle with groups of high and low voices (measures 59–63), and their "mirthful tunes" are suggested by short melodic motives that pass back and forth between voices. These depictions range from the clever and subtle to the kind of obvious translation of words to music that has earned the term *madrigalism*.

Weelkes treated the final phrase, "Long live fair Oriana," in a most extraordinary manner, surpassing all his other images. The words are set to a motive (first heard in measures 79–80) that enters forty-nine times in a variety of circumstances—in all voices, in seven different transpositions, outlining both major and minor triads, and with varied intervals of time between one entrance and the next. The effect is as if a great crowd is hailing Elizabeth again and again, from every direction. The long life wished for the queen is illustrated both by the length of this section, occupying almost the last third of the madrigal, and by augmentation of the motive in the bass by a factor of eight (at measure 83) and later by four (measure 102). If most of the word-painting is clever or conventional, the impact in this final section is also deeply meaningful.

Although undoubtedly performed for the queen, this madrigal, like most, was intended primarily for amateurs to sing at home for their own pleasure. This piece must have been particularly entertaining to sing because it combines wordplay and wit with attractive melodies, noble sentiments, and interesting textures that change from homophony to imitative polyphony and from one grouping of voices to another.

# JOHN DOWLAND (1563–1626)

*Flow, my tears*

*Air or lute song*

CA. 1600

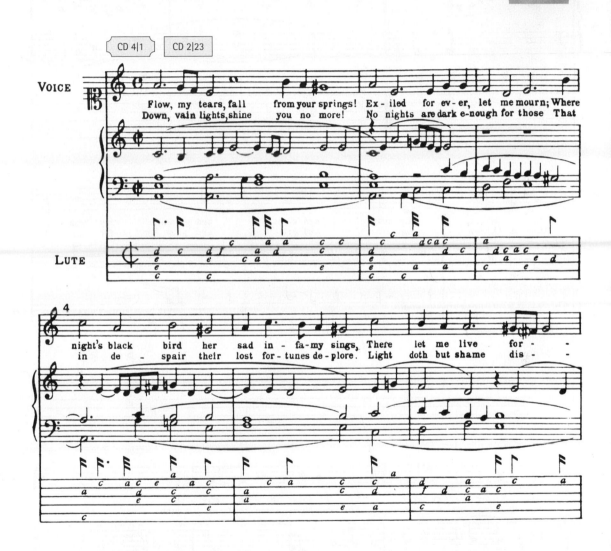

John Dowland published his lute song *Flow, my tears* in his *Second Book of Songs* (1600). He adapted it from his most popular piece for lute, a pavane titled *Lachrimae* (Tears), which he later arranged for viol consort and published in a collection called *Lachrimae or Seaven Teares* (1604). Many other composers wrote arrangements or variations on this same piece, including William Byrd (see NAWM 61). Such reworking of existing music into new forms was typical during the Renaissance and has parallels in the many arrangements of popular tunes published during recent decades.

A pavane (or pavan) is a slow processional dance with three repeated strains in the form AABBCC. Most sixteenth-century pavanes were functional dance music, but Dowland's pavanes are more contrapuntal than those of earlier composers, and he apparently intended them primarily as abstract instrumental music for the enjoyment of the player or of listeners. In the lute song arrangement of *Flow, my tears*, Dowland set the topmost melody in the vocal line with a poem in five strophes—two for the statement and repetition of the first strain, two for the second strain, and the last sung twice to the third strain.

The opening motive of *Lachrimae* is the basis for the entire piece: a stepwise descent through a fourth that suggests a falling tear and thus earned the pavane its name. The motive appears many times in various forms and in all four contrapuntal parts (here, including the top, middle, and bass lines of the lute accompaniment as well as the voice). In arranging the piece as a song, Dowland (or perhaps an anonymous poet) capitalized on this motive by setting appropriate words to it at the opening, "Flow, my tears, fall from your springs!" The association of this motive with tears then brings new meaning to later phrases of text that are not obviously about tears but come to life when linked with that image through this motive; this occurs at the phrases "[sad] infamy sings," "There let me live forlorn," "Down, vain lights," and so on, through "they that in hell" in the last stanza (measures 19–20). The rising motive in measures 11–12 clearly conveys the text of both verses, demonstrating that although concrete painting or expression of individual words and phrases is usually not possible in songs where more than one strophe is sung to the same music, it is possible to arrange the poetry to evoke feelings that suit the gestures in the music.

Although there is a tendency for modern listeners to hear this piece in the key of A minor, it exhibits traits of the modal system of the Renaissance. Old-fashioned sixth-to-octave cadences (in measures 8–9 and 19) occasionally appear alongside the more modern form with a falling fifth in the bass (as in measures 6–7), and even the latter form follows modal voice-leading with a sixth-to-octave cadence between melody and tenor (the middle part in the lute). The long series of harmonies that rise by third or fifth in measures 11–14 (d–F–a–C–G–d–a) would be unlikely to occur in a tonal piece, where root motion is directional, normally moving *down* by third or fifth (rather than up) or up by second or fourth. The melody ranges from a fifth below to a fifth above the final A, placing it in the plagal mode on A (mode 10 or Hypoaeolian).

The lute tablature, shown here below the transcription, indicates which strings are to be played, which frets the fingers should be placed at to stop the strings, and what rhythm to play. Those who are accustomed to tablature find it easier to use than standard notation, but anyone who is not a lute player will likely find it a curious and confusing code. What looks like a musical staff is actually a sign for the six main pairs (or *courses*) of strings, tuned from bottom up $G$–$c$–$f$–$a$–$d'$–$g'$. (A seventh, tuned to $D$, is needed for notes below $G$; see measures 11 and 14–15 for examples.) The letter $a$ means to play the string below the letter as an open string, $b$ to stop it at the first fret (producing a note a half-step above the open string), and so on. Thus, in the first chord, the low string tuned to $G$ is stopped at its second fret (shown by the letter $c$), producing the note $A$; the strings tuned to $c$ and $f$ are both stopped at the fourth fret (the letter $e$), producing the notes $e$ and $a$ respectively; and the string tuned to $a$ is stopped at the third fret, producing the note $c'$. The rhythmic signs above the six strings indicate what durations to use (one flag is a half note, two flags a quarter note, and so on); to keep the notation simple, a duration stays in force until another one is indicated (compare the tablature in measure 1 to the transcription above it). Lute players throughout Europe used various systems, but all were based on these same principles.

# PIERRE ATTAINGNANT (PUBLISHER) (CA. 1494–CA. 1552)

## Dances from *Danseries a 4 parties, second livre*

*Dances*

CA. 1547

(a) No. 1: Basse danse

From *Danseries a 4 parties, second livre* (Paris, 1547), ed. Raymond Meylan (Paris: Heugel & Cie., 1969), 1 and 38–39. Reproduced by permission of Theodore Presser, Inc. Note values reduced by half. Barlines through the entire brace mark the *quaternions* of the choreography; triple-time measures are set off by barlines through the staff; in the *basse danse*, after every seventh minim of a *quaternion* a broken line appears, indicating the hemiola effect.

(b) No. 36: Branle gay, *Que je chatoulle ta fossette*

Pierre Attaingnant was not a composer but an editor and printer who became the first music publisher to achieve mass production, using a single-impression printing process that was faster and cheaper than the triple-impression process used by Petrucci. He issued many collections of chansons and of dance music, including the 1547 anthology that contains these two anonymous dances.

The first is a *basse danse*, a stately couple dance that reached the height of its popularity during the fifteenth century and had almost disappeared by the 1540s. It consisted of a series of figures, each performed within a four-measure phrase called a *quaternion*. In this transcription, each quaternion is marked off by a barline through the entire score, and individual measures are delineated by barlines through each staff. In this basse danse, the eighth beat in each quaternion is emphasized with a long note in two or more voices, creating a repeating pattern of beat groupings (3 4 2 3) that results in a hemiola effect; the editor has indicated this pattern by omitting the barline before the third $\frac{3}{4}$ measure in each quaternion and inserting broken barlines between the staves one beat later.

The music consists of two sections, each repeated. This structure, called *binary form*, later became the standard form for dances in the seventeenth and eighteenth centuries, and it was expanded upon in various ways to create sonata form, rondo form, and other standard formal patterns in the mid- to late-eighteenth century. One phrase repeats exactly (measures 9–12 repeat measures 1–4), but otherwise each section is full of variety, with some repetition and variation of only the initial rhythmic ideas.

One of the basic steps of the basse danse was the *branle*, a side step with a swaying shift of weight from the right to the left foot. The branle later became an independent dance, and several varieties emerged. The *branle double* and *branle simple* were in duple meter and in moderate tempo, and the *branle gay* was in a relatively fast triple meter.

The branle gay included here is composed of a limited number of melodic four-measure phrases, some of which are inconclusive and others cadential, allowing for various antecedent-consequent combinations. The distribution of these phrases creates the overall shape of an ABA' form. The A section (measures 1–12) presents two phrases in an abb' pattern; the B section (measures 13–28) varies two new phrases in the pattern cc'dd'; and the A' section (measures 29–48) is in the form ababb'. As in the basse danse, the usual long-short rhythm common in triple meter is sometimes reversed in a short-long pattern, giving the music an extra bounce and sometimes suggesting a hemiola effect. Branles were often identified by the text that was sung to the top line, in this case *Que je chatoulle ta fossette.*

These instrumental dances were published in partbooks, with one bound booklet for each of the four players. Each partbook included only the music for a single part, and no full score was available. The instrumentation was not specified; rather, the choice was left up to the players. These dances could be played by ensembles with four instruments of the same type in different sizes to suit the ranges of the parts, such as a *consort* of bass, tenor, alto, and soprano recorders, or a similar consort of viols. They could also be played by a *broken consort*, with a different type of instrument on each part. The players were free to embellish the music and did so especially at cadences. Percussion was never notated, but artwork from the period shows that drums or other percussion instruments were used at least some of the time. The freedom that the players had to decide how to perform pieces has more in common with modern practice for popular music than with current standards for performing classical music, where scrupulous adherence to the score is expected.

# LUIS DE NARVÁEZ (FL. 1526–49)

## From *Los seys libros del Delphin*

*Intabulation and variation set*

CA. 1538

(a) *Cancion Mille regres*, intabulation of Josquin's *Mille regretz*

CD 4|7

60 LUIS DE NARVÁEZ  From *Los seys libros del Delphin*

(b) *Cuatro diferencias sobre "Guárdame las vacas"* [Four Variations on "Guárdame las vacas"], variation set

Adapted from Luys de Narváez, *Los seys libros del Delphin,* ed. Emilio Pujol, Monumentos de la Música Española 3 (Barcelona: Consejo Superior de Investigaciones Cientificas, 1945), 85–87.

Luis de Narváez was apparently a native of Granada in southern Spain, although nothing is known of his early years. He was employed from about 1526 by Francisco de los Cobos, secretary to Emperor Charles V, and after his patron's death in 1547 he entered the service of the royal family. Narváez is best known for *Los seis libros del Delphin* (The Six Books of the Dauphin), published in Vallidolid, Spain, in 1538. It is a collection of pieces for *vihuela* (a Spanish plucked string instrument that was closely related to the viol and to the lute) that testify to Narváez's skill as a vihuelist and as a composer. The contents include fantasias, sets of variations, arrangements of vocal pieces, songs, and a contrapuntal setting of a basse danse melody. Two of those genres are illustrated here: arrangements and variations.

*Cancion Mille regres* is an arrangement—called an *intabulation* because it was written in tablature—of *Mille regretz* (NAWM 41), the chanson attributed to Josquin. Comparing the original to Narváez's version shows that the latter is not a simple transcription but an imaginative reworking of the piece for a new medium.

Narváez preserved the four-voice texture of the original but changed some notes and added many figures. The vihuela cannot sustain tones the way that voices can, since a plucked string rapidly loses volume; to compensate and to make the rhythm more lively, Narváez added scales, turns, and other figuration. Such figures were called *divisions* or *diminutions* because they divided the long notes into smaller durations.

Some figures fill in large intervals with stepwise motion—for example, the sixteenth notes in the first half of measure 2 bridge the gap between *c'* and *f'*, and those in measure 6 fill in the rising fifth from *d* to *a*. Other figures ornament what were sustained tones in the original, like those in the second half of measure 2 and in measure 7. Through such embellishments Narváez drew attention to the movement of different voices at different times, often emphasizing important beats and cadences. The constant variations in texture and figuration sustain the interest of player and listener alike.

*Los seys libros del Delphin* was the first publication to contain sets of variations, called *diferencias* in Spanish. It includes two sets of variations on *Guárdame las vacas,* a standard air for singing poetry that consists of a simple melodic outline over a bass progression:

This variation set does not begin with the melody in unadorned form, as would become common in later theme-and-variation movements. Rather, it comprises a succession of four variations in which the original bass is readily apparent, but the melody is richly elaborated, although the melodic outline remains perceptible underneath the elaborate decoration. Each variation introduces a new figuration while preserving the phrase structure, harmonic plan, and cadences of the theme. These characteristics became standard for variation sets. Narváez added a four-measure phrase at the end of the fourth variation to confirm the cadence and reinforce the conclusion.

One interesting difference between vihuela or lute music and vocal music is the notation of accidentals. Singers were expected to alter pitches by half steps up or down as called for by the rules of musica ficta, so manuscripts and printed vocal music often omitted those accidentals. It is up to modern editors to suggest where such alterations would likely have been made. Unlike composers of vocal music, intabulators had to specify each note exactly, by indicating on which fret the finger would be placed, so that there would be no ambiguity. A comparison of Narváez's intabulation of *Mille regretz* to the original chanson demonstrates that Narváez regularly expanded the minor sixth to a major sixth at cadences by sharping the upper note, as at measures 4, 5, and 9; these alterations would have been made by singers according to the rules of musica ficta (although they are not always indicated by the editor of the chanson in NAWM 41). The exact notation of intabulations often suggests what typical practice may have been, but it is not certain whether singers would have consistently used the same alterations as instrumentalists.

# WILLIAM BYRD (CA. 1540–1623)

*Pavana Lachrymae*

*Pavane variations*

CA. 1600

From *The Fitzwilliam Virginal Book*, ed. J. A. Fuller Maitland and W. Barclay Squire, vol. 2 (Leipzig: Breitkopf & Härtel, 1899), 42–46.

10   30

11   31

12 32
Rep.

61 WILLIAM BYRD *Pavana Lachrymae*

Several composers reworked or wrote variations on John Dowland's lute pavane *Lachrimae* (Tears), among them Dowland himself in his lute song *Flow, my tears* (NAWM 58) and in other forms. William Byrd wrote his version for keyboard, *Pavana Lachrymae*, around 1600, and it was included in the Fitzwilliam Virginal Book, a manuscript collection copied between 1609 and 1619.

A comparison between Byrd's keyboard arrangement and Dowland's song demonstrates how Byrd reworked the model's material. (Note that Byrd's arrangement is transposed a fourth higher and that, although there are more frequent barlines in the Byrd, the note values are equivalent in the two pieces.) Byrd varied each strain, then added a second variation to each strain, marked "Rep." (reprise) in the score. In the first variant of each strain, Byrd retained the outline of the tune in the right hand but added short accompanimental motives or decorative turns, figurations, and scale work imitated between the hands. Especially notable are the many references to the opening motive of Dowland's song, echoed several times in the middle voices in measures 1–3. In the second variation of each strain, the relationship to Dowland's model is more subtle. There are rhythmic displacements and the melody is less obvious, yet the harmony is retained and the melody can usually be traced in some part of the texture. In the second strain, at the words "And tears and sighs and groans" (NAWM 58, measures 11–12), where Dowland imitated the melody in his bass line, Byrd followed his example (measures 32–34 and 44–46), gradually adding notes to the pattern to create a sense of intensification.

The preferred instrument for this piece was the *virginal*, the English name for harpsichord. As in the pieces that Narváez composed for vihuela (NAWM 60), the embellishing figures help to compensate for the inability of a plucked string instrument to sustain pitches. The double diagonal line drawn through the stem of a note indicates an ornament, but contemporary writings do not tell us exactly how to perform it; most likely, this sign indicated a *shake*, a brief trill oscillating between the designated note and the note above it, perhaps only once or twice. On the accompanying recording, the repeat marks are not observed; as a result, the form is AA'BB'CC', reflecting the original form of the pavane.

# GIOVANNI GABRIELI (CA. 1555–1612)

*Canzon septimi toni a 8*, from *Sacrae symphoniae*

*Ensemble canzona*

CA. 1597

From Giovanni Gabrieli, *Opera Omnia*, vol. 10, *Instrumental Ensemble Works in "Sacrae symphoniae"* *(Venice, 1597), Printed Anthologies and Manuscript Sources*, ed. Richard Charteris, Corpus Mensurabilis Musicae 12 (American Institute of Musicology, Hänssler-Verlag, 1998), 11–21. Used by permission of A-R Editions, Inc.

62 GIOVANNI GABRIELI  *Canzon septimi toni a 8, from Sacrae symphoniae*

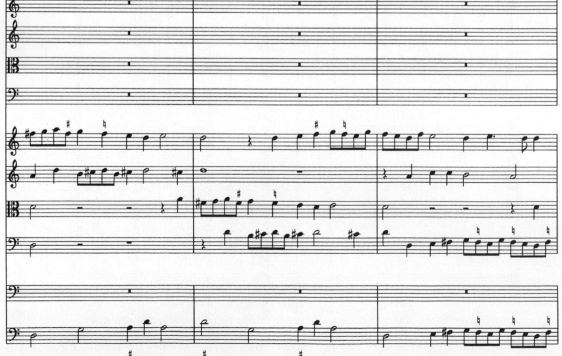

Giovanni Gabrieli's *Sacrae symphoniae* (Sacred Symphonies), published in 1597, was a collection of ensemble works ("symphonies" in the sense of "sounding together") that he had composed over the previous decade or so as part of his work as organist and composer at St. Mark's Church in Venice and at the Scuola Grande di San Rocco. The collection contained works for singers with instruments (forty motets, three mass movements, and two Magnificats) and for instruments alone (fourteen canzonas and two sonatas). Both vocal and instrumental works were conceived for divided choirs (called *cori spezzati*), ensembles divided into subgroups that engaged in dialogue and joined together for glorious climaxes.

The *Canzon septimi toni a 8* (Canzona in the Seventh Tone for Eight Parts) exemplifies Gabrieli's style and use of divided choirs. The "eight parts" are divided into two groups called first choir (*primus chorus*) and second choir (*secundus chorus*), each with four players in cantus, altus, tenor, and bassus range. Each choir is accompanied by an organ, as explained below. The "seventh tone" is the authentic mode on G, the Mixolydian mode, clearly defined in this piece by the opening and closing sonorities, the frequent cadences on G, and the ranges of the cantus and tenor parts. As is typical in this mode (but quite untypical in the key of G major), sonorities on C are about as prominent as those on D, and F is almost as common a note as F♯.

The first instrumental canzonas were transcriptions of French chansons (both the Italian *canzona* and the French *chanson* mean "song"). One legacy from that heritage is the opening rhythm of this and many other canzonas composed in the late sixteenth century—a half note followed by two quarter notes—which echoes the opening rhythm of many chansons (see *Tant que vivray*, NAWM 54). Also like the chanson, the canzona unfolds in a series of sections, some imitative and some largely homophonic. Typically, each section is based on different melodic material, but variation or repetition of material may also occur. The textures are relatively transparent, the music moves quickly, and the motives are strongly rhythmic.

This canzona features a refrain that appears three times, creating the following formal plan:

| Measure | Section | Musical Description |
|---|---|---|
| 1 | A | choir 1 alone, then choir 2 alone |
| 18 | B | Refrain: dialogue in triple meter, then together in duple |
| 26 | C | choir 1 alone, then short dialogue, then choir 2 alone |
| 39 | B | Refrain |
| 47 | D | choir 2 and choir 1 in dialogue, then together |
| 60 | B | Refrain |
| 69 | E | choirs together with some imitation between them |

Most of the piece is in duple meter, but the refrain begins in triple meter, setting it apart. The refrain is the same at each appearance: short phrases in homophony are presented in one choir and immediately echoed in the other, then the two choirs join in a homophonic passage with a running scale figure in imitation between the two bass parts.

The sections before and after the refrains differ from each other in musical material, but they create a sense of direction from complete separation to integration of the two choirs. In the opening section, choir 1 plays a point of imitation, and choir 2 then presents its own completely different material (measure 11). The section after the first refrain has a similar shape, but the two choirs engage briefly in dialogue, as if tossing ideas back and forth, before choir 2 takes over (measures 30–32). The next time (at measure 47), choir 2 begins, but its subject is soon taken up by choir 1, and after a brief dialogue they join together in a passage that mixes homophony with imitation between the upper lines of the two choirs (measures 56–60). After the last refrain, the choirs continue playing together with brief imitation between them. Metaphorically, what began as two people on opposite sides of the room speaking in monologues concludes with them engaged in eager conversation, echoing each other's ideas. Such a logical series of events, framed by the refrains, exemplifies the newfound freedom of instrumental music in the late sixteenth century. No longer bound by the forms and rhythms of dance (as in NAWM 59 and 61) or song (as in NAWM 60a and 60b), composers were free to create entirely new forms based on abstract ideas.

Gabrieli did not specify the instrumentation for this piece, although he did for the *Sonata pian' e forte* (Soft and Loud Sonata) in the same collection. One likely instrumentation, used on the accompanying recording, features violins on the top two lines in choir 1, cornetts (wooden instruments blown like a brass instrument but fingered like a recorder) on the top two lines in choir 2, and sackbuts (early trombones) on the bottom two lines in each choir. The original clef for each line, shown at the beginning of the score, indicated the range for which a suitable instrument would be found. The editor has marked the specific range for each part at the beginning of the piece. Today Gabrieli's canzonas and sonatas are often played by ensembles of modern brass instruments.

The staves marked "basso per l'organo" (bass for the organ) are for the two organs—one associated with each choir of instruments. Each organ plays a bass line derived from the lowest notes sounded in that choir by any instrument; thus, at the beginning, the organ for choir 1 (the upper of the two organ staves) plays with the cantus line for one measure, then with the altus, then with the tenor, and finally with the sextus starting in measure 6. The organ for choir 2 (the bottom staff) enters at measure 11 with its choir. The organist was expected to fill in the harmony above the notated bass line, guided at times by figures below the staff. The practice of writing out the bass line and leaving the player to add the appropriate chords became very common in the seventeenth and eighteenth centuries and was known as *basso continuo* (continuous bass). This particular type of bass line, following the lowest note sounded in the ensemble, became known as a *basso seguente* (following bass, or uninterrupted bass). The piece can be played without the organs, as it usually is today.

# CLAUDIO MONTEVERDI (1567–1643)

*Cruda Amarilli*

*Madrigal*

LATE 1590S

First published in Claudio Monteverdi, *Il quinto libro de madrigali a cinque voci* (Venice, 1605). This edition from Claudio Monteverdi, *Opera omnia*, vol. 6, *Madrigali a 5 voci: Libro quinto*, ed. Maria Caraci (Cremona: Fondazione Claudio Monteverdi, 1984), 107–10. Used by permission.

Cruda Amarilli che col nome ancora
D'amar, ahi lasso, amaramente insegni.
Amarilli del candido ligustro,
Più candida e più bella,
Ma dell'aspido sordo
E più sorda e più fera e più fugace.
Poi che col dir t'offendo
I mi morò tacendo.

Cruel Amaryllis, who with your very name
teach bitterly of love, alas!
Amaryllis, than the white privet flower
paler and more beautiful,
but deafer than the asp
and fiercer and more elusive.
Since by speaking I offend you,
I shall die in silence.

—GIOVANNI BATTISTA GUARINI

The text of this madrigal is one of eleven in Claudio Monteverdi's fifth book of madrigals (1605) that are drawn from Giovanni Battista Guarini's pastoral verse play *Il pastor fido*. Here, in the second scene from the first act, Mirtillo complains that Amarilli is spurning his love. His speech begins with a pun on the name Amarilli, whose stem "amar" can be a contraction either of "amare" (to love) or "amaro" (bitter). With her name, Mirtillo protests, Amarilli teaches bitterly of how to love (or, in other possible translations, teaches how to love bitterly or teaches that *she* loves bitterly).

Monteverdi expressed the bitter mood of the opening words "Cruda Amarilli" with striking dissonances that break the rules of normal counterpoint. For example, in the second measure the bass skips down to E, creating a seventh against the canto; the rules of proper counterpoint require dissonances to be entered by step, meaning that there should be a passing tone between the G and E in the bass. When the suspension in the canto resolves down to C, the bass has already moved on to B, creating an even more biting dissonance of a minor ninth plus a minor seventh with the alto. This sonority includes all the first five notes of the Mixolydian scale (G–A–B–C–D). The rules of counterpoint call for passing tones to fall on weak beats, so here the canto and alto notes should appear one quarter note earlier to create consonances on the third beat over the bass note B. The same phrase is repeated a fourth higher, and then Monteverdi echoes the text's sardonic humor by setting the next half line in a dancelike dotted rhythm that continues without a pause into the following line, which mixes the jeering laughter of sixteenth notes with the crudest dissonances in the piece.

This madrigal was already in circulation in 1598, the date of an imaginary dialogue in which these violations of the rules of counterpoint for the treatment of dissonance were discussed in Giovanni Maria Artusi's *L'Artusi overo delle imperfettioni della moderna musica* (The Artusi, or Of the Imperfections of Modern Music), published in 1600. In the dialogue, one speaker particularly objects to the dissonance in measures 12–14, pointing out that the soprano part in measure 13 fails to agree with the bass. The A in the soprano line, a ninth above the bass, seems to appear out of nowhere and leaps to a seventh, F. The other speaker defends the passage, arguing that if one imagines a G on the first beat of the soprano part, the figure is like an *accento*, an improvised embellishment common at this time, with the stepwise motion G–F–E embellished as G–A–F–E. Such written-out embellishments, or *passagi*, as they were called, also season the harmony with runs in measure 12 that include an augmented octave between F in the bass and F♯ in the quinto part.

Although some of Monteverdi's dissonances may thus be rationalized as embellishments, his real motivation for including them was to convey through harmony, rather than through the graphic melodic images of some earlier madrigals, the meaning and feeling of the poet's message. In his preface to the fifth book of madrigals, Monteverdi described his approach as that of a second practice (*seconda pratica*) by which, for the sake of expressing a text, composers were free to violate some of the strict rules of the first practice taught in the manuals on counterpoint. Indeed, asserting the dominance of the words over the music virtually required doing violence to the music in order to convey the strength of the emotions and images. A listener who recognized the violations to the rules of music had to search for explanations in the text, just as one might react to a friend's sudden outburst by trying to understand the emotions that motivated it.

Several other passages show the same use of rule-breaking as a rhetorical device, including the settings of "amaramente" (bitterly) in measures 19–23 and "l'aspido" (the asp) in measures 36–38. Throughout, *Cruda Amarilli* typifies the flexible, animated, evocative, and variegated style of Monteverdi's polyphonic madrigals.

By the time this madrigal was published in 1605, a new fashion had emerged for solo or ensemble madrigals to be accompanied by basso continuo. Thus, although it was conceived for five solo voices without accompaniment, *Cruda Amarilli* was published with a basso continuo part, marked "B.S." for basso seguente (see explanation in NAWM 62). This arrangement made the piece more flexible, for with the basso continuo it could be performed with one singer alone (on the top line) or with any number of the other voices added. However, the basso continuo remained only an option, not a necessary part of the music, and this madrigal was no doubt often sung unaccompanied.

# GIULIO CACCINI (CA. 1550–1618)

*Vedrò 'l mio sol*

*Solo madrigal*

CA. 1590

First published in *Le nuove musiche* (Florence, 1602). This edition from *Giulio Caccini: Le nuove musiche,* ed. H. Wiley Hitchcock, Recent Researches in the Music of the Baroque Era 9 (Madison, Wisc.: A-R Editions, 1970), 81–85. Reprinted by permission. Abbreviations used in the score: *senza mis. (senza misura),* freely, without beating the measure; *escl. (esclamazione),* a decrescendo after attacking a note, followed by a sforzando.

Vedrò 'l mio sol, vedrò prima ch'io muoia
Quel sospirato giorno
Che faccia 'l vostro raggio à me ritorno.
O mia luce, o mia gioia,
Ben più m'è dolc' il tormentar per vui
Che 'l gioir per altrui.
Ma senza morte io non potrò soffrire
Un sì lungo martire;
E s'io morrò, morrà mia speme ancora
Di veder mai d'un sì bel dì l'aurora.

I'll see my sun; I'll see before I die
that wished-for day
when your ray returns to me.
O my light, O my joy,
much sweeter is my torment for you
than delight in others.
But without death I cannot suffer
such a long martyrdom.
And if I die, will die my hope
to see ever again the dawn of such a beautiful day.

—GIOVANNI BATTISTA GUARINI
OR ALESSANDRO GUARINI

*Vedrò 'l mio sol* is one of over two dozen songs for solo voice with basso continuo that Giulio Caccini wrote in or before the 1590s and published in his collection *Le nuove musiche* (The New Music, 1602). In his foreword, he boasted that this madrigal was among those received "with loving applause" when performed around 1590 for the Camerata, the group of gentlemen, scholars, and musicians who met in Count Giovanni de' Bardi's palace in Florence to discuss literature, science, and the arts and to hear new music.

This song is classified as a madrigal rather than an aria or other form because it is through-composed rather than strophic. Solo madrigals set texts similar to those of polyphonic madrigals, but afforded solo singers greater opportunity to display emotion and virtuosity.

Each poetic line is set as a separate phrase, ending with a cadence, sustained note, or pair of notes. This convention was common in airs improvised on melodic formulas throughout the sixteenth century, as well as in polyphonic madrigals. The many repeated notes in speech rhythm are typical of solo airs, but can also be found in some polyphonic madrigals that were composed late in the century, as the declamatory style of text setting became more common. Thus, this piece draws on two long-standing traditions: madrigal settings and solo singing.

For emotional effect, Caccini borrowed from oratory the device of heightened repetition, as in measures 35–37 and 43–48. He repeated the text and music of the last lines, as was customary in the polyphonic madrigal. However, he abandoned contrapuntal part-writing for a simple chordal accompaniment so that the words and melody would strike the listener with greater force.

At a number of the cadences, Caccini wrote out the embellishments that singers customarily would have added—for example, at the words "muoia" (measure 7) and "aurora" (measures 70–72). Caccini, himself a singer, notated the ornaments because he did not trust others to improvise appropriately. Other refinements that Caccini considered essential to performance—although not always indicated in the score—were crescendos and decrescendos, trills and turns (called *gruppi or groppi*), rapid repetitions of the same pitch (called *trilli*), *esclamazioni* ("exclamations," performed with a decrescendo after attacking a note, followed by a sforzando), and departures from strict observance of the printed note values (now called *tempo rubato* or "stolen time"). He described these refinements and gave examples of some of them in his foreword to *Le nuove musiche*. The editor of this edition of *Vedrò 'l mio sol* has suggested the placement of some of these effects in brackets.

The accompaniment is a basso continuo, specifically a *figured bass*, in which the composer has added numbers and flat or sharp signs below the bass notes to indicate what notes are to be played. Caccini claimed to have invented the practice of figuring the basso continuo, and indeed *Le nuove musiche* contains some of the earliest examples of scores with specific figuration. The editor has supplied one possible *realization* of the figured bass in smaller notes in the treble staff just above the bass. If there is no figure, the presumption is that the third and fifth above the bass note should be played (as in the first measure), although passing and other ornamental tones are allowed. Caccini's 11–$\sharp$10 figures in the second measure indicate that a G and F$\sharp$ are to be sounded in succession, exactly an eleventh and tenth above the D in the bass; later composers would simply have written 4–$\sharp$3 in the same circumstance, leaving it to the player to determine the correct octave for the G–F$\sharp$ suspension. A sharp without a number indicates that the third of the chord should be major, as in measure 25; a flat indicates that the third is minor, as in measures 32–33. The continuo player is welcome to introduce figuration as long as it does not overwhelm the singer. For example, the editor suggests imitating the singer's figure in measures 33 and 37, and playing a scale leading up to the singer's next note in measures 16 and 45.

The basso continuo can be played by one or more instruments. The most likely accompaniment would have been a lute or a *theorbo*, a large lute with extra bass strings. Caccini intended for the singer to accompany himself or herself (an indication of the high level of training required to perform his songs), but in recent times very few performers are trained both as singers and as lutenists.

# Jacopo Peri (1561–1633)

*Le musiche sopra l'Euridice*: Excerpts

*Opera*

1600

(a) Prologue: *Io, che d'alti sospir*, strophic aria

TRAGEDY

1. Io, che d'alti sospir vaga e di pianti,
   Spars' or di doglia, hor di minaccie il volto,
   Fei negl'ampi teatri al popol folto
   Scolorir di pietà volti e sembianti.

I, who with deep sighs and tears am smitten,
my face, covered now with grief, now with menace,
once in ample theatres crowded with people
made their faces turn pale with pity.

Edited from Peri, *Le musiche sopra l'Euridice* (Florence, 1601), 2, 11–12, and 14–17. Note values reduced by half. Original barring retained. Time signatures added by the editor are in brackets; editorial accidentals are above the staff. In the Prologue, the composer intended that rhythmic adjustments be made in the strophes.

2. Non sangue sparso d'innocenti vene,
   Non ciglia spente di tiranno insano,
   Spettacolo infelice al guardo umano,
   Canto su meste e lagrimose scene.

   Not of blood spilled from innocent veins,
   nor of eyes put out by an insane tyrant,
   a spectacle unhappy to human sight,
   do I sing on this sad and tearful stage.

3. Lungi via, lungi pur da' regi tetti
   Simulacri funesti, ombre d'affanni:
   Ecco i mesti coturni e i foschi panni
   Cangio, e desto ne i cor più dolci
     affetti.

   Stay far from under this royal roof,
   dismal images, shadows of anguish.
   Behold, the gloomy buskins and the dark rags
   I transform, and awaken in the hearts
     sweeter affections.

4. Hor s'avverrà che le cangiate forme
   Non senza alto stupor la terra ammiri.
   Tal ch'ogni alma gentil ch'Apollo inspiri
   Del mio novo cammin calpesti l'orme,

   Now, it will happen that the changed forms
   not without great amazement the world will admire,
   so that every gentle genius whom Apollo inspires
   takes up the tracks of my new path,

5. Vostro, Regina, fia cotanto alloro,
   Qual forse anco non colse Atene, o Roma,
   Fregio non vil su l'onorata chioma,
   Fronda Febea fra due corone d'oro.

   Yours, Queen, will be so much laurel
   that perhaps not even Athens or Rome won more,
   no mean ornament on the honored head,
   a leafy branch of Phoebus between two crowns.

6. Tal per voi torno, e con sereno aspetto
   Ne' reali Imenei m'adorno anch'io,
   E su corde più liete il canto mio
   Tempro, al nobile cor dolce diletto.

   Thus for you I return, and with a serene countenance
   at this royal wedding I too adorn myself,
   and with happier notes my song
   I temper, for the noble heart's sweet delight.

7. Mentre Senna real prepara intanto
   Alto diadema, onde il bel crin si fregi
   E i manti e' seggi de gl'antichi regi,
   Del Tracio Orfeo date l'orecchie al canto.

   Meanwhile the royal Seine prepares
   a lofty diadem with which the beautiful hair to crown
   and the cloaks and thrones of ancient kings;
   to the song of the Thracian Orpheus, lend your ears.

(b) Aria: *Nel pur ardor*

TIRSI

| | |
|---|---|
| Nel pur ardor della più bella stella | With the pure flame of the brightest star |
| Aurea facella di bel foc'accendi, | light the golden torch with beautiful fire |
| E qui discendi su l'aurate piume, | and here descend on golden wings, |
| Giocondo Nume, e di celeste fiamma | O happy god, and with celestial fire |
| L'anime infiamma. | the souls inflame. |
| | |
| Lieto Imeneo d'alta dolcezza un nembo | Happy Hymen, let your shower of lofty sweetness |
| Trabocca in grembo a' fortunati amanti | overflow into the breasts of the fortunate lovers |
| E tra bei canti di soavi amori | and, amidst pretty songs of delightful loves, |
| Sveglia nei cori una dolce aura, un riso | stir in their hearts a gentle breeze, a smile |
| Di Paradiso. | of Paradise. |

(c) Dialogue in recitative: *Per quel vago boschetto*

dom - bri    E dal pro-fon-do co-re    Con un so-spir mor-ta-le    Si spa-ven-to-so ohi-mè so-spin-se

fuo - re.    Che, qua-si a-ves - se l'a - le, Giun-se o-gni Nin - fa    al do-lo-ro - so suo - no,    Et

el - la in ab-ban-do - no    Tut-ta la-scios - si all'or    nel-l'al - trui brac - cia.    Spar-gea il bel vol-

to, e le do-ra - te chio - me    Un su-dor viè più fred-d'as-sai___ che giac - cio.    In - di s'u-dio'l tuo

no - me    Tra le·lab-bra so-nar    fred-d'e're-man - ti    E, vol-ti gl'oc-chi al cie-lo,    Sco-lo-

DAFNE

| | |
|---|---|
| Per quel vago boschetto, | In the beautiful thicket, |
| Ove, rigando i fiori, | where, watering the flowers, |
| Lento trascorre il fonte degl'allori, | slowly courses the spring of the laurel, |
| Prendea dolce diletto | she took sweet delight |
| Con le compagne sue la bella sposa, | with her companions—the beautiful bride— |
| Chi violetta o rosa | as some picked violets, others roses, |
| Per far ghirland' al crine | to make garlands for their hair, |
| Togliea dal prato o dall'acute spine, | in the meadow or among the sharp thorns. |
| E qual posand' il fianco | Others lying on their sides |
| Su la fiorita sponda | on the flowered bank, |
| Dolce cantava al mormorar dell' onda; | sang sweetly to the murmur of the waves. |
| Ma la bella Euridice | But the lovely Eurydice |
| Movea danzando il piè sul verde prato | dancingly moved her feet on the green grass |
| Quand'ahi ria sorte acerba, | when—O bitter, angry fate!— |
| Angue crudo e spietato | a snake, cruel and merciless, |
| Che celato giacea tra fiori e l'erba | that lay hidden among flowers and grass |
| Punsele il piè con si maligno dente, | bit her foot with such an evil tooth |
| Ch'impalidì repente | that she suddenly became pale |
| Come raggio di sol che nube adombri. | like a ray of sunshine that a cloud darkens. |
| El dal profondo core, | And from the depths of her heart, |
| Con un sospir mortale, | a mortal sigh, |
| Si spaventoso ohimè sospinse fuore, | so frightful, alas, flew forth, |
| Che, quasi avesse l'ale, | that, almost as if they had wings, |
| Giunse ogni Ninfa al doloroso suono. | every nymph rushed to the painful sound. |
| Et ella in abbandono | And she, fainting, |
| Tutta lasciossi all'or nell'altrui braccia. | let herself fall in another's arms. |
| Spargea il bel volto e le dorate chiome | Then spread over her beautiful face and her golden tresses |
| Un sudor viè più fredd'assai che giaccio. | a sweat colder by far than ice. |
| Indi s'udio 'l tuo nome | And then was heard your name, sounding |
| Tra le labbra sonar fredd'e' tremanti | between her lips, cold and trembling, |
| E volti gl'occhi al cielo, | and her eyes turned to heaven, |
| Scolorito il bel volto e' bei sembianti, | her beautiful face and appearance discolored, |
| Restò tanta bellezza immobil gielo. | this great beauty was transformed to motionless ice. |

ARCETRO

| | |
|---|---|
| Che narri, ohimè, che sento? | What do you relate, alas, what do I hear? |
| Misera Ninfa, e più misero amante, | Wretched nymph, and more unhappy lover, |
| Spettacol di miseria e di tormento! | spectacle of sorrow and of torment! |

ORPHEUS

| | |
|---|---|
| Non piango e non sospiro, | I do not weep, nor do I sigh, |
| O mia cara Euridice, | O my dear Eurydice, |
| Ché sospirar, ché lacrimar non posso. | for I am unable to sigh, to weep. |
| Cadavero infelice, | Unhappy corpse, |
| O mio core, o mia speme, o pace, o vita! | O my heart, O my hope, O peace, O life! |
| Ohimè, chi mi t'ha tolto, | Alas, who has taken you from me? |
| Chi mi t'ha tolto, ohimè! dove sei gita? | Who has taken you away, alas? Where have you gone? |
| Tosto vedrai ch'in vano | Soon you will see that not in vain |
| Non chiamasti morendo il tuo consorte. | did you, dying, call your spouse. |
| Non son, non son lontano: | I am not far away; |
| Io vengo, o cara vita, o cara morte. | I come, O dear life, O dear death. |

—OTTAVIO RINUCCINI

*Le musiche sopra l'Euridice* (The Music on The Euridice, or simply *Euridice*) is the earliest opera to survive in a complete score. Ottavio Rinuccini wrote the text (called the *libretto*), and Jacopo Peri set it to music. The opera was produced in Florence on October 6, 1600 for the wedding of King Henry IV of France and Maria de' Medici, niece of the grand duke of Tuscany. In that first performance, some of the music was replaced by Giulio Caccini's setting of the same libretto. Peri himself sang the role of Orfeo, and a boy soprano sang the part of Dafne, the messenger in the third excerpt given here. Caccini rushed his version into print that December, and Peri's was published the following February.

The plot of *Euridice* centers on the powers of music—an ideal topic for the first operas. According to the story, on the wedding day of the half-god musician Orpheus and his beloved Eurydice, the bride-to-be dies from a snakebite. Orpheus goes down to the underworld and wins her back through the beauty of his singing and playing on the lyre. The original story had a tragic ending, but Rinuccini altered the plot to end happily since the opera was to be performed in celebration of a wedding.

The three excerpts reprinted here from Peri's *Euridice* illustrate three styles of *monody*, or solo singing, found in this work. Two of the excerpts reflect styles commonly used by composers during the previous century, and the other exhibits a new style that was developed by Peri specifically to suit the new form of opera.

The Prologue (a) is a strophic aria similar to those used in the sixteenth century for singing poetry. Each stanza has four lines of eleven syllables each. The music for each line except the last consists of recitation on a repeated pitch and a cadential pattern ending in two sustained notes; the last line is more varied. The singer was expected to adjust the rhythm in each strophe to suit the text, as can be heard on the accompanying recording (on which only three of the seven stanzas are included). After each strophe is a *ritornello*, a brief instrumental refrain. In the prologue, the figure of Tragedy links the opera to the ancient Greek tragedy on which it was modeled, but she reassures the audience that since *Euridice* was written for a joyous occasion, it will awaken "sweeter affections" than the combination of pity and horror for which the classic tragedy aimed. Tragedy further explains that if others in the future imitate the new genre of opera, it will increase the renown of the bride for whose wedding this opera was first presented.

Tirsi's song (b) to Hymen, god of marriage, is also an aria, in the sense of a strophic song. But its style is quite different from that of the Prologue, with a more tuneful and rhythmically marked melody similar to that of a canzonetta. It is framed by music that was referred to as a *sinfonia*, a term that then simply meant a piece for instrumental ensemble. Despite its brevity, this sinfonia is the longest purely instrumental interlude in Peri's score. The undulating parallel thirds above a drone indicate the pastoral setting for the drama, a rural landscape populated by shepherds. Instruments are not specified, but the pastoral associations strongly suggest the use of two flutes or recorders, as in the performance on the accompanying recording.

Finally, Dafne's speech and the reactions to it of Arcetro and Orfeo (c) are examples of the new style of *recitar cantando*, later known as *recitative*, which Peri claimed to have pioneered and which was fundamental to the new genre of opera. In this style, the voice imitates the inflections and rhythms of speech, and the chords specified by the basso continuo simply provide support, having no rhythmic profile or formal plan of their own. The voice returns frequently to pitches consonant with the harmony on the main accents of the poetic line. But, in order to imitate the gliding contours of the natural speaking voice, the melody wanders from the chordal tones of the accompaniment on syllables that would not be sustained in a spoken recitation (for example, see measures 3 and 21–22). In order to highlight the meaning of the text, some dissonances are emphasized, particularly to convey strongly negative emotions, as at "Angue crudo e spietato" (cruel and merciless snake, measures 23–34) and "maligno dente" (evil tooth, measures 26–27). Only some line endings are marked by cadences; many are elided, which again suggests a naturalistic depiction of speech.

The dramatic style of recitative is especially appropriate for the text of this scene. In the midst of preparations for the wedding of the famed musician Orfeo and the nymph Euridice, Dafne reports that Euridice, while picking flowers to make a garland for her hair, was bitten by a snake and died. There is a natural progression in Dafne's speech. At first, it is emotionally neutral, consonant, and with slow-changing harmonies. As she tells of Euridice's fatal snakebite, it becomes more excited, with more dissonances, sudden changes of harmony, fewer cadences, and more rapid movement in the bass.

The responses to the news by the shepherd Arcetro and by Orfeo are also in the new recitative style. Peri made these melodies more lyrical and tuneful through varied repetitions and sequences. But the dissonances are even stronger than those in Daphne's speech, expressive of their grief, as at "Misera Ninfa" (wretched nymph, measures 58–59) and "Che sospirar" (to sigh, measure 67). Peri used melodic chromaticism to heighten emphasis on the words "miseria" and "tormento" (sorrow and torment, measures 62–63), and used chromatically contrasting chords to intensify the harmony, as at the change from an E-major triad on "o pace, o vita!" (oh peace, oh life!) to G minor on "Ohimè" (alas, at measures 72–73). When Orfeo vows to go down to the underworld to retrieve Euridice from the land of the dead (measures 80–87), the music returns to diatonicism, with several successive cadences that symbolize his resolve.

# Claudio Monteverdi (1567–1643)

*L'Orfeo*: Excerpt from Act II

*Opera*

1607

(a) Aria/canzonetta: *Vi ricorda o boschi ombrosi*

27

Vissi già mesto e do_len_te, vis_si già mesto e do_lente Hor gio_i_sco e quegli af_

(Più tranquillo)

30

_fan_ni che sof_fer_ti ho per tan_t'an_ni  fan più ca_ro il ben pre_

32

_sen_te. Vis_si già me_sto e do_len_te, vis_si già mesto e do_

(b) Song: *Mira, deh mira Orfeo*

(c) Dialogue in recitative: *Ahi, caso acerbo*

**1)** The character's name is missing, but it is a shepherd.

4

(d) Recitative: *Tu se' morta*

98
se' da me par_ti _ ta per mai più,  mai più non torna_re ed io ri_man_

100
_go,  no,  no,  che se i ver_si al_cu_na co_sa pon_no,

102
n'andrò si_cu _ ro a più profon_di a_bis_si  e in _ te_ne_ri _ to il

104
cor  del Re  de l'om_bre  me_co trar_rot_ti  a ri_ve_der le

106
stel _ le,  O se ciò ne_ghe_rammi em_pio de_sti _ no,

108

ri_marrò te_co    in compagnia    di mor_te    a dio ter_ra

111

a  dio cie_lo    e  So_le,    a  Di_o.

(e) Choral madrigal: *Ahi, caso acerbo*

# CHORO

41  46

(Andante)

Ahi  ca_so a_cer_bo, Ahi fat'em_pio e cru_de_le,  Ahi stel_le ingiu_rio_

Ahi  ca_so a_cer_bo,    Ahi  fat'em pio e cru_de_le,  Ahi stel_le ingiu_rio_

Ahi  ca_so a_cer_bo,  Ahi  fa_t'em_pio e cru_de_le,  Ahi  stel_le ingiu_rio_

Ahi  ca_so a_cer_bo,  Ahi  fa_t'em_pio e cru_de_le,  Ahi stel_le ingiu_rio_

Ahi  ca_so a_cer_bo,  Ahi  fa_t'em_pio e cru_de_le, Ahi  stel_le ingiu_rio_

ORPHEUS

| | |
|---|---|
| Vi ricorda, o boschi ombrosi, | Do you remember, O shady woods, |
| de' miei lungh' aspri tormenti, | my long, bitter torments, |
| quando i sassi ai miei lamenti | when the stones to my laments |
| rispondean, fatti pietosi? | replied, being moved to pity? |
| | |
| Dite, all'hor non vi sembrai | Say, then did I not appear to you |
| più d'ogn'altro sconsolato? | to be more disconsolate than any other? |
| Hor fortuna ha stil cangiato | Now Fortune has changed her tune |
| et ha volto in festa i guai. | and has turned to joys my troubles. |
| | |
| Vissi già mesto e dolente. | I once lived sad and sorrowful. |
| Hor gioisco e quegli affanni | Now I rejoice, and those difficulties |
| che sofferti ho per tant'anni | that I suffered for so many years |
| fan più caro il ben presente. | make more dear my present blessings. |
| | |
| Sol per te, bella Euridice, | Only because of you, beautiful Eurydice, |
| benedico il mio tormento; | do I bless my torment; |
| dopo il duol vi è più contento, | after grief, one is more content, |
| dopo il mal vi è più felice. | after misfortune, one is more happy. |

SHEPHERD I

| | |
|---|---|
| Mira, deh mira, Orfeo, che d'ogni intorno | Behold, ah, behold, Orpheus, how all around |
| ride il bosco e ride il prato. | the woods laugh and the meadows laugh. |
| Segui pur col pletr' aurato | Continue then, with golden plectrum |
| d'addolcir l'aria in si beato giorno. | to sweeten the air on such a blessed day. |

MESSENGER

| | |
|---|---|
| Ahi, caso acerbo, ahi, fat' empio e crudele! | Ah, bitter event, ah, fate wicked and cruel! |
| Ahi, stelle ingiuriose, ahi, cielo avaro! | Ah, malicious stars, ah stingy heavens! |

SHEPHERD II

| | |
|---|---|
| Qual suon dolente il lieto di perturba? | What mournful sound disturbs the happy day? |

MESSENGER

| | |
|---|---|
| Lassa, dunque debb'io, | Alas, therefore must I, |
| mentre Orfeo con sue note il ciel consola, | while Orpheus with his notes delights heaven, |
| con le parole mie passargli il core? | with my words pierce his heart? |

SHEPHERD II

| | |
|---|---|
| Questa è Silvia gentile, | This is gentle Sylvia, |
| dolcissima compagna | sweetest companion |
| della bell' Euridice. O quanto è in vista | of the beautiful Euridice. O how her face looks |
| dolorosa! Hor che fia? Deh, sommi Dei, | sorrowful! Now what has happened? Ah, great Gods, |
| non torcete da noi benigno il guardo. | do not turn from us your benign gaze. |

MESSENGER

| | |
|---|---|
| Pastor, lasciate il canto, | Shepherd, leave off your song, |
| ch'ogni nostra allegrezza in doglia è volta. | for all our mirth is turned to grief. |

ORPHEUS

| | |
|---|---|
| D'onde vieni? Ove vai? Ninfa, che porti? | Whence do you come? Where do you go? Nymph, what news do you bring? |

MESSENGER

| | |
|---|---|
| A te ne vengo Orfeo, | To you I come, Orpheus, |
| messaggera infelice | unhappy messenger |
| di caso più infelice e più funesto. | of tidings yet more unhappy and more tragic. |
| La tua bella Euridice . . . | Your beautiful Eurydice . . . |

ORPHEUS

| | |
|---|---|
| Ohimè, che odo? | Alas, what do I hear? |

MESSENGER

| | |
|---|---|
| La tua diletta sposa è morta. | Your beloved wife is dead. |

ORPHEUS

| | |
|---|---|
| Ohimè. | Alas! |

MESSENGER

| | |
|---|---|
| In un fiorito prato | In a flowered meadow |
| Con l'altre sue compagne | with her companions |
| Giva cogliendo fiori | she was going about gathering flowers |
| Per farne una ghirlanda a le sue chiome, | to make a garland for her hair, |
| Quand'angue insidioso, | when a treacherous serpent |
| Ch'era fra l'erbe ascoso, | that was hidden in the grass |
| Le punse un piè con velenoso dente: | bit her foot with venomous tooth: |
| Ed ecco immantinente | then at once |
| Scolorirsi il bel viso e nei suoi lumi | her face became pale, and in her eyes |
| Sparir que lampi, ond'ella al sol fea scorno. | those fires that vied with the sun grew dim. |
| All'hor noi tutte sbigottite e meste | Then we all, frightened and sad, |
| Le fummo intorno, richiamar tentando | gathered around calling, tempting |
| Li spirti in lei smarriti | the spirits that were smothered in her |
| Con l'onda fresca e con possenti carmi; | with fresh water and powerful charms. |
| Ma nulla valse, ahi lassa! | But nothing helped, alas, |
| Ch'ella i languidi lumi alquanto aprendo, | for she, opening her languid eyes slightly, |
| E te chiamando Orfeo, | called to you, Orpheus, |
| Dopo un grave sospiro | and, after a deep sigh, |
| Spirò fra queste braccia, ed io rimasi | expired in these arms, and I remained |
| Piena il cor di pietade e di spavento. | with heart full of pity and terror. |

SHEPHERD I

| | |
|---|---|
| Ahi caso acerbo, ahi fat' empio e crudele! | Ah, bitter event, ah, fate wicked and cruel! |
| Ahi stelle ingiuriose, ahi cielo avaro! | Ah, malicious stars, ah, stingy heavens! |

SHEPHERD III

| | |
|---|---|
| A l'amara novella | The bitter news |
| rassembra l'infelice un muto sasso, | has turned the unfortunate one into a mute stone; |
| che per troppo dolor non può dolersi. | from too much pain, he can feel no pain. |

SHEPHERD I

| | |
|---|---|
| Ahi ben havrebbe un cor di Tigre o d'Orsa | Ah, he must have the heart of a tiger or a bear |
| Chi non sentisse del tuo mal pietate, | who did not feel pity for your loss, |
| Privo d'ogni tuo ben, misero amante! | as you are bereft of your dear one, wretched lover. |

ORPHEUS

| | |
|---|---|
| Tu se' morta, mia vita, ed io respiro? | You are dead, my life, and I still breathe? |
| Tu se' da me partita | You have departed from me, |
| Per mai più non tornare, ed io rimango? | never to return, and I remain? |
| No, che se i versi alcuna cosa ponno, | No, for if verses have any power, |
| N'andrò sicuro a' più profondi abissi, | I shall go safely to the most profound abyss, |
| E intenerito il cor del Re de l'Ombre | and having softened the heart of the King of the Shades |
| Meco trarrotti a riveder le stelle, | I shall bring you back to see the stars once again, |
| O se ciò negherammi empio destino | and if this is denied me by wicked fate, |
| Rimarrò teco in compagnia di morte, | I shall remain with you in the company of death. |
| A dio terra, a dio cielo, e sole, a dio. | Farewell earth, farewell sky and sun, farewell. |

CHORUS

| | |
|---|---|
| Ahi caso acerbo, ahi fat'empio e crudele! | Ah, bitter event, ah, fate wicked and cruel! |
| Ahi stelle ingiuriose, ahi cielo avaro! | Ah, malicious stars, ah stingy heavens! |
| Non si fidi huom mortale | Trust not, mortal man, |
| Di ben caduco e frale | in goods fleeting and frail, |
| Che tosto fugge, e spesso | for they easily slip away, and often |
| A gran salita il precipizio è presso. | after a steep ascent the precipice is near. |

—ALESSANDRO STRIGGIO

Monteverdi's *L'Orfeo* was first performed in 1607 for the Accademia degli Invaghiti in Mantua, where Monteverdi was maestro di cappella for Duke Vincenzo I. The academy was an aristocratic arts club (*invaghirsi* means to take a fancy to something) whose members included Francesco Gonzaga of the ducal family and Alessandro Striggio (ca. 1573–1630), who wrote the libretto. Striggio, the son of a Florentine musician and composer, expanded the story of Rinuccini's *Euridice* into a five-act play. Likewise, Monteverdi built on Peri's achievement, but used his own experience as a madrigal composer to create a musically and dramatically more satisfying form. The score was published in Venice in 1609, two years after the premiere in Mantua.

This extended excerpt from the middle of Act II exhibits Monteverdi's use of varied forms and styles for dramatic purposes. After a series of celebratory arias and ensembles at the beginning of the act, Orfeo sings a strophic aria in the style of a canzonetta, *Vi ricorda o boschi ombrosi* (a). In spirit, it resembles Peri's aria for Tirsi (NAWM 65b), but the ritornello is in five-part counterpoint. A note in the score explains that the ritornello should be played from behind the scene by five *viole da braccio* (viols played like violins), a contrabass, two harpsichords, and three *chitaroni* (theorbos) on the basso continuo. In this song, Orfeo recalls his earlier unhappiness, which has turned to joy now that he has won Euridice to be his bride.

A shepherd then sings a brief, tuneful song (b) in which he claims that even the woods and fields are laughing on this blessed day. But ironically he is interrupted when the Messenger arrives with her cry, *Ahi, caso acerbo* (Ah, bitter event) (c). Here the basso continuo accompaniment changes character through a change in orchestration from strings to an organ with wooden pipes and a theorbo, evoking a much more somber mood. The tonal center changes too, from the happy tones of the shepherd's Hypoionian (the plagal mode on C), similar to C major, to Hypoaeolian (the plagal mode on A), which sounds to modern ears like A minor. In the ensuing dramatic dialogue, Monteverdi imitated the recitative style developed by Peri, but he introduced a greater variety of melodic styles and used the harmony as a dramatic and formal device. Throughout the dialogue, the Messenger maintains her mournful mode and instrumentation, while the shepherds remain in their same more cheerful tonal and timbral realm, illustrating their lack of understanding of her grief. When Orfeo asks from where she comes and what news she brings (measures 39–41), he quickly moves up the circle of fifths from their tonal region to hers, adopting her tone of concern. When the messenger tells him that Euridice is dead, there is a stark contrast between the E-major triad in her tonal realm and the G- and C-minor triads in Orfeo's interjection, "Alas, what do I hear?" (measures 46–47). This use of chromaticism resembles that of the madrigal tradition and suggests the deep emotional impact of her words.

The Messenger then relates the events leading to Euridice's death, varying her style from simple narration on repeated notes (as at "In un fiorito prato," measure 50) to highly emotive speech (as at the leaps on "ahi lassa," measure 68, and "Orfeo," measure 72). The tonal center wanders in this section, allowing more expressive uses of chromaticism and striking harmonic juxtapositions to convey the strong feelings and images of the text. A shepherd then repeats the Messenger's opening cry of despair (at measure 77), which returns several more times as a kind of ritornello framing the rest of the act.

In Orfeo's lament (d), Monteverdi attained a new lyricism that far surpassed that of the first monodic experiments. In the passage that begins "Tu se' morta," each phrase builds greater intensity through rising pitches, chromatic alterations, and rhythmic changes. When necessary, Monteverdi repeated words and phrases from the libretto to further exploit these musical techniques. By this process and by harmonic means, he linked the fragments of recitative into coherent arches of melody. Particularly notable is the setting of the last line, "a dio terra" (measures 110–113). Here the rhythmic parallelism, the chromaticism, the rising pitch to the climax on "e sole," and the leap down to a note sounding a seventh against the bass convey the depth of Orfeo's grief.

Monteverdi composed the first section of the chorus with the melody of the Messenger's opening cry in the bass (with slight rhythmic modifications) and with the other four parts built above it. In essence, Monteverdi merged the expressive recitative style of Peri with the expressive polyphony of the madrigal tradition. As in the *kommos* of ancient Greek tragedy, which was a lament by the chorus in dialogue with one or more characters on stage, here the chorus joins Orfeo and the shepherds in bemoaning Euridice's death. Then, in the second section (after the double bar), the chorus assumes its traditional function of offering moralizing reflections on the stage action. Humankind, it sings, should not trust in the goods and pleasures of the world, for they are elusive and pass quickly. Monteverdi here adopted the methods of word-painting that were commonly used in polyphonic madrigals: all voices speed up for the idea of flight at "che tosto fugge" (that soon fly away), rise at "gran salita" (steep ascent, rendered in some versions as "gran fatica," great effort), and leap down at "il precipizio" (the precipice).

Most of Monteverdi's score is explicit about which instruments are to play in each section, which was still rare at the time *L'Orfeo* was composed. The great number and variety of instruments was no doubt made possible by the opera's aristocratic sponsors, and may have been made explicit in the printed score to lend prestige to their musical connoisseurship. The score and libretto are less clear about which passages are to be sung by which shepherd; the indications given here in the text and translation follow the accompanying recording. The editor of this edition has added tempo and dynamic markings, which do not appear in the original score.

# CLAUDIO MONTEVERDI (1567–1643)

## *L'incoronazione di Poppea*: Act I, Scene 3

*Opera*

1642

1) Copied up a 3rd (surely by mistake!) in both MSS.

POPPEA

| Signor, deh non partire, | My lord, please don't go. |
|---|---|
| Sostien, che queste braccia | Allow these arms |
| Ti circondino il collo, | to encircle your neck, |
| Come le tue bellezze | as your beauties |
| Circondano il cor mio. | encircle my heart. |

NERO

| Poppea, lascia ch'io parta. | Poppea, let me go. |

POPPEA

| | |
|---|---|
| Non partir, Signor, deh non partire. | Don't leave, my lord, please don't go. |
| Appena spunta l'alba, et tu che sei | The dawn is barely breaking, and you, who are |
| L'incarnato mio sole, | my sun made flesh, |
| La mia palpabil luce, | my light made palpable, |
| E l'amoroso dì de la mia vita, | and the loving day of my life, |
| Vuoi sì repente far da me partita? | want to part from me so quickly? |
| Deh non dir | Please don't say |
| Di partir, | that you're leaving. |
| Che di voce sì amara a un solo accento, | It is such a bitter word that from one hint of it, |
| Ahi, perir, ahi spirar quest'alma io sento. | ah, dying, ah, I feel my soul expiring. |

NERO

| | |
|---|---|
| La nobiltà de' nascimenti tuoi | The nobility of your birth |
| Non permette che Roma | does not permit that Rome |
| Sappia che siamo uniti. | should know that we are together, |
| In sin che Ottavia non rimane esclusa | until Ottavia is set aside, |
| Col repudio da me. | repudiated by me. |

POPPEA

| | |
|---|---|
| Vanne, ben mio. | Go, my dear. |

NERO

| | |
|---|---|
| In un sospir, che vien | Within a sigh that rises |
| Dal profondo del sen | from the depths of my breast |
| Includo un bacio, o cara, ed un addio: | I enclose a kiss, dearest, and a farewell. |
| Si rivedrem ben tosto, idolo mio. | We shall see each other soon, my idol. |

POPPEA

| | |
|---|---|
| Signor, sempre mi vedi, | My lord, you see me constantly; |
| Anzi mai non mi vedi. | or better still, you never see me. |
| Perchè s'è ver, che nel tuo cor io sia, | Because, if it's true that I am in your heart, |
| Entro al tuo sen celata, | hidden in your breast, |
| Non posso da' tuoi lumi esser mirata. | I cannot by your eyes be viewed. |

NERO

| | |
|---|---|
| Adorati miei rai, | My adored rays, |
| Deh restatevi omai! | please stay, then; |
| Rimanti, o mia Poppea, | remain, O my Poppea, |
| Cor, vezzo, e luce mia. | my heart, my charm, my light. |

POPPEA

| | |
|---|---|
| Deh non dir | Please don't say |
| Di partir, | that you're leaving. |
| Che di voce sì amara a un solo accento, | It is such a bitter word that from one hint of it, |
| Ahi, perir, ahi spirar quest'alma io sento. | ah, dying, ah, I feel my soul expiring. |

NERO

| | |
|---|---|
| Non temer, tu stai meco a tutte l'ore, | Do not fear; you stay with me at all times, |
| Splendor negl'occhi, e deità nel core. | splendor of my eyes, and goddess of my heart. |

| | POPPEA |
| --- | --- |
| Tornerai? | Will you return? |

| | NERO |
| --- | --- |
| Se ben io vò | Even if I go, |
| Pur teco io sto. | yet with you I stay. |

| | POPPEA |
| --- | --- |
| Tornerai? | Will you return? |

| | NERO |
| --- | --- |
| Il cor dalle tue stelle | My heart from your stars [eyes] |
| Mai non si divelle; | never can tear away; |

| | POPPEA |
| --- | --- |
| Tornerai? | Will you return? |

| | NERO |
| --- | --- |
| Io non posso da te viver disgiunto | I can no more live separated from you |
| Se non si smembra la unità del punto. | than the unity of a point can be divided. |

| | POPPEA |
| --- | --- |
| Tornerai? | Will you return? |

| | NERO |
| --- | --- |
| Tornerò. | I'll return. |

| | POPPEA |
| --- | --- |
| Quando? | When? |

| | NERO |
| --- | --- |
| Ben tosto. | Very soon. |

| | POPPEA |
| --- | --- |
| Ben tosto, | Very soon, |
| Me'l prometti? | you promise me? |

| | NERO |
| --- | --- |
| Te'l giuro. | I swear it. |

| | POPPEA |
| --- | --- |
| E me l'osserverai? | And you'll keep your promise? |

| | NERO |
| --- | --- |
| E s'a te non verrò, tu a me verrai. | And if I do not come to you, you will come to me. |

| | POPPEA |
| --- | --- |
| Addio, Nerone, addio. | Goodbye, Nero, goodbye. |

NERO

| | |
|---|---|
| Addio, Poppea, ben mio. | Goodbye, Poppea, my darling. |

—GIOVANNI FRANCESCO BUSENELLO

In his seventy-fourth year, Monteverdi wrote this opera based on a libretto by Giovanni Francesco Busenello (1598–1659) for performances during Venice's carnival season in 1642–43. The opera was not published at the time, although the libretto was; indeed, throughout the seventeenth and early eighteenth centuries, an opera's librettist was generally considered more important than the composer. Two manuscript copies of *L'incoronazione di Poppea* survive, one apparently used for the Venice performances and the other associated with a revival of the opera in Naples in 1651. The editor of the edition included here has collated the two versions and has labeled variants found in only one manuscript with *N* for Naples or *V* for Venice.

Act I, Scene 3 marks the first time in the opera that we meet Nero, emperor of Rome, and his mistress Poppea. But we have already heard much about them from Poppea's cuckolded husband Ottone and from two soldiers whom Nero left as guards while he spent the night with Poppea. In this scene the lovers emerge from Poppea's house as she begs Nero not to leave, showing the combination of seduction and flattery that has already won her the emperor's devotion.

Their dialogue progresses through many moods that are reflected in Monteverdi's setting by a variety of styles, including several types of recitative, arioso, and aria. Aria style is characterized by a clear meter, a steadily moving bass line, and a tuneful melody in the voice; recitative has a slower, freely moving bass and speechlike rhythms in the voice; and arioso is characterized by a mixture of elements from the other two styles. By the time Monteverdi composed *Poppea*, there was an emerging tradition of separating recitatives and arias into longer sections, often with a recitative leading to an aria. Recitative texts were usually in unrhymed lines known as blank verse (*versi sciolti*), sometimes ending in a rhymed couplet, and aria texts were in rhymed verse, often in strophic or other closed forms. But Monteverdi dealt very freely with the libretto's formal structure. Content rather than poetic form, and the urge to heighten emotional expression rather than the desire to charm and dazzle, determined the shifts between recitative style and aria style, and from one level of speech-song to another.

For example, the librettist wrote the dialogue at the beginning of this scene in blank verse, and accordingly Monteverdi set it in speechlike recitative, with a slightly more active bass for Nero's words "let me go" (measures 13–14) to suggest his attempt to leave. But when Poppea's text changes to rhymed couplets at "Deh non dir/ Di partir" (measure 30), calling for an aria, Monteverdi instead uses a highly expressive recitative style that recalls Orfeo's lament (NAWM 66d). The insistent repeated B♭ against an A in the bass, the chromatic motion between B♭ and B♮, and the uncanny alternation of half and whole steps in the vocal descent to the cadence (measures 34–37) perfectly express Poppea's mournful, pleading tone. Indeed, this style of recitative more clearly conveys her mood than any aria melody could do. Conversely, Poppea's speech at "Signor, sempre mi vedi" (measure 90), though written in blank verse by Busenello, is set by Monteverdi in aria style, complete with an opening ritornello, quickly moving bass, melodic sequences, and repeating phrases. Monteverdi composed it as such because the aria style more effectively conveys the appropriate emotion of coy flirting. Similarly, Poppea bursts into aria style at "vanne, ben mio" (measures 53–58), a passage that in both librettos seems to belong to Nero's recitative. As would have been expected, Nero then sings an aria to the rhymed couplets at "In un sospir" (measure 59), but he switches briefly to impassioned recitative for the emotional words "a kiss, dearest, and a farewell" and "my idol" (measures 78–80 and 85–89).

When appropriate, Monteverdi repeated or reordered the text to heighten the drama. For example, as Nero speaks of his wife Ottavia, Poppea interrupts, repeating his words and egging him on until he says that he will repudiate Ottavia to be with Poppea (measures 38–52). In the original libretto, shown here following the music, these words are all Nero's, written as a recitative in blank verse. Poppea also interrupts in a later passage with rhymed couplets that suggest the librettist meant for Nero to sing another aria (see measures 136–71); instead of waiting until after his aria to ask "Will you return?," as the librettist intended, Poppea asks it repeatedly, after every couplet, sometimes in aria style and sometimes recitative, until Nero finally promises he will return. These interruptions make Poppea seem to be a much stronger character and reveal her as the driving force in their relationship, who pushes Nero until she gets whatever she wants.

Because *Poppea* was written for a public opera house, a money-making operation, Monteverdi used a much smaller and less varied group of instruments than he used for *Orfeo*, which was written for aristocratic patrons. The instrumental parts other than the basso continuo are found only in the Naples manuscript, but it seems likely the ritornellos were played by an ensemble in Venice as well. The focus in Venetian opera was always on the singers. Monteverdi provided several opportunities for vocal display, but the singers also likely added expressive ornaments and decorative embellishments, especially at cadences. The part of Nero was written for a *castrato*, a male singer castrated before puberty to preserve his high vocal range. By the mid-seventeenth century, the leading male roles in many operas were sung by castratos, who were prized for their brilliant sound and powerful voices. In modern performances these roles are performed by mezzo-sopranos (as on the accompanying recording); are sung by countertenors or male contraltos; or are pitched down an octave and performed by tenors or baritones.

# ANTONIO CESTI (1623–1669)

*Orontea*: Excerpt from Act II

*Opera*

1656

(a) Scene 16: *E che si fa?*

From Antonio Cesti, *Orontea*, ed. William Holmes, Wellesley Edition 11 (Wellesley, Mass.: Wellesley College, 1973), 156–62.

Par——ti, fuggi di quà.

non Gelo—ne ____.

Par—to, fug-go,spari—sco,  e che sa—rà?

(b) Scene 17, opening aria: *Intorno all' idol mio*

Oron.

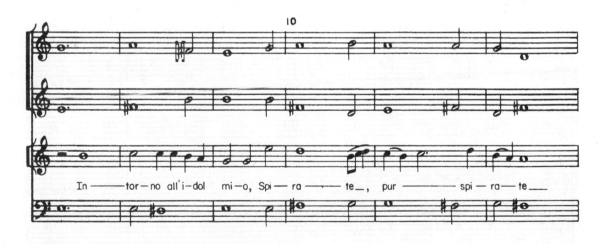

In ——tor—no all'i-dol  mi—o, Spi——ra——te_, pur ——— spi—ra—te___

Au—re___, au—re__ so—a—vi e gra———te_____, E__ nel·le guan—ce e—

—let—te Ba——cia———te–lo per me___, cor—te—si, cor—te—si au—ret———te_

———. E__ nel·le guan—ce e—let—te Ba——cia———te–lo per me___, ba——cia——te–lo per

-la — te—li per me___, lar ————————————— ve d'a—mo————re___.

|  | ORONTEA | |
| --- | --- | --- |
| E che si fa? | What are you doing? | |

|  | GELONE | |
| --- | --- | --- |
| Ohimè, io sfibbiavo costui per carità. | Oh! I unbuckled him for charity's sake. | |

|  | ORONTEA | |
| --- | --- | --- |
| Ove fosti fin ora? | Where were you until now? | |

|  | GELONE | |
| --- | --- | --- |
| All' altro mondo. | In the other world [i.e., dead drunk]. | |

|  | ORONTEA | |
| --- | --- | --- |
| S'obbedisce così? | Is this how you obey me? | |

GELONE

| | |
|---|---|
| Se delle mie dimore | If of my delays |
| Bacco fu la cagione, | Bacchus was the cause, |
| La botte ch'il versò | the bottle that he poured for me |
| Si punisca, O Signora, e non Gelone. | should be punished, O Lady, and not Gelone. |

ORONTEA

| | |
|---|---|
| Parti, fuggi di quà. | Leave, get out of here. |

GELONE

| | |
|---|---|
| Parto, fuggo, sparisco, e che sarà? | I leave, I flee, I disappear, and then what? |

ORONTEA

| | |
|---|---|
| Intorno all' idol mio | Around my idol |
| Spirate, pur spirate | breathe, just breathe, |
| Aure soave e grate | breezes sweet and pleasant, |
| E nelle guance elette | and on the favored cheeks |
| Baciatelo per me, cortesi aurette. | kiss him for me, gentle breezes. |

| | |
|---|---|
| Al mio ben che riposa | To my darling, who sleeps |
| Su l'ali della quiete | on the wings of calm, |
| Grati sogni assistete, | happy dreams induce; |
| E 'l mio racchiuso ardore | and my hidden ardor |
| Svelateli per me, larve d'amore. | unveil to him, phantoms of love. |

—GIACINTO ANDREA CICOGNINI

Antonio Cesti established himself as an opera composer by writing for the public opera houses in Venice. Beginning in 1652 he was employed by the archduke of Tyrol (a region in Austria), who was a great fan of Italian opera. Cesti's *Orontea*, with a libretto by Giacinto Andrea Cicognini, was first performed in 1656 at the archduke's newly built Venetian-style opera house in Innsbruck, and it became one of the most frequently staged operas of the mid-1600s both in Italy and abroad.

The opera tells the story of Orontea, an unmarried queen of Egypt who is reluctant to acknowledge her love for a painter named Alidoro until she discovers him painting a portrait of a rival lady of the court. Upon this discovery, Orontea realizes that she is about to lose Alidoro and resolves to marry him despite their difference in social status. In Act II, Scene 16, she encounters Alidoro asleep and the drunken servant Gelone, a comic figure in the opera, picking through Alidoro's pockets in search of money. The style of recitative in this scene is far different from the style common earlier in the century, which could serve a range of purposes from narration to intense emotional expression. The newer style of recitative, which became standard for the next hundred years, is simply a vehicle for rapid dialogue, and the vocal line usually includes many repeated notes on chord tones. The harmony maintains interest and suggests the progress of a conversation through frequent secondary dominants and changes of key.

After Orontea sends Gelone packing, she watches Alidoro sleeping, and in the first aria of Scene 17 she confesses her love for him. This aria is more elaborate than those in the early operas. The two violins play throughout, not merely in ritornellos before and after the singer's strophes. Moving away from the strict monody common in earlier operas, Cesti used a new texture of voice with instruments over basso continuo. Thus, he reestablished counterpoint in the upper parts as a standard practice in opera by blending elements of older polyphonic music with the new style. The form is strophic, as in earlier arias, but the music is adjusted to fit the text of the second strophe. There are only two strophes, compared to four or more in earlier arias by Peri (NAWM 65a) and Monteverdi (NAWM 66a), and the music for each strophe is longer, with many repetitions of words and whole phrases of text. This aria exhibits a new style of vocal music that was cultivated in Venice and is characterized by tuneful, mostly stepwise, mainly diatonic, and rhythmically simple melodic lines. The smooth contours of the vocal line contrast with and thereby throw into relief the more markedly expressive melodic and harmonic gestures, such as the leap down of a diminished seventh in measure 23 and the unprepared harmonic seventh in the following measure. This passage is heard in the opening ritornello and returns several times. After this aria, the scene continues with a monologue in recitative and another aria in which Orontea further expresses the complexity of her feelings through contrasting sentiments and styles.

# Barbara Strozzi (1619–1677)

*Lagrime mie*

*Cantata*

1650s

Published in Barbara Strozzi, *Diporti di Euterpe overo Cantate* & *ariette a voce sola*, Op. 7 (Venice: Alessandro Magni, 1659). From Carol MacClintock, ed., *The Solo Song 1580–1730* (New York: W. W. Norton & Company, 1973), 81–88, corrected by reference to the 1659 edition. © 1973 by W. W. Norton & Company, Inc. Used by permission of W. W. Norton & Company, Inc. Half-brackets indicate colored notation for hemiola.

re, Che mi to-glie'l re - spi-ro e op-pri — me il co -

- - - re; Che mi to-glie'l re - spi-ro e op-pri — me il co -

20

- - - - - - re. Li - dia, che tant'a -

25

- do - - ro,___ Per-chè un guar-do pie to - - so, ahi -

-mè,____ mi do-nò, Il pa-ter-no ri-gor,_____ il pa-ter-no ri-

-gor_____ l'im-prig-gio-nò.  Tra due mu-ra rin-chiu-sa  stà la bel-la  in-no-

-cen  -  te  Do-ve giun-ger non può  rag-gio di so  -  le,  E quel che più mi

duo  -  le ed ac-cresc' il mio mal,  tor-men  -  ti e pe-ne,  È

che per mia ca - gio-ne, per mia ca - gio-ne pro-va ma - le il ____ mi - o be -

- ne. ____ E voi lu - mi do - len - ti, do-

-len - ti, e voi lu - mi do - len - ti, do - len - ti, non pian -

-ge - - - - - - -

spi-ro, per cui spi - ro  E pur____ non mo - - ro. Stà co-lei tra du-ri
pre-go, ve ne pre - go)  a - spre mi e pe - - ne. Dhè to-glie-te-mi la

mar-mi, per cui spi-ro, per cui spi - ro  E pur____ non mo - - ro.
vi - ta, (ve ne pre-go, ve ne pre - go)  a - spre mi e pe - - ne.____

**1.**  **2.**

**Adagio**

Ma ben m'ac-cor - go,  che per tor-men-tar - - mi mag - gior-men-

-te, La sor - te mi nie - ga an - co la mor - te, mi nie - ga an - co, mi

**95**

nie-ga an-co la mor - te.    Se dun - qu'è ve - ro, o____ Di -

**100**                                                      **105**

- o,  è  ve - ro,  è  ve - ro,  o  Di - o,  Che sol del pian - -

**110**

- to, del pian - - to, del pian - - to____ mi -

| Lagrime mie, à che vi trattenete, | Tears of mine, what holds you back, |
| Perchè non isfogate il fier' dolore, | why don't you give vent to the fierce pain |
| Chi mi toglie 'l respiro e opprime il core? | that takes away my breath and weighs on |
| | my heart? |
| | |
| Lidia, che tant' adoro, | Lidia, whom I adore so much, |
| Perchè un guardo pietoso, ahimè, mi donò, | because of a pitying glance, alas, that she |
| | gave me, |
| Il paterno rigor l'impriggionò. | paternal severity has imprisoned her. |
| Tra due mura rinchiusa | Locked up between two walls, |
| Stà la bella innocente, | remains the innocent beauty, |
| Dove giunger non può raggio di sole, | where no ray of sun can reach, |
| E quel che più mi duole | and what most pains me |
| Ed accresc'il mio mal, tormenti e pene, | and increases my discomfort, torments, |
| | and anguish, |
| È che per mia cagione | is that because of me |
| Prova male il mio bene. | my beloved suffers. |
| E voi lumi dolenti, non piangete! | And you, pained eyes, do not weep! |
| Lagrime mie, à che vi trattenete? | Tears of mine, what holds you back? |
| | |
| Lidia, ahimè, veggo mancarmi. | Lidia, alas, I feel myself failing. |
| L'idol mio, che tanto adoro, | My idol, whom I adore so much |
| Stà colei tra duri marmi | remains between hard marble walls, |
| Per cui spiro e pur non moro. | her for whom I sigh and yet I don't die. |
| | |
| Se la morte m'è gradita, | If death suits me, |
| Or che son privo di spene, | now that I am deprived of hope, |
| Dhè, toglietemi la vita | Oh, take away my life— |
| (Ve ne prego) aspre mie pene. | I beg you—my bitter sufferings. |

| | |
|---|---|
| Ma ben m'accorgo, che per tormentarmi | Still I realize that to torment me |
| Maggiormente, la sorte | the more, destiny |
| Mi niega anco la morte. | even denies me death. |
| Se dunqu'è vero, o Dio, | If it is true then, O God, |
| Che sol del pianto mio, | that only for my tears |
| Il rio destino ha sete, | does cruel fate thirst, |
| [Lagrime mie, à che vi trattenete?] | [tears of mine, what holds you back?] |

Barbara Strozzi was one of the most important women composers of the seventeenth century and was especially well known as a composer of cantatas. In 1659 *Lagrime mie* appeared in her third published collection of cantatas and arias, *Diporti di Euterpe* (Pleasures of Euterpe, the Muse of music and lyric poetry). The poet may have been her adoptive (and perhaps natural) father Giulio Strozzi, who came from a Florentine noble family but resided in Venice. Partly to give her an outlet for her performances and compositions, he founded a society called the Academy of the Unisoni, and she undoubtedly composed and sang this cantata for that group.

The cantata's form is similar to that of most solo cantatas composed during the mid-seventeenth century, with sections in recitative, arioso, and aria styles that alternate corresponding to changes between narrative and lyric poetry in the text. Except for two lyric stanzas of four eight-syllable lines each, which Strozzi set as a strophic aria (measures 71–87), the text is in madrigal-type verse with seven- and eleven-syllable lines that do not follow a regular rhyme scheme.

Strozzi divided this free-form verse into sections according to content. In the first three lines, the poet addresses his tears; she composed this section as a lament in impassioned recitative style, with long expressive melismas. The next ten lines are a narration about Lidia, the object of the poet's love; Strozzi set this section as an *arioso*, which combines recitative with some elements of aria style, including passages that feature florid runs, a quickly moving bass, or rhythmic regularity. As the poet recalls the weeping eyes at "E voi lumi dolenti" ("And you, pained eyes," beginning at measure 49), Strozzi invokes the conventional emblem of the lament—the descending bass in triple meter. With the return of the opening line, "Lagrime mie, a che vi trattenete?" ("Tears of mine, what holds you back?," at measure 63), Strozzi repeats the opening musical passage as a kind of refrain. After the Aria (so marked in the original publication), a short recitative leads to a triple-time section built on a descending-fourth bass. The final line receives two parallel settings, the first cadencing on G (measure 116) and the second on the tonal center E, on which most of the earlier sections also closed. Although the music ends here, the poetry strongly implies a return to the opening line, which rhymes with the closing line ("sete" and "trattenete") and completes the thought (beginning at "Se dunqu'è vero," "If it is indeed true"). The performers on the accompanying recording reprise the entire first section of the cantata (measures 1–22); an alternative would be to sing the refrain at measures 63–70, which repeats only the first line but closes on the tonal center E.

The dry declamatory style of theatrical dialogue did not suit such intimate poetic texts, so composers softened, sweetened, and intensified the style of their recitatives in these cantatas meant for chamber performance. In the opening recitative, Strozzi very artfully exploited many of the rhetorical devices that the Roman composers Luigi Rossi (1597–1653) and Giacomo Carissimi (1605–1674) had introduced into cantata recitative. For example, the hesitations on the disso-nant D♯, A, and F♯ over the opening E-minor harmony, together with the C♮ of the harmonic-minor scale, create a moving and vivid projection of the lamenting lover's weeping and sobbing. In the Arioso, the tasteful word-inspired runs at "adoro" (adore, measure 25), "pietoso" (pitying, measure 27), and "rigor" (sever-ity, measures 30 and 32), the delicate chromaticism at "tormenti" (torments, measure 42), and the compelling seventh chords and suspensions—particularly over the descending basses—demonstrate Strozzi's mastery in applying music to express the affective vocabulary of this genre.

The cantata is scored for solo voice with continuo, played on a harpsichord on the accompanying recording. In accordance with the performing practice of Strozzi's time, both the singer and the continuo player add improvised embellishments.

# ALESSANDRO GRANDI (1586–1630)

## O quam tu pulchra es

*Solo motet (sacred concerto)*

CA. 1625

Values halved in triple meter. Published in *Ghirlanda sacra, Libro primo . . . per Leonardo Simonetti* (Venice, 1625). Edited by Rudolf Ewehart in *Drei Hohelied Motetten*, Cantio sacra 23 (Cologne: Verlag Edmund Bieler, 1960), 7–9. Reprinted by permission.

| | |
|---|---|
| O quam tu pulchra es, | O how beautiful you are, |
| amica mea, columba mea, formosa mea. | my love, my dove, my beauty. |
| Oculi tui columbarum, | Your eyes are like doves, |
| capilli tui sicut greges caprarum | your hair like a flock of goats, |
| et dentes tui sicut greges tonsarum. | and your teeth like a flock of ewes newly shorn. |
| Veni de Libano, amica mea, | Come with me from Lebanon, my love, |
| columba mea, formosa mea, | my dove, my beauty, |
| veni, coronaberis. | come, make a garland. |
| Surge, propera, sponsa mea, | Arise, hasten, my bride, |
| dilecta mea, immaculata mea. | my delight, my spotless one. |
| Surge, veni, quia amore langueo. | Arise, come, for I grow weak with love. |

—ADAPTED FROM SONG OF SONGS,
4:1–2, 4:8, 2:10, 5:2, AND 2:5

Alessandro Grandi was serving as deputy choirmaster under Monteverdi at St. Mark's Basilica in Venice when he wrote this motet, published in an anthology in 1625. He drew the text from various verses of the Song of Songs, an ancient love poem that was included in the Bible because its erotic imagery was understood to represent the love between God and those who worship him. It was a popular source for musical settings in the seventeenth century, in part because the words invited a rich and varied musical treatment. This setting for solo voice with continuo was considered a motet because it served the same function as Renaissance motets; like them, it was a setting of a Latin text other than the Mass Ordinary that was appropriate for use during a Mass or Office service. But, like Caccinni's solo madrigal in NAWM 64, this work uses the new styles of monody to realize a text that in previous generations would have been set polyphonically.

Grandi's solo motet is a religious composition that incorporates elements from dramatic recitative, solo madrigal, and aria. The sections alternate between styles in the same manner as in a cantata (such as Strozzi's *Lagrime mie* in NAWM 69) or in an operatic scene (like the scene from Monteverdi's *L'incoronazione di Poppea* in NAWM 67), demonstrating that the structure of the motet had changed fundamentally from that of its polyphonic predecessors. The first twenty-one measures are recitative, but of a more melodious, rhythmic style than that of recitative used in the theater. Marco Scacchi coined the term "hybrid recitative" (*recitativo inbastardito*) to describe this mixed style, which he found more appropriate for church music. The opening phrase, "O quam tu pulchra es" (O how beautiful you are) recurs several times as a kind of refrain. In the following passage, triple-time aria style (measures 22–34) represents greater activity at the words "Veni, veni de Libano" (Come, come from Lebanon). Next follow five measures of recitative that recall the opening section. The triple-time aria style then returns (measures 40–51), again symbolizing activity at "Surge, propera" (Arise, hasten). The rest of the motet features a new refrain on "Surge, veni" (Arise, come) in duple-time aria style that suggests motion through quickly moving bass and vocal lines. This refrain alternates with languid, drawn-out recitative settings for the words "Quia amore langueo" (For I grow weak with love). Pieces composed during this period in the concertato medium (voices with obligatory instrumental accompaniment) often had refrains, so Grandi's use of textual repetition to create two refrains reflects a practice that was common among his contemporaries.

By this period, representing words through music in motets was a century-old tradition. However, Grandi's use of the new monodic styles pioneered in opera and vocal chamber music to express text in motets was novel. It is interesting to note that many more listeners were likely to have encountered these new styles in sacred music than in operas or cantatas, whose audiences were relatively small and elite.

This motet could have been performed in church services or in devotions at the confraternities that were an important part of social life in Venice. The continuo part could be performed on an organ, but theorbo, lute, and harpsichord were also used for playing continuo in churches at this time. On the accompanying recording the continuo is performed on a harpsichord, supported by a cello that sustains the bass notes. The singer adds appropriate embellishments, especially at cadences.

# GIACOMO CARISSIMI (1605–1674)

*Historia di Jephte*: Excerpt

*Oratorio*

CA. 1648

(a) Recitative: *Plorate colles*

Edited by Gottfried Wolters, figured bass realized by Mathias Siedel (Wolfenbüttel: Möseler Verlag, 1969), 29–39.

Is - ra - el et glo - ri - a pa - tris me - i, e - go si - ne

fi - li - is vir - go, e - go fi - li - a u - ni - ge - ni - ta

mo - ri - ar et non vi -

vam. Ex - hor - re - sci - te ru - pes, ob - stu - pe - sci - te col - les,

val - les et ca - ver - nae in so - ni - tu hor - ri - bi - li re - so -

*me - am       et    Jeph - te    fi - li-am u - ni - ge - ni-tam in car - mi-ne do -*

*lo -      ris          la - men - ta - - - mi - ni,          et*

*Jeph - te    fi - li-am u - ni - ge - ni-tam   in   car - mi - ne do -*

*lo -      ris          la - men - ta - - mi - ni.*

## (b) Chorus: *Plorate filii Israel*

375/403  3

380/408

DAUGHTER

Plorate colles, dolete montes
et in afflictione cordis mei ululate!

Weep, hills; grieve, mountains;
and in the affliction of my heart, wail!

ECHO

Ululate!

Wail!

DAUGHTER

Ecce moriar virgo
et non potero morte mea
meis filiis consolari,
ingemiscite silvae,
fontes et flumina,
in interitu virginis lachrimate!

See, I shall die a virgin
and I shall not be able at my death
to be consoled by my children.
Groan, forests;
springs and rivers,
for the death of a virgin, weep!

ECHO

Lachrimate!

Weep!

DAUGHTER

Heu me dolentem
in laetitia populi,
in victoria Israel
et gloria patris mei,
ego sine filiis virgo,
ego filia unigenita
moriar et non vivam.
Exhorrescite rupes, obstupescite colles,
valles et cavernae
in sonitu horribili resonate!

Woe is me, sorrowful,
amidst the people's joy
in Israel's victory
and my father's glory.
I, without children, a virgin,
I, an only daughter,
will die and not live.
Shudder, crags; be stupefied, hills;
valleys and caves,
with the horrible sound resound!

ECHO

Resonate!

Resound!

DAUGHTER

Plorate filii Israel,
plorate virginitatem meam
et Jephte filiam unigenitam
in carmine doloris lamentamini.

Weep, sons of Israel,
bewail my virginity
and Jephtha's only daughter
lament in songs of sorrow.

CHORUS

Plorate filii Israel,
plorate omnes virgines
et filiam Jephte unigenitam
in carmine doloris lamentamini.

Weep, sons of Israel;
weep, all virgins,
and Jephtha's only daughter
lament in songs of sorrow.

The *oratorio* is a genre that first developed in Rome during the seventeenth century as a musical setting of a sacred narrative or dialogue in either Latin or Italian. Such works were not used in church services, but were performed in church halls known as oratories, from which the new genre got its name. Oratorios resembled operas without staging, costumes, or action, and they used similar forms of monody, such as recitative and aria. But oratorios differed from operas by sometimes including a narrator and by giving a greater role to the chorus, which had associations both with Greek tragedy and with liturgical polyphony. Oratorios were performed during Lent, the period of penitence before Easter, and they emphasized subjects appropriate to that season.

This excerpt from Giacomo Carissimi's *Jephte* exhibits some of the common characteristics of oratorios. The biblical story, drawn from Judges 11:29–40, emphasizes the Lenten themes of suffering and obedience to God. Jephtha, the military leader of the Israelites, is victorious in battle and owes the victory to a promise he made to the Lord. He vowed that if allowed to defeat the Ammonites, on his return home he would sacrifice the first person to come out of his house. It is his daughter, his only child, who first runs out to meet him with timbrels and dances. Despite his grief, he must keep his vow, but he allows her two months to wander the mountains and bewail her fate.

A contemporary writer, perhaps a priest at the Jesuit college in Rome where Carissimi was maestro di cappella, expanded the brief biblical narrative with additional text, including the closing scene reprinted here. The daughter's lament is a long, sorrowful recitative that is sweetened with arioso passages. Carissimi repeated words and phrases of the text for rhetorical effect, as at "Plorate" (Weep) in measures 287–88 and "et in afflictione cordis mei ululate!" (and in the affliction of my heart, wail!) in measures 291–98. He intensified the effect of text repetition by repeating the melodic gesture a step higher (at "Plorate") or by repeating an entire phrase up a fourth, in what would now be considered a sequence (measures 287–91 and 291–98). The frequent flatting of melodic notes (as at measures 297, 299, and 296) conveys pathos. Two other singers, who echo some of the daughter's cadential phrases, represent her companions.

Carissimi's recitative uses expressive dissonances in a way that recalls early Florentine opera, but they exist in a more chordally conceived environment. For example, the A in measure 292 is not simply a free dissonance, but a member of a chord, and the F♯ in measure 302 is part of a D chord over a G pedal point. Similarly, the skip to the seventh over the bass in measures 308–9 and the Neapolitan sixth chord in measure 310 and elsewhere (featuring a lowered note a minor sixth above the bass and a semitone above the subsequent cadential note) are harmonic rather than purely melodic effects. These passages demonstrate how much the emotional intensity of this scene is expressed through harmonic as well as melodic means.

The oratorio closes with a magnificent six-voice chorus of lamentation. In what became an emblem of lament during the seventeenth century, the bass line descends repeatedly by step through a fourth (measures 358–63 and 367–70); a chromatic variant of the same figure appears in Dido's lament at the end of Purcell's *Dido and Aeneas* (NAWM 79b). Especially striking is how Carissimi conveys the intensification of grief by building from single suspensions (measures 377–78) to double suspensions (measures 38off) and even a triple suspension (measure 381), combining powerful dissonances with a mournful descending gesture.

On the accompanying recording, the continuo is played on theorbo, and the chorus is sung by six solo voices, as was probably the performing practice of the time. As suggested by the editor (with the mark "*Vi- -de*"), measures 413–24 are omitted from the performance on the recording.

# HEINRICH SCHÜTZ (1585–1672)

*O lieber Herre Gott*, SWV 287, from *Kleine geistliche Konzerte I*

*Sacred concerto*

CA. 1636

72

CD 5|4

O lie - ber Her - - re Gott we - cke uns auf, dass wir be - reit sein, we - cke uns auf, dass wir be - reit sein, wenn dein Sohn kömmt, o lie - ber

O lie - ber Her - -

First published in *Erster Theil kleiner geistlichen Concerten* (Leipzig, 1636). Edition adapted from *Heinrich Schütz Sämtliche Werke*, ed. Philipp Spitta, vol. 6, *Kleine geistliche Konzerte* (Leipzig: Breitkopf & Härtel, 1887), 13–15. "SWV 287" indicates that this work is number 287 in the *Schütz-Werke-Verzeichnis* [Schütz Works Catalogue], ed. Werner Bittinger (Kassel: Bärenreiter, 1960).

| | |
|---|---|
| O lieber Herre Gott, | O dear Lord God, |
| wecke uns auf, dass wir bereit sein, | wake us up, so that we are ready, |
| wenn dein Sohn kömmt, | when your Son comes, |
| ihn mit Freuden zu empfahen | him with joy to receive |
| und dir mit reinem Herzen zu dienen, | and you with a pure heart to serve, |
| durch denselbigen, deinen lieben Sohn, | through him, your dear Son, |
| Jesum Christum, Amen. | Jesus Christ, Amen. |

—MARTIN LUTHER

Heinrich Schütz wrote the pieces in his *Kleine geistliche Konzerte* (Small Sacred Concertos) during the 1630s for church services at Dresden, where he was chapel master. As the composer mentions in his preface, the chapel had been greatly reduced in size due to the Thirty Years' War then raging through Germany and draining his patron's treasury, so Schütz scored the concertos for fewer singers than in most of his previous works and used no instruments beyond the continuo. These two collections of pieces for one to five solo voices with continuo, published in 1636 and 1639, were quite popular throughout Germany because they met the need for small works suitable for performance in Lutheran churches.

Schütz had studied in Venice with Giovanni Gabrieli in 1609–12 and visited there again in 1628–29 when Monteverdi and Grandi were at St. Mark's, so he was quite familiar with Italian innovations in music. Like Grandi's motet (NAWM 70), this duet uses contrasts between recitative, arioso, and aria styles to convey the text. The long notes in the opening phrase convey wonder at standing before God in prayer, and the poignant descent of a diminished fourth from B♭ to F♯ calls attention to the words "lieber Herre" (dear Lord). The next phrase, beginning at measure 6, depicts the words "wecke uns auf, dass wir bereit sein" (wake us up, so that we are ready) through a faster-moving arioso with upward leaps on "auf" (up) and "bereit" (ready), and repetitions of the text and music in sequence over a rising chromatic bass. The second singer then repeats these two phrases while the first adds imitative counterpoint. "Herre" is highlighted with an augmented triad, a striking, unusual sonority, which resolves irregularly (measure 15); this departure from traditional counterpoint exemplifies the *stile moderno* (modern style) that Schütz had learned in Italy.

A new section begins in measure 28. At the words "ihn mit Freuden" (him with joy [to receive]), the music conveys joy through aria style in triple meter and increases its intensity through imitation and a rising sequence. A brief recitative ensues, and then both aria and recitative passages repeat varied and transposed, again intensifying the words. More text repetition, imitation, and sequences combine in the final section (beginning at measure 67), building to a peak of activity through the sixteenth-note figuration on "Amen." Throughout, the sense of the words determined the types of settings that Schütz composed.

In the seventeenth century, women did not perform in church services. The treble parts in this piece would have been sung by boys whose voices had not yet changed. On the accompanying recording, the duet is sung by two boy sopranos, and the continuo is realized on an organ, supported by a cello playing the bass line.

# HEINRICH SCHÜTZ (1585–1672)

*Saul, was verfolgst du mich*, SWV 415, from *Symphoniae sacrae III*

*Sacred concerto*

CA. 1650

First published in *Symphoniarum sacrarum tertia pars, worinnen zubefinden sind deutsche Concerten*, Op. 12 (Dresden, 1650), No. 18. This edition is by Werner Breig, *Neue Ausgabe samtlicher Werke*, vol. 21, *Symphoniae Sacrae III (1650)* (Kassel: Barentreiter, 2002), 95–110. Used by permission.

*)The dynamic markings in Violin I and Cantus I apply to both violins and the six solo voices.

*)From here on the dynamic markings in Tenor I are independent from the echo-dynamics of the other voices.

| Saul, Saul, was verfolgst du mich? | Saul, Saul, why do you persecute me? |
| Es wird dir schwer werden, | It will be hard for you |
| wider den Stachel zu löcken. | to kick against the thorns. |

After the end of the Thirty Years' War in 1648, Heinrich Schütz once again had the full resources of the Dresden chapel at his disposal, and he returned to writing large-scale works. *Saul, was verfolgst du mich* is in the grand polychoral style of Gabrieli, with whom Schütz had studied decades earlier. The text is from one of the most dramatic episodes in the New Testament, Paul's description of how he was converted to Christianity:

> Thus I journeyed to Damascus with the authority and commission of the chief priests. At midday, O king, I saw on the way a light from heaven, brighter than the sun, shining round me and those who journeyed with me. And when we had all fallen to the ground, I heard a voice saying to me in the Hebrew language, "Saul, Saul, why do you persecute me? It hurts you to kick against the goads." (Acts 26:12–14, Revised Standard Version)

According to the Bible, Saul, a Jew, had been sent to Damascus to fetch Christian prisoners, and the voice he heard in the desert was that of Christ. The experience led to Saul's conversion and to his career (under the name Paul) as an advocate for Christianity.

The concerto is set for six solo voices (the ensemble Schütz called *favoriti*, or favored ones), two violins, two four-voice choirs (possibly with one singer per part), and continuo. Other instruments may have doubled the choral parts. At the opening of the piece, the two-note chords from the D-minor triad rise from the depths of the solo basses through the tenors. The same music is then heard shifting to an A-minor triad in the sopranos, and finally the violins present an F-major triad before returning to cadence on D. Christ's question "Was verfolgst du mich?" (Why do you persecute me?) is set to grinding, dissonant anticipations and suspensions that break the rules of traditional counterpoint in order to highlight the harshness of the text. Through all this, the repetition of the very brief text reinforces its intensity.

Thus far in the piece, the texture has been that of a concerto for few voices. Now the polychoral medium conveys the same musical material on a bright D-major triad (measure 17), and the choruses and soloists together reverberate with echoes, suggesting the effect of Christ's voice bouncing off rocky projections in the desert. The dynamic markings—*forte* when the choruses enter, *mezzopiano* for the first echo, and *pianissimo* for the second—are printed in the original publication, showing Schütz's attention to detail for the sake of creating an impressive effect. The slight metric shift in measures 21–23 and the wavering between major and minor triads on G reinforce the effect by creating the sense of the echoing sound being distorted as it caroons off nearby cliffs.

The following section is in a contrasting style, a recitative on the words "Es wird dir schwer werden, wider den Stachel zu löcken" (It will be hard for you to kick against the thorns). Here, Schütz demonstrates his skill at text depiction with a large melodic leap downward and a circling melisma on "kick," suggesting a flailing, ultimately fruitless gesture of resistance. After a varied reprise of the choral "Saul, Saul" as a refrain (measure 34), the recitative material is developed in imitation (beginning at measure 39), and then the polychoral and recitative ideas are combined (measure 60). At the final return of the "Saul, Saul" chorus, one tenor voice, perhaps representing Christ's clarion call, sounds out "Saul, Saul, Saul" in long notes (measure 66), gradually rising in pitch as the chorus repeats its cry and is echoed by the other soloists, until with a last echo the piece ends quietly.

Original performance practice likely called for all the parts to be sung by men and boys, but on the accompanying recording women sing the upper parts. They are joined by organ and cello performing the continuo, with theorbo added to highlight the contrast in style for the sections on "Es wird dir schwer warden."

# GIROLAMO FRESCOBALDI (1583–1643)

## Toccata No. 3

*Toccata*

CA. 1615, REV. 1637

First published in Girolamo Frescobaldi, *Toccate e partite d' intavolatura di cimbalo . . . Libro primo* (Rome, 1615); printed in this revised form in *Toccate d'intavolatura di cimbalo et organo libro 1* (Rome, 1637). This edition from Frescobaldi, *Orgel- und Klavierwerke,* ed. Pierre Pidoux, vol. 3, *Das erste Buch der Toccaten, Partien usw. (1637)* (Kassel: Bärenreiter-Verlag, 1954), 11–13. Reprinted by permission of Bärenreiter Music Corporation.

Although Girolamo Frescobaldi wrote music in a variety of genres, he made his international reputation with his keyboard music. His 1615 collection entitled *Toccate e partite d' intavolatura di cimbalo . . . Libro primo* (Toccatas and Partitas Intabulated for Harpsichord . . . Book I) was the first that he conceived exclusively for keyboard. The pieces in it, including an early version of this toccata, are idiomatically suited to the harpsichord; the music fits easily under two hands at the keyboard, and Frescobaldi avoided the long sustained notes common in his organ music because they decay too quickly on the plucked strings of the harpsichord. The revised toccata shown here was published in a later collection, *Toccate d'intavolatura di cimbalo et organo libro 1* (Toccatas Intabulated for Harpsichord and Organ Book 1), published in 1637.

A toccata is a piece in improvisatory style, in which the player explores a range of harmonies and figurations. *Toccata* means "touched" in Italian, referring to the act of touching the keys, as if improvising. Toccatas were often played as preludes to other pieces, and one function of a toccata was to clearly define the mode of the piece that it preceded. This toccata is in the transposed Dorian mode on G. The music is constantly approaching a cadence on either G or the modal tenor D, but in most cases the composer evades or weakens the sense of a cadence through harmonic or rhythmic effects, or through continued motion in one or more part. As a result, the music maintains forward momentum until the final cadence on G.

Like most of Frescobaldi's toccatas, this one unfolds as a series of brief phrases or sections, each closed with a cadence or similar punctuation. Each section treats a distinctive figure that is passed between voices, as in measures 1–2, or varied in some other way, like the sequence in measures 5–6. The style shifts frequently, further distinguishing the sections. At the outset, the toccata breathes the spirit of recitative, with jagged lines and nervous rhythms. At measure 5 there is a short arioso passage with chains of suspensions over a walking bass. A rapid run in the bass in measure 7 leads to an imitative section in measures 8–11. Figurations and textures continue to change every two or three measures throughout the rest of the piece, which gradually builds in intensity as sixteenth-note rhythms come to predominate. The sectional quality of a toccata derives from its purpose as a prelude or as music to play on the harpsichord for one's own enjoyment, for as Frescobaldi observed, the performer may stop at any cadence that seems appropriate, tailoring the length of the piece to suit the situation.

In accordance with the improvisatory spirit of the toccata, Frescobaldi noted in the preface to this collection that the harpsichordist need not play in strict time, but may accelerate or retard the tempo as prompted by the music, and particularly should play more slowly at cadences. The performer on the accompanying recording follows this suggestion. He also freely arpeggiates chords and adds ornaments, in accordance with the performing practice of Frescobaldi's time.

# GIROLAMO FRESCOBALDI (1583–1643)

## Ricercare after the Credo from *Mass for the Madonna*, in *Fiori musicali*

*Ricercare*

CA. 1635

From Girolamo Frescobaldi, *Fiori musicali,* ed. Christopher Stembridge (Padua: Armelin Musica, 1997), 68–69. Used by permission.

\* The sharp indicates that the last chord is major, with B natural (not G sharp).

Girolamo Frescobaldi spent most of his career as organist at St. Peter's Cathedral in Rome, but *Fiori musicali* (Musical Flowers, 1635) was his only published collection to contain only music intended specifically for church services. The collection consists of three *organ masses,* each of which comprises all the music that an organist would need to play for the celebration of Mass in a major church or cathedral. This included a toccata before the Mass, settings of parts of the Kyrie played in alternation with the choir, a canzona after the Epistle, a ricercare after the Credo, a toccata at the Elevation of the Host, and a few other pieces. Included here is the Ricercare after the Credo from the Mass for the Madonna, used for feasts of the Blessed Virgin Mary.

By the early seventeenth century, a *ricercare* was an imitative composition based on the continuous development of a single subject, sometimes with a countersubject. The subject of this ricercare is easy to pick out of the texture because of its distinctive shape, with a rising minor sixth, dotted rhythm, downward leap, and rising chromatic line in deliberate half notes. It appears several times in the first half of the piece, in all four voices, and usually in counterpoint with the lively countersubject that first appears in measure 4. After a cadence in measure 24, the subject appears in augmentation, and a variant of the countersubject in original and inverted form weaves around it. The ricercare is in G Dorian, confirmed by the strong cadences on G and by the subject, which most often either enters on G and rises chromatically to D (as in measures 1–4) or enters on D and rises to G (as in the bass at measures 5–7). The player has the option to end the piece at the fermata in measure 24 if a shorter ricercare is desired.

Although Frescobaldi conceived *Fiori musicali* for organ, he published the compositions in score rather than organ tablature, and the edition included here maintains that appearance. Such scores were common for organ music around this time in both the Italian and the German tradition, and Frescobaldi commented in his preface to *Fiori musicali* that any accomplished organist should be able to play from a score. The symbol after the barline at the end of each staff indicates the next note that part is to play.

The performance on the accompanying recording is on an organ that was built during the mid-sixteenth century at a convent in Milan, Italy. The organ has been preserved almost intact, allowing us to hear the piece on a type of instrument that Frescobaldi would have known.

This organ is tuned in mean-tone temperament, the most common tuning system for keyboard instruments during the sixteenth and seventeenth centuries. It differs from equal temperament in that the most common intervals and chords are much closer to pure tuning, and the thirds especially are sweeter. However, the half steps are not all the same size, as they would be in equal temperament. As a result, modern listeners may find the chromatic lines particularly bracing, even unsettling. If the organ seems "out of tune," that is evidence of how accustomed we have become to equal temperament.

# BIAGIO MARINI (1594–1663)

*Sonata IV per il violino per sonar con due corde*

*Sonata for violin and continuo*

CA. 1626

From Biagio Marini, *String Sonatas from Opus 1 and Opus 8.* Transcribed and edited by Thomas D. Dunn; continuo realization by William Gudger. Collegium Musicum: Yale University, Second Series, vol. 10 (Madison, Wisc.: A-R Editions, Inc. 1981), 115–21. Used with permission.

76 BIAGIO MARINI *Sonata IV per il violino per sonar con due corde*

groppo al alta

The sonata for one or two instruments with basso continuo became an important genre in the seventeenth century, signifying a shift in instrumental music that paralleled the increased focus on solo singing in the new vocal genres of the time. Among the first significant sonatas for violin and continuo are the four Biagio Marini included in his Op. 8 (1629), a compendium of his instrumental works in various genres that was published while he was serving as violinist and composer for the ducal court of Neuburg in southern Germany. Marini's sonatas are notable for taking advantage of the idiomatic possibilities of the violin and for borrowing expressive gestures and figuration from vocal monody.

*Sonata IV per il violino per sonar con due corde* (Sonata IV for the violin to play on two strings) takes its name from its use of double stops (playing on two strings simultaneously). The first published work to make use of this effect was Marini's Op. 2 (1618), published while he was working with Monteverdi at St. Mark's in Venice. Like a canzona (see NAWM 62), the sonata presents a series of contrasting sections, each distinguished by a particular figuration and sometimes by different moods, meters, or tempos. Changes of style between recitative-like and aria-like sections recall similar stylistic alternations in the vocal music of Monteverdi (NAWM 67), Strozzi (NAWM 69), and Grandi (NAWM 70). In sonatas composed later in the century, these contrasting sections would be separated to form individual movements (see NAWM 83).

The first section, marked *Tardo* (slow), begins with an expressive melody in the style of a solo madrigal or recitative above a slowly moving bass. At measure 6, the texture changes to rapid figures that are idiomatic for the violin, and then the two styles alternate. In measures 20–26, the range of the melody expands beyond two octaves, and there are leaps of a seventh, ninth, twelfth, and even larger. The extensive range and large leaps would be difficult or impossible for a singer to perform, so the use of these effects helped to distinguish the new violin idiom from the vocal monody that inspired it.

The second section (at measure 31) moves at a more regular pace, like an aria. It presents material in double stops, first moving mostly in parallel thirds or sixths, and then in imitation between two voices. In the next section (at measure 51), the violin plays scale figures, trills, and large leaps, as the tempo alternates between *Tardo* (Slow) and *Presto* (Quickly). The *affetti* marking at measure 70 indicates that the player should draw the most intense possible emotion from the passage by using unusual playing techniques or adding highly expressive ornamentation; the violinist on the accompanying recording does so with a variety of elaborate embellishments.

The brief section at measure 83 is distinguished by a change to triple meter and fast tempo, as the violin executes jagged leaps that extend to a range of two and a half octaves. A return to a slow recitative-like melody in quadruple meter at measure 95 leads to an aria-like passage (measure 102) in which the bass moves steadily while the violin spins out a short phrase through transposition and variation.

There follows another rhapsodic section, marked by scalar figures. The final section, comprising an aria in triple meter (measure 127) and a slow arioso-like conclusion (measure 148), is marked to be repeated, providing the listener with some welcome repetition after the many varied styles and figurations in the sonata, and giving the performers the opportunity to embellish the repetition.

The sonata is in mode 9, the Aeolian mode on A. Each section fits into an overall structure of tonal areas: the first section opens and closes on A, the second on G, and the rest of the sections alternate closing on C and on A.

In the performance on the accompanying recording, the continuo is played on an organ and a theorbo (a large lute with extra bass strings, also called *chitarrone*). The violinist emphasizes the contrast between the recitative-like and aria-like sections by playing with much greater rhythmic freedom in the former. Both soloist and theorbist add embellishments, especially at cadences, as was customary performance practice during the period.

# JEAN-BAPTISTE LULLY (1632–1687)

*Armide*: Excerpts

*Opera (tragédie lyrique)*

1686

(a) Overture

Edited by Robert Eitner, *Publikationen älterer praktischer und theoretischer Musikwerke*, 14 (Leipzig: Breitkopf & Härtel, 1885), 1–3 and 100–104.

25 60

(Lentement, zweite Ausg.)

(b) Act II, Scene 5: *Enfin il est en ma puissance*

27  62

Armide. *(tenent un dard à la main.)*

En - fin    il est en ma puis-san - ce.   Ce fa-tal en-ne - mi,    ce su-per - be vain -

queur.    La char-me du som - meil - le liv - re à ma ven-gean - ce;   je vais per-cer son in-vin-ci - ble

28  63

*(Armide*

coeur.    Par lui tous mes cap-tifs sont sor-tis d'es-cla - va - ge; qu'il é-prou-ve tou-te ma ra - ge.    Quel

té de lui ra-vir le jour! A ce jeu-ne hé-ros tout cè - de sur la ter - re. Qui croi-

rait qu'il fut ne seu-le-ment pour la guer-re? Il sem - ble e - tre fait pour l'a - mour.

Ne puis - je me ven - ger à moins qu'il ne pé - ris - se? Hé! ne suf-fit - il

pas que l'a-mour le pu - nis - se? Puis-qu'il n'a pu trou - ver mes yeux as - sez char-

\* On the recording, the music returns to measure 71, continues through measure 90, and again repeats measures 86–90.

ARMIDE
*(holding a dagger in her hand)*

| | |
|---|---|
| Enfin il est en ma puissance, | Finally he is in my power, |
| Ce fatal ennemi, ce superbe vainqueur. | this mortal enemy, this superb conqueror. |
| Le charme du sommeille livre à ma vengeance; | The charm of sleep delivers him to my vengeance; |
| Je vais percer son invincible coeur. | I will pierce his invincible heart. |
| Par lui tous mes captifs sont sortis d'esclavage; | Through him all my captives have escaped from slavery. |
| | |
| Qu'il éprouve toute ma rage. | Let him feel all my anger. |
| Quel trouble me saisit? qui me fait hésiter? | What confusion grips me? What makes me hesitate? |
| Qu'est-ce qu'en sa faveur le pitié me veut dire? | What in his favor does pity want to tell me? |
| Frappons . . . Ciel! qui peut m'arrêter? | Let us strike . . . Heavens! Who can stop me? |
| Achevons . . . je frémis! vengeons–nous . . . je soupire! | Let us get on with it . . . I tremble! Let us avenge . . . I sigh! |
| Est ce ainsi que je dois me venger aujourd'hui? | Is it thus that I must avenge myself today? |
| Ma colère s'éteint quand j'approche de lui. | My rage is extinguished when I approach him. |
| Plus je le voi, plus ma vengeance est vaine; | The more I see of him, the more my vengeance is ineffectual. |
| | |
| Mon bras tremblant se refuse à ma haine. | My trembling arm denies my hate. |
| Ah! quelle cruauté de lui ravir le jour! | Ah! What cruelty, to rob him of the light of day! |
| A ce jeune héros tout cède sur la terre. | To this young hero everything on earth surrenders. |
| Qui croirait qu'il fut né seulement pour la guerre? | Who would believe that he was born only for war? |
| Il semble être fait pour l'Amour. | He seems to be made for love. |
| Ne puis-je me venger à moins qu'il ne périsse? | Could I not avenge myself unless he dies? |
| Hé! ne suffit-il pas que l'amour le punisse? | Oh, is it not enough that Love should punish him? |
| Puisqu'il n'a pu trouver mes yeux assez charmants, | Since he could not find my eyes charming enough, |
| Qu'il m'aime au moins par mes enchantements. | let him love me at least through my sorcery, |
| Que, s'il se peut, je le haïsse. | so that, if it's possible, I may hate him. |
| | |
| Venez, venez, seconder mes désirs, | Come, come support my desires, |
| Démons, transformez-vous en d'aimables zéphirs. | demons; transform yourselves into friendly zephyrs. |
| | |
| Je cède à ce vainqueur, la pitié me surmonte. | I give in to this conqueror; pity overwhelms me. |
| Cachez ma foiblesse et ma honte | Conceal my weakness and my shame |
| Dans les plus reculés déserts. | in the most remote desert. |
| Volez, volez, conduisez-nous au bout de l'univers. | Fly, fly, lead us to the end of the universe. |

—JEAN-PHILIPPE QUINAULT

*Armide* was one of Jean-Baptiste Lully's last operas, produced in Paris in 1686. The libretto was written by his longtime collaborator, playwright Jean-Philippe Quinault. In the early 1670s, the two had developed a new French form of opera known as *tragédie en musique* (tragedy in music), later called *tragédie lyrique* (lyric tragedy), by combining elements of classical French drama with ballet, the French song tradition, and a new form of recitative. The orchestra consists of strings divided into five parts rather than the four that later became standard; some of the parts may have been doubled by winds in some performances.

The opera begins with an *ouverture*, or overture, in the form and genre known as the *French overture*. There are two sections, each marked with a repeat. The first part is in a relatively slow duple meter and is mostly homophonic. It has a majesty suitable to the king of France, whose entrance into the theater the overture usually accompanied when he was in attendance. Dotted rhythms pervade the texture, some notated and others played in accordance with a French performing convention of the time called *notes inégales* (unequal notes), whereby even eighth notes in slow or moderate tempos were performed as unequal, with the first somewhat longer than the second. Most modern performers interpret this as dotted-eighth-sixteenth figures, though there is reason to believe that contemporary performers kept a fluid ratio between longer and shorter notes. A related convention encouraged "over-dotting," the playing of singly dotted quarter notes as somewhat longer than notated, which modern performers tend to interpret as double-dotted. In this section of the overture, applying both conventions causes the short notes in the bass to align with those in the upper voices. The second section of the overture begins in a faster tempo and in compound triple meter, with imitative entrances leading to development of the opening motive. The slower tempo and duple meter return at the end of the overture, recalling the mood and figuration of the first section.

The second excerpt is a monologue that includes one of the most impressive recitatives in all of Lully's operas. Armide is an enchantress who captures knights of the Crusades, casts a spell over them, and holds them for her pleasure in her palace. The knight Renaud has incited her anger by freeing her captives, yet against her will she has fallen in love with him. In this scene, she intends to slay him as he sleeps. Her dagger is ready, but because of her love, Armide cannot bring herself to kill him.

The orchestra introduces this scene with a tense prelude that has some characteristics similar to those of the slow section of a French overture. Armide, accompanied only by continuo, then sings in a form of recitative that later became known as *récitatif simple* (simple recitative). In this style, the music alternates freely between measures of two, three, and four beats to create a natural declamation for the text, with the two main accents found in each poetic line falling on downbeats. All the line endings and some caesuras within the lines are marked by rests. Lully also uses rests dramatically, as in the passages where Armide hesitates, her revenge interrupted by warm feelings for Renaud (for example, "Let us get on with it . . . I tremble! Let us avenge . . . I sigh!" at measures 38–42). Finally, she decides to use her magic to make him love her (measures 65–71). Suggesting her new resolve, the style here changes to *récitatif mesuré* (measured recitative), a more regular, metrical style with a more active bass. Like most of Lully's recitatives, this one is more melodious than its Italian counterparts, with melodic lines driven by a more active harmonic background.

The recitative leads directly to an *air*, a full-fledged song with regular meter and phrasing. In it, Armide calls on her demons to transform themselves into zephyrs and transport her and Renaud to some remote desert, where her shame and weakness will not be observed. The meter, rhythm, and tempo are those of the minuet, a dance that during Lully's time was associated with surrendering to love and thus was perfectly suited to the dramatic situation. The orchestra introduces the entire melody, and then Armide sings the air accompanied by continuo alone, repeating the first period and the final phrase. The text-setting is syllabic, and overall the air is simpler in style than the contemporary Italian arias, which feature more florid passages and more repetition of text. Yet Armide's changing emotions are aptly conveyed by Lully's simple yet rhetorically powerful style and by the structure of the scene—a combination of orchestral preludes and two types of recitative, culminating in a dance-like air.

On the accompanying recording, drums announce the overture, and flutes double the top violin line. Trills and other ornaments, called *agréments*, are added where appropriate, whether notated or not (on these, see NAWM 78). During the orchestral introduction to Armide's monologue, a wind machine is used to suggest the swirling winds aroused by her magic. The rhythm of Lully's recitatives is meant to be flexible. It follows a notational convention whereby measures of two beats (such as measure 35) are in cut time, with the half note receiving one beat, but in measures of three or four beats, the quarter note receives one beat. On the recording, the orchestral introduction to the air (measures 71–90 of the scene) is repeated after the air, with an added repetition of the last phrase for finality.

# ELISABETH-CLAUDE JACQUET DE LA GUERRE

**78**

(1665–1729)

Suite No. 3 in A Minor, from *Pièces de clavecin*

*Keyboard suite*

CA. 1687

(a) Prelude

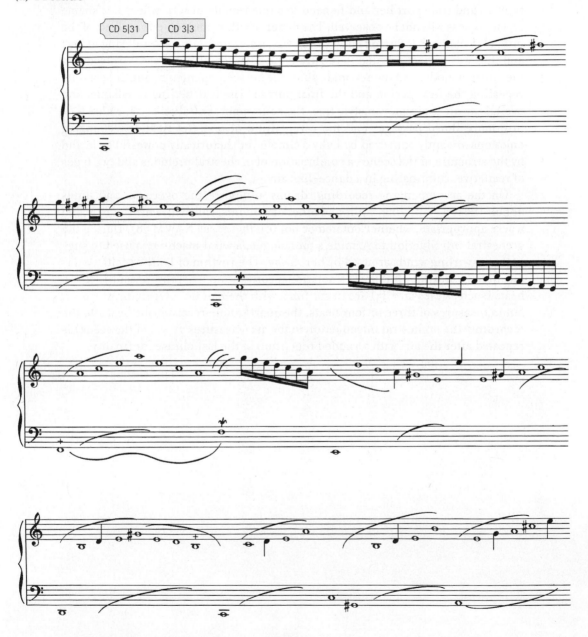

From Elisabeth-Claude Jacquet de la Guerre, *Pièces de Clavecin,* ed. Carol Henry Bates (Paris: Heugel, 1982), 28–39. Reprinted by permission of Theodore Presser, Inc. The second courante is not included on the recording.

## (b) Allemande

(c) Courante I and II

[2ᵉ] **Courante** [not on recording]

(d) Sarabande

(e) Gigue

(f) Chaconne

(g) Gavotte

(h) Menuet

Elisabeth-Claude Jacquet de la Guerre was a child prodigy in music and a favorite of King Louis XIV, to whom she dedicated almost all of her works. Her first publication, issued when she was 22, was a collection called *Pièces de clavecin* that included four suites for harpsichord. Keyboard suites of the time were intended for amateurs to play for their own enjoyment or for family and friends. They consisted primarily of stylized dances, most of which were in *binary form*, with two sections that were each repeated, the first moving from the tonic to a cadence on the dominant (or, in minor keys, sometimes the relative major) and the second returning to close on the tonic. Jacquet de la Guerre's Suite No. 3 in A Minor is typical of the genre and includes all of the most common types of dance.

As in most French harpsichord music of the time, the composer used figuration borrowed from the style that musicians used for playing the lute, known as the *style luthé* (lute style) or *style brisé* (broken style). Rather than plucking all the notes at once, lutenists usually picked out one or two notes at a time, arpeggiating chords and alternating between melody and harmony. A similar texture is evident throughout this harpsichord suite—for example, in the arpeggiated closing chords of each section (see allemande, measures 8 and 17) and in the frequent alternation between voices (see allemande, measures 10–16, where three or four voices are present but rarely are more than two notes struck simultaneously).

Many notes are marked with ornaments, called *agréments*, of which the most important are these:

Agréments compensate for the quick decay of plucked string tones on a harpsichord and draw attention to notes that deserve emphasis, including active tones that propel a melody forward and cadential notes that draw a phrase to a close. The player is also free to add appropriate ornaments, within the limits of taste.

Like many suites, the Suite in A Minor begins with a prelude in an improvisational style similar to that of a toccata. Here, de la Guerre follows the French tradition of the *unmeasured prelude*, in which a special notation without meter is used to allow greater rhythmic freedom. Arpeggiated chords are written in whole notes with occasional quarter notes interspersed to indicate notes that are played but not held, such as passing tones. Most melodic passages are in eighths and sixteenths, although the rhythm remains somewhat free. Perhaps most striking to the eye are the slurs, used to show sustained notes or phrase groupings. Typical of preludes, there are no repetitions or notable melodies. Instead, the player explores the key and its available harmonies, moving to the dominant and gradually returning to the tonic. This exploration of the key recalls the original function of the prelude as a means to establish the keynote before a song or to test and adjust a lute's tuning before playing a dance.

The first four dances—allemande, courante, sarabande, and gigue—are those most frequently used in suites. Indeed, in Germany (though not in France), the standard suite contained these four dances in this order, often preceded by a prelude and with some other dances added near the end. Each of the four dances has a different meter, character, and national origin, providing a great deal of variety.

The *allemande* (meaning "German"), presumably of German origin, developed from a fast couple dance based on a repeating pattern of walking three steps and then lifting the free foot in the air. By the seventeenth century, the allemande was no longer danced, and the music became slower and highly stylized—far from the dance that was its source. Allemandes are in a moderate $\frac{4}{4}$ meter, always begin with an upbeat, and progress almost continuously in eighth and sixteenth notes. Within these parameters, de la Guerre created a striking variety of rhythms and textures. In some passages, the contrapuntal voices contract or expand in contrary motion (as in measures 1–2), and in other passages, the voices rise or fall together (as in measures 10–11). As a result of these variations in texture, the sonorities are constantly changing.

The *courante* ("running" or "flowing") was a French dance whose choreography included bending the knee on the upbeat or offbeat and rising on the beat, often followed by a step or glide. The music is in moderate triple or compound meter and always begins with an upbeat. In many courantes, including the two in this suite, the meter shifts back and forth between $\frac{3}{2}$ and $\frac{6}{4}$, sometimes with different voices simultaneously implying different meters. Although the composer included two courantes in this suite, only one is performed on the accompanying recording—a reminder that the performer had the discretion to omit dances if he or she so desired.

The *sarabande* originated in Latin America as a fast dance-song with ribald lyrics, but in the seventeenth century, French composers modified the form to be slow and dignified in triple meter with a stress on the second beat. The rhythmic figure in the first measure of the sarabande from this suite (a dotted quarter note on beat two and an eighth leading into the downbeat) is particularly characteristic. In the second half of the dance, de la Guerre shifts this figure forward one beat (to the first two beats of the measure). However, since the harmony tends to resolve on the third beat of the measure, as if that were the downbeat, the characteristic sarabande rhythm can still be heard. This device creates an intriguing dissonance between notated and perceived meter.

The *gigue* ("jig") originated in England and Ireland as a solo dance distinguished by rapid footwork. Introduced into France in the mid-seventeenth century, it was stylized as a dance in fast compound meter. The wide leaps and fugal imitation at the beginning of both sections of this gigue are typical, as is the almost constant motion.

The remaining three dances are also common in suites. The *chaconne* originated as a triple-time Spanish dance-song, probably from the New World. In Italy, it evolved into a form for variations over an ostinato bass, while in France it developed into a stately dance that was often shaped by repetition rather than variation. Like many French chaconnes, this one is in *rondeau form*, with a four-measure chaconne theme (repeated each time it is played) that alternates with contrasting eight-measure periods called *couplets*, each with its own figuration and harmonic scheme. Each couplet is more active than the preceding one, and the progressive increase in activity gives a satisfying shape to the piece. Since the repetitions of the theme are exact, in the original score they were not written out in full. However, in the present edition, the editor has supplied the missing measures in brackets.

The *gavotte* was a vigorous dance in duple time with a characteristic rhythm of two quarter notes leading to a half note on the downbeat. The choreography of the dance included bending the knee prior to the beat, jumping on the downbeat, and then taking one or two steps. The music was often simpler and more repetitive than the heavily stylized allemande or courante, as seen in the varied repetition from phrase to phrase in this suite's gavotte.

Simplest of all dances was the *minuet*, an elegant couple-dance in moderate triple meter. Still danced through the early eighteenth century, the minuet was the one dance from the Baroque suite that became part of Classic-era genres such as the symphony and string quartet (see NAWM 103). Minuets were danced using various patterns of four steps within a basic rhythmic unit of two measures. As a result, the sense of two-measure units is stronger in the minuet than in any of the other dances in the suite. The last eight measures of the second section are a varied repetition of the first section, producing a *rounded binary form*, which became one of the most common forms in the eighteenth century and is the direct ancestor of sonata form.

This sequence of dances in contrasting meters, tempos, and textures offered a variety of moods and styles, as was valued in the seventeenth century. Furthermore, all were presented with the elegance and emotional restraint prized at Louis XIV's court and in French culture of the period.

In nearly all the dances of this suite, as in many publications of the time, the word *Reprise* (repetition) is printed at the beginning of the second half. This serves as a visual cue to help the performer locate the point to return to for the repetition of the second strain, after playing through it for the first time.

# Henry Purcell (1659–1695)

## *Dido and Aeneas*: Conclusion

*Opera*

1689

(a) Recitative: *Thy hand, Belinda*

From *The Works of Henry Purcell*, vol. 3, *Dido and Aeneas*, rev. ed. Margaret Laurie (Sevenoaks, Kent: Novello, 1979), 94–99. Words by Nahum Tate. Music by Henry Purcell. Arranged by Margaret Laurie & Thurston Dart. Copyright © 1961 (Renewed) by Novello & Co., Ltd., 8/9 Frith Street, London W1D 3JB. International copyright secured. All rights reserved. Reprinted by permission of G. Schirmer, Inc. (ASCAP).

(b) Lament (ground bass aria): *When I am laid in earth*

(c) Chorus: *With drooping wings*

The first known performance of Henry Purcell's *Dido and Aeneas* was given in 1689 by pupils at Josias Priest's boarding school for young gentlewomen in Chelsea, a suburb of London. Priest's school offered training in the arts to the daughters of London's rich and powerful. Students there had previously performed *Venus and Adonis*, a masque by John Blow that had been written for the king and premiered at the royal court. Purcell had several royal appointments, including as organist at the Chapel Royal, and his librettist, Nahum Tate, was soon to be appointed as poet laureate (court poet). These connections between its creators, its performers, and the royal court suggest that *Dido and Aeneas* may have been written for performance at court, perhaps for the coronation of William and Mary that year. It has been suggested that the opera's prologue refers allegorically to the Glorious Revolution of 1688, when the new rulers deposed Mary's brother James II. The music for the prologue is lost, but the libretto describes how Phoebus, the Sun, crossed the sea and was then joined by Venus, just as William invaded from the Continent, followed by Mary. Yet there is no record of any performance of *Dido and Aeneas* at court, or even plans for one, leaving the reasons Purcell and Tate wrote their opera a matter for speculation.

The plot of *Dido and Aeneas* is derived from the fourth book of Virgil's *Aeneid*, but with some added twists. Dido, queen of Carthage, loves the visiting hero Aeneas, who is fleeing the destruction of Troy and is destined to found Rome.

Although he returns her affection, a sorceress plots to destroy the romance by sending an elf disguised as Mercury to remind Aeneas of his destiny. He is persuaded and agrees to depart. When Aeneas appears at court to say farewell, Dido condemns him for his weakness and deception, and she orders him away even after he has a last-minute change of heart. Then, in the scene included here, Dido realizes she cannot live without him. She sings a lament before dying broken-hearted, and the chorus mourns as cupids appear and scatter roses on her tomb.

Dido's recitative that begins the scene, addressed to her confidante Belinda, conveys her despair through an evocative melisma on "darkness" and sighing figures on "bosom," "would," "Death," and "now." Purcell used a distinctively English style of recitative that he had helped to develop. It resembles the expressive recitatives of Monteverdi (see NAWM 66d and 67) and Strozzi (NAWM 69), and is quite unlike the rapid Italian recitative of the time (NAWM 68a and 82a) or the wholly syllabic French style of Lully (NAWM 77b). Through its slow, stepwise descent of a seventh, the melody portrays the dying Dido and prepares listeners for the lament.

Dido's lament is one of the landmarks of seventeenth-century music, a justly famous adaptation of technique to expression. Purcell followed an Italian opera tradition of setting laments over a basso ostinato, or ground bass. The bass grows out of the descending fourth common to laments, but changes the usual diatonic pattern (G–F–E♭–D) to chromatic (G–F♯–F♮–E♮–E♭–D) and adds a cadential extension (B♭–C–D–G) to create a five-measure pattern that is heard eleven times. Over these inexorable repetitions, symbolizing her inevitable fate, Dido's melody conveys great tension by following an independent course. Purcell intensifies the dissonances by re-attacking suspended notes on strong beats, as in measures 7, 10, 12, and 13. We feel a further jolt when, several times, dissonances are resolved by skip instead of step, as on the word "trouble" in measures 12 and 13. When Dido hammers out a relentless D against the changing harmonies on the words "Remember me!" (measures 17–20 and 28–31), we gain a sense of her obstinacy and pride. The violins augment the grieving effect with added suspensions, sighing figures, and other dissonances, and close with a chromatic descent through an octave.

As was customary in the early Italian operas and many French operas, the act and the opera end with a chorus, in emulation of the choruses of ancient Greek tragedy. Here, the slowly sinking lines of the preceding recitative and aria reach their culmination in the repeated descending minor-scale figures on "drooping wings" and the sighs on "soft" (measures 14–20). Text-painting is notable throughout, including eighth-note undulations on "scatter roses" (measures 11–13) and dramatic rests to mark "Keep here your watch, and never part" (measures 22–30). But it is the recurring stepwise descending motions that link the elements of this entire scene and convey the mournful mood so powerfully.

The edition reprinted here includes both the original basso continuo and, for the recitative and closing chorus, a realization by the editor. In the aria, possible rhythmic variants through double-dotting are indicated by stems and flags above those notes that could be delayed and shortened. Accidentals, ornaments, and dynamics suggested by the editor are printed in small type and slurs added by the editor are marked through with a vertical line.

# TOMÁS DE TORREJÓN Y VELASCO (1644–1728)

*La púrpura de la rosa*: Excerpt

*Opera*

1701

del monte, en tu coturno,
todo el bello matiz,
que en cintas de esmeralda
son lazos de rubí;

del abril, en tu seno,
o blanco, o carmesí,
todo el candor, y nácar
del clavel, y el jazmín:

de suerte que dejando
sin ti el sol sin lucir,
la aura sin respirar,
el monte sin vestir,

From Tomás de Torrejón y Velasco and Juan Hidalgo, *La púrpura de la rosa*, ed. Louise K. Stein, Musica
Hispana, ser. A, vol. 25 (Madrid: Instituto Complutense de Ciencias Musicales, 1999), 74–80.

y el abril, en efecto,
sin lograr y pulir
las flores ciento a ciento,
las rosas mil a mil,

que ya desde esta parte
le deja descubrir
de atalaya un laurel
que abraza amante vid,

todo es amor, por señas
que dél a recibir
a su deidad, las ninfas
en alegre festín

salen al paso; y tú,
para llegar aquí,
no temes las fierezas,
y las bellezas sí.

*Adonis*    ¡Ay!, que no sé qué afecto ...
*Venus*    No has de pasar de aquí.
*Adonis*    ... Me hace no obedecer.
*Venus*    Y agradecer a mí.

**45**

**Múdase el teatro en el de jardín, y por las puertas salen cantando y bailando las Ninfas, y Celfa y Chato**

*[The set changes to that of the garden, and the nymphs enter singing and dancing, and Celfa and Chato]*

**I**

Co-rred, co-rred, cris-ta - les; plan-tas, vi - vid, vi - vid; a-ves, can - tad, can-tad;
Co-rred, co-rred, cris-ta - les; plan-tas, vi - vid, vi - vid; a-ves, can - tad, can-tad;
Co-rred, co- rred, cris-ta - les; plan-tas, vi - vid, vi - vid; a-ves, can - tad, can-tad;
Co- rred, co- rred, cris-ta - les; plan-tas, vi - vid, vi - vid; a-ves, can - tad, can-tad;

**10**

flo-res, lu - cid, lu - cid; pues que vuel - ve Ve - nus, her - mo-sa y gen - til, tra - yen-do des-
flo-res, lu - cid, lu - cid; pues que vuel - ve Ve - nus, her - mo-sa y gen - til, tra - yen-do des-
flo-res, lu - cid, lu - cid; pues que vuel - ve Ve - nus, her - mo-sa y gen - til, tra - yen-do des-
flo-res, lu - cid, lu - cid; pues que vuel - ve Ve - nus, her - mo-sa y gen - til, tra - yen-do des -

po - jos del a - mor tras    sí,    por - que na - die pue - de e - xen - to de - cir que vi-

po - jos del a - mor tras    sí,    por - que na - die pue - de e - xen - to de - cir que vi-

po - jos del a - mor tras    sí,    por - que na - die pue - de e - xen - to de - cir que vi-

po - jos del a - mor tras    sí,    por - que na - die pue - de e - xen - to de - cir que vi-

vir no a - man - do se lla - ma vi - vir. Co - rred,    vi - vid,    can - tad,    lu - cid.

vir no a - man - do se lla - ma vi - vir. Co - rred,    vi - vid,    can - tad,    lu - cid.

vir no a - man - do se lla - ma vi - vir. Co - rred,    vi - vid,    can - tad,    lu - cid.

vir no a - man - do se lla - ma vi - vir. Co - rred,    vi - vid,    can - tad,    lu - cid.

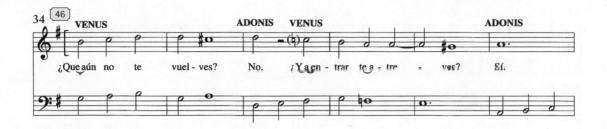

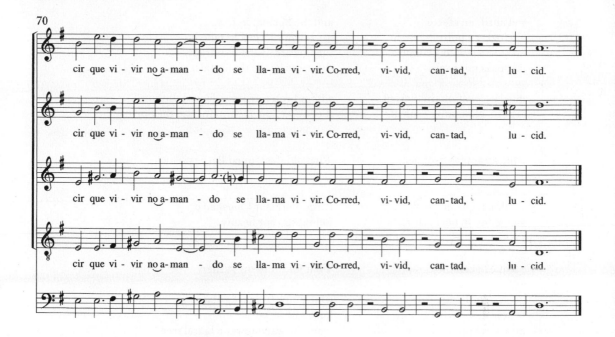

cir que vi-vir no a-man - do se lla-ma vi-vir. Co-rred, vi- vid, can- tad, lu- cid.

**VENUS**

| | |
|---|---|
| Y bien, ¿qué es lo que adviertes? | Well, what is it that you notice? |

**ADONIS**

| | |
|---|---|
| Que te llevas tras ti, | That you carry behind you, |
| en tus rizos, del sol | in your curls, all the sun |
| todo el nevado [dorado] Ofir; | of snowy [or golden] Ophir; |
| | |
| del aura, en tus alientos, | in your breath, |
| todo el humor [humo] sutil, | all the delicate humor [or vapor] of the breeze, |
| que en destiladas gomas | that in any distilled gums |
| cualquiera es ámbar gris; | is ambergris; |
| | |
| del monte, en tu coturno, | in your buskin [high boot], |
| todo el bello matiz, | all the beautiful colors of the mountain, |
| que en cintas de esmeralda | so that in ribbons of emerald |
| son lazos de rubí; | there are bows of ruby; |
| | |
| del abril, en tu seno, | in your bosom, |
| o blanco, o carmesí, | whether white or crimson, |
| todo el candor, y nácar | all the innocence, and the pearl-colored |
| del clavel, y el jazmín; | carnations, and the jasmine of Spring; |
| | |
| de suerte que dejando | so that being left |
| sin ti el sol sin lucir, | without you leaves the sun unable to shine, |
| la aura sin respirar, | the breeze unable to breathe, |
| el monte sin vestir, | the mountain without covering, |

| | |
|---|---|
| y el abril, en efecto, | and the Spring, in fact, |
| sin lograr y pulir | unable to succeed in polishing |
| las flores ciento a ciento, | the flowers by the hundreds, |
| las rosas mil a mil, | the roses by the thousands; |
| | |
| quedan mustios sin ti el sol, | without you remain withered the sun, |
| el aura, el monte y el abril. | the breeze, the mountain, and the Spring. |

VENUS

| | |
|---|---|
| ¡Qué atrasadas lisonjas! | What old-fashioned flattery! |

ADONIS

| | |
|---|---|
| Perdona, que he de ir | Pardon me, for I must go on |
| siguiendo tu hermosura. | following your beauty. |

VENUS

| | |
|---|---|
| ¿A qué? si en mi jardín, | What for? if in my garden, |
| | |
| que ya desde esta parte | which now from this place |
| le deja descubrir | lets us observe |
| de atalaya un laurel | from the watchtower a laurel tree |
| que abraza amante vid, | that a loving vine embraces, |
| | |
| todo es amor, por señas | there are signs that all is love, |
| que dél a recibir | while from there, to receive |
| a su deidad, las ninfas | their deity, the nymphs |
| en alegre festín | in joyful celebration |
| | |
| salen al paso; y tú, | come out; and you, |
| para llegar aquí, | in coming here, |
| no temes las fierezas, | do not fear the cruel, |
| y las bellezas sí. | but only the beautiful. |

ADONIS

| | |
|---|---|
| ¡Ay!, que no sé qué afecto . . . | Ah! I know not what emotion . . . |

VENUS

| | |
|---|---|
| No has de pasar de aquí. | You must not enter here. |

ADONIS

| | |
|---|---|
| . . . Me hace no obedecer. | . . . makes me disobey. |

VENUS

| | |
|---|---|
| Y agradecer a mí. | And makes me grateful. |

*[The scene changes to a garden, and through the doors enter nymphs singing and dancing, along with Celfa and Chato.]*

ALL

| | |
|---|---|
| Corred, corred, cristales; | Flow, flow, crystal fountains; |
| plantas, vivid, vivid; | plants, live, live; |
| aves, cantad, cantad; | birds, sing, sing; |
| flores, lucid, lucid, | flowers, shine, shine; |
| pues que vuelve Venus, | since Venus returns, |
| hermosa y gentil, | beautiful and graceful, |
| trayendo depojos | bringing the spoils |
| del amore tras sí, | of love behind her, |
| porque nadie puede | so that no one can |
| exento decir | freely say |
| que el vivir no amando | that to live without loving |
| se llama vivir. | can be called living. |
| Corred, vivid, cantad, lucid. | Flow, live, sing, shine. |

VENUS

¿Que aún no te vuelves?          You are not yet leaving?

ADONIS

          No.                                                    No.

VENUS

¿Y a entrar te atreves?          And you dare to enter?

ADONIS

          Sí.                                                    Yes.

VENUS

Entra, pues; y vosotras          Enter, then; and you others
alegres proseguid.               continue your merriment.

ALL

Corred, corred, cristales . . .          Flow, flow, crystal fountains . . .

—PEDRO CALDERÓN DE LA BARCA

*La púrpura de la rosa* was the first opera composed and produced in the New World. It was commissioned by the viceroy of Peru and performed at his palace in Lima, Peru on October 19, 1701, to celebrate Philip V's eighteenth birthday and his first year as king of Spain. The libretto, by Spanish playwright Pedro Calderón de la Barca, was originally set by Juan Hildalgo for an opera performed in Madrid, Spain, in 1660 on the occasion of the marriage of Philip V's grandparents, Louis XIV of France and Spanish princess Maria Teresa. The plot, about the erotic love of Venus and Adonis, was appropriate for a royal wedding and also appealing for a colonial audience. An unknown poet adapted the libretto to suit the celebration for Philip V. The composer of the Lima version was Tomás de Torrejón y Velasco, who had come to Peru as a young man, served as chapelmaster at the Lima Cathedral, and became the most famous composer in the New World.

Patron, librettist, and composer were all thoroughly familiar with the conventions of Spanish opera, which were quite different from those of Italy, France, or England. In the Spanish opera tradition, almost all the roles, male and female, were sung by women, excepting only the role of the male member of a peasant couple, who offered comic relief. The sound of the accompaniment in Spanish operas was distinctive as well, for the continuo was usually realized by harps, guitars, and viols rather than by lute or keyboard. But the greatest difference was in the dominance of lyrical song. Rather than setting dialogue in recitative and emotional moments in arias, Spanish composers set both in strophic songs.

In the excerpt included here, Adonis praises Venus's beauty and then follows her into her garden, where they are welcomed by a chorus of nymphs and the peasant couple Chato and Celfa. Adonis begins his song in response to a question from Venus, then sings five short stanzas to a melody that is only five measures long (measures 5–9). The second stanza would start in measure 10, but since the music simply repeats, the composer included only a few notes and a *dal segno* sign to indicate the repetition to be used for the later stanzas. To orient modern musicians unaccustomed to these performing conventions, the editor included some repeated music in brackets, and the measures in the excerpt are numbered as if all of the music were written out.

Adonis closes his song with a couplet that introduces a new melodic idea (measures 31–37), which is expanded into a twelve-measure melody (measures 38–49) that serves as the basis of the next song. The middle stanzas are a solo for Venus, but the first and fifth stanzas present a dialogue between Venus and Adonis, who sing phrases in alternation. Here, there is no musical distinction between dialogue and monologue or between recitative and aria. Rather, the music flows in unbroken song, accommodating the libretto's mostly unrhymed poetry. This is characteristic of the Spanish style, as are the lilting syncopations in the melody. The effect of the frequently repeating short melodies is hypnotic and, in the context of this scene, erotic, offering a pleasure unlike that of other operatic traditions.

The closing chorus is simple and almost entirely homophonic, as are many choruses in French opera. But the rhythms here are borrowed from the syncopated dances and songs of Latin America. Any of the three beats in triple meter may receive a text accent or long note, creating a vibrant and unpredictable flow. Between two statements of the chorus, Venus and Adonis engage in a last, brief dialogue, set to the same melody as before, and then they enter Venus's garden together.

# JUAN DE ARAUJO (1646–1712)

## Los coflades de la estleya

*Villancico*

LATE SEVENTEENTH CENTURY

81

Original parts written a fourth higher.

Edited by Robert Stevenson in *Inter-American Music Review* 6, no. 2 (Spring–Summer 1985): 37–45. Used by permission of Robert Stevenson. Translation by Jules Whicker, from liner notes to *New World Symphonies: Baroque Music from Latin America,* performed by Ex Cathedra, conducted by Jeffrey Skidmore (London: Hyperion Records CDA67380, 2003).

*added.

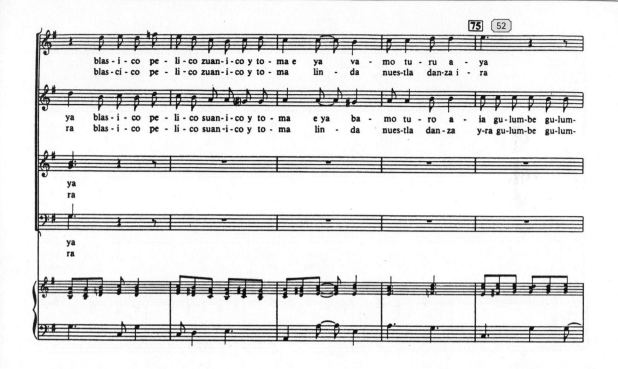

*Estribillo:*

a  Los coflades de la estleya
   vamo turus a Beleya
   y velemo a ziola
   beya con ziolo en lo poltal.
   Vamo, vamo currendo ayá.
   Oylemo un viyansico
   que lo compondlá Flasico
   ziendo gayta su fosico
   y luego lo cantalá Blasico,
   Pellico, Zuanico i Tomá,
   y lo estliviyo dilá:

   Fellow brothers of the Star
   let us all go to Bethlehem,
   and we shall see Our beautiful Lady,
   with Our Lord in the manger.
   Let's go, let's run there.
   We shall hear a villancico
   that Francisco will compose,
   piping in his little voice,
   and then Blasico will sing it
   with Perico, Juanico, and Tomás,
   and the *estribillo* [refrain] will go:

B  Gulumbé gulumbé gulumbá
   Guache moleniyo de Safala.

   Gulumbé, gulumbé, gulumbá,
   Poor boys, black boys from Safala.

c  Bamo abel que traen de Angola

   a ziolo y a ziola
   Baltasale con Melchola
   y mi plimo Gasipar.
   Vamo, vamo currendo ayá.

   Let us go and see what they have
       brought from Angola
   for Our Lord and Our Lady,
   Balthasar and Melchior
   and my cousin Caspar.
   Let's go, let's run there!

B  Gulumbé gulumbé gulumbá
   Guache moleniyo de Safala.

   Gulumbé, gulumbé, gulumbá,
   Poor boys, black boys from Safala.

*Copla 1:*

d  Vamo siguiendo la estleya          *eya*
   lo negliyo coltezano                *vamo*
   pus lo Rey e cun tesuro             *turo*
   de calmino los tlesban              *ayá.*

   Let us follow the star,            *Come on!*
   we black courtiers,                *Let's go!*
   since the Three Kings              *All of us!*
   are coming with treasure.          *That way!*

   Blasico, Pellico, Zuanico i Tomá,
   eyá! vamo turo ayá.

   Blasico, Perico, Juanico, and Tomás,
   come on! let's all go there!

B  Gulumbé gulumbé gulumbá
   Guache moleniyo de Safala.

   Gulumbé, gulumbé, gulumbá,
   Poor boys, black boys from Safala.

d'  Vamo turuz los Neglios             *plimos*
    pues nos yeba nostla estleya       *beya*
    que sin tantuz neglos folmen       *noche*
    mucha lus en lo poltal             *ablá.*

    Let's go, all the black boys,      *my cousins!*
    since our Star is leading us,      *beautiful!*
    even though we're all as black     *as night,*
    on the manger, plenty of light     *there'll be.*

    Blasico, Pellico, Zuanico i Tomá,
    plimos beya noche ablá.

    Blasico, Perico, Juanico, and Tomás,
    cousins, it will be a beautiful night!

B   Gulumbé gulumbé gulumbá
    Guache moleniyo de Safala.

    Gulumbé, gulumbé, gulumbá,
    Poor boys, black boys from Safala.

*Copla 2:*

d  Vaya nuestra cofladia *linda*     Let's go, all our brotherhood *fine!*
   Pues que nos yeba la eztleia *nueztla*     Since the star leads us, *ours!*
   tlas lo Rey e pulque aya *danza*     after the kings, and since *a dance*
   que pala al niño aleglan *yra.*     to cheer the child there *will be.*

   Blasico, Pellico, Zuanico i Tomá,     Blasico, Perico, Juanico, and Tomás,
   linda nuestla danza yra.     Our dance will be so fine!

B  Gulumbé gulumbé gulumbá     Gulumbé, gulumbé, gulumbá,
   Guache moleniyo de Safala.     Poor boys, black boys from Safala.

d' Vamo alegle al poltariyo *plimo*     Let's go merrily to the stable *cousins.*
   velemo junto al peseble *bueye*     We'll see next to the manger *oxen.*
   que sin tantuz neglos folmen *neglo*     Even though we're all jet *black,*
   mucha lus en lo poltal *ezá.*     on the manger, plenty of light *there is!*

   Blasico, Pellico, Zuanico i Tomá,     Blasico, Perico, Juanico, and Tomás,
   plimo neglo buey e ezá.     black cousins, here are the oxen.

B  Gulumbé gulumbé gulumbá     Gulumbé, gulumbé, gulumbá,
   Guache moleniyo de Safala.     Poor boys, black boys from Safala.

ANONYMOUS                    TRANS. JULES WHICKER

The villancico began its career in the Renaissance as a secular song in mock-peasant style (see NAWM 48), but by the seventeenth century it had become a sacred genre associated particularly with Christmas and other important feasts. While preserving the popular style, villancico composers in both Spain and the New World incorporated new techniques of the Baroque era, including the con-certato medium, continuo accompaniment, monody, polychoral or other anti-phonal effects, and, in some works, instrumental ritornellos. Composers in Latin America also adapted the rhythms of native and West African dances, pro-ducing a fresh and vivacious style of religious music.

One of the most well-known composers of villancicos in the New World was Juan de Araujo, who was born in Spain but trained in Peru and active as a choir-master in Lima and in La Plata, Bolivia. Of his 158 extant compositions, 142 are villancicos. He delighted in the possibilities of syncopation within a $\frac{6}{8}$ meter, as is evident in the example shown here, *Los coflades de la estleya.*

Renaissance villancicos represented the lives of peasants for the entertain-ment of aristocrats, and class distinctions play a part in the text of this villancico as well. Although the poet was probably of Spanish heritage and of an educated class, the words are in dialect and speak from the perspective of what he calls "poor boys, black boys." If we interpret the text from an Old World perspective, the "black boys" would have been Ethiopians going to Bethlehem to see the Christ child, and the mention of Angola in southern Africa also evokes that continent. But in the Spanish colonies of the New World, the term might have been used to describe descendants of African slaves, descendants of South American natives, or people of mixed ancestry, for all were sometimes referred to as black. The words of the poem are in a vernacular dialect perhaps meant to imitate the speech patterns of people from these groups. In the Spanish colonies, there was a strict social and economic hierarchy in which full-blooded Europeans ranked at the top and pure-blooded Indians and Africans ranked at the bottom. Some of the language in this poem is now considered offensive ("even though we're all as black as night, on the manger [there will be] plenty of light"), but the poet's intent seems to have been to include even the poorest and least privileged in celebrating the birth of Jesus, who indeed was poor himself.

The form of the seventeenth-century villancico resembles that of its Renaissance ancestor, with a refrain, called an *estribillo*, that precedes and follows one or more stanzas, called *coplas*, which typically end with the same music as the refrain. But seventeenth-century villancicos are often much longer and therefore more complex than those composed during the Renaissance. Here, the *estribillo* is sixty measures long and is subdivided into two parts by its own brief internal refrain, creating the form aBcB (as marked next to the text above, with B beginning in measures 27 and 50). The same internal refrain recurs in the *coplas* (at measures 75 and 101), dividing them in a similar manner and producing the following form for the entire piece: aBcB dBd'B dBd'B aBcB.

Araujo scored this villancico for two treble soloists (on the upper two staves), choir (on the next two staves), and continuo. There are frequent exchanges between soloists and choir, especially in the *coplas*, where the choir interjects single words—taken from the last line before the internal refrain—between phrases sung by the soloists, creating new meanings through the juxtaposition (see for instance measures 61–71, and compare the words sung in measures 73–75). The rhythmic syncopations are influenced by Spanish, Cuban, West African, and South American rhythms. The rhythmic patterns in measures 2 and 3 recur frequently and become especially challenging to perform when displaced by half a measure, as in measures 6–9. It is difficult to imagine an amateur choir correctly singing the offbeat interjections in the *coplas* without a great deal of rehearsal. But the effect is a wonderful musical evocation of boys running eagerly, almost stumbling over each other in their impatience to see the newborn child.

On the accompanying recording, the treble soloists are women, although performing practice of the time would have called for boys to sing the upper parts. In accord with Spanish tradition, the continuo group includes guitar and harp. Latin American percussion instruments including maracas and small drums are added in some passages, especially during the internal refrains.

# ALESSANDRO SCARLATTI (1660–1725)

## *Clori vezzosa, e bella*: Conclusion

Cantata

CA. 1690–1710

(a) Recitative: *Vivo penando*

CD 5|56

Vi-vo, vi-vo pe-nan-do, è ver; ma son con-ten-to dell' is-tes-so tor-men-to

per-chè, per-chè se pen-so che tu so-la sei cag-ion di tan-ti, e

tan-ti af-fa-ni miei, di-ven-ta mio gio-ir-e, la pe- na ed il mar-ti-re,

e più e più pe-nar-vor-rei per pa-le-sar-ti più gl'af-fet-ti mi-ei.

*Originally

From Alessandro Scarlatti, *Three Cantatas for Voice and Cello with Keyboard*, ed. Peter Foster, Nona Pyron, and Timothy Roberts (Fullerton, Calif.: Grancino Editions, 1982), 16–19.

(b) Aria: *Sì, sì ben mio*

Vivo penando, è ver; ma son contento
dell'istesso tormento,
perchè se penso che
tu sola sei cagion
di tanti affanni miei,
diventa mio gioire
la pena ed il martire,
e più penar vorrei
per palesarti più, gl'affetti miei.

I live suffering, it is true; but I am content
with that same torment,
because if I think that
you alone are the cause
of so many of my troubles,
it becomes my joy,
that suffering and that torture,
and I would like to suffer more
to reveal to you more of my feelings.

Sì, sì ben mio, sì, sì
ancor vorrei per te più pene al core.

Yes, yes, my love, yes, yes,
I would like, through you, still more
    torments for my heart.

Pietosa al mio dolore,
forse diresti un dì:
"Chi vidde maggior fè, più fido amore?"

Feeling pity at my pain,
perhaps you will say one day:
    "Who ever saw greater faith, or a
    more devoted love?"

Alessandro Scarlatti was the most prolific composer of cantatas, with over six hundred to his credit. Typical of the cantatas that Scarlatti composed after about 1690, *Clori vezzosa, e bella* has two recitative-aria pairs and is scored for voice and continuo. The poetry freely alternates lines of six, seven, and eleven syllables with an irregular rhyme scheme.

As in most cantatas of the time, the text is a pastoral love poem in the form of a monologue, written as though it were a portion of a drama in which one character is speaking to another, with each section conveying a different reflection on the central theme. Here, the protagonist is a shepherd addressing the nymph Clori. In the first recitative, he swears that he loves only her, and in the following aria, he declares that he suffers from a burning passion. In the second recitative-aria pair, included here, he claims that he is glad for his pain since Clori is the cause, and he then asks for more suffering, hoping that perhaps some day she will see how faithful he is to her.

Scarlatti used a wide range of harmonic vocabulary in the recitative to portray the lover's torments. The key modulates quickly from A minor to G minor and F minor (measure 43), and then a chromatically rising bass line leads to cadences in A minor and finally F major. At several of the cadences, the local dominant is preceded by a diminished seventh chord (measures 39, 46, and 49), a type of dissonance that was still unusual for the time but that Scarlatti used frequently to add harmonic intensity and suggest strong emotions. The rhythms in the vocal line imitate natural speech, but emotionally charged words are highlighted with melodic effects such as a short melisma on "pena" (suffering) and an emphasis on semitone motion at "penando" (suffering), "dell'istesso tormento" (with that same torment), "gioire" (rejoice), and "affetti" (feelings).

The aria follows the *da capo* form that became standard around 1690 and remained the most common aria form for almost a century. The term derives from the words "Da capo" ("from the head," meaning "over again"), which are written in the music at the end of the second section (measure 87) to indicate that the performers should return to the beginning of the aria and repeat the first section, creating an overall form of ABA. The text for a da capo aria is typically in two sentences or segments that express related but different thoughts. In the A section of this aria, the shepherd welcomes more torments of love, and in the B section (at measure 74), he expresses the hope that Clori may someday feel pity and recognize his devotion. Throughout, words and phrases are repeated many times as the composer spins out the musical material with variations, extensions, and sequences. The quick gigue rhythm and bouncy melodic gestures produce a witty irony by suggesting that the lover's feelings are at least as pleasurable as they are painful.

As in most da capo arias, the A section is itself a small two-part form: the text is set twice, preceded each time by an instrumental ritornello. In the first vocal statement (measure 54), the voice repeats and develops a motive from the ritornello and then cadences in the subdominant. The continuo repeats a segment of the ritornello in the new key (measure 59), and then in the second vocal statement, the voice develops the material further, eventually modulating back to the tonic D minor.

The B section offers contrasts of key and mood, beginning in F major and modulating to several new keys. The bass continues to vary the ritornello theme while the voice introduces several new but related ideas.

On the accompanying recording, this cantata is sung by a *countertenor*, a high male voice, and the continuo is played by cello, archlute, and harpsichord. As was customary in Scarlatti's time, the singer embellishes many of the cadences in the recitative with added appoggiaturas and varies some phrases during the reprise of the aria's A section.

# ARCANGELO CORELLI (1653–1713)

## Trio Sonata, Op. 3, No. 2

*Trio sonata*

1680s

(a) Grave (first movement)

Arcangelo Corelli, *Historisch-kritische Gesamtausgabe der musikalischen Werke*, vol. 1, *Sonate da chiesa, Opus I und III*, ed. Max Lütolf (Laaber: Laaber-Verlag, 1987), 123–29.

**(b) Allegro (second movement)**

(c) Adagio (third movement)

(d) Allegro (fourth movement)

83 ARCANGELO CORELLI  Trio Sonata, Op. 3, No. 2

Arcangelo Corelli composed his *Sonate a tre*, Op. 3, while he was employed by Cardinal Pamphili in Rome as music master, composer of instrumental music, and orchestra director. A set of twelve trio sonatas, the collection was published in Rome in 1689. Corelli dedicated it to another of his patrons, Francesco II, Duke of Modena.

Biagio Marini's Sonata IV (NAWM 76) featured a series of sections contrasting in tempo, figuration, and mood. In Corelli's sonatas, the sections have been expanded to form separate movements. The sonatas in Op. 3 are in *sonata da chiesa* (church sonata) format, and No. 2 in D major features the slow-fast-slow-fast succession of movements typical in church sonatas. Although Corelli avoided obvious secular connotations, this sonata bears a resemblance to the stylized dance suite: the last movement is a gigue, and the third hints at the rhythm of the sarabande. The four movements are thematically independent, and all are in D major except for the third movement, which is in the relative minor, B minor.

*Grave*, the marking at the beginning of the first movement, does not merely designate the tempo but also indicates that the character of the music is serious, intense, and profound. The intensity is expressed by the determined march of the walking bass and the suspended dissonances on most downbeats. By Corelli's time, suspensions, passing tones, neighbor tones, and similar dissonances were understood as nonchord tones sounding against a chordal background, rather than as part of a contrapuntal web regulated by the rules of sixteenth-century counterpoint. As a result, voices in the texture were free to leap between the chord tones against the dissonances (as the bass does in measure 2) or even to leap from a suspension down to a chord tone and then up to the note of resolution (as in measures 15 and 17, and also in measures 24 and 46–48 of the second movement). Typical of Corelli's music are the chains of suspensions created by the two violins as their lines meet, cross, and separate, accompanied by a series of sequences created by the steadily walking bass. The forward momentum of suspensions and sequences contributes to the strong sense of harmonic direction that Corelli is known for. Marini's Sonata IV reveals elements of Renaissance modality, but Corelli's sonata is fully tonal. The first movement moves from the tonic to cadences on V (A major), V of V (E major), and vi (B minor, the relative minor) before returning to to close on the tonic.

The first Allegro is fugal, as in most of Corelli's church sonatas, and the basso continuo participates fully in the imitation. Indeed, the bass is the first to answer the subject in direct motion, the second violin having answered with an inverted, incomplete variant of the subject. This movement is remarkable in its nearly complete exclusion of nonthematic material. After the subject, its inversion, and its counterpoints are introduced, they return in numerous permutations and variations. The harmony explores the same harmonic regions as in the first movement, cadencing on A major, B minor, and E major before returning to D.

The Adagio resembles a passionate vocal duet in which two singers alternately imitate each other and proceed in parallel thirds. Syncopations and suspensions on the first and second beats of the triple-time measures emphasize the second beat, as in a sarabande rhythm, through both resolution and dissonance. The dance character is reinforced by hemiola passages at cadences (measures 19–21 and 36–39). A half cadence at the end of the Adagio causes listeners to expect B minor, but instead the finale returns to D major.

The final movement is labeled Allegro, but it shares many characteristics with movements marked by Corelli as gigues. It involves all three instrumental parts in fugal imitation, as was customary for gigues, and it is in the binary form of a dance. The subject of the second half is an inversion of that in the first half, a technique typical of many later gigues. Additionally, there are two sequential episodes of the kind found in later fugues (measures 8–10 and 28–32). The extensive use of contrapuntal devices such as inversion, *stretto* (imitating the subject in close succession, as in measures 32–35), and pedal point (measures 15–18) demonstrates the influence of the Bologna school, in which such techniques were cultivated and where Corelli was trained.

Trio sonatas (especially in the *da chiesa* tradition) were normally performed by at least four players: one on each violin line; a cello or bass viola da gamba to play the bass line; and a lute or keyboard instrument to play continuo, doubling the bass line and filling in the harmonies. Either an organ or harpsichord could be used to play continuo, but the organ was more typical for church performances. On the accompanying recording, the continuo is performed by organ and cello. On rare occasions, the cello and continuo parts diverge, as in the last movement, where Corelli apparently considered the sixteenth notes in the subject too fast for the continuo (see measures 7 and 22). Throughout all four movements, the two violin parts are almost equally active and avoid the embellishments and virtuosic display common in solo sonatas such as Marini's. Trio sonatas such as this were also occasionally played by orchestras, with more than one player on each string part.

# DIETERICH BUXTEHUDE (CA. 1637–1707)

## Praeludium in E Major, BuxWV 141

*Organ prelude*

LATE SEVENTEENTH CENTURY

From Dietrich Buxtehude, *Sämtliche Orgelwerke,* ed. Josef Hedar, vol. 2, *Präludien und Fugen* (Copenhagen: Wilhelm Hansen, 1952), 79–84. Copyright © 1951 (Renewed). Edition Wilhelm Hansen AS, Copenhagen. All Rights for US & Canada controlled by G. Schirmer, Inc. (ASCAP). International Copyright Secured. All Rights Reserved. Reprinted by permission. "BuxWV 141" indicates that this work is number 141 in the *Buxtehude-Werke-Verzeichnis* [Buxtehude Works Catalogue], ed. Georg Karstädt (Wiesbaden: Breitkopf & Härtel, 1974; rev. ed., 1985).

84 DIETERICH BUXTEHUDE Praeludium in E Major, BuxWV 141

For almost forty years, Dieterich Buxtehude served as organist at St. Mary's Church in Lübeck, in northern Germany. As in most Lutheran churches, services there began with a substantial prelude for organ, and several later portions of the service were also introduced with preludes. Buxtehude likely played his Praeludium in E Major as an opening prelude, and he may also have used it as a challenging assignment for his organ students. Unlike some of his contemporaries, he did not seek to publish his organ music, and none of his original manuscripts survive. The earliest source for this piece dates from after his death.

Although this piece is called a Praeludium (Latin for "prelude"), it is in the style of a toccata, in which free and fugal sections alternate. Here, there are five free sections, of which the first two are the most substantial, the next two are shorter transitions, and the last is a climactic coda on a motive from the final fugue. The fugal sections differ from each other in subject, meter, tempo, character, style, and treatment. The contrasts between free and fugal textures and between different sections of the same type create tremendous variety within the piece. But it is unified by the key of E major and by the sense of continuity from one section to the next; each of the fugues blends into the following free section without a cadence, and only the first and last sections close on the tonic.

The piece begins with a three-measure flourish in the right hand that serves a grand upbeat to the first E-major chord. The next eight measures explore a number of figurations while the harmony moves slowly to the dominant and back to the tonic. This and the other free sections sound improvisatory because of frequent and unpredictable changes in rhythm, melodic direction, harmony, phrasing, and texture.

The next section exhibits all the typical characteristics of a seventeenth-century fugue. The fugue subject (measure 13) is imitated in all four voices in turn, in Buxtehude's favorite order of soprano–alto–tenor–bass. A series of entries like this is called an *exposition*. As usual, the second entrance, called the *answer*, is altered intervallically to fit the key, and later voices alternate subject and answer. If the subject begins on the dominant note (as here), the answer begins on the tonic, and vice versa. In Buxtehude's Praeludium, a second four-voice exposition (measures 24–32) is followed by a brief *episode* that is built on the end of the subject and modulates to the dominant. Then a final series of entrances end with an embellished variant in the tenor (measures 45–46). Throughout the fugue, the part for pedal keyboard is a full participant in the counterpoint, and the sixteenth-note passages demonstrate that Buxtehude was a virtuoso with his feet as well as his hands.

Before the fugue reaches a final cadence, a free toccata section begins (measure 47), full of exuberant runs that take the pitch to the highest point in the piece. After the tonic chord finally arrives, there are two "long trills" (so marked in the score) in the pedal part (measures 51 and 53) that create new energy.

The second fugal section, marked *Presto* (measure 60), breaks up into imitations of a short figure after only two entries of the subject. A brief, suspenseful transition reestablishes the tonic for the third fugal section (measures 75–86), a three-voice fugue in gigue rhythm and tempo on a subject that is derived from the subject of the first fugue. Neither of these middle fugues includes the pedal. A transitional Adagio leads to the final fugue, which returns to a four-voice texture that includes the pedals and features another subject derived from the first. In the coda, the opening motive of the final fugue alternates between the pedal and the other voices, bringing the prelude to a rousing close.

# Antonio Vivaldi (1678–1741)

## Concerto for Violin and Orchestra in A Minor, Op. 3, No. 6

*Violin concerto*

CA. 1710

**85**

(a) Allegro (first movement)

85 ANTONIO VIVALDI   Concerto for Violin and Orchestra in A Minor   CD 6   CD 3

(b) Largo (second movement)

(c) Presto (third movement)

Antonio Vivaldi's *L'estro armonico* (The Harmonic Inspiration, Op. 3), published in Amsterdam in 1711, established the composer's European reputation and became the most influential collection of music published during the early eighteenth century. The twelve concertos it contains are written for a variety of soloists with orchestra: four feature solo violin, and the others feature combinations of two to five instruments (two concertos each for two violins, two violins with cello, four violins, and four violins with cello). The solo violin concertos and most of the others have three movements in the order fast–slow–fast, which became the most common structure for concertos, but a few begin with one or two added slow movements. Concerto No. 6 for Violin and Orchestra in A Minor was among the first of Vivaldi's concertos to become popular, circulating through reprintings and manuscript copies. It exhibits many of the characteristics that are typical of his concerto style.

For the fast movements of his concertos, Vivaldi used *ritornello form,* in which ritornellos played by the full orchestra alternate with episodes that feature the soloist or soloists. The opening ritornello statement is made up of several small units. The subsequent ritornellos may repeat this entire opening statement, but most repeat only one or some of its smaller units, often varied. In Vivaldi's concertos, the ritornellos form the pillars of the movement's tonal structure: the first and last ritornellos are in the tonic, at least one ritornello (usually the first to be in a new key) is in the dominant, and others are usually in closely related keys. The episodes feature virtuosic, idiomatic passages for the soloists, either developing material drawn from the ritornello or presenting new ideas. A solo episode typically drives the music forward by modulating to a new key that is then confirmed by the next ritornello. Within these general guidelines, Vivaldi's ritornello forms show almost limitless invention.

In the first movement, the opening ritornello presents three ideas: A, the opening phrase; B, a related motive treated in sequence (measures 3–7); and C, an arpeggiated figure (measures 7–9) that is immediately varied (measures 10–12). The second ritornello varies A, and then the third states A, B, and a variant of A in the key of the minor dominant. All the later ritornellos are in the tonic, presenting phrases A or C. Over a light accompaniment played by the orchestra, the episodes spin out material that focuses either on elements from the ritornellos (A in the first ritornello, B in the last) or on new figuration. Motives are often treated in sequence over changing harmonies, with motion around the circle of fifths frequently used for modulations (as at measures 51–55). In the last quarter of the movement, the complete material of the opening ritornello reappears in the tonic, but spread out through three ritornellos and an episode. The form of the movement can be diagrammed as follows:

| Section: | Rit | Epi | Rit | Epi | Rit | Epi | Rit | Epi | Rit | Epi | Rit |
|---|---|---|---|---|---|---|---|---|---|---|---|
| Motives: | ABCC' | A, A' | A'' | new, A' | ABA''' | new | A | new | C' | B' | CC' |
| Key: | a | mod | a | mod | e | mod | a | mod | a | | |
| Measure: | 1 | 13 | 21 | 24 | 35 | 45 | 58 | 60 | 68 | 71 | 75 |

The finale differs from the first movement in that its opening ritornello (measures 95–124) has more segments, the subsequent ritornellos are more varied in the material they repeat, and the key structure is somewhat different. Typically, modulation is common in episodes, and ritornellos are stable in key, but one of the ritornellos in this finale actually modulates through three keys, from the relative major through the minor dominant and back to the tonic (measures 185–203). The last ritornello (measures 209–32) repeats all the material of the opening ritornello in order, but several short segments are presented by the soloist rather than by the orchestra, further confusing the distinction between ritornellos and episodes. The freedom with which Vivaldi deploys the ritornello principle in this finale and the differences between the finale and first movement only begin to suggest the variety of formal structures he achieved in his ritornello-form movements.

Both the ritornellos and the episodes feature almost constant motion in eighth and sixteenth notes. This driving, motoric rhythm is characteristic of Vivaldi's fast movements and of much music from the late Baroque period, but very different from the rhythmically varied, constantly changing music of early Baroque composers like Monteverdi or Frescobaldi.

The slow middle movement is a rhapsodic interlude for solo violin over sustained chords in the orchestral violins and violas, with the cellos, basses, and continuo silent. The effect is dreamlike, with the soloist's smoothly flowing figures treated in sequence over chromatic progressions in the other instruments. Although the omission of continuo is unusual, light scoring and emphasis on the soloist are typical of Vivaldi's slow movements, offering a strong contrast to the outer movements. Also typical of his middle movements is the use of a different but closely related key—here, D minor, the subdominant of A minor.

Vivaldi wrote his concertos for string orchestras of about twenty to twenty-five players performing on instruments with gut strings and directed by the leader of the violins. They can be and often are played by larger orchestras on modern instruments with metal strings and led by a conductor. However, in the last several decades it has become common for performers to attempt to recreate the sound, performing forces, and performing practices that would have been familiar to Vivaldi, as on the accompanying recording.

# FRANÇOIS COUPERIN (1668–1733)

*Vingt-cinquième ordre*: Excerpts

*Keyboard suite*

CA. 1730

(a) *La visionaire*

From François Couperin, *Pièces de clavecin,* Book 4, ed. Kenneth Gilbert (Paris: Huegel, 1970).

(b) *La muse victorieuse*

François Couperin published twenty-seven *ordres,* or suites, for harpsichord between 1713 and 1730. They were intended for amateurs to play for their own entertainment. The two movements reprinted here are from Couperin's twenty-fifth ordre, which was included along with seven others in his fourth book of harpsichord suites, published in 1730. The ordres were made up mostly of stylized dances in binary form, like earlier keyboard suites, but the dances did not follow any particular sequence.

Couperin gave fanciful and suggestive titles to the movements in his ordres. Those in his twenty-fifth ordre include *La visionaire* (The Dreamer), *La misterieuse* (The Mysterious One, an allemande), *La monflambert* (a gigue, probably named after Anne Darboulin, who married the king's wine merchant Monflambert in 1726), *La muse victorieuse* (The Victorious Muse), and *Les ombres errantes* (The Roving Shadows). Of these five movements, the first and fourth are included here. Unlike Jacquet de la Guerre's Suite in A Minor (NAWM 78), in which every dance is in the same key, Couperin's ordre includes movements in three different keys: Eb major for the opening movement (despite the key signature with two flats), C major for the second and fourth, and C minor for the third and last.

*La visionaire,* the first movement of this ordre, is a whimsical take on the conventions of the French overture. In the slow opening section, labeled *Grave et marqué* (solemn and marked), Couperin embellished the traditional dotted rhythms of the overture style by replacing many of the short notes with fast triplets. After modulating to the dominant in measure 14, the music confirms the new key with a momentary turn to the dominant minor. The second half, marked *Viste* (fast), begins with imitation between the hands, a tribute to the traditional imitative fast second section of the French overture. The movement then lapses into an allemande style, haunted by memories of the majestic first half.

*La muse victorieuse*, marked *Audacieusement* (audaciously or boldly), is a *passepied*, a faster relative of the minuet that is typically written in $\frac{3}{8}$ meter with an upbeat, four-measure phrases, and cadences marked by hemiola rhythms (for example, see measures 26–28 and especially measures 30 and 74, where the hemiola is written out as a measure in $\frac{3}{4}$ meter). The last eleven measures of the first half of the movement are paralleled at the end of the second half, transposed down a fifth to create a final cadence in the tonic C major rather than in the dominant. Such a musical rhyme creates a close relationship between the two halves. This formal device was common in binary movements by Couperin and, later, Domenico Scarlatti (see NAWM 98).

Throughout the ordre, Couperin used agréments and other forms of ornamentation to stress important notes, maintain forward momentum, and achieve an elegant line. Refined elegance, emotional restraint, vibrant energy, and logical clarity in harmony, melody, and form made Couperin's suites very appealing to the courtiers and amateurs of his time.

In all the dances of this ordre, as in Jacquet de la Guerre's suite (NAWM 78), the word *Reprise* is printed at the beginning of the second strain as a visual aid to the performer, highlighting the point to which the eye must return for the repetition of the second half. However, all the marked repetitions are omitted from the accompanying recording.

# JEAN-PHILIPPE RAMEAU (1683–1764)

*Hippolyte et Aricie*: Conclusion of Act IV

*Opera*

1733

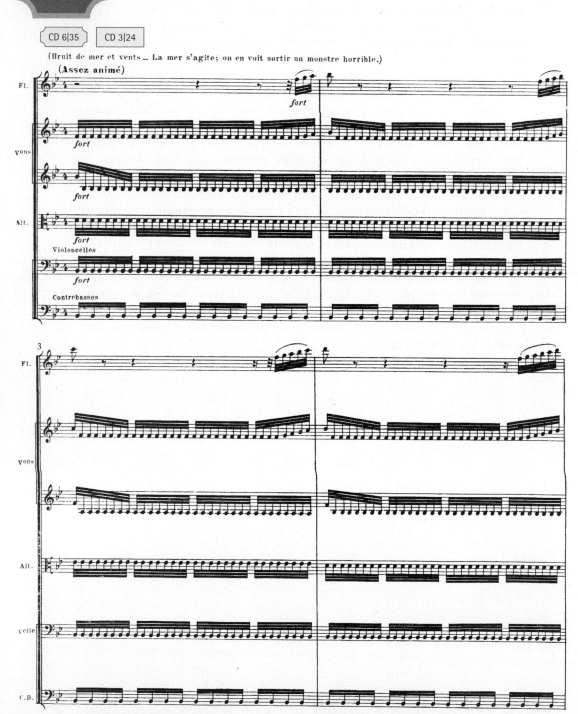

(Bruit de mer et vents — La mer s'agite; on en voit sortir un monstre horrible.)

(Assez animé)

From Jean Philippe Rameau, *Oeuvres complètes*, vol. 6, *Hippolyte et Aricie*, ed. Vincent d'Indy (Paris: Durand, 1900), 306–27.

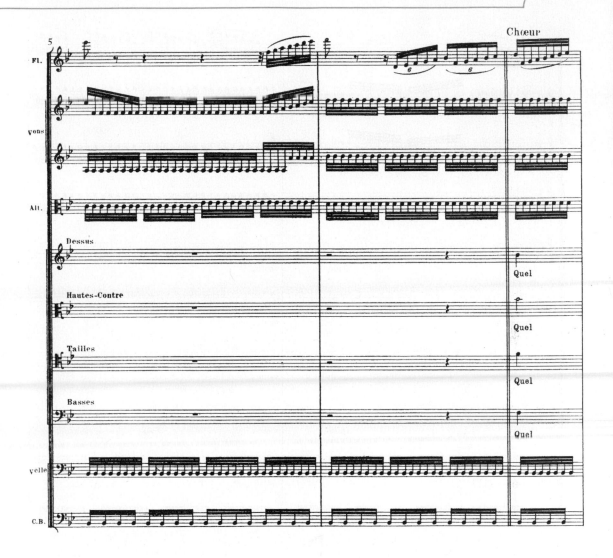

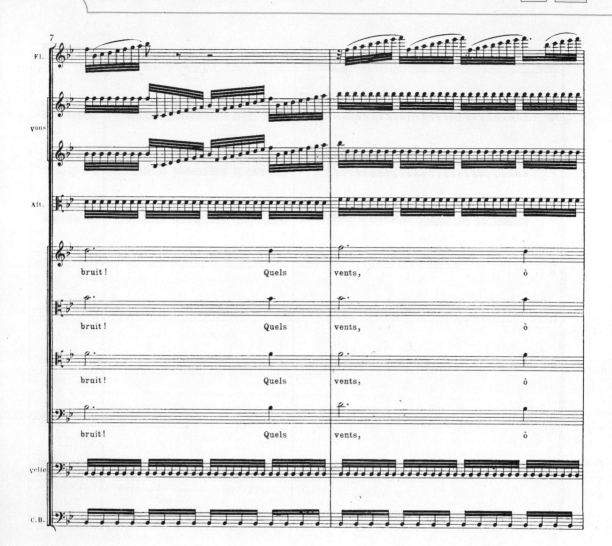

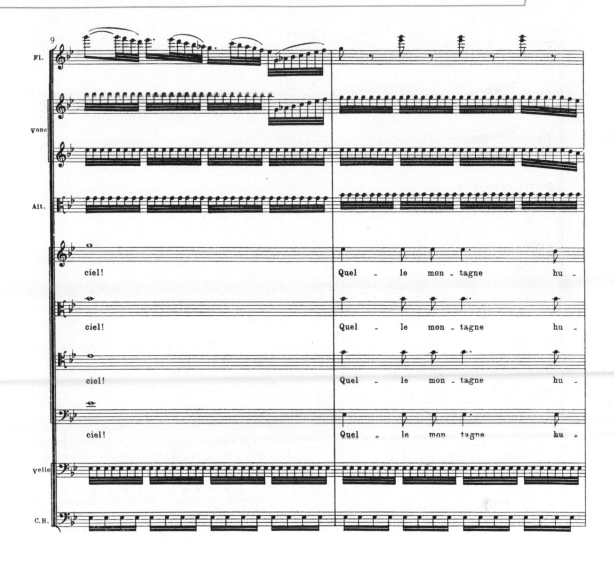

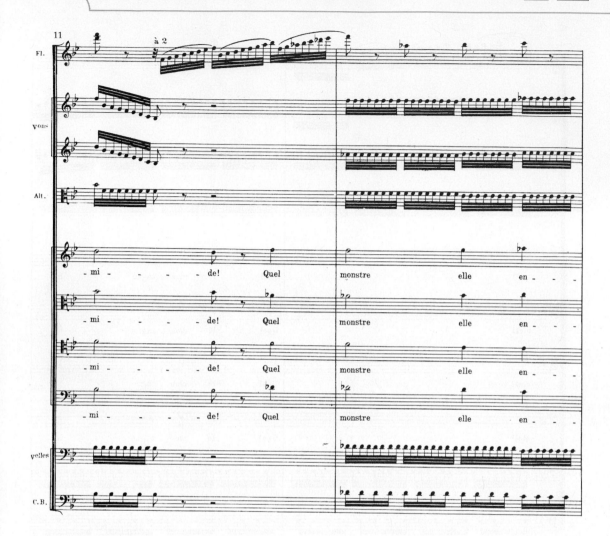

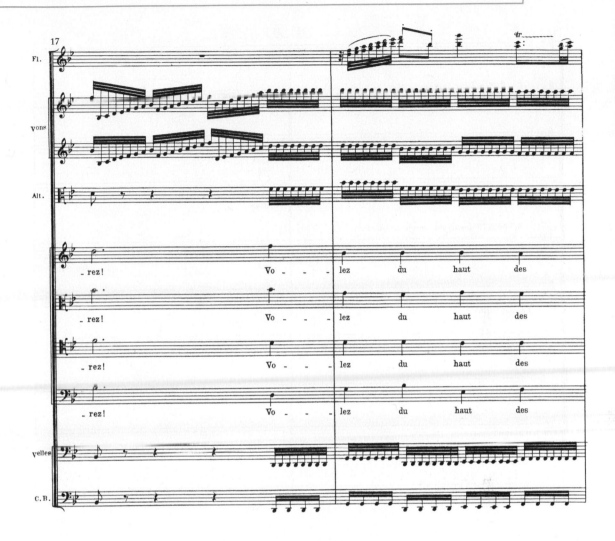

37　26

**Scène IV** — PHÈDRE, troupe de chasseurs et chasseresses

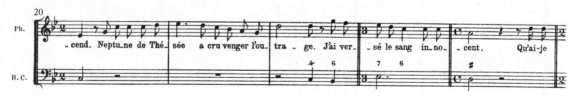

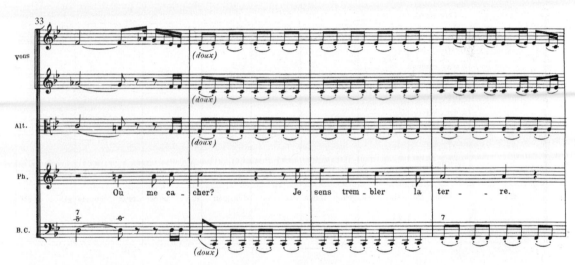

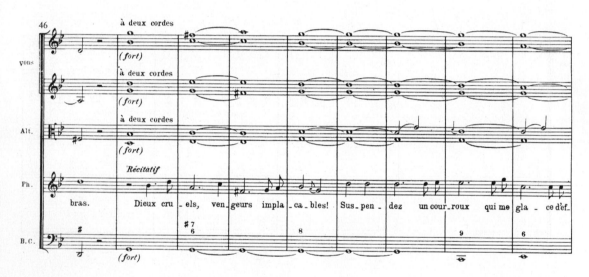

*(Noise of sea and winds. The sea becomes agitated,*
*and out of it comes a horrible monster.)*

CHORUS

Quel bruit! Quels vents, ô ciel! Quelle
　montagne humide!
Quel monstre elle enfante à nos yeux!
O Diane, accourez! Volez du haut des
　cieux!

What noise! What winds, O heavens!
　What a mountain of water!
What a monster it bears to our eyes!
O Diana, hasten [to help us]! Fly down
　from the top of the heavens!

HIPPOLYTE

*(going toward the monster)*

Venez! qu'a son défaut je vous serve de guide.

Come! in her absence I will serve you as guide.

ARICIE

Arrête, Hippolyte, où cours-tu?
Que va-t-il devenir! Je frémis, je frissonne.
Est-ce ainsi que les Dieux protègent la vertu?
Diane même l'abandonne.

Stop, Hippolyte, where are you going?
What will happen! I tremble, I shudder.
Is this how the gods protect virtue?
Even Diana deserts him.

CHORUS

Dieux! Quelle flamme l'environne!

Gods! What a flame envelops him!

ARICIE

Quels nuages épais!
Tout se dissipe . . .
Hélas! Hippolyte ne parait pas . . .
Je meurs . . .

What thick clouds!
All is clearing . . .
Alas! Hippolyte does not appear . . .
I am dying . . .

CHORUS

O disgrâce cruelle,
Hippolyte n'est plus . . .

O cruel disfavor,
Hippolyte is no more . . .

SCENE IV

*(Phèdre enters)*

PHÈDRE

Quelle plainte en ces lieux m'appelle?

What lament calls me to this place?

CHORUS

Hippolyte n'est plus.

Hippolyte is no more.

PHÈDRE

Il n'est plus! ô douleur mortelle!

He is dead! O mortal grief!

CHORUS

O regrets superflus!

O useless regrets!

PHÈDRE

Quel sort l'a fait tomber dans la nuit éternelle?

What fate cast him into eternal darkness?

CHORUS

| | |
|---|---|
| Un monstre furieux, sorti du sein des flots, | A raging monster, which came out from the bosom of the deep, |
| Vient de nous ravir ce héros. | Just now snatched this hero from us. |

PHÈDRE

| | |
|---|---|
| Non, sa mort est mon seul ouvrage. | No, his death is my handiwork alone. |
| Dans les Enfers c'est par moi qu'il descend. | It is because of me that he descends into the underworld. |
| Neptune de Thésée a cru venger l'outrage. | Neptune thought to avenge the affront to Thésée. |
| J'ai versé le sang innocent. | I have shed innocent blood. |
| Qu'ai-je fait? Quel remords! Ciel! J'entends le tonnerre. | What have I done? What remorse! Heavens! I hear the thunder. |
| Quel bruit . . . Quels terribles éclats! | What a noise . . . What terrible flashes! |
| Fuyons! Où me cacher? Je sens trembler la terre. | Flee! Where shall I hide? I feel the earth quaking. |
| Les Enfers s'ouvrent sous mes pas. | Hades opens under my feet. |
| Tous les Dieux, conjurés pour me livrer la guerre, | All the gods, conspiring to wage war against me, |
| Arment leurs redoutables bras. | take up their formidable armaments. |
| Dieux cruels, vengeurs implacables! | Cruel gods, implacable avengers! |
| Suspendez un courroux qui me glace d'effroi! | Cease your wrath that freezes me with dread! |
| Ah! si vous êtes équitables, | Ah! if you are fair-minded, |
| Ne tonnez pas encor sur moi! | do not thunder any more at me! |
| La gloire d'un héros que l'injustice opprime, | The glory of a hero whom injustice oppresses |
| Vous demande un juste secours. | demands your rightful aid. |
| Laissez-moi révéler à l'auteur de ses jours | Let me reveal to the author of his days [his father] |
| Et son innocence et mon crime! | Both his innocence and my crime! |

CHORUS

| | |
|---|---|
| O remords superflus! | O useless remorse! |
| Hippolyte n'est plus. | Hippolyte is no more. |

—SIMON-JOSEPH PELLEGRIN

*Hippolyte et Aricie* was Jean-Philippe Rameau's first opera. It premiered in Paris in 1733 and provoked a stormy debate between Rameau's admirers, who became known as *Ramistes*, and supporters of the older French style of Lully, known as *Lullistes*. The libretto had a distinguished pedigree: its author Abbé Simon-Joseph Pellegrin drew heavily on the drama *Phèdre* (1677), by Jean Racine, the leading author of tragedies in seventeenth-century France, and Racine in turn had drawn on ancient plays by Euripides and Seneca.

According to the story, Phèdre is attracted to Hippolyte, son of her husband Theseus, but when she approaches Hippolyte, he refuses her advances and raises his sword to protect himself. Theseus discovers the two in the midst of this encounter, and when neither will explain what was going on, Theseus assumes that Hippolyte was trying to force himself on Phèdre. Left alone, Theseus calls on his own father, Neptune, god of the sea, to avenge the wrong by killing Hippolyte. Shamed by the encounter with Phèdre, Hippolyte resolves to flee with his beloved Aricie. They encounter hunters and huntresses who celebrate Diana, goddess of the hunt, in a *divertissement* (an interlude for dances, songs, and choruses that was a standard part of each act of French operas in the Lully mold).

At the beginning of the excerpt included here, the revels for Diana are interrupted by a raging sea, from which emerges a great fire-breathing monster. As the chorus cries to Diana for aid, Rameau uses the style of descriptive orchestral writing that French audiences prized, depicting the wind and waves with rapid pulsations and scales in the strings and flute. When Hippolyte rushes to fight the monster and Aricie begs him to stop, the orchestral effects continue in a texture of accompanied recitative similar to that of Italian opera. Hippolyte is engulfed by flames, again depicted by the orchestra, and when the smoke clears, he is gone. He is mourned in a moving, brief statement by the chorus that is highlighted by appoggiaturas and by one of the most eloquent silences in all of opera.

In an exchange marked by heart-breaking simplicity, Phèdre enters the scene and the chorus tells her what happened. She realizes that she alone caused the disaster, since the monster must have been sent by Neptune, and she resolves to reveal to Theseus her guilt and Hippolyte's innocence. Her monologue begins in *récitatif simple*, accompanied by continuo alone as she admits her guilt (scene 14, measure 16); changes to accompanied *récitatif mesuré* when she senses thunder, lightning, and an earthquake, all imitated by the orchestra (measure 25); and closes with dignified resolve in accompanied *récitatif simple* (measure 47), capped by a final comment from the chorus. This scene has long been recognized as one of the most moving and remarkable in all of eighteenth-century opera.

Rameau conveys the anguish of Aricie, Phèdre, and the chorus through harmony highly charged with dissonances that propel it forward. Many chords feature sevenths, ninths, diminished fifths, and augmented fourths (evident in the figured bass, where a line through a figure indicates a diminished fifth, augmented fourth, or chromatically altered interval), and dissonant appoggiaturas are common.

This edition was prepared by the prominent nineteenth-century composer Vincent d'Indy, who looked to Rameau, Couperin, and other early French composers as the embodiment of a distinctively French tradition. The edition preserves some of the old C clefs, notably the alto clef (which marks the middle line as middle C) for Hippolyte and the choral altos, and the tenor clef (which marks the second line from the top as middle C) for the choral tenors. In other ways, d'Indy modernized the score, changing the bass violas to cellos, reinforcing the flute with parallel octaves in oboes and bassoons (omitted here) to balance the larger Romantic string section, and making other alterations. He also added tempo and dynamic markings in parentheses. The performers on the accompanying recording add a few expressive embellishments, especially appoggiaturas on cadential notes, which heighten the tragic tone.

# JOHANN SEBASTIAN BACH (1685–1750)

## Prelude and Fugue in A Minor, BWV 543

*Organ prelude and fugue*

CA. 1715

From Johann Sebastian Bach, *Neue Ausgabe sämtlicher Werke*, series 4, *Orgel Werke*, vol. 5, ed. Dietrich Kilian (Kassel: Bärenreiter, 1972), 186–97. Reprinted by permission of Bärenreiter Music Corporation. "BWV 543" indicates that this work is number 543 in the *Bach-Werke-Verzeichnis* [Bach Works Catalogue], ed. Wolfgang Schmieder (Wiesbaden: Breitkopf & Härtel, 1950; rev. ed., 1990).

Johann Sebastian Bach is believed to have composed the organ Prelude and Fugue in A Minor while at Weimar (1708–17), where he served as court organist and later as concertmaster. During these years, he became fascinated with the new style of concerto developed by Vivaldi and other Italian composers. Bach copied many of their concertos by hand, a traditional method for thoroughly learning a piece, and he arranged several for organ or harpsichord solo. As a result, his own style began to change. In his toccatas (or preludes) and fugues, he blended elements of the Italian concerto with the tradition he had inherited from Buxtehude and other north German organists, as is evident in this piece.

Buxtehude's Praeludium in E Major (NAWM 84) contained a series of alternating toccata-like and fugal sections. In contrast, Bach's standard practice was to compose only two main sections, a prelude and a fugue, each much longer than a similar section in a Buxtehude work. Like the first section of Buxtehude's prelude, but on a greatly enlarged scale, Bach's prelude begins with virtuosic passagework confirms the tonic, and then ranges through the harmonies in the key before returning to the tonic at the end. There are pedal points (as at measures 10–23), pedal solos (measures 25–28 and 46–47), dialogues between the pedals and the upper voices (measure 40–44), and even some passages of fugal imitation (measures 36–37 and 47–48), all reminiscent of Buxtehude. But much of the figuration is violinistic, modeled on the solo episodes in Vivaldi concertos. For instance, the opening figure imitates a common pattern that violinists perform by moving rapidly back and forth between the strings. The figure sinks chromatically in a manner that is typical neither of Buxtehude nor of Vivaldi, but rather of Bach's own rich harmonic style. Vivaldi's influence is also evident in the many sequences, circle-of-fifth progressions, and repetitions of the opening material in contrasting keys.

Like the prelude, the fugue (marked *Fuga*) features violinistic figuration. The surprisingly long fugue subject (measures 1–5 of the fugue) includes a motive, treated in sequence, that jumps between a repeated high note and a moving lower line. This type of figuration is idiomatic for the violin, on which it would be played by alternating between strings. The form of the fugue is analogous to that of a fast movement in a Vivaldi concerto, with the subject serving the function of a ritornello. In the opening exposition, each of the four fugal voices states the subject on either the tonic or the dominant minor, in the order soprano–alto–tenor–bass. The following episode (measure 31–43) and others later in the fugue are similar to the solo episodes in a concerto movement, moving rapidly through sequences or around the circle of fifths while elaborating motives from the subject and new material.

Later entrances of the subject—some of them disguised by embellishments to the opening figure—establish the tonal structure of the piece. The subject appears on the tonic A minor (measure 44), dominant E minor (measure 51), and other closely related keys, including C major (measure 62), G major (measure 71), and D minor (measure 78). Near the end of the fugue, the subject returns on A minor (measure 96), E minor (measure 113, echoing the opening motive in other voices before continuing), and A minor again (measure 131). Between these statements are additional episodes that each develop the material in a different way, and most of which modulate to a new key that is confirmed by the next entrance of the subject.

Bach's adaptation of ritornello form to the fugue allowed him to write fugues that maintained coherence but were much longer and more varied than those by earlier composers. This ritornello-like structure, alternating expositions of the subject with extended episodes, became typical of Bach's fugues, and because of Bach's prominence as a model composer of fugal works, it soon became a standard characteristic of fugue. After the last statement of the subject, this fugue breaks off at a moment of high dissonance (measure 139), followed by a toccata-like coda. Such a return to toccata style at the end of a fugue is reminiscent of Buxtehude (see NAWM 84).

# Johann Sebastian Bach (1685–1750)

## Chorale Prelude on *Durch Adams Fall*, BWV 637

*Chorale prelude*

CA. 1716

From *Johann Sebastian Bach's Werke*, vol. 25/2, *Orgelwerke*, vol. 2 (Leipzig: Bach-Gesellschaft, 1875), 53.
Chorale edited from Joseph Klug, *Geistliche Lieder auffs new gebessert* (Wittemberg, 1535), after Johannes
Zahn, *Die Melodien der deutschen evangelischen Kirchenlieder* (Gütersloh, 1892), vol. 4, No. 7549.

In his last years at Weimar (1716–17), Bach began to compile a collection he called *Orgelbüchlein* (Little Organ Book) that contained short chorale preludes for organ. Chorale preludes were designed to be played during church services as a way to introduce the tune of a chorale before the congregation sang it. This prelude is on the chorale *Durch Adams Fall*, first published in 1524:

| Durch Adams Fall ist ganz verderbt | Through Adam's fall are entirely spoiled |
|---|---|
| Menschlich Natur und Wesen; | both human nature and character. |
| Dasselb Gift ist auf uns geerbt, | The same venom was by us inherited, |
| Daß wir nicht mochten g'nesen | so that we could not recover from it |
| Ohn Gottes Trost, der uns erlöst | without God's solace, which saved us |
| Hat von dem grossen Schaden, | from great harm; |
| Darein die Schlang' hienam bezwang | for the serpent somehow managed |
| Gotts Zorn auf sich zu laden. | to take unto itself God's anger. |

—LAZARUS SPENGLER

Like many chorales, the tune is in bar form, consisting of a repeated section (two *Stollen*, each with two lines of text) and a closing section (*Abgesang* of four lines). In Bach's day, chorale melodies that originally included long and short notes in irregular patterns with rests between phrases, like this one, were often sung in even quarter notes with fermatas marking the ends of phrases. It is this smoother rhythmic version of the tune that Bach uses in this prelude, in which the fermatas are not intended to be observed as pauses, but simply indicate cadential notes.

As in the other chorale preludes in the *Orgelbüchlein*, the melody is heard once in complete, continuous, and readily recognizable form. It appears in the top line with only a few brief embellishments. The other voices portray the images in the poem through some of Bach's most graphic representations. Large, dissonant leaps in the pedals depict the idea of Adam's fall; several of them depart from a consonant chord and fall into a dissonant one, as if from innocence into sin. The twisting, chromatic line in the alto suggests the slithering of the serpent. The tenor repeatedly slides downward and then struggles upward again, perhaps representing the pull of temptation, the sorrow of sin, and the struggle to overcome them. As the congregation prepared to sing, each member holding up the text of the first verse, such musical imagery must have seemed particularly vivid. Like a short musical sermon, the prelude would bring the minds of the worshipers to the meaning and import of the words they were about to sing.

The chorale tune is modal, and its cadential notes largely determine the harmonic structure of the piece. This accounts for the prominent cadences on D minor, F major, and G major, and the infrequent appearances of the ostensible tonic, A minor.

# JOHANN SEBASTIAN BACH (1685–1750)

*Nun komm, der Heiden Heiland*, BWV 62

*Cantata*

1724

(a) No. 1, Chorus: *Nun komm, der Heiden Heiland*

Nun komm, der Heiden Heiland,
Der Jungfrauen Kind erkannt,
Des sich wundert alle Welt:
Gott solch Geburt ihm bestellt.

—MARTIN LUTHER

Now come, Savior of the heathens,
child, known to be born of the Virgin,
at which all the world marveled
that God such a birth for him ordained.

(b) No. 2, Aria (tenor): *Bewundert, o Menschen*

Bewundert, o Menschen, dies große Geheimnis:
Der höchste Beherrscher erscheinet der Welt.

Hier werden die Schätze des Himmels entdecket,
Hier wird uns ein göttliches Manna bestellt,
O Wunder! die Keuschheit wird gar nicht beflecket.

Admire, O humankind, this great mystery:
the supreme ruler appears to the world.

Here are the treasures of Heaven revealed,
here is a divine manna prepared for us,
O wonder! Virginity is not at all defiled.

**(c) No. 3, Recitative (bass):** *So geht aus Gottes Herrlichkeit und Thron*

So geht aus Gottes Herrlichkeit und Thron    Thus goes out from God's glory and throne
Sein eingeborner Sohn.                        His only-begotten Son.
Der Held aus Juda bricht herein,              The hero from Judah appears,
Den Weg mit Freudigkeit zu laufen             to run the course with joy
Und uns Gefallne zu erkaufen.                 and to redeem us fallen creatures.
O heller Glanz, o wunderbarer Segensschein!   O brilliant radiance, O marvelous light of blessing!

**(d) No. 4, Aria (bass):** *Streite, siege, starker Held!*

Streite, siege, starker Held,
Sei vor uns im Fleische kräftig!

Sei geschäftig,
Das Vermögen in uns Schwachen
Stark zu machen!

Struggle, triumph, mighty hero!
Be strong for us in the flesh.

Be active,
that the abilities of us weak creatures
will be made strong!

(e) No. 5, Accompanied recitative (soprano and alto): *Wir ehren diese Herrlichkeit*

Lip-pen, was du uns zu-be - reit; die Dun-kel-heit ver-stört uns nicht und sa-hen dein un-end-lich Licht.

Lip-pen, was du uns zu-be - reit; die Dun-kel-heit ver-stört uns nicht und sa-hen dein un-end-lich Licht.

| | |
|---|---|
| Wir ehren diese Herrlichkeit | We honor this glory |
| Und nahen nun zu deiner Krippen | and now approach your manger |
| Und preisen mit erfreuten Lippen, | and praise with joyful lips |
| Was du uns zubereit; | what you have prepared for us; |
| Die Dunkelheit verstört uns nicht | the darkness does not trouble us, |
| Und sahen dein unendlich Licht. | for we have seen your endless light. |

## (f) No. 6, Chorale: *Lob sei Gott, dem Vater, ton*

ein'-gen Sohn, Lob sei Gott, dem Heil - gen Geist, im - mer und in E - wig - keit!

| Lob sei Gott, dem Vater, ton, | Praise be to God the Father, |
|---|---|
| Lob sei Gott, sein'm ein'gen Sohn, | praise be to God his only Son, |
| Lob sei Gott, dem Heilgen Geist, | praise be to God the Holy Spirit |
| Immer und in Ewigkeit! | forever and in eternity! |

One of Bach's duties as cantor and music director in Leipzig (1723–50) was to provide a large vocal composition each week to be performed between the Gospel reading and the sermon during the main Sunday morning service at either St. Thomas's or St. Nicholas's, the two largest churches. Following the general pattern introduced by Lutheran theologian and poet Erdmann Neumeister in 1700, Bach composed each sacred work in several movements, to a text that combined verses from chorales or the Bible with poetic texts set as recitatives and arias. Neumeister adopted the Italian term *cantata* for such pieces, although Bach typically referred to them by other terms, such as "the principal composition" or simply "the music." Such works share with the Italian secular cantata (see NAWM 82) the use of recitatives and arias, but include choral movements and chorales as well.

During his first years in Leipzig, Bach wrote three (or perhaps four) complete cycles that each included cantatas for the entire church year. For his second cycle, composed in 1724–25, he based each cantata on a chorale. *Nun komm, der Heiden Heiland*, BWV 62 is the cantata from that cycle for the first Sunday in Advent. First performed on December 3, 1724, this cantata was based on Martin Luther's Advent chorale *Nun komm, der Heiden Heiland* (NAWM 42b).

The anonymous author of the cantata's text preserved the first and last of Luther's eight stanzas for the opening and closing movements, both sung by the chorus, as was customary in Bach's church cantatas. The poet paraphrased the remaining stanzas in poetry that was suitable for arias (with regular meter and rhymes) and recitatives (somewhat more irregular), which Bach used for the four middle movements. The cantata thus took this form:

| Chorale stanzas | Movement and voices | Movement type | Key |
|---|---|---|---|
| 1 | 1. Chorus | Chorale motet | b |
| 2–3 | 2. Tenor soloist | Da capo aria, with orchestra | G |
| 4–5 | 3. Bass soloist | Recitative with continuo | mod |
| 6 | 4. Bass soloist | Da capo aria, continuo with unison orchestra | D |
| 7 | 5. Soprano and alto soloists | Accompanied recitative | mod |
| 8 | 6. Chorus | Chorale harmonization | b |

Within this structure, Bach included maximum variety. Each of the four vocal soloists is featured in a type of movement that is borrowed from Italian opera. The two recitatives—one with continuo alone and one accompanied by the orchestra—encompass the two standard types of the time. One aria features the full orchestra, and the other is essentially a continuo aria (for voice and continuo alone) in which the upper strings play in octave unison with the basso continuo. Only the third and fourth movements adopt the recitative-aria pairing for the same soloist that was typical in Italian operas and cantatas; the tenor aria and soprano-alto recitative are free-standing. The two choral movements are the only sections that incorporate the tune of the chorale, but Bach also made them as different from one another as possible. One is an elaborate chorale motet and the other is a simple harmonization in four parts. The choral movements retain the minor mode of the chorale, so the cantata opens and closes in the same key. The other movements are in closely related keys, with major mode in the rejoicing, active arias and rapid modulations in the recitatives.

The opening chorus is always the weightiest movement in Bach's chorale cantatas, and in them Bach often combines traditional genres in ingenious ways. Here, the movement blends the ritornello structure and instrumental writing of a concerto with the cantus-firmus counterpoint of a chorale motet. The sopranos, reinforced by the horn, sing the chorale in long notes in the style of a cantus firmus (see measures 22, 33, 43, and 63). The other voices weave imitative counterpoint beneath the soprano line. The first and last phrases of the chorale are introduced by a point of imitation based on the chorale melody (measures 17 and 56). The four phrases of the chorale are framed by an instrumental ritornello whose sequences, idiomatic string figuration, and vigor recall Vivaldi and whose rising motives suggest the optimism and anticipation of Advent. The opening ritornello (measures 1–16) remains in the tonic

B minor, but later ritornellos change keys to follow the tonal progress of the chorale. After the last phrase of the chorale, the opening ritornello is repeated (marked with a da capo). The ritornello and chorale are not kept separate, but are linked through counterpoint. The first phrase of the chorale appears in most of the ritornellos (for instance, in the first ritornello at measures 3–5 and 15–17), and the orchestra develops ideas from the ritornello as accompaniment to each segment of the chorale.

The tenor aria follows the traditional structure of a da capo aria. The A section begins and ends with a substantial ritornello that frames two vocal statements (at measures 24 and 56) separated by an abbreviated ritornello (measure 52). The first statement modulates to the dominant D major, and the second wends its way back to the tonic G major. The B section, which also features two vocal statements punctuated by the orchestra, explores new tonal realms, including E minor, B minor, and C major. The meter and phrasing resemble a minuet, with two- and four-measure units in triple time. This secular dance rhythm and its associations with bodily movement reinforce the text's focus on the mystery of the incarnation (God's embodiment in human form). Long melismas and melodic high points call attention to the important words "höchste Beherrscher" (supreme ruler).

The bass recitative is typical of Bach in its angular melody, large intervals, and text-painting, which includes a quickly rising scale on "laufen" (run), a falling seventh on "Gefallne" (the fallen), and rapid motion on "heller" (brilliant). The following aria adopts a heroic, martial style that is well suited to its text, with many arpeggiations, brilliant runs, large leaps, and the orchestra playing in octaves throughout. The form is similar to that of the tenor aria.

In the final recitative, the soprano and alto soloists sing mostly in parallel thirds and sixths that combine with the soft, slowly changing chords in the strings to create an aura of reverence and mystery appropriate to the words and to the season of Advent.

The closing chorale is set in four-part harmony, though Bach energizes the harmonization with eighth notes that appear almost continuously in at least one part. The entire orchestra plays *colla parte*, doubling the vocal parts, with all the winds reinforcing the chorale melody. By beginning with the most elaborate movement and ending with a simple chorale, Bach's church cantatas tend to move from complexity to simplicity, closing with a musical thought that is like an aphorism, a brief statement that sums up what has come before. Here, the text of the final verse of the chorale is the German translation of the Lesser Doxology (see NAWM 3a and 4a), a centuries-old formula of praise for the Trinity.

Bach drew on a wide range of styles and genres for this cantata, including Lutheran chorale and chorale motet, Italian opera, cantata, and concerto, and French dance. The variety evident here demonstrates Bach's tendency to assimilate all the types of music he knew, blend them together, and elaborate on them.

At the beginning of each movement in this edition of the score, the editor shows the first note of each part in the original notation. In Bach's time, the singers sang from individual parts, not from a choral score as is the custom today, and Bach used soprano, alto, tenor, and bass clefs rather than the mix of treble and bass clefs that singers are accustomed to today. We know from Bach's records and from the surviving parts that the chorus was small, no more than twelve singers, although modern performances often use more.

# GEORGE FRIDERIC HANDEL (1685–1759)

*Giulio Cesare*: Act II, Scenes 1–2

*Opera*

1724

(a) *Eseguisti*

From *George Friedrich Händels Werke: Ausgabe der Deutschen Händelgesellschaft*,
ed. Friedrich W. Chrysander, vol. 68, 51–58. Bärenreiter Music Corporation.

## SCENA II.

NIRENO, e poi CESARE.

Qùì s'ode vaga Sinfonia di varj stromenti.

66

Qùì s'apre il Parnasso, e vedesi in trono la Virtù,
assistita delle nove Muse.

(b) *V'adoro pupille*

Pie _ to _ se vi bra _ ma   il  me _ sto mio  co _ re, ch'ogn'

o _ ra vi  chia _ ma  l'a _ ma _ to _ suo ben, __ ch'ogn' o _ ra vi  chia _ ma  l'a _ ma _ to suo ben.

*(Fine.)*

CESARE.

Non ha in cie _ lo il To _ nante  me _ lo _ dia, che pa _ reggi  un sì bel can _ to.

*Aria du Capo.*

SCENE 1

CLEOPATRA

| Eseguisti, oh Niren, quanto t'imposi? | Did you carry out, Nireno, what I commanded? |

NIRENO

| Adempito è il commando. | The order has been executed. |

CLEOPATRA

| Giunto è Cesare in corte? | Has Caesar arrived in the court? |

NIRENO

| Io vel condussi, ed ei | I led him here, and he |
| Già a queste soglie il piè rivolge. | is already directing his steps toward this threshold. |

CLEOPATRA

| Ma dimmi: è in pronto | But tell me, is the |
| La meditata scena? | projected stage-set ready? |

NIRENO

| Infra le nubi l'alta regia sfavilla; | Among the clouds the lofty kingdom sparkles; |
| Ma che far pensi? | but what are you thinking of doing? |

CLEOPATRA

| Amore | Cupid |
| Già suggerì all'idea | gave me the idea— |
| Stravagante pensier; ho già risolto | an extravagant thought; I have resolved |
| Sotto finte apparenze | in disguise |
| Far prigionier d'amor chi 'l cor m'ha tolto. | to make prisoner of love him who has stolen my heart. |

NIRENO

| A lui ti scoprirai? | Will you reveal yourself to him? |

CLEOPATRA

| Non è ancor tempo. | It's not time yet. |

NIRENO

| Io che far deggio? | What must I do? |

CLEOPATRA

| Attendi | Wait for |
| Cesare in disparte: indi lo guida | Caesar aside, then lead him |
| In questi alberghi, e poi lo guida ancora | to these quarters, and afterwards show him |
| Colà nelle mie stanze, e a lui dirai | to my chambers, and I will tell him |
| Che, per dargli contezza | that—to give him an account |
| Di quanto dal suo Rè gli si contende, | of the nature of the dispute with his king— |
| Pria che tramonti il sol Lidia l'attende. | before the sun sets Lidia will be waiting for him. |

*(Cleopatra exits.)*

SCENE 2

NIRENO

| | |
|---|---|
| Da Cleopatra apprenda chi è seguace | From Cleopatra, let those who follow Love |
| D'amor l'astuzie e frodi. | learn [his] tricks and deception. |

CESARE

| | |
|---|---|
| Dov'è, Niren, dov'è l'anima mia? | Where is she, Nireno, where is my soul? |

NIRENO

| | |
|---|---|
| In questo loco in breve | Here in this place shortly |
| verrà Lidia, Signor. | will come Lidia, my Lord. |

*(A Sinfonia of various instruments is faintly heard.)*

CESARE

| | |
|---|---|
| Cieli! E qual delle sfere | Heavens! What harmonious sound |
| Scende armonico suon, che mi rapisce? | descends from the spheres and enchants me? |

NIRENO

| | |
|---|---|
| Avrà di selce il cor chi non languisce. | He has a heart of stone who does not surrender. |

*(Parnassus opens and we see Virtue in her throne, accompanied by the nine Muses.)*

CESARE

| | |
|---|---|
| Giulio, che miri? | Julius, what do you see? |
| E quando con abisso di luce | When, in a blaze of light, |
| scescro i Numi in terra? | did the gods descend to earth? |

CLEOPATRA
*(in costume as Virtue)*

| | |
|---|---|
| V'adoro pupille, | I adore you, pupils, |
| Saette d'Amore, | Cupid's darts. |
| Le vostre faville | Your sparks |
| Son grate nel sen; | are welcome to the heart. |
| Pietose vi brama | Pitiable, for you longs |
| Il mesto mio core, | my gloomy heart, |
| Ch'ogn'ora vi chiama | which every hour calls you, |
| L'amato suo ben. | its beloved treasure. |

CESARE

| | |
|---|---|
| Non ha in cielo il Tonante melodia, | Jupiter in heaven has no melody |
| Che pareggi un si bel canto. | that matches such beautiful song. |

CESARE

| | |
|---|---|
| V'adoro pupille, etc. | I adore you, pupils, etc. |

—NICOLA HAYM

Between 1711 and 1741, George Frideric Handel composed about forty operas for performance in London. His *Giulio Cesare*, produced in 1724, was one of his greatest successes and has become probably his best known opera. The libretto is by Nicola Haym (1679–1729), a cellist and composer as well as a producer and poet.

The opera begins with Julius Caesar's arrival in Egypt. Cleopatra, in her official capacity as co-ruler of Egypt (with her brother Ptolemy), welcomes Caesar, and she quickly falls in love with him. Not wishing to reveal her weakness, she tries to seduce him disguised as her handmaiden Lidia. In this scene, Cleopatra's confidant Nireno leads Caesar to a grove where a woman is singing to the accompaniment of an orchestra. It is Cleopatra in costume as Virtue, surrounded by the nine Muses.

The standard elements of an operatic scene from this period are present: dialogue in simple recitative accompanied by continuo, followed by a da capo aria introduced by the orchestra. But these elements are slightly rearranged to create greater realism and enhance the drama. Instead of presenting a static orchestral introduction and aria, Handel intersperses the recitative with the sections of the aria so that the plot advances continuously throughout the scene.

According to the stage directions, the orchestral sinfonia is faintly heard during the preceding recitative, as if Caesar (and the audience) were hearing from a distance a performance already in progress. As the scene is revealed and Caesar beholds Virtue on her throne in Parnassas, the sinfonia is played in full. It anticipates the main figure of the aria to follow, as if it is an opening ritornello. But Caesar breaks in after the sinfonia with his reaction in recitative: "Julius, what do you see? When, in a blaze of light, did the gods descend to earth?" By breaking the conventional link between orchestral prelude and aria, Caesar surprises the audience and thus conveys his own surprise and awe. Then Cleopatra begins her aria, drawing on material from the orchestral sinfonia. The A section includes the usual two vocal statements of the text (the second begins at measure 18), but there is no ritornello between them, as if we are so charmed by Cleopatra that we could not stand to have her stop singing.

After the brief closing ritornello, the B section modulates through several minor keys (D minor, G minor, and A minor) and introduces contrasting material suited to the more wistful text of this section. We expect the repetition of the A section to follow immediately, but instead Cleopatra simply stops. We are transfixed. Caesar comments in recitative, "Jupiter in heaven has no melody that matches such beautiful song." Caesar's interjection brings us to a new level of realization; our recognition of his total enchantment with Cleopatra makes the reprise of the A section not only a conventional formal device but a deepening of the dramatic situation.

Both the opening sinfonia and the accompaniment to Cleopatra's aria are scored like a concerto with multiple soloists, contrasting a small ensemble of oboe, two muted violins, viola, viola da gamba, harp, theorbo, bassoon, and cello with the full orchestra of strings and oboes. The sinfonia begins with the solo ensemble alone, and then the orchestra joins in varying the four-note motive that will open Cleopatra's aria. In the aria, the small ensemble continually accompanies the voice, and the orchestra punctuates and complements this accompaniment during the A section and remains silent during the B section. Handel rarely used such a division of soloists contrasted with the orchestra; here it achieves a magical, ethereal effect.

The vocal line grows from a four-note motive into paired antecedent-consequent four-measure phrases, as in a dance. The word "saetta" (Cupid's arrow) probably inspired the flirting, darting motive. The sinfonia and the A section of the aria have the rhythmic character of a sarabande, with emphasis on the second of the three beats in each measure, suggesting associations of dignity and of allure. The combination of French and Italian influences—a French dance style in a da capo aria form with concerto-like texture—is typical of many German composers. It is especially characteristic of Handel, whose upper-class English audience appreciated both the grand French style (associated with the monarchy in England as well as France) and the newer, more dramatic Italian style. The B section contrasts markedly in rhythm, featuring almost constant eighth-note motion in the accompaniment. As was customary, the singer on the accompanying recording embellishes the vocal line in the aria, especially during the repetition of the A section.

# GEORGE FRIDERIC HANDEL (1685–1759)

*Saul*: Act II, Scene 10

*Oratorio*

1738

(a) No. 66, Accompanied recitative: *The Time at length is come*

From *Hallische Händel-Ausgabe*, ser. 1, vol. 13 (Kassel: Bärenreiter, 1962), 213–40. Used by permission.

(b) No. 67, Recitative: *Where is the Son of Jesse?*

(c) No. 68, Chorus: *O fatal Consequence of Rage*

75   53

Andante larghetto

92 GEORGE FRIDERIC HANDEL *Saul*

92 GEORGE FRIDERIC HANDEL *Saul*

End of the Second Act

Handel composed *Saul* from July to September 1738, and it premiered at the King's Theatre in the Haymarket on January 16, 1739. It was one of Handel's first English oratorios, preceded only by *Esther* in 1732, and *Deborah* and *Athalia* in 1733. The success of *Saul* encouraged Handel to shift the focus of his efforts from opera to oratorio. Charles Jennens, who also wrote librettos for *Messiah* and other oratorios, here dramatized the Bible's First Book of Samuel, Chapters 16 to 20, 24, 28, and 31, and Chapters 1 and 2 of the Second Book.

David, who played the harp to calm Saul during his fits of anger, became a military hero by defending the Israelites against Goliath and other enemies. In Act I, at a victory celebration for David, a chorus of women praises him for having slain "ten thousands," compared to Saul's "thousands." This and similar incidents arouse Saul's jealousy. The scene included here is set at a banquet during which Saul plans to take his revenge. When David wisely does not attend, Saul becomes so angry that he throws the javelin meant for his rival at his own son Jonathan, David's beloved friend.

In Saul's accompanied recitative (No. 66), he expresses his resolve to have David killed. Between the lines of rhymed poetry, the violins and violas simulate bellicose trumpet fanfares.

The continuo recitative (No. 67) is set to unrhymed verse, mostly in ten-syllable lines. Saul's fury intensifies as he listens to the excuses Jonathan makes for David's absence. The accompaniment, en route from the initial D minor to its dominant, passes through alien chords of G♯ major, C♯ minor and major, F♯ minor, and E major. In the many seventh chords, the seventh of the chord is often in the bass, so that the resolution is to a first-inversion chord and the harmonic tension is maintained. Finally, Saul orders Jonathan to capture David, to face his death. But when Jonathan again pleads David's innocence, Saul threatens: "Dar'st thou oppose my Will? Die then thy self." He throws the javelin at Jonathan, who manages to dodge it and escape. In this score, the editor has indicated the traditional appoggiaturas that singers customarily add to the cadential note at the end of each sentence.

The chorus, "O fatal Consequence of Rage" (No. 68), which Jennens modeled on choruses from Greek tragedy, reflects on the morality of the situation and closes the act. The chorus comprises a succession of three fugues, each of which ends with majestic homorhythmic passages. Such systematic use of homophony, stemming from the English choral tradition, distinguishes Handel's choral writing from the complex polyphonic web that Bach spins in his choral movements (compare NAWM 90a).

The first fugue in the chorus is based on "Quos pretioso sanguine," from the *Te Deum* by Antonio Francesco Urio (ca. 1631–ca. 1719), and is one of six passages in *Saul* that feature material borrowed from Urio's *Te Deum*. Such borrowing was a frequent practice for Handel, as for other Baroque composers, but he usually repaid with interest, developing the existing material in new ways. Like Urio's fugue, Handel's begins with a stretto, in which the voices enter in quick succession rather than after the entire subject has been heard. This is a device that composers usually saved for the final climactic effect rather than using it in the first entries. Handel undoubtedly chose to borrow from Urio's fugue because the downward leap of a tritone or sixth, combined with the stretto, is an apt fit for the words, suggesting anger, agitation, and grief. The similarity between Handel's and Urio's fugues ends at the first exposition (measures 1–6). Handel then treats the subject in another point of imitation in which he explores new ways to combine the subject with itself in counterpoint. Next, he alternates fugal expositions with homophonic declamation.

The second fugue aptly illustrates the furious assailant, who goes blindly "from Crime to Crime," with a subject that, after a rising second, leaps down a minor seventh (measure 56), and an episode that meanders over a chromatic bass (measures 73–78). The last fugue portrays Saul's headstrong drive to self-destruction. A partial return of the previous fugue and full repetition of the last one lead to the final denouement, as the chorus pronounces the moral of the tale in forceful homophony.

# INSTRUMENT NAMES AND ABBREVIATIONS

The following tables set forth the English, Italian, German, and French names used for the various musical instruments in these scores, and their respective abbreviations.

## WOODWINDS

| English | Italian | German | French |
|---|---|---|---|
| Piccolo (Picc.) | Flauto piccolo (Fl. Picc.); Ottavino (Ott.) | Kleine Flöte (kl. Fl.) | Petite flûte |
| Flute (Fl.) | Flauto (Fl.), pl. Flauti; Flauto grande (Fl. gr.) | Flöte (Fl.), pl. Flöten; Große Flöte (gr. Fl.) | Flûte (Fl.) |
| Alto flute | Flauto alto (Fl. alto); Flauto contralto (fl.c-alto) | Altflöte | Flûte en sol |
| Oboe (Ob.) | Oboe (Ob.) | Hoboe (Hb.); Oboe (Ob.), pl. Oboen | Hautbois (Hb.) |
| English horn (E.H.) | Corno inglese (C. ing., Cor. ingl., C.i.) | Englisches Horn (engl. Horn) | Cor anglais (C.A.) |
| Sopranino clarinet | Clarinetto piccolo (clar. picc.) | | |
| Clarinet (C., Cl., Clt., Clar.) | Clarinetto (Cl., Clar.), pl. Clarinetti | Klarinette (Kl., Klar.), pl. Klarinetten; Clarinette (Cl.) | Clarinette (Cl.) |
| Alto clarinet (A. Cl.) | | | |
| Bass clarinet (B. Cl.) | Clarinetto basso (Cl. b., Cl. bas., Cl. basso, Clar. basso) | Bass Klarinette (Bkl.), Bassclarinette (Basscl.) | Clarinette basse (Cl. bs.) |
| Contrabass clarinet (Cb. Cl.) | | | |
| Saxophone (Sax.) [alto, tenor, baritone, bass] | Sassofone | Saxophon | Saxophone |
| Bassoon (Bsn., Bssn.) | Fagotto (Fag,. Fg.), pl. Fagotti | Fagott (Fag., Fg.), pl. Fagotte | Basson (Bssn., Bon.) |
| Contrabassoon (C. Bsn.); Double bassoon (D. Bsn.) | Contrafagotto (Cfg., C. Fag., Cont. F.) | Kontrafagott (Kfg.) | Contrebasson (C. bssn.) |

## BRASS

| English | Italian | German | French |
|---|---|---|---|
| Horn, French horn (Hr., Hn.) | Corno (Cor., C., Cr.), pl. Corni | Horn (Hr.), pl. Hörner (Hrn.) | Cor; Cor à pistons |
| Trumpet (Tpt., Trpt., Trp., Tr.) | Tromba (Tr., Trb.), pl. Trombe (Trbe., Tbe.); Clarino, pl. Clarini | Trompete (Tr., Trp., Tromp.), pl. Trompeten | Trompette (Tr.) |
| Piccolo trumpet | Tromba piccola (Tr. picc.) | | |
| Bass trumpet | Tromba bassa (Tr. bas.) | | |
| Cornet | Cornetta | Kornett | Cornet à pistons (C. à p., Pist.) |
| Trombone (Tr., Tbe., Trb., Trm., Trbe.) [alto, tenor, bass] | Trombone (Trbn.), pl. Tromboni (Tbni., Trbni., Trni.) | Posaune (Ps., Pos.), pl. Posaunen | Trombone (Tr.) |
| Contrabass trombone | Cimbasso (Cimb.) | | |
| Baritone horn (Baritone, Bar.) | | | |
| Tenor tuba | | Tenortuba | |
| Tuba (Tb.) | Tuba (Tb., Tba.) | Tuba (Tb.); Basstuba (Btb.) | Tuba (Tb.) |

## STRINGS

| English | Italian | German | French |
|---|---|---|---|
| Violin (V., Vl., Vn., Vln., Vi.) | Violino (V., Vl., Vn., Vln., Viol.), pl. Violini (Vni.); Viola da braccio | Violine (V., Vl., Vln., Viol.), pl. Violinen; Geige (Gg.), pl. Geigen | Violon (V., Vl., Vln., Von.) |
| Viola (Va., Vl., pl. Vas.) | Viola (Va., Vla., Vl.) pl. Viole (Vle.) | Bratsche (Br.), pl. Bratschen | Alto (A., Alt.) |
| Violoncello, Cello (Vcl., Vc.) | Violoncello (Vc., Vcl., Vcll., Vcllo.), pl. Violoncelli | Violoncell (Vc., Vcl.), pl. Violoncelli | Violoncelle (Vc., Velle., Vcelle.) |
| Double bass (D. Bs.); String bass; Bass viol | Contrabasso (Cb., C. B.), pl. Contrabassi or Bassi (C. Bassi, Bi.); Violon, violone [may also designate or include cello or bass viola da gamba] | Kontrabass (Kb.), pl. Kontrabässe; Bass | Contrebasse (C. B.) |
| Viola da gamba; Viol; Gamba | Viola da gamba | Gambe | Viole |

## PERCUSSION

| English | Italian | German | French |
|---------|---------|--------|--------|
| Percussion (Perc.) | Percussione | Schlagzeug (Schlag.) | Batterie (Batt.) |
| Timpani (Timp.); Kettledrums (K. D.) | Timpani (Timp., Tp.) | Pauken (Pk.) | Timbales (Timb.) |
| Snare drum (S. D., Sn. Dr.) | Tamburo piccolo (Tamb. picc.); Tamburo militare (Tamb. milit.) | Kleine Trommel (Kl. Tr.) | Caisse claire (C. cl.); Tambour militaire (Tamb. milit.) |
| Tenor drum | Cassa rullante | Rührtrommel | Caisse roulante |
| Indian drum | | | |
| Tom-tom | | | |
| Bass drum (B. drum, Bass dr., Bs. Dr.) | Gran cassa (Gr. Cassa, Gr. C., G. C.) | Große Trommel (Gr. Tr.) | Grosse caisse (Gr. c.) |
| Tambourine (Tamb.) | Tamburino (Tamb.) | Schellentrommel, Tamburin | Tambour de Basque (T. de B., Tamb. de Basque) |
| Cymbals (Cym., Cymb.) | Piatti (P., Ptti., Piat.) | Becken (Beck.) | Cymbales (Cym.) |
| Suspended cymbal (Sus. cym., Susp. cymb.) | | | |
| Sizzle cymbal (Sizz. cym.) | | | |
| Tam-Tam (Tam-T.); Gong | Tam-Tam (Tam-T.) | Tam-Tam | Tam-Tam |
| Triangle (Trgl., Tri.) | Triangolo (Trgl.) | Triangel (Trgl.) | Triangle (Triang.) |
| Glockenspiel (Glocken.) | Campanelli (Cmp.) | Glockenspiel (Glsp.) | Carillon |
| Bells; Tubular bells (Tub. bells); Chimes | Campane (Cmp.) | Glocken | Cloches |
| Antique Cymbals | Crotali, Piatti antichi | Antiken Zimbeln | Cymbales antiques (Cym. ant.) |
| Xylophone (Xyl., Xylo.) | Xilofono | Xylophon (Xyl.) | Xylophone |
| Vibraphone | | | |
| Marimba | | | |
| Claves | | | |
| Raspador | | | |
| Gourd | | | |
| Maraca | | | |

## OTHER INSTRUMENTS

| English | Italian | German | French |
|---------|---------|--------|--------|
| Harp (Hp., Hrp.) | Arpa (A., Arp.) | Harfe (Hrf.) | Harpe (Hp.) |
| Piano | Pianoforte (P.-f., Pft., Pfte.) | Klavier | Piano |
| Celesta (Cel.) | Celesta | | Céleste |
| Harpsichord | Cembalo (Cemb.); Clavicembalo | Cembalo | Clavecin |
| Organ (Org.) | Organo (Org.) [Organo di legno is an organ with wooden pipes] | Orgel | Orgue |
| Guitar | Chitarra | Gitarre (Git.) | Guitare |
| Lute | Lauto, leuto, liuto | Laute | Luth |
| Theorbo | Teorba; Chitarrone | Theorb; Chitarron | Téorbe |
| Archlute | Arcileuto | Erzlaute | Archiluth |
| Banjo | | | |

# GLOSSARY OF SCORE AND PERFORMANCE INDICATIONS

For a glossary of general music terms, see *A History of Western Music*, 7th ed.

**a, à** The phrases a 2 (à 2), a 3 (à 3), and so on, indicate that the music is to be played or sung by 2, 3, or more players or singers.

**A** Alto or altus.

**à deux cordes** On two strings; double stop, playing on two strings simultaneously.

**a tempo** At the (basic) tempo; marks a return to the main tempo, usually after a ritardando or other temporary change.

**a tempo giusto** At a moderate tempo.

**accompagnato (accomp.)** In a continuo part, this indicates that the chord-playing instrument resumes (cf. tasto solo).

**adagio** Slow, leisurely.

**ad libitum (ad lib.)** An indication giving the performer liberty; for example, to vary from strict tempo or to include or omit the part of some voice or instrument.

**affetti** Add expressive ornamentation (see p. 511).

**allegretto** A moderately fast tempo (between allegro and andante).

**allegro** A rapid tempo (between allegretto and presto).

**alto, altus (A.)** The deeper of the two main divisions of women's (or boys') voices; in vocal music in four or more parts, a part above the tenor and below the highest voice.

**andante** A moderately slow tempo (between adagio and allegretto).

**animé** Animated.

**assai, assez** Very.

**audacieusement** Audaciously.

**avec** With.

**B** Bass, basso, bassus, or basse-contre.

**bass, basso, bassus, basse-contre (B.)** The lowest part in a vocal or instrumental work, or a low male voice.

**basse-continue, basso continuo (B.C.)** See *continuo*.

**basso per l'organo** Basso seguente played on the organ.

**basso seguente (B.S.)** Continuo part, usually optional, that follows the lowest note sounding in the ensemble.

**B.S.** Basso seguente.

**burden** In English polyphony, a refrain.

**C** Cantus or canto.

**cantabile (cant.)** In a singing style.

**cantus, canto (C.)** In Renaissance and seventeenth-century music, the highest part in a vocal work.

**capella** Choir or group of singers.

**chiuso** Closed ending; see *open and closed endings*.

**choeur** Chorus.

**chorus** Group of singers or instruments; normally several on a part, but in Renaissance and Baroque music, may also indicate a group of performers who sing or play one on a part.

**cinquiesme** Fifth part in a polyphonic vocal work.

**con** With.

**con discrezione** With discretion, or ad libitum.

**continuo (Con., Cont.)** An instrumental accompaniment consisting of a bass line, usually together with figures designating the chords to be played above them. In general practice, the chords are played on a lute, theorbo, harpsichord, or organ, and often a viola da gamba or cello doubles the bass notes.

**contra** Contratenor.

**contratenor (Co., Ct.)** In medieval and Renaissance music, the name given to the third voice part that was added to the basic two-voice texture of cantus and tenor, having the same range as the tenor, which it frequently crosses.

**contratenor altus, contratenor bassus** In Renaissance polyphony, contratenor parts that lie relatively high (altus) or low (bassus) in comparison to the tenor; also simply called *altus* and *bassus.*
**corda, corde** String on a string instrument.
**coro** Chorus.
**couplet** In a rondeau, a passage heard between statements of the refrain.
**crescendo (cresc.)** Increasing in volume.

**D** Duplum, discantus, or dessus.
**da capo (D.C., D.C. al Fine)** Repeat from the beginning, usually up to the indication Fine (end).
**dal segno (D.S.)** Repeat from the sign, usually up to the indication Fine (end).
**déclamation mesurée** Measured declamation, in tempo.
**decrescendo (decresc., decr.)** Decreasing in volume.
**dessus** Treble.
**discantus** In Renaissance polyphony, the highest part in a vocal work; cantus.
**doux** Gentle, soft.
**duplum (D., Du.)** In medieval polyphonic music, the first voice composed over the tenor.

**e** And.
**ergänzt** Restored or completed by the editor.
**esclamazione (escl.)** An embellishment consisting of a decrescendo on a note, followed by a sforzano.
**et** And.

**fauxbourdon (faulx bourdon)** Three-voice texture in the Renaissance in which two voices are written, moving mostly in parallel sixths and ending each phrase on an octave, while a third unwritten voice is sung in parallel perfect fourths below the upper voice.
**fine** End, close; marks the end of a piece in which the first section repeats after a later section is heard.
**forte, fort (*f*)** Loud.
**fortissimo (*ff*)** Very loud.

**giusto** Moderate.
**grave** Slow, solemn.
**gravement** Gravely, solemnly.
**groppo, groppo al alta** Trill on the upper note.

**haute-contre** Contratenor altus or alto part in vocal music.

**larghetto** Slightly faster than largo.
**largo** A very slow tempo.
**lentement** Slowly.
**lento** A slow tempo (between andante and largo).
**letterale** Literally; shows the original reading of the musical source, which the editor has determined is a misprint.

**ma** But.
**ma non troppo** But not too much.
**marqué** Marked, with emphasis.
**mezzo forte (*mf*)** Moderately loud.
**mezzo piano (*mp*)** Moderately soft.
**motetus** In medieval polyphonic music, especially in motets, the texted voice part just above the tenor.
**M.S.** Manuscript.

**non** Not.

**octavus** Eighth part in a polyphonic vocal or instrumental work.
**open and closed endings** In medieval music, two different endings for a repeated section, the first (open, ouvert, verto) ending on a pitch above the final of the mode, the second (closed, clos, chiuso) ending with a full cadence on the final.
**orchestra** Ensemble of strings with more than one player on each string part, often with other instruments as well.
**organal voice (vox organalis)** In an organum, the voice that is added above or below the original chant melody.

**pedal** On an organ, the pedals are a keyboard played with the feet.
**pes** In English medieval polyphony, a tenor, not from chant, usually with a short repeating melody.
**pianissimo (*pp*)** Very soft.
**piano (*p*)** Soft.
**più** More.
**plus** More.
**poco (un poco)** Little, a little.
**presto** A very quick tempo, faster than allegro.
**prima, primus, primum** First.
**principale (pr.)** Principal, solo.

**principal voice (vox principalis)** In an organum, the voice that carries the original chant melody.

**pupitre** Music stand; in an orchestra, "un pupitre" (one stand) is two players of a string instrument.

**Q** Quadruplum, quintus, or quinto.

**quadruplum (Q.)** In medieval polyphony, the fourth voice, added to tenor, duplum, and triplum.

**quintus, quinto (Q.)** Fifth part in a polyphonic vocal or instrumental work.

**R** Ritornello.

**rechant** Refrain.

**recitative, récitatif (recit.)** A vocal style designed to imitate and emphasize the natural inflections of speech; or a passage in that style.

**refrain** Recurring line(s) of text set to a recurring melody or passage.

**reprise (Rep.)** A repetition. In Byrd's variations (NAWM 61), "Rep." marks a varied repetition of a strain; in French Baroque dances, "Reprise" is used to highlight the point to which the player must return to begin the repetition of the second half of the dance.

**ritardando (rit., ritard.)** Gradually slackening in speed.

**ritenuto** Held back; implies a more sudden slowing than ritardando.

**ritornello (R., ritor.)** In a fourteenth-century madrigal or caccia, the closing section; in sixteenth- and seventeenth-century vocal music, instrumental introduction or interlude between sung stanzas; in an aria or similar piece, an instrumental passage at the beginning that recurs several times, like a refrain; in a concerto fast movement, the recurring thematic material played at the beginning by the full orchestra and repeated in shortened or varied form throughout and at the end of the movement.

**S** Soprano or superius.

**secondus, secundum** Second, as in the second violin part.

**segno** Sign in form of 𝄋 indicating the beginning and end of a section to be repeated.

**sempre** Always, continually.

**senza** Without.

**senza misura (senza mis.)** Free of regular meter.

**septimus** Seventh part in a polyphonic vocal or instrumental work.

**sextus** Sixth part in a polyphonic vocal or instrumental work.

**sforzando, sforzato (sfz, sf)** With sudden emphasis.

**solo, solus** Part for one singer or instrumentalist; also used to alert the accompanying part, such as the continuo, of a solo passage.

**soprano (Sop., S.)** The uppermost part, or the voice with the highest range.

**sordino, sordini (sord.)** Mute.

**superius** The uppermost part in a polyphonic vocal work.

**T** Tenor, tenore, or taille.

**tacet** Be silent; rest.

**taille** In French vocal music, the tenor part.

**tardo** Slow.

**tasto solo** In a continuo part, this indicates that only the string instrument plays; the chord-playing instrument is silent.

**tenor (T., ten.)** (1) In medieval and some Renaissance polyphony, the main structural voice, usually the lowest voice, carrying the chant or other borrowed melody if there is one, and serving as the foundation for the other voices. (2) In later polyphony and choral music, the second voice from the bottom of the texture. (3) Relatively high male voice or part.

**tenor bassus** The lower of two tenor parts in a polyphonic work.

**tenore** Italian for tenor (2) or tenor (3).

**tiple** Spanish for treble.

**todas** All, tutti.

**tous** All, tutti.

**tranquillo** Quiet, calm.

**treble (Tr.)** (1) The highest part in a polyphonic vocal work. (2) A high voice, especially a soprano, or a part written for high voice or soprano.

**très** Very.

**trill (trillo, tr., t.)** The rapid alternation of a given note with the note above it.

**trillo (tr.)** In Italian vocal music of the late sixteenth and very early seventeenth centuries, a vocal ornament consisting of rapid repetition on a single note.

**triplum** In medieval polyphonic music, a voice part above the tenor and duplum.

**troppo** Too much.

**tutti** Literally, "all"; usually means all the instruments in a given category as distinct from a solo part.

**V** Verse, as in a psalm verse in Gregorian chant.

**verse** (1) In Gregorian chant, setting of a psalm verse or similar text. (2) Stanza of a hymn or strophic song, whether or not the song has a refrain.

**verto** Open ending; see *open and closed endings.*

**vite, viste** Fast.

**zweite Ausgang (zweite Ausg.)** The second time through a repeated section; used to indicate a change (such as tempo or dynamic) on the repetition.

# INDEX OF COMPOSERS

# INDEX OF TITLES

# INDEX OF FORMS AND GENRES